Founded
in
1888

CHILTON'S Repair and Tune-Up Guide

Outboard Motors Under 30 Horsepower

ILLUSTRATED

Prepared by the

Automotive Editorial Department

Chilton Book Company

401 Walnut Street
Philadelphia, Pa. 19106
215—WA 5-9111

managing editor **JOHN D. KELLY**; assistant managing editor **PETER J. MEYER**; editor **KERRY A. FREEMAN**; technical editors **Robert J. Brown, Philip A. Canal**

CHILTON BOOK COMPANY PHILADELPHIA NEW YORK LONDON

First Edition

Published in Philadelphia by Chilton Book Company
and simultaneously in Ontario, Canada, by Thomas
Nelson & Sons, Ltd.
Manufactured in the United States of America

Library of Congress Cataloging in Publication Data

Chilton Book Company. Automotive Editorial Department.
Chilton's repair and tune-up guide outboard motors,
under 30 horsepower.

1. Outboard motors—Maintenance and repair.
I. Freeman, Kerry A., ed. II. Title. III. Title:
Repair and tune-up guide outboard motors.
VM348.C48 1973 623.87'23'4 72-10846
ISBN 0-8019-5723-0
ISBN 0-8019-5802-4 (pbk)

ACKNOWLEDGEMENTS

CHILTON BOOK COMPANY expresses appreciation to the following firms for their generous assistance and technical information:

BELK'S MARINE SUPPLY (MERCURY), *Holmes, Pennsylvania*

THE BOATING INDUSTRY ASSOCIATION, *Chicago, Illinois*

CHAMPION SPARK PLUG COMPANY, *Toledo, Ohio*

CHRYSLER OUTBOARD CORPORATION, *Hartford, Wisconsin*

J & J MARINA (JOHNSON), *Stone Harbor, New Jersey*

KIEKHAEFER MERCURY, *Fond du Lac, Wisconsin*

OUTBOARD MARINE CORPORATION (EVINRUDE), *Milwaukee, Wisconsin*

OUTBOARD MARINE CORPORATION (JOHNSON), *Waukegan, Illinois*

UNITED STATES COAST GUARD

The editorial content of this book has been compiled from authoritative sources by skilled Automotive Editors. While every effort is made to attain accuracy, the Publisher cannot be responsible for manufacturing changes, typographical errors, or omissions.

Contents

1 · General Information and Maintenance

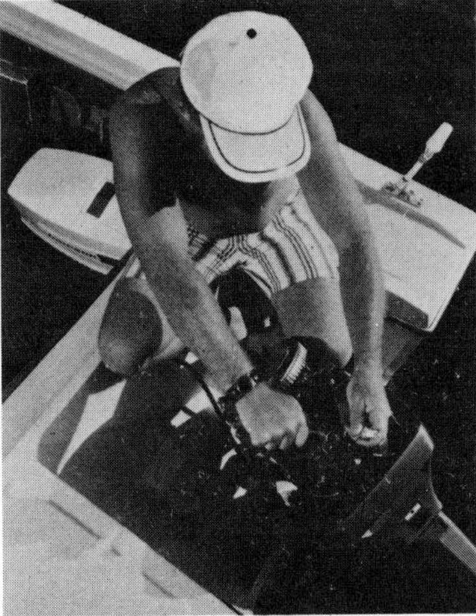

Introduction

This Repair and Tune-Up Guide is intended to contain the basic information necessary to repair and/or adjust the functioning systems of each specific outboard motor. Before attempting any service to your motor, it would be wise to read through the procedures and familiarize yourself with both the procedures and tools needed to complete the operation. A basic understanding of the operation of your motor will also aid in attempts to repair it. The use of special factory tools has been avoided wherever possible, although in some cases these tools are necessary. This book also assumes that the reader has, at hand, a reasonable number of common tools and other equipment.

If you are in doubt concerning any operations in this book, consult either an authorized service facility or your owner's manual.

Most outboards, given proper care, require little service other than periodic maintenance and adjustment. While common sense should dictate most normal maintenance, specific procedures are detailed for mid- and pre-season service and winterizing. Tune-up procedures and specific recommended maintenance are covered in the manufacturer's section. Specific procedures for removal, overhaul, and replacement of components is also covered in the manufacturer's section.

Most procedures in this book are recommended by the manufacturer or the Boating Industry Association. In some cases it was necessary to substitute more common tools for special factory tools; however, the usage of the special tool was kept in mind when selecting an alternate tool. If in doubt concerning the service of a motor, consult a dealer or, in minor cases, the factory authorized owner's manual.

Mounting the Motor on the Boat

Before buying a new or used outboard, it is wise to consult a dealer concerning the actual mounting dimensions and clearances. The following chart may help in determining whether a motor will fit a given transom.

NOTE: *This chart is taken from the Boating Industry Association's Marine Service Manual of Recommended Practices and is reproduced with the permission of the Boating Industry Association.*

Transom and Motor Well Dimensions

Motor (hp)	Transom Thickness Dimension A (in.) Min	Max	Motor Clearance (in.) Dimension B	Cover Height (in.) Dimension C	Transom Height (Vertical) (in.) Dimension D Short Shaft	Long Shaft	Cutout Length (in.) Dimension E ①
Under 5.5	1¼	1¾	14	18	14½–15	19½–20	21½
5.5–12	1⅜	1¾	17	22½	14½–15	19½–20	21½
12–61	1⅜	2	21	29	14½–15	19½–20	21½
61–91	1⅝	2¼	28	32½	——	19½–20	24
Over 91	1⅝	2¼	28	32½	——	19½–20	30

① If the transom cap strip extends more than 1/16 in. aft of the transom, the aft surface of the transom should be built up to bring the extension of the strip into tolerance.

As a safety measure, add 3 in. to Dimension E when the inboard section of the motor cutout is formed by the back of the seat.

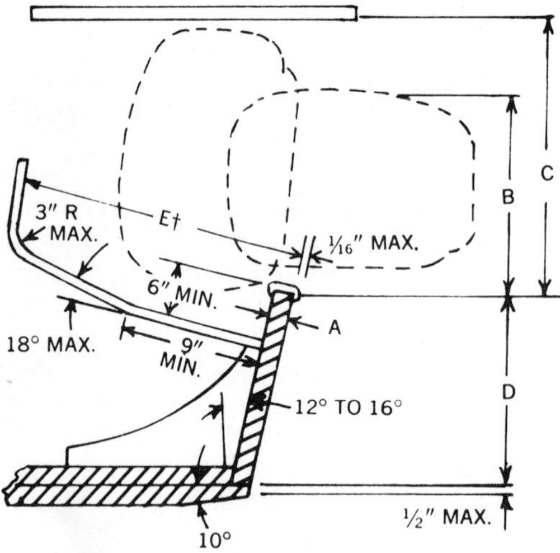

†The Fisher Pierce 55 H.P. requires an E dimension of 25 in.

Transom and motor well dimensions (© Boating Industry Association)

Most outboards, except very small models, have a provision for bolting the motor to the transom. Large outboards use this method exclusively, while intermediate-size models are equipped with bolt holes in the mounting bracket which serve as a safety feature, in addition to the screw clamps on the mounting bracket.

Due to the weight involved with large outboards, installation is best left to a dealer who is equipped with a hoist to handle the motor during installation. If a hoist or chainfall is available, however, the owner can satisfactorily mount the motor himself.

Usually the motor is mounted with the boat on the trailer, eliminating the possibility of the motor becoming submerged. Be sure that the boat is securely attached to the trailer, preferably by the bow winch line and several hold-down straps. Raise and support the front of the trailer so that the boat is on an even keel. Place jacks or cinder blocks with large timbers (4 in. x 4 in.) under the rear crossmember of the trailer to support the weight of the motor when it is lowered onto the transom. It is a good practice to use new thru-bolts (preferably brass), nuts, and washers at the beginning of each season. Use the largest diameter bolt that will fit through the holes in the mounting bracket. It is also a good practice to install wood or rubber transom plates between the inside faces of the mounting bracket and the transom. These plates, available commercially, serve the dual purpose of acting as vibration dampers and protecting the transom.

Lift the motor (it is advisable to use the lifting ring available from the dealer) and carefully lower the motor onto the transom, aligning the bolt holes in the transom with those in the mounting bracket. *Do not remove the lifting apparatus.* If the motor is being installed for the first time, carefully center the motor on the transom. Carefully mark the locations of the bolt holes. Be sure that the motor rests with full weight on the transom.

NOTE: *If there is any doubt concerning placement of the motor on the transom, consult a dealer for special mounting instructions.*

Remove the motor from the transom, and centerpunch and drill the holes. Lower the motor onto the transom and fasten it securely with thru-bolts and lockwashers. Be sure that the rear half of the mounting bracket rests flush against the transom. Tighten the screw clamps if they are provided.

If no bolt holes are provided on the mounting bracket, it is a good idea to install a safety chain, which is connected through an eye-bolt, through the transom, and attached to the motor.

NOTE: *It is not advisable to attach a safety chain to larger motors, since a motor which has vibrated loose could damage the transom.*

Be sure that the chain does not interfere with the steering gear. See the manufacturer's section for any specific mounting procedures.

General Care and Maintenance

Given proper care and maintenance, most outboard motors will reward the owner with years of reliable and relatively trouble-free service. If abused, however, the condition of an outboard motor will quickly deteriorate. Following are suggestions which should help maintain the original condition of an outboard motor. (Most outboard manufacturers also provide an owner's manual, which provides manufacturers suggestions to properly maintain their outboards.)

NOTE: *See the manufacturer's section for specific periodic maintenance. The following information ("Mid-Season Service," "Off-Season Service," and "Pre-Season Preparation") is taken from the Boating Industry Association's Marine Service Manual of Recommended Practices and is reproduced with the permission of the Boating Industry Association.*

WARNING: *Disconnect the battery before servicing ignition (particularly CD) systems.*

OUTBOARD MOTOR MAINTENANCE

The following checks should be made in mid-season or every fifty hours.

1. Drain and flush the gearcase and refill it to the corect level, using the manufacturer's recommended lubricant.
2. Remove and clean the fuel filter bowl. Replace the fuel bowl element. Always use a new filter bowl gasket.
3. Clean and gap the spark plugs to the recommended gap. Replace worn or burnt spark plugs. (Use new gaskets and torque the plugs to the manufacturer's recommendations.)
4. Check the propeller for correct pitch. If the propeller is worn, chipped, or badly bent replace it.
5. Lubricate all of the grease fittings, using the manufacturer's recommended lubricant.
6. Check the remote-control box, cables, and wiring harness.
7. Check the steering controls and lubricate the mechanical steering assembly.
8. Lubricate all carburetor and magneto linkages with the manufacturer's recommended lubricant.
9. Adjust the tension of the magneto or generator drive belts.
10. Clean and coat the battery terminals with grease or a special protective compound.
11. Check the operation of the water pump and thermostat.
12. Check the breaker points' condition and timing.
13. Check the carburetor and ignition synchronization.
14. Check the carburetor adjustment.

OFF-SEASON STORAGE

Operate the motor in a test tank or on the boat, at part throttle with the shift lever in Neutral. Rapidly inject rust preventive oil (with a pump-type oil can) into the carburetor air intake(s) until the motor is smoking profusely. Stop the motor immediately to prevent burning the oil out of the cylinders. This will lubricate and protect the internal parts of the powerhead, while the motor is in storage. If your motor was last operated in salt water, run it in fresh water before preparing it for storage.

1. Place the motor on a stand in the normal upright position. Remove the motor cover.

2. Retard the throttle all the way and disconnect the spark plug leads. Manually rotate the motor flywheel several times to drain any water from the water pump.

3. Drain the carburetor float chamber and remove the fuel filter bowl. Drain, clean, and replace the fuel filter element and gasket.

4. Clean and lubricate the electric starter drive mechanism.

5. Completely drain and clean the fuel tank.

6. Remove the propeller and check it for overall condition and pitch. Clean and liberally lubricate the propeller shaft. Replace the propeller drive pin if it is bent or worn. Replace the propeller using a new cotter pin or tab-lock washer.

7. Drain and refill the gearcase, using the manufacturer's recommended lubricant.

8. Wipe over the entire external motor surface with a clean cloth that has been soaked in light oil.

9. Store your motor in an upright position in a dry, well-ventilated room. To prevent accidental starting, leave the spark plug leads disconnected.

10. Remove the battery from the boat and keep it charged while in storage.

PRE-SEASON PREPARATION

1. Remove, clean, inspect, and properly gap the spark plugs. Replace any defective plugs. (Use new gaskets and torque the plugs to the manufacturer's recommendations.)

2. Remove the oil level plug from the gearcase and check for the proper oil level.

3. Thoroughly clean and refinish surfaces as required.

4. Check the battery for full charge and clean the terminals. Clean and inspect the battery cable connections. Check the polarity before installing the battery cables. Cover the cable connections with grease or a special protective compound to prevent corrosion.

5. If possible, run the motor in a test tank prior to installing the motor on the boat. Check the operation of both the water pump and the thermostat.

SALT WATER CARE

Motors which are used in salt water present special problems and require meticulous care. The aluminum alloys used in outboard motors are highly resistant to corrosion by oxidation (breakdown of metal, caused by its combination with oxygen) but are very susceptible to galvanic action (electrical process of depositing atoms of one metal, in solution, on the surface of a different metal). Although oxidation cannot occur under water, it is very prevalent in warm, humid climates. Aluminum parts are protected from galvanization by anodizing (the process of coating metal with a hard shell of aluminum oxide). This covering is, however, only protective if it remains unbroken. Following are suggestions for the care of all motors used in salt water.

1. After each use, tilt the motor out of the water and flush the entire motor with cool, fresh water.

2. If possible, periodically flush the motor, following the manufacturer's recommendations in the appropriate chapter.

3. Be sure that the motor is adequately protected with an *approved* paint.

NOTE: *Do not use anti-fouling paints, since these contain copper or mercury and can hasten galvanic corrosion.*

4. Check frequently to be sure that no aluminum parts are left unprotected. Bare metal should be protected quickly.

5. A small, self-sacrificing block of susceptible metal, placed near the part to be protected, will sometimes spare a valuable part.

NOTE: *Consult a dealer before attempting to install such a device.*

Submerged Motor Service

Occasionally, through accident or negligence, an outboard motor may be subjected to complete submersion. Mechanical damage could result from the inability of water to compress; however, a more obvious damage is corrosion, especially in the presence of salt water. Corrosive action can start immediately, although it is far more extensive in the presence of heat and oxygen, after the motor is recovered.

Submerged motors must be recovered, cleaned and disassembled as quickly as possible. The following procedure can be used as a guide for handling a submerged motor. Consult the specific manufacturer's section for disassembly procedures.

1. Recover the motor as quickly as possible.

2. If some time must elapse before the motor is serviced (it should be serviced within twenty-four hours), it is best to keep the motor submerged in fresh water. If the motor is too large to be entirely submerged, remove the powerhead and submerge it.

3. Wash the entire motor with clean, fresh water to remove all weeds, mud, and other debris.

4. Remove the carburetor, spark plugs, and reed valve (if possible).

5. Remove water from the cylinders by pointing the spark plug ports down and operating the manual starter (turning the flywheel will do).

CAUTION: *If the motor does not turn over freely, do not force it. This condition indicates mechanical damage, such as a bent connecting rod.*

6. Pour alcohol into the cylinders (alcohol will mix with water). Operate the manual starter again to remove the remaining water and alcohol.

NOTE: *Most manufacturers recommend special engine cleaners in place of alcohol. Engine cleaners frequently contain some type of lubricant also.*

7. Lubricate the internal parts by pouring oil through the spark plug ports. Operate the manual starter.

8. Disassemble the entire motor and wash in hot, soapy water and air-dry it.

9. Immerse all parts (excluding gaskets, which are renewed, and sensitive electrical components) in oil or spray them with an oil mist until they are completely covered.

NOTE: *Alcohol will best protect electrical components.*

10. Ball and roller bearings which cannot be disassembled should be replaced with new ones. Even minute traces of silt and sand will quickly ruin bearings and will necessitate replacement.

11. Check the crankshaft journals (especially the lower one) for traces of moisture or sand scoring.

12. Assemble the motor, using new parts as necessary, along with new gaskets and rubber parts.

13. If in doubt concerning the serviceability of any part, consult a dealer.

Repairing Damaged Threads

In spite of their light weight and high resistance to oxidation, the aluminum alloys used in the construction of outboard motors have two deficiencies; aluminum has insufficient thread strength to hold attaching bolts of stronger metals, and the possibility of seizure involving dissimilar metals, due to galvanic action, is always present. The latter process is only hastened by the presence of salt water and salt air. Because of the peculiar characteristics of aluminum, manufacturers have carefully chosen outboard components. It is not advisable to substitute small components such as nuts, bolts, and washers. Sealants or waterproof grease should be used wherever possible to prevent seizure and torque specifications should be adhered to carefully.

In the event that an aluminum thread is damaged, do not despair; it is not a major disaster. Heli-Coil thread repair kits are available through most dealers and jobbers. These stainless steel wire inserts are precision-formed coils of various sizes, tailored to accept a bolt or stud of the original size. When inserted into the hole, the

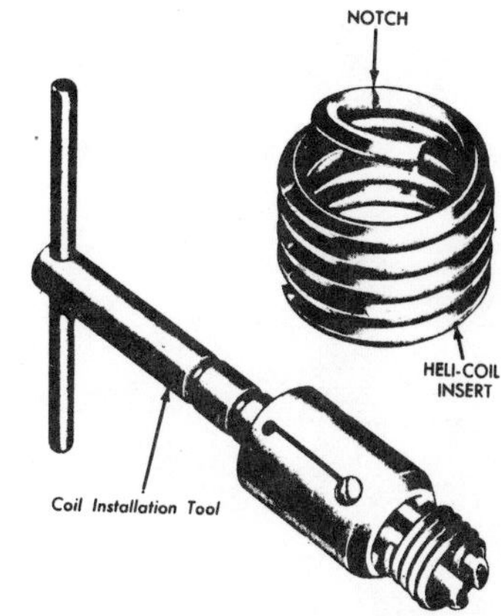

Heli-Coil insert and installation tool

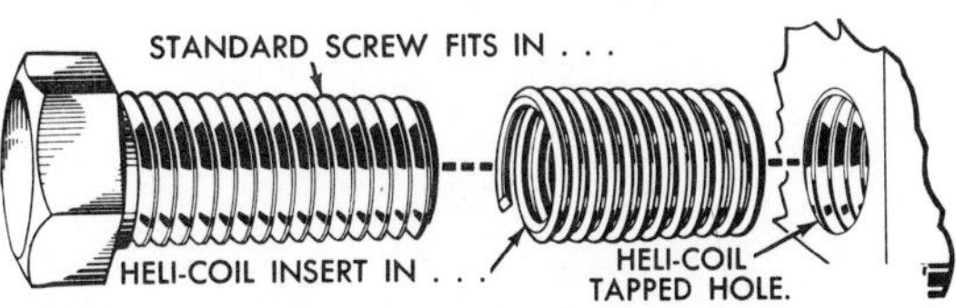

Heli-Coil insert and standard screw (© Chrysler Corp.)

diamond-shaped wire forms internal threads of nominal diameter which are stronger than the original aluminum threads. For convenience, inserts are packaged in kits of the most popular sizes, containing inserts of a given thread size, a special tap and inserting tool, a T-handle to drive the inserting tool, and a pressure plate to ease starting the inserts. Thread inserts are available in the following sizes: all National Coarse (USS) sizes from no. 4—1½ in.; National Fine (SAE) sizes from no. 5—1½ in., and metric sizes: 5 mm x 0.9 mm, 6 mm x 1.0 mm, 8 mm x 1.25 mm, 10 mm x 1.5 mm, and 12 mm x 1.25 mm. Inserts for repairing 14 mm and 18 mm spark plug ports are also available. The chart below may be helpful in replacing some common size threads.

To repair damaged threads, the following procedure should be followed carefully.

1. Drill the damaged threads out of the stripped hole. Use the same drill size as the outside diameter of the bolt thread. For example, use a 5/16 in. drill for a 5/16—18 thread.

2. Select the correct special tap supplied with the kit. The tap is marked for the size and thread desired. As an example, the special tap marked 5/16—18 will not cut the same thread as a standard 5/16—18 tap. It will, however, form a thread large enough to accept the coiled insert.

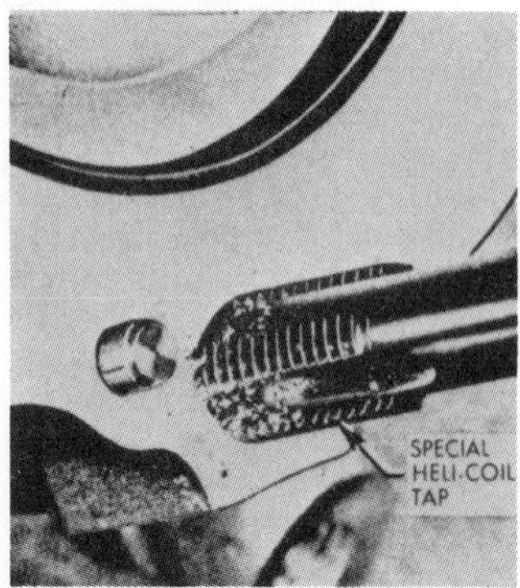

Cutting thread for the insert with the special tool supplied with Heli-Coil kit

3. Select the correct thread inserting tool. These tools are marked for the hole and thread size to be restored. Place the thread insert on the tool and adjust the sleeve for the correct length for the insert being used.

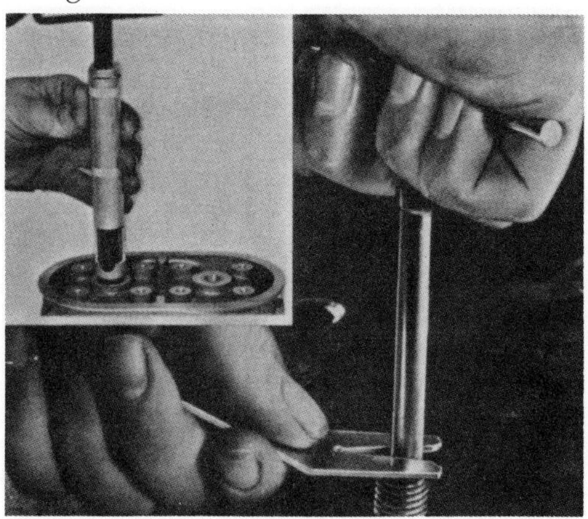
Installing the Heli-Coil insert (© Kiekhaefer Mercury)

4. Press the insert against the face of the tapped hole while turning the tool clockwise. This will wind the insert into the drilled hole. Continue this action until the insert is one-half turn below the surface of the work.

5. Reaching below and through the thread insert, bend the insert tang straight up and down until it breaks off at the notch.

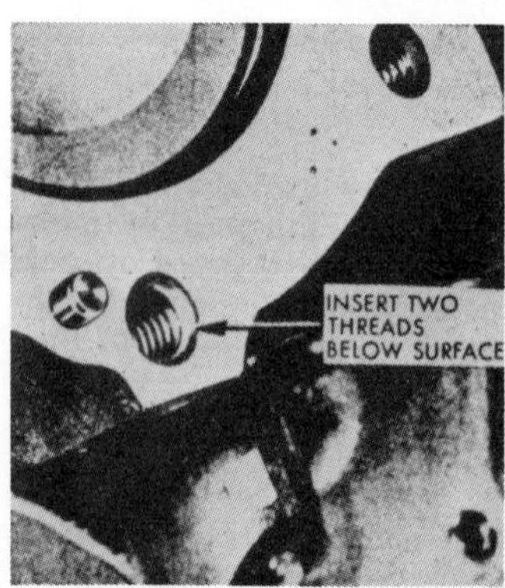

Heli-Coil insert installed

Thread Size	*Heli-Coil Insert* Part No.	Insert Length (in.)	Drill Size (in./mm)	Tap Part No.	Insert Tool Part No.	Extracting Tool Part No.
¼—20	1185—4	⅜	17/64 (0.266)	4 CPB	528—4N	1227—6
5/16—18	1185—5	15/32	Q (0.332)	5 CPB	528—5N	1227—6
⅜—16	1185—6	9/16	X (0.397)	6 CPB	528—6N	1227—6
7/16—14	1185—7	21/32	29/64 (0.453)	7 CPB	528—7N	1227—16
½—13	1185—8	¾	33/64 (0.516)	8 CPB	528—8N	1227—16

6. If an error has been made or if the results are unsatisfactory, the insert can be removed with the extractor tool. Place the extractor tool in the insert until the blade contacts the top turn of the coil, one-quarter to one-half turn from the end. Tap the tool solidly with a hammer. This will cause the blade to cut into the insert. Press downward on the tool and turn it counterclockwise until the insert is removed.

Boat Performance and Propeller Selection

Many variables will influence, if not dictate, the performance characteristics of any boat. Some, of course, will have a greater influence than others. Assuming that the motor itself is in good condition and properly tuned, the following factors must be considered (not necessarily in order) when attempting to influence or evaluate boat performance.

HULL DESIGN

Hull designs are of two basic types: displacement hulls or planing hulls. In practice, however, pleasure craft are a variation of one of the two basic types. The displacement hull, common to larger yachts, is characterized by a round bottom which forces its way through the water. The center of gravity is very low, providing a smooth, stable ride in heavy seas. Since the amount of water displaced by this type of hull remains practically the same, regardless of speed, this has the effect of reducing the maximum speed capability. Simply as a matter of interest, the maximum speed of a displacement-type hull is fixed by the length of the waterline. No matter how much horsepower is applied to drive the hull, its speed (mph) will not exceed $1\frac{1}{2}$ times the square root of its waterline. The following formula will calculate the maximum speed of a large displacement hull.

$$\text{Speed (mph)} = \frac{3\sqrt{\text{waterline length}}}{2}$$

Planing hulls are designed to gain speed by lifting out of the water. Because the lifting effect supports only part of the weight of the boat, displacement and frictional resistance are decreased, resulting in an increased speed. In theory, planing hulls are perfectly flat. In practice, however, perfect planing hulls do not exist because of poor maneuverability at slow speeds when the hull is not planing. Practical design combinations of displacement and planing hulls supply the answer to speed and maneuverability problems for pleasure craft.

V-type hulls employ planing characteristics and are much faster than true displacement hulls. *V*-type hulls tend to sta-

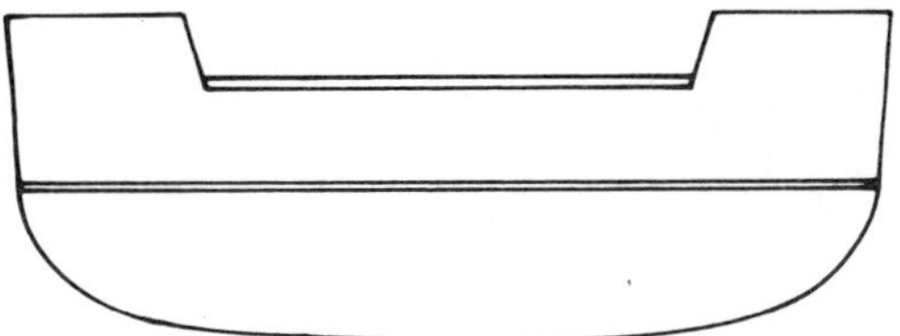

Schematic representation of the aft portion of a planing hull

Aft portion of a slightly modified planing hull

Bow section of a *V*-type hull slightly altered by overextended chines. On most of the smaller pleasure craft using this type bow, a planing type aft section is employed.

bilize themselves at high speeds, but act as inefficient displacement hulls at lower speeds.

Modified *V* hulls are combinations of displacement and *V*-type hulls. The bow section is characteristic of a displacement hull, while the aft tapers off to a flat *V* shape. These hulls are much better for use in rough water, since the displacement-type bow tends to cut through the water, rather than rise above swells and then slap down. At higher speeds, the planing-type aft section provides lift and stability.

Deep *V* hulls have a much sharper rise from the keel to the chine (where the bottom meets the side) than a traditional *V*-bottom design. The V shape is present along the entire length of the boat and provides good stability in heavy seas. The modified V-type is much faster in calm water because of its planing-type aft section.

Aft view of a deep *V*-type hull

Catamarans were the forerunner of the modern tri-hull or trihedral design. A trihedral will not reach planing speed as fast as *V*-bottom craft; however, this disadvantage is offset by their inherent lateral stability and vast amount of useful space, particularly in the bow.

Bow section of a modern trihedral hull

CENTER OF GRAVITY

For maximum speed, move the weight aft until the boat just begins to porpoise. This will reduce wetted surface to a minimum, only the aft portion being actually in the water.

TRANSOM HEIGHT

Pleasure craft manufactured specifically for use with outboard motors have transoms ranging from approximately fifteen to twenty inches high. A motor leg that is too short or a transom that is too high will cause the motor to cavitate, particularly in sharp turns. This is due to the motor running wild in an air pocket, rather than in water. The effect of transom height is small at low speeds, but quite important at high speeds. It is important that the proper motor (short-leg or long-leg) is used for a given transom height. See the "Transom and Motor Well Dimensions" chart for general recommendations. As a general rule, for average use, the motor cavitation plate should be one-half to one inch below the bottom of the keel at the transom or, if there is no keel, the bottom of the boat. In the event that the motor and transom cannot be satisfactorily matched to cure cavitation, cutting a notch in the transom to lower the motor will sometimes prove satisfactory.

TILT PIN ADJUSTMENT

The tilt pin, located on the outboard side of the mounting bracket at the bottom, controls the angle of the motor in relation to the transom. In general, the tilt pin should be adjusted so that the motor cavitation plate is about parallel to the water. The speed of boats with their weight located forward will sometimes be improved by tilting the engine out one pin hole. This will tend to raise the bow of the boat and reduce wetted surface. If the motor is tilted in, the boat will ride with the bow down, wetting more of the bottom and reducing speed. This will generally improve operation in rough water. It should be noted that experimentation is necessary to determine the optimum tilt pin setting. Variations in design, power, weight distribution, and transom angle will dictate the correct tilt pin setting.

NOTE: *If it is found that the tilt pin cannot be satisfactorily adjusted, check for water in the bottom of the boat,*

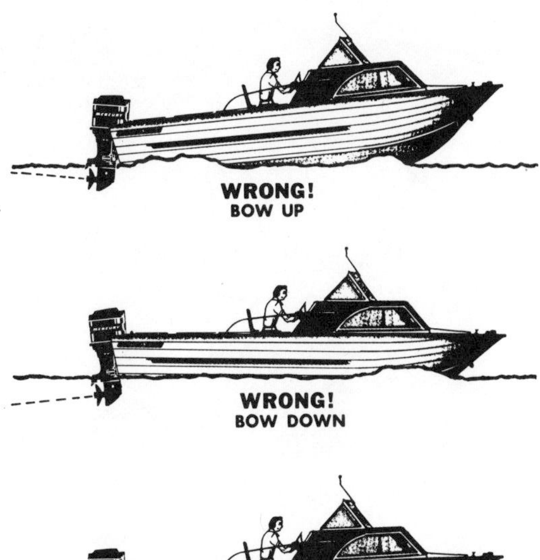

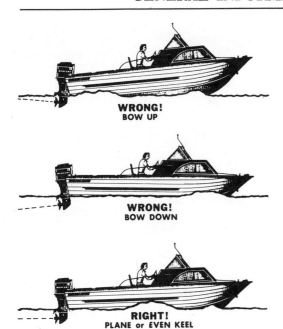

Effects of tilt pin adjustment on planing angle (© Kiekhaefer Mercury)

since this will cause a constantly shifting mass of weight with a constantly changing weight distribution.

BOTTOM CONDITION

Surface Roughness

Moss, barnacles, and other surface irregularities that increase friction will cause a considerable loss of speed. It was found in one specific test that a boat that was anchored in salt water for forty days suffered almost a fifty percent reduction in speed, due to marine growth on the hull.

Hook

The bottom is said to "hook" if it is concave in the fore and aft direction when viewed from below. When the boat is planing, this causes more lift on the bottom near the transom and allows the bow to drop. This greatly increases wetted surface and reduces speed. A hook will be more likely to occur near the transom and is the result of supporting the boat too far forward of the transom while on a trailer or in storage. Minor hooks can be corrected when the boat is wet by applying pressure to the hook and leaving it to dry. It is best to remove the floorboards and to support the boat on sawhorses with suitable lateral bracing. Use a timber, braced from the ceiling, to force the hook down. After the boat drys for several days, the hook should be corrected.

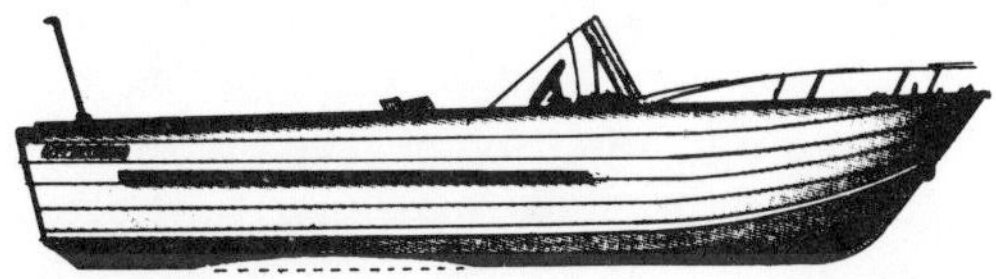

Extreme example of hook (© Kiekhaefer Mercury)

Method of correcting a hook (© Boating Industry Association)

Rocker

A boat is said to have a "rocker" if the bottom is convex in the fore and aft direction. A boat with a rocker will exhibit a

Extreme example of rocker (© Kiekhaefer Mercury)

Method of correcting a rocker (© Boating Industry Association)

strong tendency to porpoise. Minor rockers can be corrected in the same manner as was used for hooks. Turn the boat upside down with the gunwales resting on saw-horses. Using a timber, braced from the ceiling, force the rocker down and leave it to dry for several days.

PROPELLER SELECTION

NOTE: *The following information on propeller selection is taken from the Boating Industry Association's Marine Service Manual of Recommended Practices and is reproduced with the permission of the Boating Industry Association.*

The only way to be absolutely sure that the engine will achieve its full horsepower, and will operate efficiently and safely, is to use a reliable tachometer to test the engine rpm at full throttle. Knowing that the engine will turn up to the manufacturer's recommended test wheel range, select a propeller from one of the many charts supplied by your engine or propeller supplier. Make a few test runs at full throttle, with the same load as the rig will normally carry, and note the average rpm reading indicated on the tachometer. If the reading is above or below the manufacturer's indicated operating range, it is imperative that you change propellers.

Since the diameter of the propeller is generally limited by the lower unit design of the engine, the pitch and blade area will be of the greatest concern. Pitch is the theoretical distance that the propeller will travel in a solid substance if it made one complete revolution, without slippage. Increasing the pitch reduces rpm at full throttle, while reducing the pitch will increase rpm at full throttle.

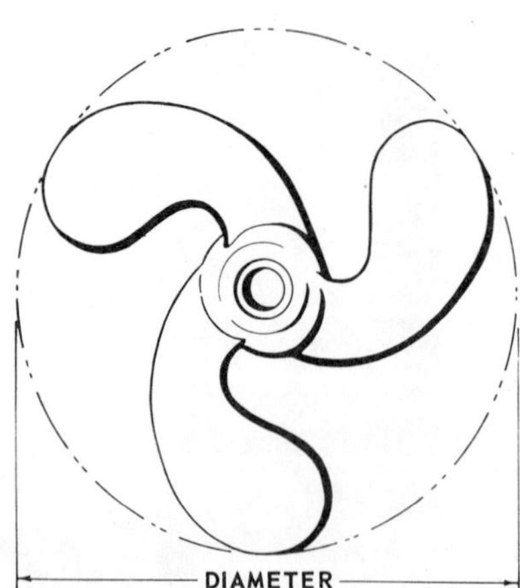

Propeller diameter

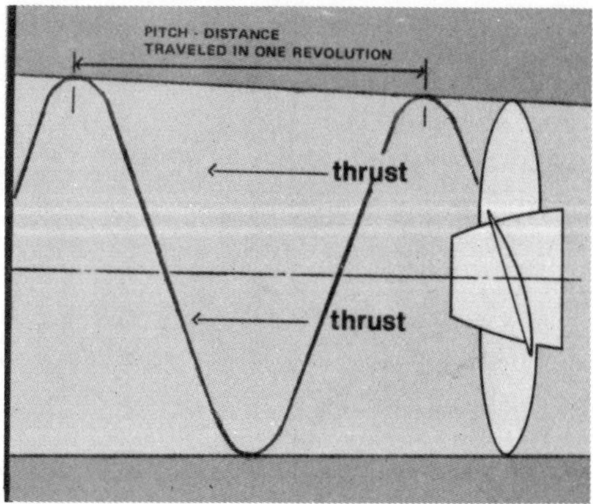

Propeller pitch

Keeping the preceding information in mind, if the full throttle tachometer reading is below the manufacturer's recommended operating range, you must try propellers of less pitch until a propeller is obtained that will allow the engine to continually operate within the recommended full throttle operating range. If the full throttle tachometer reading is above the manufacturer's recommended operating range, you must try propellers of greater pitch, until a propeller is found that will allow the engine to continually operate within the recommended full throttle operating range.

The number of blades for outboard propellers generally vary from two to four. When selecting a propeller for a light boat, two-blade or three-blade props will give the best results. As the weight increases, the blade area should increase. On large, heavy boats, the blade area should be increased by using three or four blades, to obtain optimum performance.

In a situation where both two-blade and three-blade props or three-blade and four-blade props will allow the engine to operate within the full throttle operating range, choose the one that will give the greatest forward speed.

IMPORTANCE OF LOAD CHANGES

To properly complete the job of propping, the rig should be checked with both the minimum and maximum expected loads, including skiers. It will often be necessary to have several propellers available (or one variable pitch propeller) and information on when to use them and how to change them as loads vary.

Many times, however, a propeller operating at the high end of the recommended range, with light loads, will still operate within the range with a maximum load.

PROPELLER CARE

A bent or nicked propeller will set up vibrations in the motor, which will have a damaging effect on many of the operating parts. There will be a definite loss of power and efficiency with a damaged propeller. Propellers should be checked frequently to be sure that all of the blades are in good condition. Remember to check the propeller for nicks and pitch on all service jobs. Consult your engine or propeller supplier for information on propeller repairs or else familiarize yourself with the nearest repair service.

Boat Performance Troubleshooting

NOTE: *The following chart is taken from the Boating Industry Association's Marine Service Manual of Recommended Practices and is reproduced with the permission of the Boating Industry Association.*

NOTE:

These are the most common problem areas affecting performance.

1. Improper motor tilt angle or transom height
2. Incorrect propeller selection
3. Improper load distribution
4. Water under cockpit floor

BOAT REACTION	CHECK POINTS
1. Poor speed—light load	A. Incorrect propeller selection B. Load too far forward C. Motor too low in water D. Engine malfunction E. Motor tilt too far in F. Marine growth on hull or lower unit
2. Poor speed—heavy load	A. Under-powered B. Engine malfunction C. Incorrect propeller selection D. Motor tilt too far out E. Marine growth on hull or lower unit
3. Slow to plane—heavy load	A. Motor tilt too far out B. Incorrect propeller selection C. Too much load in stern D. Water under cockpit floor E. Hull has a hook
4. Speed loss	A. Water under cockpit floor B. Marine growth on hull or lower unit C. Weeds on propeller D. Damaged propeller
5. Hard ride in rough water	A. Too much load in stern B. Motor tilt too far out C. Poor speed management
6. Runs wet in rough water	A. Load too far forward B. Motor tilt too far in C. Overloaded
7. Lists on straight when heavily loaded	A. Load not evenly distributed B. Motor tilt too far in C. Water under cockpit floor D. Hull has a hook
8. Lists or rolls on straight when lightly loaded	A. Loose steering B. Water under cockpit floor C. Motor tilt too far in D. Incorrect transom height E. Load too far forward F. Hull has a hook
9. Nose heavy—catches on waves and in turns	A. Motor tilt too far in B. Load too far forward C. Hull has a hook
10. Porpoises on straight run	A. Motor tilt too far out B. Motor too low in water C. Too much load in stern D. Hull has a rocker
11. Porpoises on turns only	A. Motor tilt too far out B. Motor too low in water C. Overpowered
12. Banks too much in turns	A. Overloaded B. Load too far forward C. Motor tilt too far in D. Overpowered E. Hull has a hook
13. Excessive Cavitation	A. Incorrect propeller selection B. Motor too high on transom C. Motor tilt too far out D. Overpowered E. Load too far forward F. Water under cockpit floor G. Keel extends too far aft; thru-hull fittings disturb water flow H. Weeds on propeller

Tune-Up and Troubleshooting

Neither tune-up nor troubleshooting can be considered independently, since each has a direct relationship with the other.

An engine tune-up is a service to restore the maximum capability of power, performance, and economy in an engine, and, at the same time, assure the owner of a complete check and more lasting results in efficiency and trouble-free performance. Each year tune-up has become more important, with the increased power and performance capabilities of outboards. It is advisable to follow a definite and thorough procedure of analysis and correction of all items affecting power, performance, and economy. The extent of an engine tune-up is usually determined by the length of time since the last service; however, specific maintenance should be performed at regular intervals (see manufacturer's section for "Periodic Maintenance") depending on operating conditions.

Troubleshooting is a logical sequence of procedures which will most likely lead the owner or serviceman to the particular cause of trouble. The troubleshooting charts in this manual are general in nature, intended to apply to all two-stroke outboards. In some cases, more specific troubleshooting procedures for component parts may be found in the manufacturer's section. Service usually comprises two areas: diagnosis and repair. While the apparent cause of trouble, in many cases, is worn or damaged parts, performance problems are less obvious and the first job is to isolate the problem and cause. Once the cause has been determined through troubleshooting, refer to the manufacturer's section for removal and/or repair procedures. An orderly diagnostic procedure cannot be stressed too frequently, since this could prove invaluable in repairing a stalled or disabled motor in an emergency (on the open water) where no other help is available.

TUNE-UP

Lubrication and Fuel

Since two-cycle engines are lubricated by oil mixed with the fuel, it is important that the correct oil/fuel ratio be maintained at all times. Follow the instructions in the manufacturer's section for recommended oil/fuel ratio. When filling the fuel tank, add about a gallon of fuel and then the oil. Fill the rest of the tank with fuel and shake it thoroughly. Never add oil after the tank has been filled.

Of equal importance is the fuel used in outboard motors. Avoid the use of stale fuel, because of the harmful deposits (varnish) which build up in the engine and fuel system, and clog the small drillings and calibrated orifices in the carburetor. See the manufacturer's section for recommended grades of fuel. If no recommendations are available, use a good grade of marine white gasoline.

NOTE: *Leaded hi-test fuel is recommended for many four-stroke outboards. If in doubt, consult a dealer.*

Compression

A compression check should be the first step of any tune-up because an engine showing low or uneven compression will not respond to a tune-up. It is essential that the cause of poor compression be found and corrected before further tune-up procedures are attempted.

Compression gauge installed

Remove the spark plugs, one at a time, and disconnect the coil to prevent the engine from starting. Install a compression gauge in each spark plug hole, in turn, and crank the engine through at least four compression strokes to obtain the maximum reading. Record the compression of each cylinder and compare it to the manufacturer's specifications. If no specifications are available, compression is usually satisfactory if it is even or if there is less than 10 psi variation between the cylinders. Poor compression is usually indicative of damage to the cylinders, pistons, rings, or head gasket(s). If poor compression is found between two adjacent cylinders, check for a blown cylinder head gasket between those two cylinders.

If the powerhead shows any indication of overheating (scorched or discolored paint), inspect the cylinders through the transfer ports for scoring or wear. It is possible for a cylinder to be slightly scored and still exhibit adequate compression.

While working with the powerhead, some manufacturer's advocate soaking the cylinders (with the engine horizontal) with a recommended engine cleaner, to remove accumulated carbon deposits. When using an engine cleaner, use the manufacturer's recommended brand and follow the instructions on the container.

Spark Plugs

The recommended spark plug and gap for a particular motor is given in the "Tune-Up Specifications" chart in each manufacturer's chapter. The particular designation of a spark plug gives, among other information, the heat range. The hot or cold rating (heat range) refers to the ability of the spark plug to conduct heat away from the firing tip. The heat range has no bearing on the intensity of the spark. In general, cold plugs are required when the engine is subjected to large loads (pulling skiers, for example) and hot plugs are required for lower intensity operation (trolling).

CAUTION: *A spark plug that is too hot will not allow the electrode to cool sufficiently between power strokes and will cause the electrode to glow red-hot. This, in turn, causes excessively high temperatures, bringing about detonation and pre-ignition.*

It is best to consult a dealer before installing plugs which differ from the manufacturer's recommendations.

Conventional Spark Plugs

Each spark plug should be removed and inspected individually and compared to the spark plug diagnosis chart to determine the cause of malfunction and possible

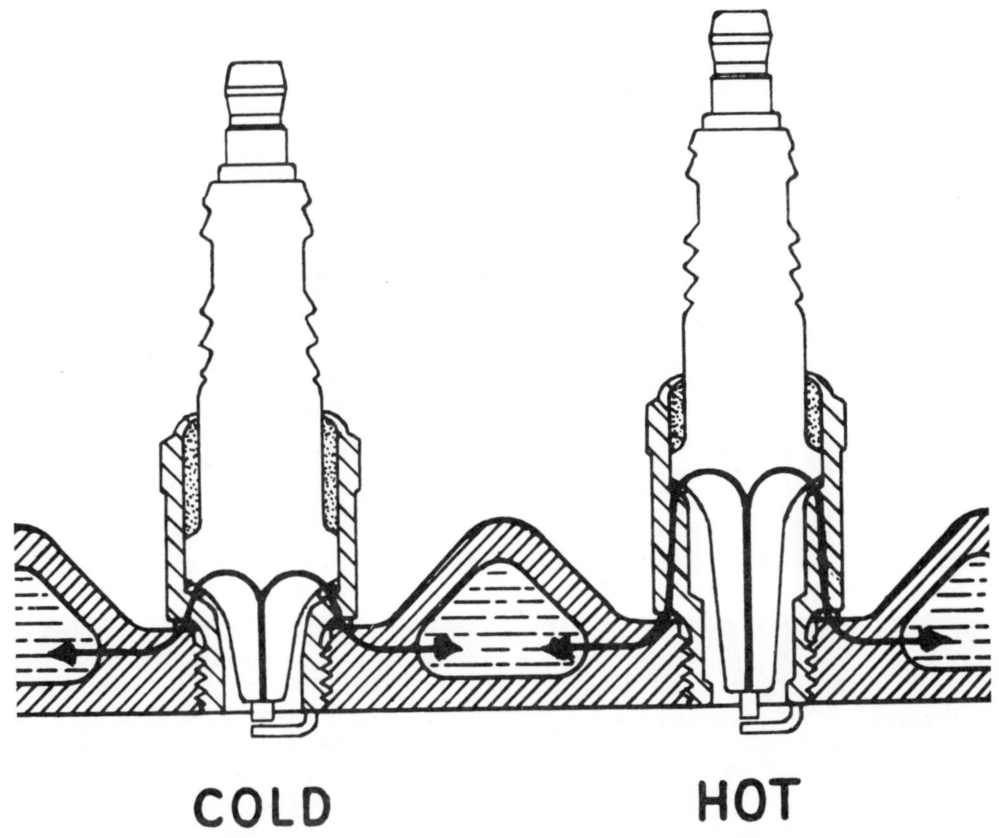

The heat range of a spark plug refers to the ability of a plug to conduct heat away from the firing tip.

A piston damaged by pre-ignition (© Kiekhaefer Mercury)

corrective measures. Replace spark plugs as necessary. In normal service, spark plugs are replaced in sets, corresponding to the number of cylinders. Inspect each spark plug for its make, type, and heat range. All plugs must be of the same make and heat range. Adjust each spark plug gap (new or old) to the manufacturer's specification, using a round feeler gauge, as illustrated. Before adjusting the gap, file the center electrode flat with a point file.

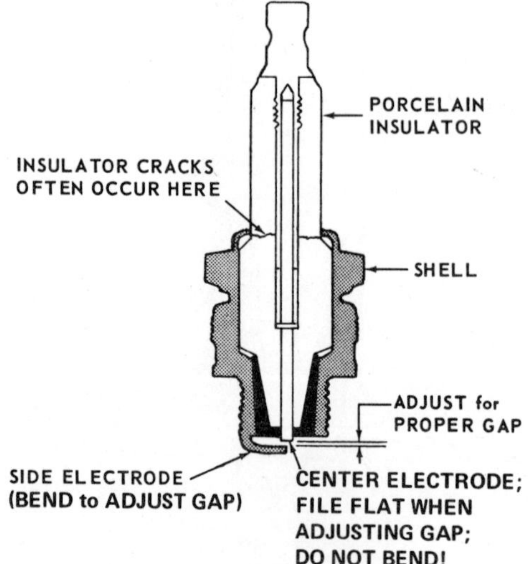

Cross-sectional view of a conventional spark plug (© Kiekhaefer Mercury)

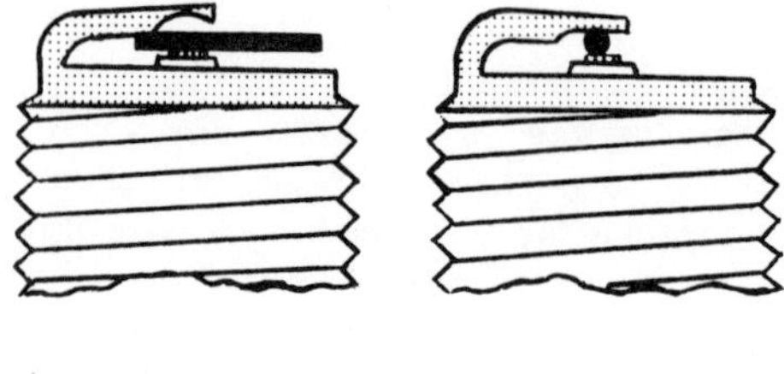

Gapping conventional spark plugs

CAUTION: *Never bend the center electrode to adjust the gap; always adjust the gap by bending the side electrode.*

Surface Gap Spark Plugs

Remove the spark plugs and inspect the center electrode as illustrated. If it is worn or burned back more than 1/32 in. (0.8 mm) below the insulator, it will not function properly. Do not replace surface gap plugs for any other reason than this. Be sure that the plugs being replaced are definitely misfiring; the accumulation of deposits can be deceiving.

CAUTION: *Due to the high voltage requirements with surface gap spark plugs, do not use this type of plug, unless specifically recommended by the manufacturer.*

Surface gap spark plug, illustrating proper gap (© Kiekhaefer Mercury)

Spark Plug Installation

Inspect the spark plug hole threads and clean them before installing the spark plugs. Crank the engine several times to blow out any material which might have been dislodged during the cleaning operation. Install the spark plugs in the powerhead with new gaskets and torque them to the manufacturer's specification. Improper installation is one of the largest single causes of unsatisfactory spark plug performance, and is generally the result of one or more of the following practices.

Cause	*Result*
Insufficient torque (to fully seat gasket)	Compression loss—early plug failure
Excessive torque	Reduced operation life—complete destruction from inability to dissipate heat
Dirty gasket seal	High temperatures—early plug failure
Corroded hole threads	Excessively high temperatures—early failure (overheating)

Always use a new gasket seal and wipe the seats in the head clean. The gasket must be fully compressed on clean seats to ensure complete heat transfer and to provide a gas-tight seal in the cylinder. For this reason, as well as the necessity of maintaining the proper plug gap, the correct torque, when installing the spark plugs, is extremely important.

Spark Plug Diagnosis

Can be identified in a negative ground system by lack of wear at the center electrode and a semicircular wear pattern at the side electrode. The primary coil leads are reversed from proper position.

Reversed coil polarity

Plugs with even-colored, tan or light gray deposits and moderate electrode wear.

Normal appearance

If one or more plugs in a set have chipped insulators, severe detonation is the probable cause. Bending the center electrode to adjust the gap can also crack the insulator. Install new plugs of the correct gap and heat range. Check for over-advanced timing.

Chipped insulator

Usually occurring in a relatively new set, splash deposits may form after a long delayed tune-up when accumulated cylinder deposits are thrown against the plugs at high rpm. Clean and install the plugs.

Splash-fouled

Results from fused deposits which appear as tiny beads or glass-like bubbles; caused by improper oil/fuel ratio and high-speed operation following sustained low speeds.

Gap-bridged

See "Gap Bridging."

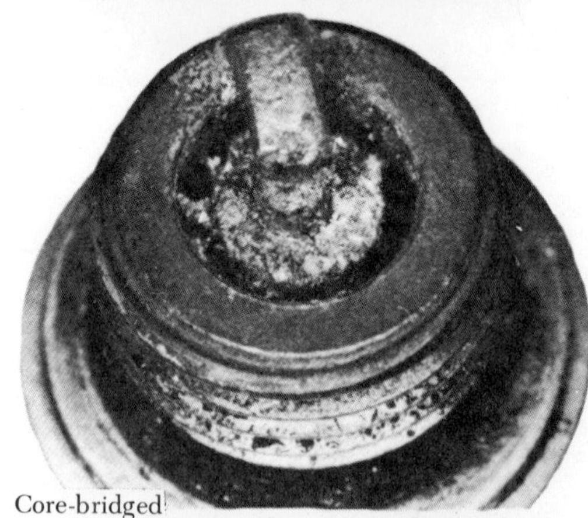
Core-bridged

Oil or wet, black carbon covering the entire end of the plug, caused by excessive oil in the fuel, too rich fuel mixture, sustained low-speed operation, or incorrect heat range plugs.

Oil-fouled

Usually caused by severe pre-ignition or detonation. Likely causes are improper heat range plugs, low octane gasoline, neglected engine maintenance (even with high octane fuel), over-advanced ignition timing, or inadequate engine cooling.

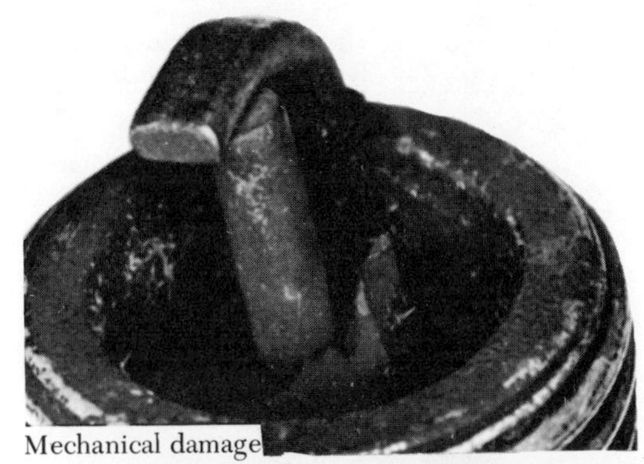
Mechanical damage

If the set of plugs has dead white insulators and badly worn electrodes, check for overadvanced ignition timing. Install plugs of the next colder heat range.

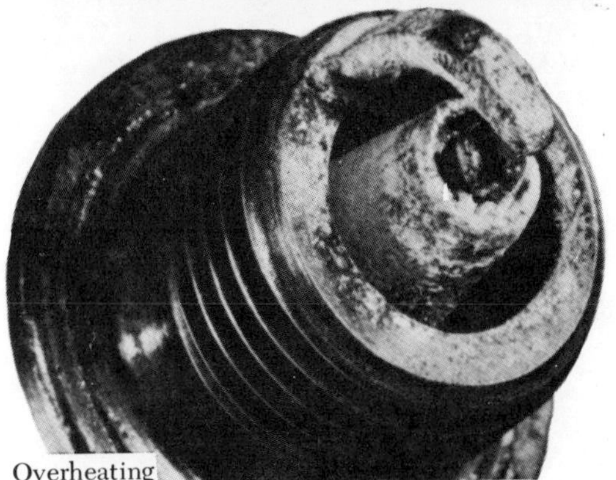
Overheating

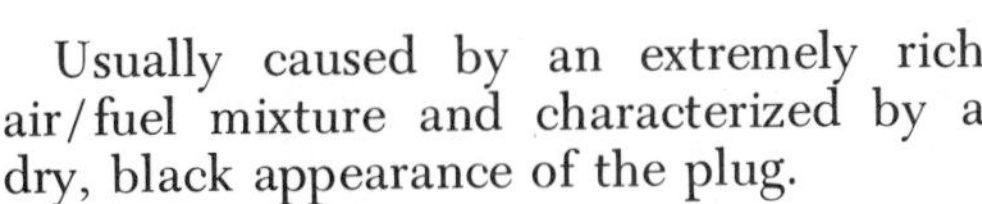
Usually caused by an extremely rich air/fuel mixture and characterized by a dry, black appearance of the plug.

Cold-fouled

Fuel System

Carburetor

The most common causes of problems in the carburetor are improper fuel and the formation of gum or varnish in the calibrated drillings and jets. Hard varnish and other deposits will build up, over a period of time, and block the calibrated drillings. The carburetor should be removed, disassembled, and thoroughly cleaned. (Refer to the manufacturer's section exploded views, and the removal and repair procedures.) Before disassembling the carburetor, thoroughly clean the external surface to remove all traces of dirt and grease. Disassemble the carburetor and soak all components (except cork washers, gaskets, and seals) in a good carburetor solvent. Blow all parts dry with compressed air or allow them to air-dry. Never attempt to clean the calibrated drillings or jets with wire, since this will only cause damage and the unnecessary replacement of parts.

Troubleshooting Pressure-Type Carburetors

Symptom	*Probable Cause*
ENGINE WON'T START 1. No fuel at carburetor	a. Empty gas tank b. Clogged fuel filter c. Restricted vent in gas tank d. Defective fuel pump e. Air leak in line from tank f. Clogged or broken fuel line
2. Fuel at carburetor	a. Flooding at carburetor b. Choke not operating c. Restricted carburetor jets d. Water in gasoline
3. Flooding at carburetor	a. Choke out of adjustment b. High float level c. Float stuck d. Excessive fuel pump pressure e. Float saturated beyond buoyancy

Symptom	*Probable Cause*
ROUGH OPERATION	a. Dirt or water in fuel
	b. Reed valve open or broken
	c. Incorrect fuel level in carburetor bowl
	d. Carburetor loose at mounting flange
	e. Throttle shutter not closing completely
	f. Throttle shutter valve installed incorrectly
ENGINE MISFIRES AT HIGH SPEED	a. Dirty carburetor
	b. Lean carburetor adjustment
	c. Restriction in fuel system
	d. Low fuel pump pressure
ENGINE BACKFIRES	a. Poor quality fuel
	b. Air/fuel mixture too lean
	c. Excessive lean or too rich mixture
	d. Improperly adjusted carburetor
ENGINE PRE-IGNITION	a. Excessive oil in fuel
	b. Poor grade of fuel
	c. Lean carburetor mixture
SPARK PLUGS BURN AND FOUL	a. Fuel mixture too rich
	b. Inferior grade of gasoline
HIGH GAS CONSUMPTION	
1. Flooding or leaking	a. Cracked carburetor casting
	b. Leaking line connections
	c. Defective carburetor bowl gasket
	d. High float level
	e. Plugged vent hole in cover
	f. Loose needle and seat
	g. Defective needle valve seat gasket
	h. Worn needle valve and seat
	i. Foreign matter clogging needle valve
	j. Worn float pin or bracket
	k. Float binding in bowl
	l. High fuel pump pressure
2. Overly rich mixture	a. Choke lever stuck
	b. High float level
	c. High fuel pump pressure
ABNORMAL SPEEDS	a. Carburetor out-of-adjustment
	b. Too much oil in fuel

Inspection

Even though wear damage is minimal on outboard carburetors, the following inspections should be made after the carburetor is disassembled and cleaned.

1. Be sure that the throttle shaft moves freely and is not worn. If the throttle shaft sticks, check further for gum or varnish on the pivot points.

2. Check the mixture adjustment needle for a groove around the tapered point. This is usually the result of overtightening the needle in its seat. If it is found that the motor will not hold an adjustment, investigate this as a possible cause. If the needle is grooved or bent, replace it with a new one.

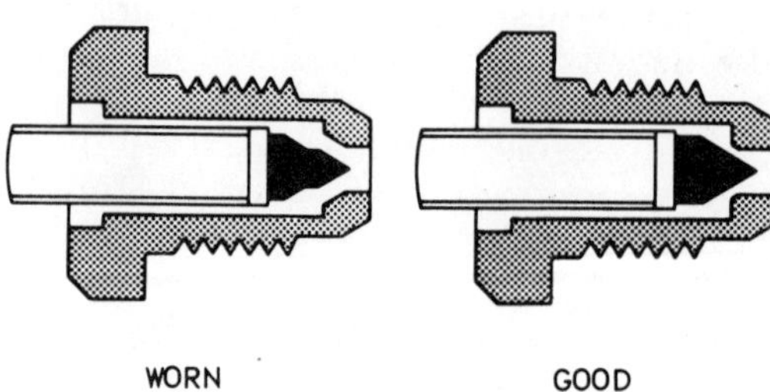

Check the mixture adjustment needle for wear in the form of a groove around the tip of the needle. (© Outboard Marine Corp.)

3. Check the needle valve seat for wear, as this may also prohibit a satisfactory adjustment.

4. Inspect the float for free movement. It should not bind or stick.

5. Check to make sure that the carburetor linkage moves freely and does not bind.

6. Be sure that the carburetor body is not cracked since this will cause carburetor flooding.

Assemble the carburetor, following the instructions in the manufacturer's section. Rather than risk unsatisfactory performance, it is standard practice to replace the jets at every disassembly. These are inexpensive and available from your local dealer. The use of carburetor overhaul kits is also suggested because these contain all of the new gaskets and seals which should be replaced at every overhaul. Be sure to adjust the float to the manufacturer's specification.

NOTE: *When installing new jets, do not overtighten them in their seats. This will damage the jets and will necessitate replacement.*

Adjustments

Refer to the manufacturer's section for all adjustments. Also included in the manufacturer's section are data on available jets for use in different altitudes.

FUEL PUMP

Most outboard motors are equipped with one or more diaphragm-type fuel pumps, operated either mechanically, electrically, or by vacuum from the crankcase.

Remove the fuel pump, disassemble it (see manufacturer's section), and wash all of the parts thoroughly (except diaphragm). Blow them dry with compressed air or air-dry them. Carefully inspect each part for wear or damage. Especially inspect the fuel pump diaphragm; problems in this area are often mistakenly diagnosed as ignition trouble. A tiny pin-hole in the diaphragm will permit gas to enter the crankcase and will wet-foul a particular cylinder at idle speed. At higher speeds this is not as noticeable as the fuel is metered and the plug will fire normally. Replace the diaphragm if conditions warrant.

Assemble the fuel pump and tighten the elbows and check valve connections firmly. After assembly, check the valves by blowing through the outlet hole. Air should be drawn through the valve, but the valve should close immediately when attempting to blow through it. Check the intake valve in a reverse manner. When installing the fuel valves and fittings, use Permatex for sealant, but do not use an excessive amount or the lines will be plugged. Always use new gaskets when assembling. If, after overhaul, poor high-speed performance is still noticeable, check the fuel pump delivery pressure as described in the manufacturer's section.

Fuel Lines and Filters

Inspect the fuel lines for kinks, leaks, or restrictions. If necessary, remove the fuel lines and blow them out with compressed air. When installing the fuel lines, be sure that they are not twisted.

Remove the fuel filters (see manufacturer's section) and wash the parts in solvent, allowing them to air-dry.

CAUTION: *Do not operate an outboard motor with the filters removed. This will only lead to frequent carburetor clogging.*

If frequent fuel starvation is encountered, check all of the above in addition to the fuel tank.

Reed Valves

If all other possibilities have been exhausted and the motor still performs poorly at low speed (but satisfactorily otherwise), an inspection of the reed valve unit is warranted. Remove the reed valve unit as described in the manufacturer's section and check for broken or bent reeds. Be sure that all other possibilities have been thoroughly checked, since the removal of the reed valves on some motors involves removal of the powerhead.

Ignition System

Breaker Points

On most outboards the breaker points are located under the flywheel and the flywheel must be removed to service the breaker points. Refer to the manufacturer's section for removal procedures. Inspect the breaker points for burning or pitting. The contacts should be clean and light gray in color. A simple test light can be constructed (see illustration) to be used as a continuity tester. Disconnect the coil lead from the points and connect one end of the tester to the points (insulated terminal) and the other to a good ground.

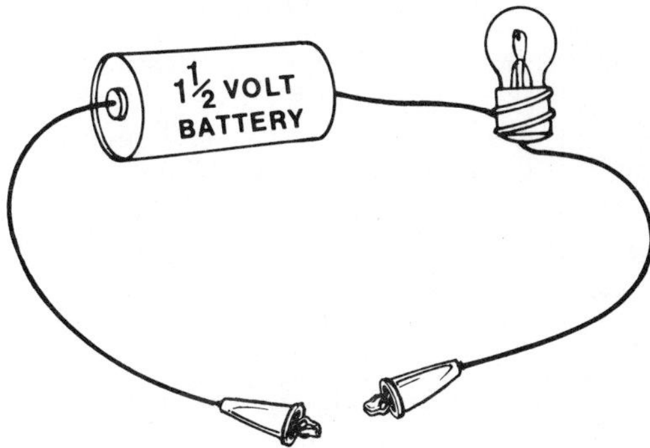

A simple test light can be constructed from readily available materials.

CAUTION: *Before servicing the ignition system (particularly CD type), disconnect the battery.*

With the points closed, the light should burn; it should go out when the points open. If this does not happen, replace the breaker points, making sure that the light oil or wax is cleaned from the points. Adjust the point gap to the manufacturer's specification. It is standard practice to replace the condenser when the points are replaced.

Maker Points

High primary voltage, in systems using maker points, will quickly roughen the maker points. This is not cause for concern, as points in this condition will continue to function satisfactorily. Do not replace maker points unless an obvious malfunction is present or the contacts are loose or burned away. See the particular manufacturer's section for maker point service (where applicable.)

Condenser

The condenser can be checked using the continuity tester described previously. Check the condenser case for cracks and remove the condenser. Connect a lead of the continuity tester to the condenser wire and the other lead to the condenser case. A short in the condenser is indicated if the light comes on. If the breaker points are observed to pit very rapidly, check the condenser as this is usually at fault.

Ignition Timing

Consult the manufacturer's section for specific timing specifications and procedures.

Magneto Air Gap

On motors where the armature and coil are mounted outside the flywheel, turn the engine to locate the flywheel magnets under the armature core legs. Measure the clearance between the armature core legs and the flywheel magneto. If the measured clearance does not meet manufacturer's specifications, loosen the armature mounting screws and adjust it to specifications.

If the armature is located under the flywheel, a slot or opening is usually provided to adjust the air gap.

Magneto Edge Gap

This is a service specification and is not usually adjustable. Magneto edge gap can, however, change due to a loose flywheel or drive key, excessive breaker cam wear, or improperly adjusted breaker points. Correction of the problem will usually bring the magneto edge gap within specifications.

Battery

Batteries in marine use are normally kept in special plastic boxes. No maintenance is normally necessary, other than keeping the charge up and keeping the terminals clean and lightly coated with petroleum jelly. Check the charge of the battery frequently with a hydrometer. Consult the chart to determine the charged condition from the specific gravity reading.

If the motor is to be unused for a long period of time, it is wise to remove the battery and store it in a cool, dry place. Be sure to keep the battery fully charged.

SPECIFIC GRAVITY READING	CHARGED CONDITION
1.260-1.280	Fully Charged
1.230-1.250	Three Quarter Charged
1.200-1.220	One Half Charged
1.170-1.190	One Quarter Charged
1.140-1.160	Just About Flat
1.110-1.130	All The Way Down

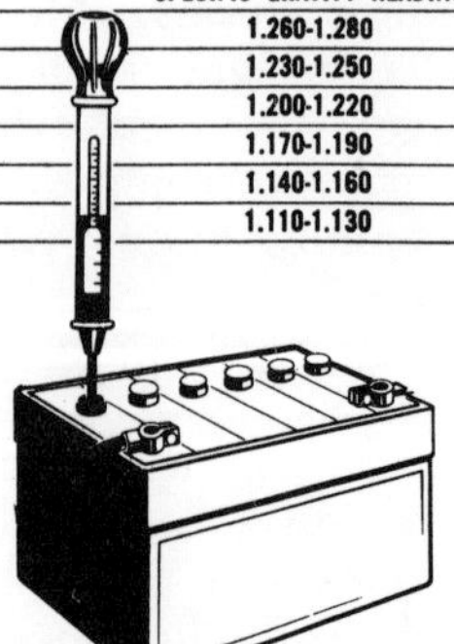

Specific gravity vs. charged condition

Cooling System

If overheating is encountered, check the water intakes for blockage. If these appear to be clear, refer to the manufacturer's section for water pump and impeller service procedures.

Lower Unit

Gearcase

Check the level and condition of the gearcase lubricant at the specified manufacturer's intervals. These can be found in the manufacturer's section, along with the specified lubricant.

Propeller

Check the propeller for nicks, gouges, or other damage which will affect performance. If the motor is equipped with shear pins, check these for wear or damage. Small nicks on the propeller may be filed smooth or hammered out with a light hammer. Be sure to place the propeller on a block of wood before attempting to correct any nicks with this method.

TROUBLESHOOTING 2 STROKE OUTBOARD MOTORS

NOTE: *The following troubleshooting chart is taken from the Boating Industry Association's Marine Service Manual of Recommended Practices and is reproduced with the permission of the Boating Industry Association.*

Start all major diagnoses with a compression test; also check the wheel rpm. Do not run the motor out of water.

MOTOR REACTION	CHECK POINTS
1. Manual starter rope pulls out, but pawls do not engage	A. Friction spring bent or burred
	B. Excess grease on pawls or spring
	C. Pawls bent or burred
2. Starter rope does not return	A. Recoil spring broken or binding
	B. Starter housing bent
	C. Loose or missing parts
3. Clattering manual starter	A. Friction spring bent or burred
	B. Starter housing bent
	C. Excess grease on pawls or spring
	D. Dry starter spindle
4. Electric starter inoperative	A. Loose or corroded connections or ground
	B. Starting circuit safety switch open or out of adjustment
	C. Under capacity or weak battery, or corroded battery terminals
	D. Faulty starter solenoid
	E. Moisture in electric starter motor
	F. Broken or worn brushes in starter motor
	G. Faulty fields
	H. Faulty armature
	I. Broken wire in harness or connector
	J. Faulty starter key, push button, or safety switch
	K. Worn or frayed insulation
5. Electric starter does not engage but solenoid clicks	A. Loose or corroded connections or ground
	B. Weak battery
	C. Faulty starter solenoid
	D. Broken wire in electric harness
	E. Loose or stripped post on starter motor
	F. See steps in number 4
6. Hard to start or won't start	A. Empty gas tank
	B. Gas tank air vent not open
	C. Fuel lines kinked or severely pinched
	D. Water or dirt in fuel system
	E. Clogged fuel filter or screens
	F. Motor not being choked to start
	G. Engine not primed—pump primer system
	H. Carburetor adjustments too lean (not allowing enough fuel to start engine)
	I. Timing and synchronizing out of adjustment
	J. Manual choke linkage bent—auto choke out of adjustment
	K. Spark plugs improperly gapped, dirty, or broken
	L. Fuel tank primer inoperative (pressurized system)
	M. Ignition points improperly gapped, burned or dirty, or triggering (CD) system inoperative
	N. Loose, broken wire or frayed insulation in electrical system
	O. Reed valves not seating or stuck shut
	P. Weak coil or condenser
	Q. Faulty gaskets
	R. Cracked distributor cap or rotor, or shorted rotor
	S. Loose fuel connector
	T. Amplifier (CD) inoperative
	U. Poor engine or ignition ground
	V. Faulty ignition or safety switch
7. Low-speed miss or motor won't idle smoothly and slowly enough	A. Too much oil—too little oil
	B. Timing and synchronizing out of adjustment
	C. Carburetor idle adjustment (mixture lean or rich)
	D. Ignition points improper (gap, worn, or fouled) or triggering (CD) system inoperative
	E. Weak coil or condenser
	F. Loose or broken ignition wires
	G. Loose or worn magneto plate
	H. Spark plugs (improper gap or dirty)
	I. Head gasket, reed plate gasket (blown or leaking)
	J. Reed valve standing open or stuck shut
	K. Plugged crankcase bleeder, check valves, or lines
	L. Leaking crankcase halves
	M. Leaking crankcase seals (top or bottom)
	N. Exhaust gases returning through intake manifold
	O. Poor distributor ground
	P. Cracked or shorted distributor cap or rotor
	Q. Fuel pump diaphragm punctured
	R. Accessory tachometer shorted or not compatible with ignition system
	S. Faulty ignition or safety switch
8. High-speed miss or intermittent spark	A. Spark plugs improperly gapped or dirty
	B. Loose, leaking, or broken ignition wires
	C. Breaker points (improper gap or dirty; worn cam or cam follower) or triggering (CD) system faulty
	D. Weak coil or condenser
	E. Water in fuel
	F. Leaking head gasket or exhaust cover gasket

MOTOR REACTION	CHECK POINTS
8. High-speed miss or intermittent spark	G. Spark plug heat range incorrect H. Engine improperly timed I. Carbon or fouled combustion chambers J. Magneto, distributor, or CD triggering system poorly grounded K. Distributor oiler wick bad L. Accessory tachometer shorted or not compatible with ignition system M. Faulty ignition or safety switch
9. Coughs, spits, slows	A. Idle or high-speed needles set too lean B. Carburetor not synchronized C. Leaking gaskets in induction system D. Obstructed fuel passages E. Float level set too low F. Improperly seated or broken reeds G. Fuel pump pressure line ruptured H. Fuel pump (punctured diaphragm), check valves stuck open or closed, fuel lines leak I. Poor fuel tank pressure (pressurized system) J. Worn or leaking fuel connector
10. Vibrates excessively or runs roughly and smokes	A. Idle or high-speed needles set too rich B. Too much oil mixed with gas C. Carburetor not synchronized with ignition properly D. Choke not opening properly E. Float level too high F. Air passage to carburetor obstructed G. Bleeder valves or passages plugged H. Transom bracket clamps loose on transom I. Prop out of balance J. Broken motor mount K. Exhaust gases getting inside motor cover L. Poor ignition—see steps in number 8
11. Runs well, idles well for a short period, then slows down and stops	A. Weeds or other debris on lower unit or propeller B. Insufficient cooling water C. Carburetor, fuel pump, filter, or screens dirty D. Bleeder valves or passages plugged E. Lower unit bind (lack of lubrication or bent) F. Gas tank air vent not open G. Not enough oil in gas H. Combustion chambers and spark plugs fouled, causing pre-ignition I. Spark plug heat range too high or too low J. Wrong propeller (pre-ignition) K. Low-speed adjustment too rich or too lean
12. Won't start, kicks back, backfires into lower unit	A. Spark plug wires reversed B. Flywheel key sheared C. Distributor belt timing off (magneto or battery ignition) D. Timing and synchronizing out of adjustment E. Reed valves not seating or broken F. Poor engine or distributor ground
13. No acceleration, low top rpm	A. Improper carburetor adjustments B. Improper timing and synchronization C. Spark plugs (improper gap or dirty) D. Ignition points (improper gap or faulty), or triggering (CD) system E. Faulty coil or condenser F. Loose, leaking, or broken ignition wires G. Reed valves not properly seated or broken H. Blown head or exhaust cover gasket I. Weeds on lower unit or propeller J. Incorrect propeller K. Insufficient oil in gas L. Insufficient oil in lower unit M. Fuel restrictions N. Scored cylinder—stuck rings O. Marine growth, hooks, rockers, or change in load of boat P. Sticky magneto plate or distributor Q. Carbon buildup on piston head at deflector R. Marginal CD amplifier
14. No acceleration, idles well but when put to full power dies down	A. High-speed or low-speed needle set too lean B. Dirt or packing behind needles and seats C. High-speed nozzle obstructed D. Float level too low E. Choke partly closed F. Improper timing and synchronization G. Fuel lines or passages obstructed H. Fuel filter obstructed. Fuel pump not supplying enough fuel I. Not enough oil in gas J. Breaker points improperly gapped or dirty K. Bent gearcase or exhaust tube L. Marginal CD amplifier M. Faulty spark plugs

MOTOR REACTION	CHECK POINTS
15. Engine runs at high speed only by using hand primer	A. Carburetor adjustments B. Dirt or packing behind needles and seat C. Fuel lines or passages obstructed D. Fuel line leaks E. Fuel pump not supplying enough fuel F. Float level too low G. Fuel filter obstructed H. Fuel tank or connector at fault
16. No power under heavy load	A. Wrong propeller B. Weeds or other debris on lower unit or propeller C. Breaker points improperly gapped or dirty D. Stator plate loose E. Ignition timing over advanced or late F. Faulty carburetion and/or faulty ignition G. Prop hub slips H. Scored cylinders or rings stuck I. Carbon buildup on piston head at deflector
17. Cranks over extremely easy on one or more cylinders	A. Low compression 1. Worn or broken rings 2. Scored cylinder or pistons 3. Blown head gasket 4. Loose spark plugs 5. Loose head bolts 6. Crankcase halves improperly sealed 7. Burned piston
18. Engine won't crank over	A. Manual start lock improperly adjusted B. Pistons rusted to cylinder wall C. Lower unit gears, prop shaft rusted or broken D. Broken connecting rod, crankshaft, or driveshaft E. Coil heels binding on flywheel F. Engine improperly assembled
19. Motor overheats	A. Motor not deep enough in water B. Not enough oil in gas or improperly mixed C. Bad thermostat D. Seals or gaskets (burned, cracked, or broken) E. Impeller key not in place or broken F. Plugged water inlet, outlet, or cavity G. Obstruction in water passages H. Broken, pinched, or leaking water lines I. Improper ignition timing J. Motor not assembled properly K. Shorted heat light wiring L. Bad water pump impeller, plate, housing, or seal

MOTOR REACTION	CHECK POINTS
20. Motor stops suddenly, freezes up	A. No oil in gas, or no gas B. Insufficient cooling water C. No lubricant in gearcase D. Rusted cylinder or crankshaft E. Bent or broken rod, crankshaft, driveshaft, prop shaft, or stuck piston F. Bad water pump or plugged water passages
21. Motor knocks excessively	A. Too much or not enough oil in gas B. Worn or loose bearings, pistons, rods, or wrist pins C. Overadvanced ignition timing D. Carbon in combustion chambers and exhaust ports E. Manual starter not centered F. Flywheel nut loose G. Flywheel hitting coil heels H. Bent shift rod (vibrating against exhaust tube) I. Loose assemblies, bolts or screws
22. Generator will not charge	A. Battery condition B. Connections loose or dirty C. Drive belt loose or broken D. Faulty regulator or cutout relay E. Field fuse or fusible wire in regulator blown F. Generator not polarized (DC generators) G. Open generator windings H. Worn or sticking brushes and/or slip rings I. Faulty rectifier diodes (AC generators) J. Faulty ammeter K. CD voltage regulator faulty L. Rectifier not grounded M. CD safety circuit grounded
23. Low generator output and a low battery	A. High resistance at battery terminals B. High resistance in charging circuit C. Faulty ammeter D. Low regulator setting E. Faulty rectifier diodes (AC generators) F. Faulty generator
24. Excessive battery charging	A. Regulator set too high B. Regulator contacts stuck C. Regulator voltage winding open D. Regulator improperly grounded E. High resistance in field coil F. Regulator improperly mounted
25. Excessive fuel consumption	A. Hole in fuel pump diaphragm B. Deteriorated carburetor gaskets C. Altered or wrong fixed jets

MOTOR REACTION	CHECK POINTS
25. Excessive fuel consumption	D. Jets improperly adjusted E. Carburetor casting porous F. Float level too high G. Loose distributor pulley
26. Shifter dog jumps	A. Worn shifter dog or worn gear dogs B. Worn linkage C. Remote control adjustment D. Gearcase loose or sprung E. Exhaust housing bent F. Linkage out of adjustment
27. Electric shift inoperative or slips	A. Improper remote control installation B. Faulty coils C. Faulty springs D. Faulty clutch and gear E. Faulty bearings F. Wrong lubricant G. Loose or sprung gearcase H. Shorted wiring

2 · Chrysler Outboard Corporation

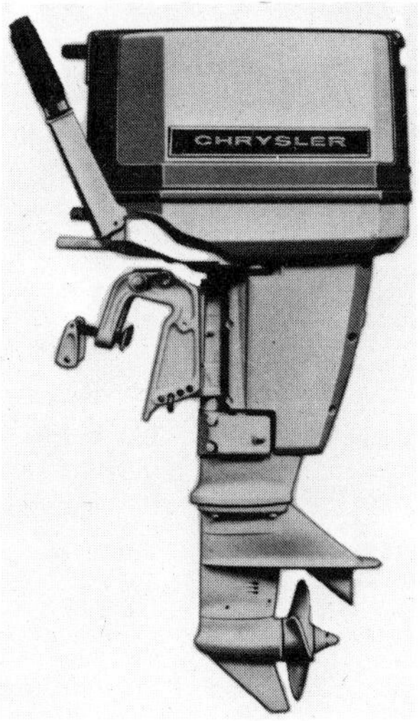

Introduction

The larger models of outboards produced by Chrysler Outboard Corporation are complemented by numerous smaller models for practically any purpose.

Smaller Chrysler outboards range in size from the ubiquitous 3.5 and 3.6 horsepower models to the larger 20 horsepower model. All 1972 Chrysler outboards are equipped with a new fuel recycling system which eliminates the overboard discharge of unburned fuel. The new system assures that excess fuel accumulations are recirculated and burned in the combustion chamber.

Chrysler lower units are protected by a spline-drive propeller and a rubber-cushioned hub which acts as a shock absorber if an underwater object is struck. A seal guard protects the splines and seal from fishline and other hazards. Other notable Chrysler features include dripless carburetors, electrical waterproofing, self-cleaning water pumps, underwater exhaust outlets, and corrosion-resistant finishes.

Do-it-yourselfers are aided by easily removable one-piece hoods, and easily accessible electrical components.

NOTE: *Chrysler factory service procedures contained in this chapter also apply to the following brands of outboard motors.*

a. Chrysler of Canada

3.5 hp	1966–69
3.6 hp	1970–72
4.4 hp	1968
5.0 hp	1969–70
6.0 hp	1966–67 and 1971–72
6.6 hp	1968
7.0 hp	1969–70
8.0 hp	1971–72
9.2 hp	1966–67
9.9 hp	1968–72
12.9 hp	1971–72
20.0 hp	1966–72

b. Wizard

3.5 hp	1966–70
6.0 hp	1966–70
9.2 hp	1966–71
20.0 hp	1966–71

c. Sea King

3.5 hp	1966–69
6.0 hp	1966–71
9.2 hp	1966–69
20.0 hp	1966–71

d. Viking (Eaton's of Canada)

3.5 hp	1966–70
6.0 hp	1966–70
9.2 hp	1966–69
20.0 hp	1967–70

e. J. C. Penney

3.5 hp	1966

Model Identification

Year	*Model (hp)*	*Model Number*	*No. of Cyls*	*Displacement (cu in.)*
1966	3.5	3601, 3611	1	5.18
	6.0	6601, 6603	2	10.60
	9.2	9601	2	11.97
	9.2 Autoelectric	9641	2	11.97
	20.0	20601, 20611	2	19.96
	20.0 Autoelectric	20641	2	19.96
1967	3.5	3701, 3711	1	5.18
	6.0	6701	2	10.60
	9.2	9701	2	11.97
	9.2 Autoelectric	9741	2	11.97
	20.0	20701, 20711	2	19.96
	20.0 Autoelectric	20741, 20751	2	19.96
1968	3.5	3018, 3118	1	5.18
	4.4	4018, 4118	2	8.99
	6.6	6018, 6118	2	10.20
	9.9	9018, 9118	2	13.15
	9.9 Autoelectric	9218, 9318	2	13.15
	20.0	20018, 20118	2	19.96
	20.0 Autoelectric	20218, 20318	2	19.96
1969	3.5	303, 313	1	5.18
	5.0	501, 511	2	8.99
	7.0	703, 713	2	10.20
	9.9	907, 917	2	13.15
	9.9 Autoelectric	923, 933	2	13.15
	20.0	2003, 2013	2	19.96
	20.0 Autoelectric	2023, 2033	2	19.96
1970	3.6	32 HA, 33 HA	1	5.18
	5.0	52 HA, 53 HA	2	8.99
	7.0	72 HA, 73 HA	2	10.20
	9.9	92 HA, 93 HA	2	13.15
	9.9 Autoelectric	94 HA, 95 HA	2	13.15
	20.0	202 HA, 203 HA	2	19.96
	20.0 Autoelectric	204 HA, 205 HA	2	19.96
1971	3.6	32 HB, 33 HB	1	5.18
	6.0	62 HA, 63 HA	2	8.99
		62 HB, 63 HB		
	8.0	82 HB, 83 HB	2	10.20
	9.9	92 HB, 93 HB	2	13.15
		92 HC, 93 HC		
	9.9 Autoelectric	94 HB, 95 HB	2	13.15
		94 HC, 95 HC		
	12.9	122 HA, 123 HA	2	13.62
		124 HB, 125 HB		
	20.0	202 HB, 203 HB	2	19.96
		202 HC, 203 HC		
	20.0 Autoelectric	204 HB, 205 HB	2	19.96
		204 HC, 205 HC		
1972	3.6	32 HB, 33 HB	1	5.18
	6.0	62 HC, 63 HC	2	8.99
	8.0	82 HC, 83 HC	2	10.20
	9.9	92 HD, 93 HD	2	13.15
	9.9 Autoelectric	94 HD, 95 HD	2	13.15
	12.9	122 HC, 123 HC	2	13.62
	12.9 Autoelectric	124 HC, 125 HC	2	13.62
	20.0	202 HD, 203 HD	2	19.96
	20.0 Autoelectric	204 HD, 205 HD	2	19.96

Serial Number

The serial number is the manufacturer's key to many engineering details and should be included in any correspondence with the factory or a dealer.

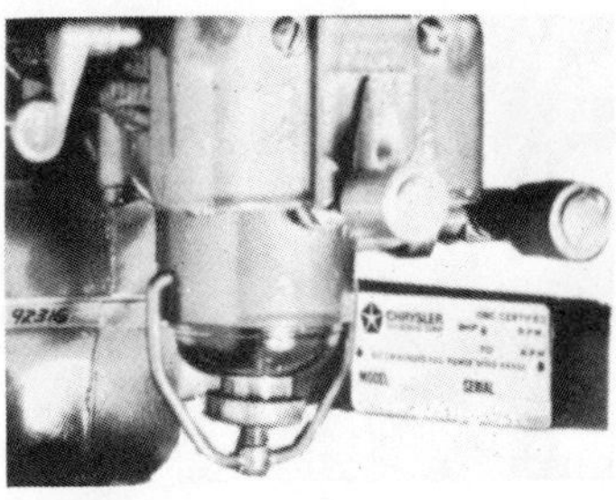

Serial number plate located on the steering handle. (© Chrysler Outboard Corporation)

Serial Number Location

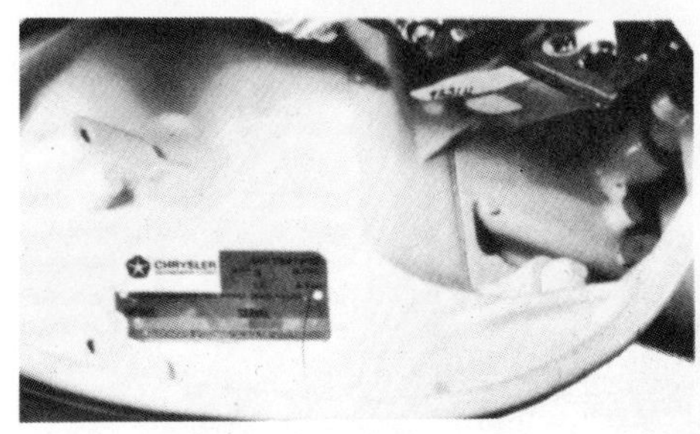

Serial number plate located under the engine cover on the forward floor support plate. (© Chrysler Outboard Corporation)

General Engine Specifications

Year	*Model*	*HP (OBC) @ rpm*	*Displacement (cu in.)*	*Full Throttle rpm Range*	*Bore (in.)*	*Stroke (in.)*
1966	3.5	3.5 @ 4500	5.18	——	2.062	1.562
	6.0	6.0 @ 4500	10.6	4000–5000	2.000	1.688
	9.2①	9.2 @ 4750	11.97	4000–5500	2.125	1.688
	20.0①	20.0 @ 5000	19.96	4500–5500	2.438	2.140
1967	3.5	3.5 @ 4500	5.18	——	2.062	1.562
	6.0	6.0 @ 4500	10.6	4000–5000	2.000	1.688
	9.2①	9.2 @ 4750	11.97	4000–5500	2.125	1.788
	20.0①	20.0 @ 5000	19.96	4500–5500	2.438	2.140
1968	3.5	3.5 @ 4500	5.18	——	2.438	2.140
	4.4	4.4 @ 4750	8.99	4300–5400	1.875	1.312
	6.6	6.6 @ 4750	10.2	4300–5400	2.000	1.625
	9.9①	9.9 @ 4750	13.15	4300–5400	2.188	1.750
	20.0①	20.0 @ 5000	19.96	4500–5500	2.438	2.140
1969	3.5	3.5 @ 4500	5.18	——	2.062	1.562
	5.0	5.0 @ 4750	8.99	4300–5200	1.875	1.625
	7.0	7.0 @ 4750	10.2	4300–5200	2.000	1.625
	9.9①	9.9 @ 4750	13.15	4300–5400	2.188	1.750
	20.0①	20.0 @ 5000	19.96	4500–5500	2.438	2.140
1970	3.6	3.6 @ 4500	5.18	4000–5000	2.062	1.562
	5.0	5.0 @ 4750	8.99	4300–5200	1.875	1.625
	7.0	7.0 @ 4750	10.2	4300–5200	2.000	1.625
	9.9①	9.9 @ 4750	13.15	4300–5200	2.188	1.750
	20.0①	20.0 @ 5000	19.96	4500–5500	2.438	2.140
1971	3.6	3.6 @ 4500	5.18	4000–5000	2.062	1.562
	6.0	6.0 @ 5000	8.99	4500–5500	1.875	1.625
	8.0	8.0 @ 5000	10.2	4500–5500	2.000	1.625
	9.9①	9.9 @ 4750	13.15	4300–5400	2.188	1.750
	12.9①	12.9 @ 5000	13.62	4500–5500	2.188	1.812
	20.0①	20.0 @ 5000	19.96	4500–5500	2.438	2.140
1972	3.6	3.6 @ 4500	5.18	4000–5500	2.062	1.562
	6.0	6.0 @ 5000	8.99	4500–5500	1.875	1.625
	8.0	8.0 @ 5000	10.2	4500–5500	2.000	1.625
	9.9①	9.9 @ 4750	13.15	4300–5400	2.188	1.750
	12.9①	12.9 @ 5000	13.62	4500–5500	2.188	1.812
	20.0①	20.0 @ 5000	19.96	4500–5500	2.438	2.140

① Specifications are same for Autoelectric models.
—— Not Available

Tune-Up Specifications

NOTE: *When checking compression look for uniformity among cylinders. Cylinder compression pressure should not vary more than 10–15 psi.*

Year	Model (hp)	Firing Order	Spark Plugs Type	Spark Plugs Gap (in.)	Breaker Point Gap (in.)	Magneto Gap (in.)
1966	3.5	Single Cyl	Ch—H8J	0.030	NA	0.020
	6.0	Alternate	Ch—H10J	0.030	0.020	NA
	9.2	Alternate	Ch—J4J	0.030	0.020	NA
	9.2 Electric	Alternate	Ch—J4J	0.030	0.020	NA
	20.0	Alternate	Ch—J4J	0.030	0.020	NA
	20.0 Electric	Alternate	Ch—J4J	0.030	0.020	NA
1967	3.5	Single Cyl	Ch—H8J	0.030	NA	0.020
	6.0	Alternate	Ch—H10J	0.030	0.020	NA
	9.2	Alternate	Ch—J4J	0.030	0.020	NA
	9.2 Electric	Alternate	Ch—J4J	0.030	0.020	NA
	20.0	Alternate	Ch—J4J	0.030	0.020	NA
	20.0 Electric	Alternate	Ch—J4J	0.030	0.020	NA
1968	3.5	Single Cyl	Ch—H8J	0.030	NA	0.020
	4.4	Alternate	Ch—L4J	0.030	0.020	NA
	6.6	Alternate	Ch—L4J	0.030	0.020	NA
	9.9	Alternate	Ch—L4J	0.030	0.020	NA
	9.9 Electric	Alternate	Ch—L4J	0.030	0.020	NA
	20.0	Alternate	Ch—L4J	0.030	0.020	NA
	20.0 Electric	Alternate	Ch—L4J	0.030	0.020	NA
1969	3.5	Single Cyl	Ch—H8J	0.030	NA	0.020
	5.0	Alternate	Ch—L4J	0.030	0.020	NA
	7.0	Alternate	Ch—L4J	0.030	0.020	NA
	9.9	Alternate	Ch—L4J	0.030	0.020	NA
	9.9 Electric	Alternate	Ch—L4J	0.030	0.020	NA
	20.0	Alternate	Ch—L4J	0.030	0.020	NA
	20.0 Electric	Alternate	Ch—L4J	0.030	0.020	NA
1970	3.6	Single Cyl	Ch—H8J	0.030	NA	0.020
	5.0	Alternate	Ch—L4J	0.030	0.020	NA
	7.0	Alternate	Ch—L4J	0.030	0.020	NA
	9.9	Alternate	Ch—L4J	0.030	0.020	NA
	9.9 Electric	Alternate	Ch—L4J	0.030	0.020	NA
	20.0	Alternate	Ch—L4J	0.030	0.020	NA
	20.0 Electric	Alternate	Ch—L4J	0.030	0.020	NA
1971	3.6	Single Cyl	Ch—H8J	0.030	NA	0.020
	6.0	Alternate	Ch—L4J	0.030	0.020	NA
	8.0	Alternate	Ch—L4J	0.030	0.020	NA
	9.9	Alternate	Ch—L4J	0.030	0.020	NA
	9.9 Electric	Alternate	Ch—L4J	0.030	0.020	NA
	12.9	Alternate	Ch—L4J	0.030	0.020	NA
	12.9 Electric	Alternate	Ch—L4J	0.030	0.020	NA
	20.0	Alternate	Ch—L4J	0.030	0.020	NA
	20.0 Electric	Alternate	Ch—L4J	0.030	0.020	NA
1972	3.6	Single Cyl	Ch—H8J	0.030	NA	0.020
	6.0	Alternate	Ch—L4J	0.030	0.020	NA
	8.0	Alternate	Ch—L4J	0.030	0.020	NA
	9.9	Alternate	Ch—L4J	0.030	0.020	NA
	9.9 Electric	Alternate	Ch—L4J	0.030	0.020	NA
	12.9	Alternate	Ch—L4J	0.030	0.020	NA
	12.9 Electric	Alternate	Ch—L4J	0.030	0.020	NA
	20.0	Alternate	Ch—L4J	0.030	0.020	NA
	20.0 Electric	Alternate	Ch—L4J	0.030	0.020	NA

NA—Not Applicable

Marine Specifications

Year	Model (hp)	Weight (lbs) ▲	Standard Propeller Diameter (in.)	Pitch (in.)	No. of Blades	Rotation (facing bow)	Recommended Transom Height Short Shaft	Long Shaft
1966	3.5	29	7½	4½	2	L	15	20
	6.0	55	7½	7½	2	R	15	20
	9.2①	55	8	8	2	R	15	——
	20.0①	77	8½	8½	3	R	15	20
1967	3.5	29	7½	4½	2	L	15	20
	6.0	55	7½	7½	2	R	15	20
	9.2①	55	8	8	2	R	15	——
	20.0①	77	8½	8½	3	R	15	20
1968	3.5	29	7½	4½	2	L	15	20
	4.4	48	7	4¾	2	R	15	20
	6.6	48	7½	6¼	2	R	15	20
	9.9①	56	8¼	8¼	2	R	15	20
	20.0①	74	8½	8½	3	R	15	20
1969	3.5	29	7½	4½	2	L	15	20
	5.0	48	7	4¾	2	R	15	20
	7.0	48	7½	6¼	2	R	15	20
	9.9①	56	8¼	8¼	2	R	15	20
	20.0①	74	8½	8½	3	R	15	20
1970	3.6	33	7½	4½	2	L	15	20
	5.0	48	7	4¾	2	R	15	20
	7.0	48	7½	6¼	2	R	15	20
	9.9①	56	8¼	8¼	2	R	15	20
	20.0①	74	8½	8½	3	R	15	20
1971	3.6	33	7½	4½	2	L	15	20
	6.0	47	8	5	2	R	15	20
	8.0	49	7½	6½	2	R	15	20
	9.9①	56	8¼	8¼	2	R	15	20
	12.9①	59	8⅛	8¼	3	R	15	20
	20.0①	79	8½	8½	3	R	15	20
1972	3.6	33	7½	4½	2	L	15	20
	6.0	47	8	5	2	R	15	20
	8.0	49	7½	6½	2	R	15	20
	9.9①	56	8½	8¼	2	R	15	20
	12.9①	59	8⅛	8¼	3	R	15	20
	20.0	79	8½	8½	3	R	15	20

▲ Depending on equipment. Actual weight may vary as much as 20–30 lbs.
① Including Autoelectric models.
—— Not Available

Standard Torque Specifications

Bolt/Screw Size	*Torque (in. lbs)*
6—32	9
10—24	30
10—32	35
12—24	45
¼—20	70
5/16—18	160
⅜—16	270

NOTE: *Due to the extensive use of white metal and aluminum to resist corrosion, torque specifications must be adhered to strictly. When tightening two or more screws on the same part, do not tighten screws one at a time. Tighten all screws evenly and gradually.*

Torque Specifications

Year	Model (hp)	Cylinder Head (in. lbs)	Flywheel (ft lbs) ▲	Main Bearing Bolts (in. lbs) Upper and Center	Main Bearing Bolts (in. lbs) Lower	Connecting Rods (in. lbs)	Gear Housing Plugs (in. lbs)	Spark Plugs (in. lbs)
1966–69	3.5	——	25	NA	NA	80	90–115	120–180
1970–72	3.6	——	25	NA	NA	80	90–115	120–180
1968	4.4	125	40	NA	NA	90	90–115	120–180
1969–70	5.0	125	40	NA	NA	90	90–115	120–180
1971–72	6.0	125	40	NA	NA	90	90–115	120–180
1968	6.6	125	40	NA	NA	90	90–115	120–180
1969–70	7.0	125	40	NA	NA	90	90–115	120–180
1971–72	8.0	125	40	NA	NA	90	90–115	120–180
1966–67	6.0	65	40	NA	NA	①	90–115	120–180
1966–67	9.2	65	40	NA	NA	①	90–115	120–180
1968–72	9.9	125	50	NA	NA	120	90–115	120–180
1971–72	12.9	125	50	NA	NA	120	90–115	120–180
1966–72	20.0	125	45	160	70	110	90–115	120–180

NOTE: *Due to the extensive use of white metal and aluminum to resist corrosion, torque specifications must be adhered to strictly. When tightening two or more screws on the same part, do not tighten screws one at a time. Tighten all screws evenly and gradually.*

—— Not available.

▲—On electric models, torque armature bolt to 25 ft lbs.

NA—Not applicable.

①—Aluminum rods, 70 in. lbs. Steel rods, 80 in. lbs.

Torque Sequences

NOTE: *After the motor has been run-in and has cooled to the touch, retorque all nuts to specification. It is recommened that cylinder head bolts be torqued in steps. Torque all bolts in sequence to 75 in. lbs, then increase in increments of 25 in. lbs until the specified torque is reached.*

Cylinder head—4.4, 5.0, 6.0, 7.0, 8.0, 9.2, 8.9, and 12.9 HP (© Chrysler Outboard Corporation)

Cylinder head—20.0 HP (© Chrysler Outboard Corporation)

Wiring Diagrams

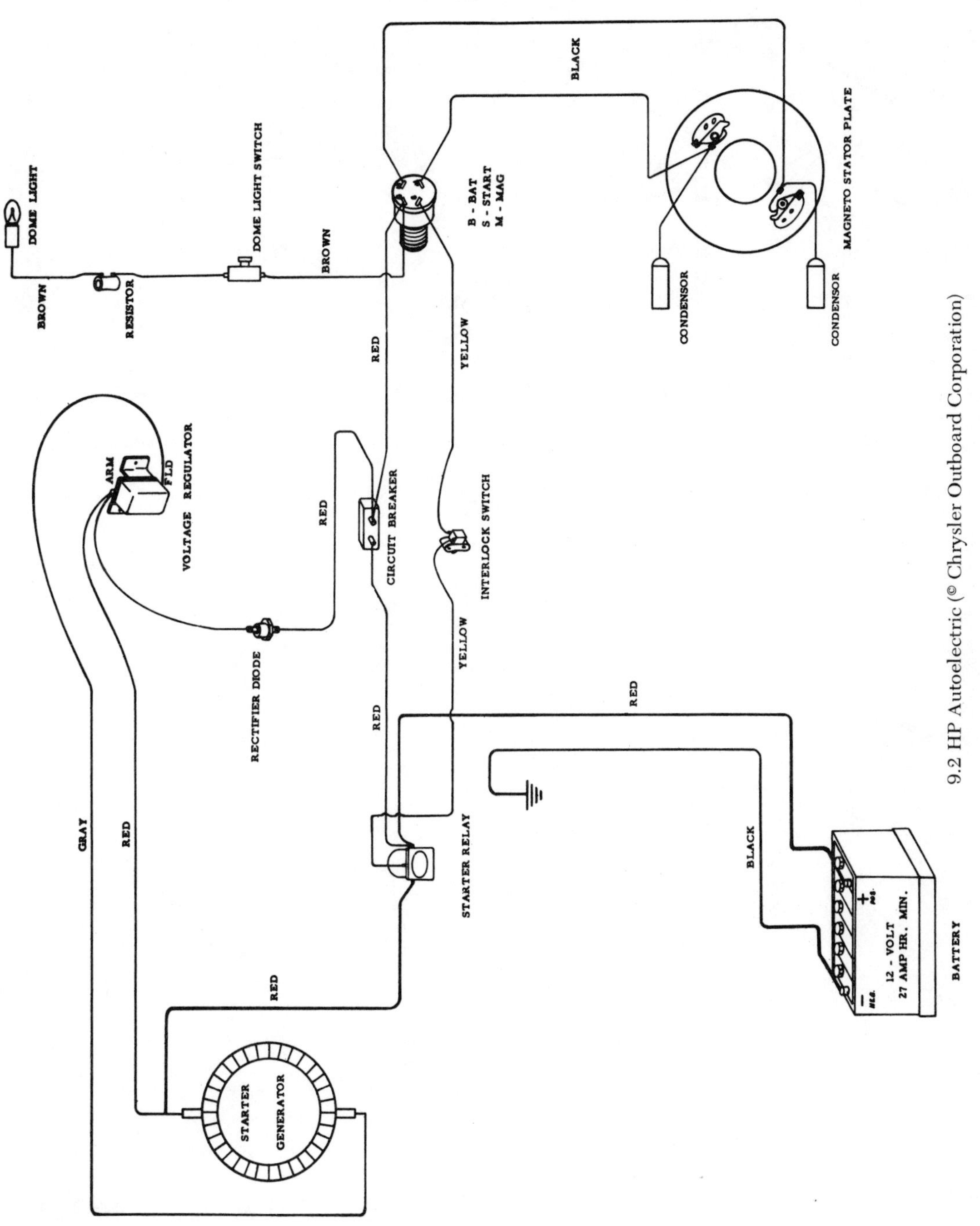

9.2 HP Autoelectric (© Chrysler Outboard Corporation)

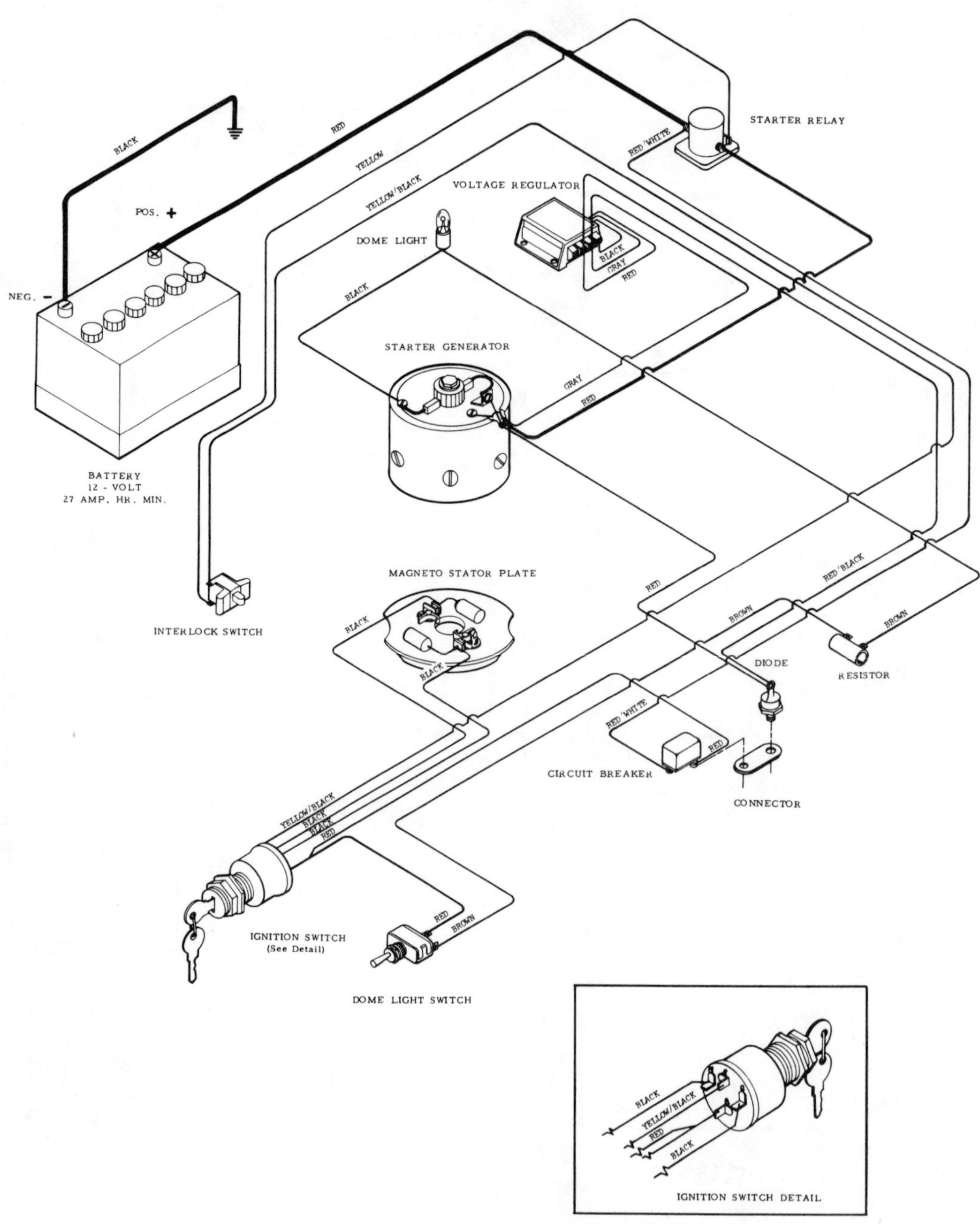

9.9 HP Autoelectric (pre-1971) (© Chrysler Outboard Corporation)

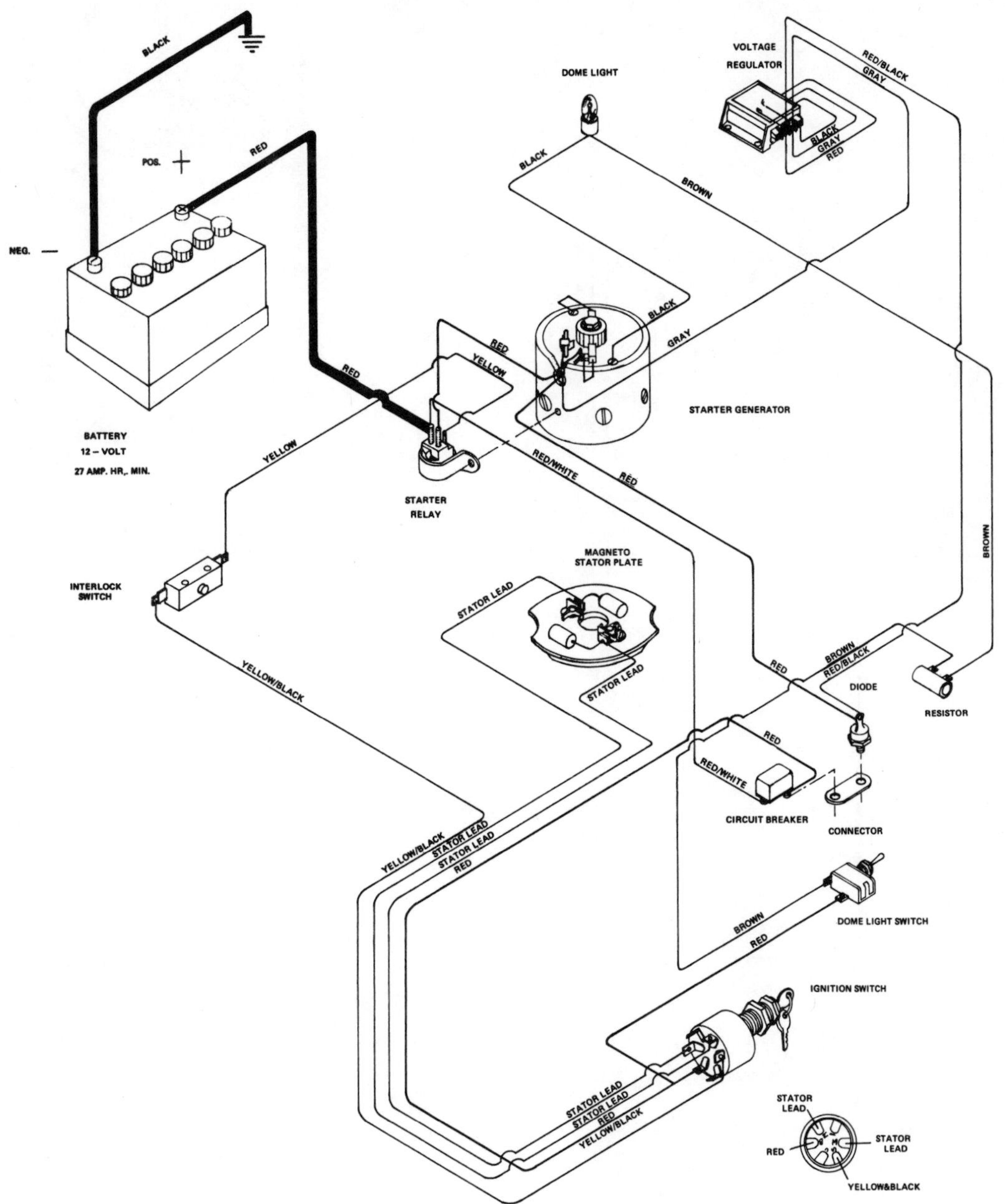

9.9 HP and 12.9 HP Autoelectric (1971–72) (© Chrysler Outboard Corporation)

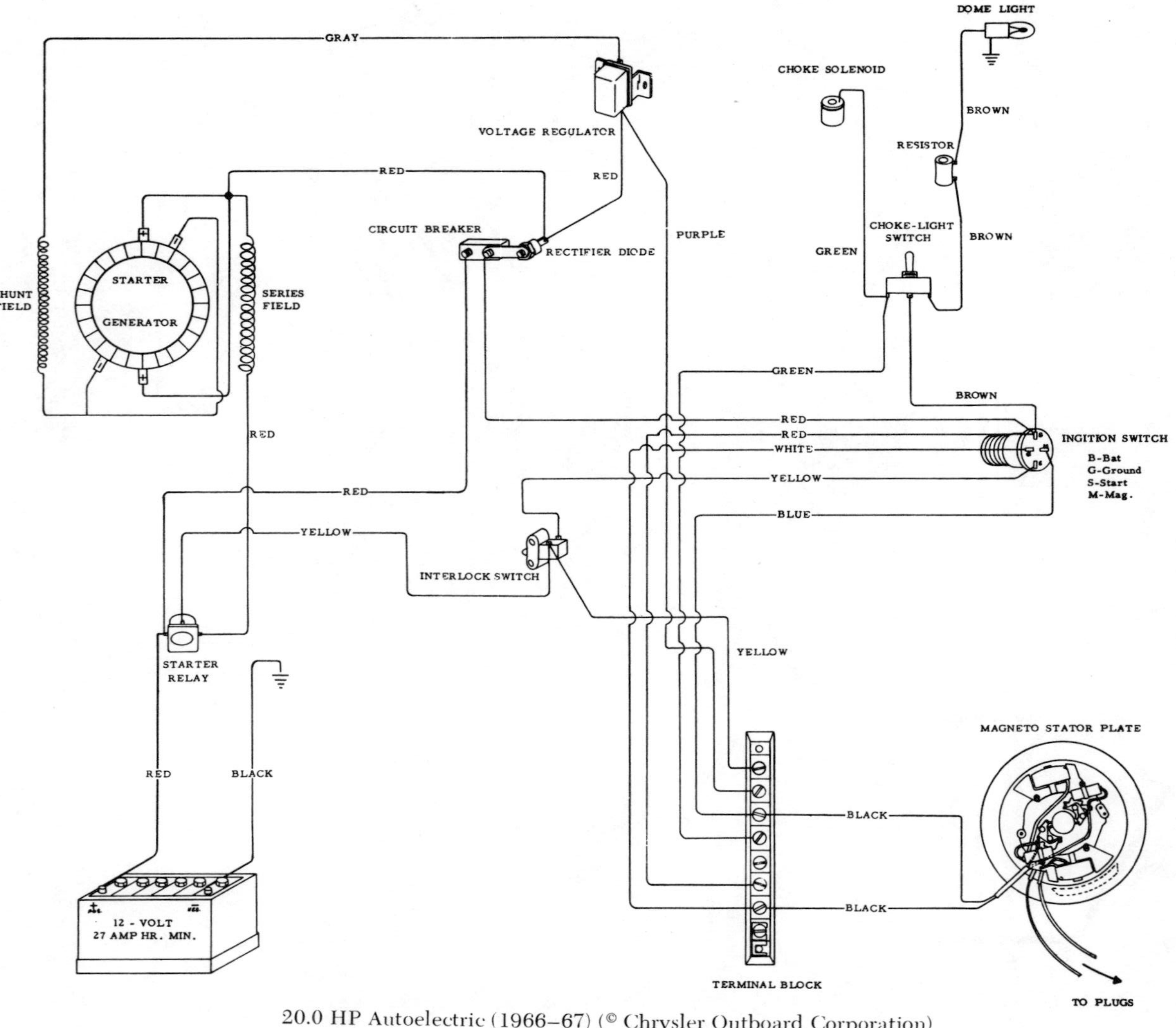

20.0 HP Autoelectric (1966–67) (© Chrysler Outboard Corporation)

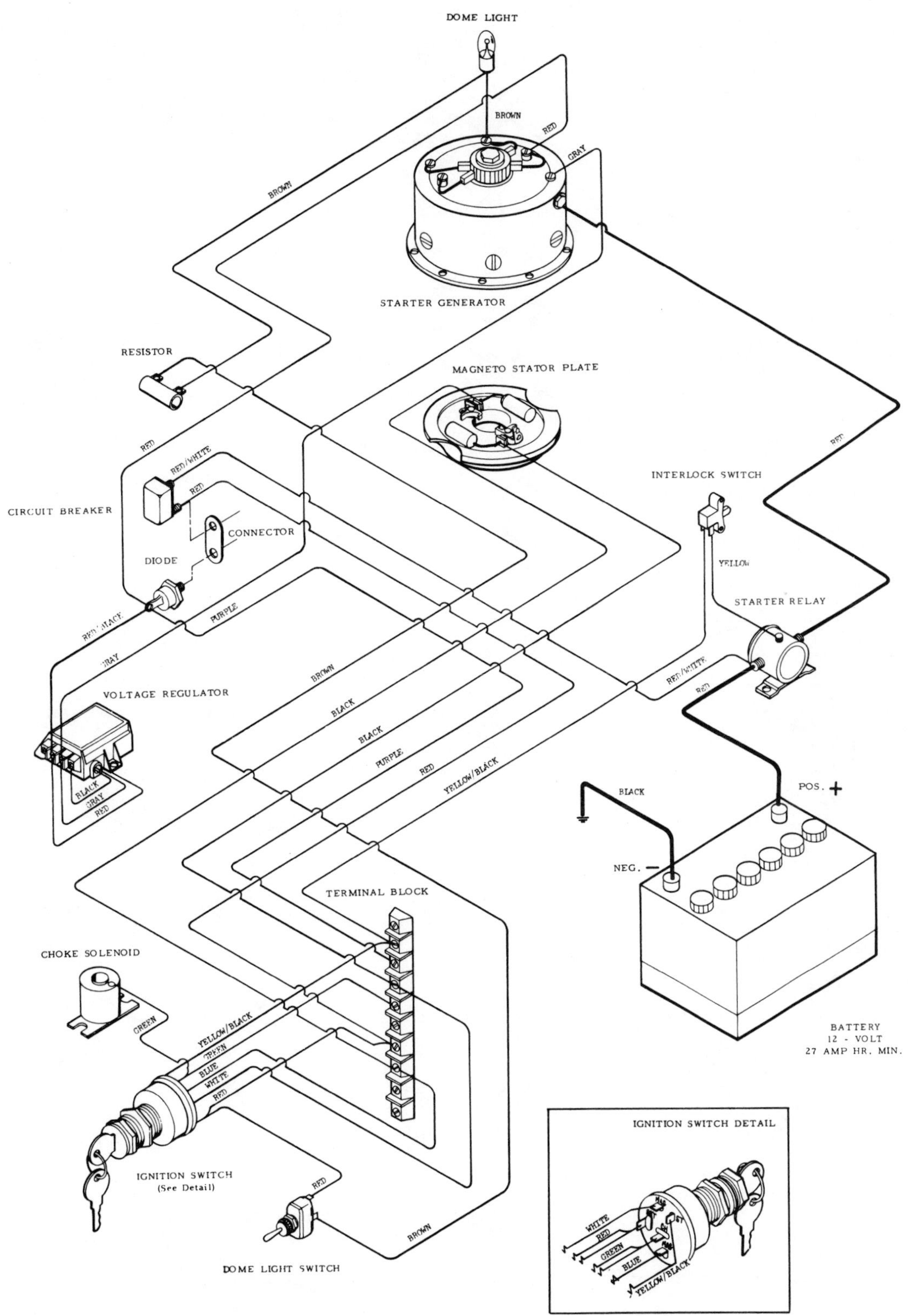

20.0 HP Autoelectric (1968–70) (© Chrysler Outboard Corporation)

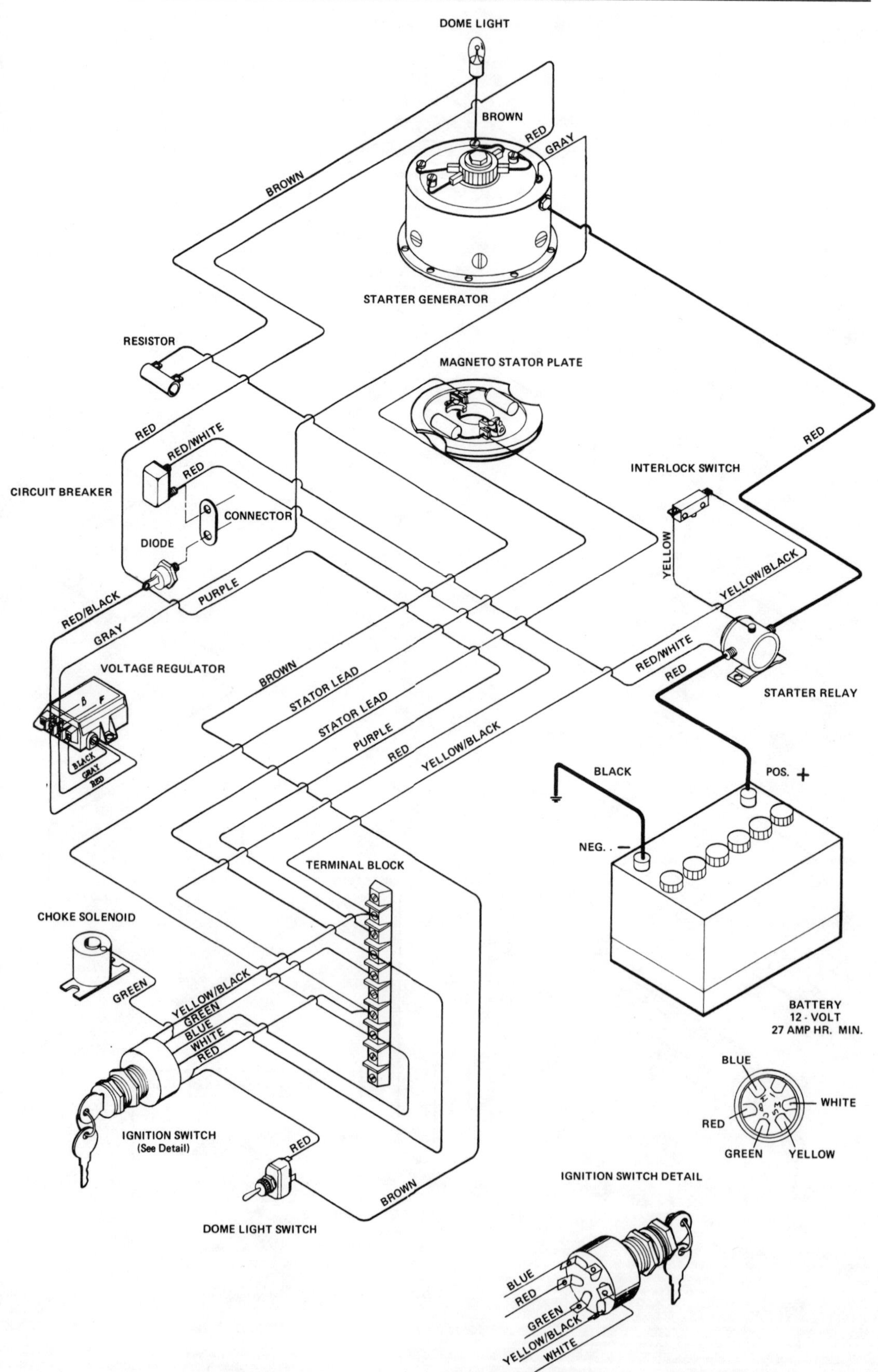

20.0 HP Autoelectric (1971–72) (© Chrysler Outboard Corporation)

General Care and Maintenance

SALT WATER

NOTE: *Not all of the procedures in this section apply to all motors. The 3.5 hp and 3.6 hp models are significantly different, being air-cooled.*

Chrysler Outboard Corporation has taken care to chemically treat all parts that contact salt water. The owner, however, must also take some special precautions after running the engine in salt water.

1. Always tilt the engine out of the water when it is not in use.

2. Periodically run the engine in fresh water to flush out salt deposits that form in the cooling system and passageways. A flushing adaptor is available from Chrysler to allow the owner to flush the motor with an ordinary garden hose.

3. Wash the engine down with fresh water at regular intervals. Apply an automotive-type wax to protect the finish.

4. Remove the propeller periodically and lubricate the propeller shaft. While you are about it, check the condition of the propeller and the lower unit. Be sure that the blades of the propeller are not nicked and that the protective coating of paint on the entire lower unit and leg is unbroken. Paint which is chipped allows the breakdown of the metal at an even faster than normal rate. Be sure you touch up those places where the paint coat is broken.

5. Whenever the engine will not be used for a day or longer, disconnect the negative battery cable to prevent battery rundown and electrolysis.

PREVENTIVE MAINTENANCE AND PERIODIC SERVICE

The following precautions and services, if heeded, should assure a long and satisfactory life for your outboard.

1. Use the type of fuel, oil, and grease specified by the manufacturer.

2. Be sure that the correct fuel/oil ratio is maintained at all times.

3. Never run the outboard motor out of water.

4. Do not overspeed clutch-type models in Neutral. The speed control should not be advanced beyond the "start" position.

5. Follow the break-in period as detailed later in this chapter.

6. Every thirty hours of use, check the gear housing and add gear lube if necessary. Completely drain and replace the grease at least once every six months.

7. Prepare the motor for off-season storage (winterizing) as directed in this chapter.

8. The propeller shaft seals should be checked at least after every year's use or immediately after contact with monofilament fishing line, nylon rope, or similar foreign material.

9. Never use the electric starter continuously for more than fifteen seconds without allowing at least three minutes for the armature and field coils to cool.

10. Shift the gears rapidly at the proper engine speed. Do not ease the gears, as this will cause excessive wear to the gears and clutch.

11. Be sure to have the authorized Chrysler dealer perform the initial ten hour inspection.

12. Check items which are subject to normal wear (water pump impeller, breaker points, spark plugs, starter ropes, starter pawls, shear pins, and items of a similar nature) at least once every season; twice a season is preferable.

13. Do not tip the motor upside down or store it in an inverted position. This practice will lead to corrosion from water seeping into the crankcase from the lower leg.

14. Perform an outboard motor tune-up at the beginning of each season or at the time of winterizing. Check the motor frequently to be sure that it is not in need of a tune-up. Periodically clean, inspect, and adjust the carburetor to ensure optimum performance.

15. Always operate the outboard motor within the recommended rpm range. See "General Engine Specifications" or the motor identification plate.

16. Be sure that your boat and motor are rated to accept each other. Power greater than that specified on the hull plate can be considered misuse and could void the warranty.

17. Be sure that the motor is adequately protected against excessive spray and backwash. Any spray or backwash that

"drowns" the motor or causes premature corrosion on electrical or carburetor parts may void the warranty.

MOTOR INSTALLATION

It is recommended that the dealer make the first installation of the outboard. The owner can, however, do this in accordance with the following suggestions and safety precautions. (See also the introductory chapter.)

1. Mount the engine at the center of the transom and tighten the stern bracket clamp screws alternately. Do not tighten them with a wrench.

2. If the engine is not centered on the transom, the torque of the propeller will cause the boat to run erratically and off course.

CAUTION: *Due to the immense amount of thrust created by the propeller, it is essential that the 20 hp model be bolted to the transom, using the holes in the mounting bracket which are there for that purpose. Be sure that the stern brackets remain parallel to each other and caulk the holes liberally to prevent leakage. Smaller motors should be mounted with the clamps only, but should be secured by a safety chain mounted on the transom (or other secure and convenient place).*

Chrysler outboards are designed to be installed on a fifteen-inch transom (standard-shaft model) or a twenty-inch transom (long-shaft model). Most outboards do not adapt well to curved or reverse-angle transoms. If the motor is to be mounted on this type of transom, contact your Chrysler dealer for special mounting instructions.

PROPELLER AVAILABILITY

Chrysler Outboard Corporation offers the propellers listed on the following chart as replacements for the standard equipment propeller. This will allow the owner to match the proper propeller to his boat for particular applications and, at the same time, operate the motor within the recommended operating range.

To match the proper propeller to your motor, refer to the material in the introductory chapter of this book under "Propeller Selection."

WINTERIZING

Before storing your motor for an extended period of time, it should be protected against rust, corrosion, and freezing. In lieu of having the motor winterized by a Chrysler dealer, the following procedure can be used.

NOTE: *The following procedure is to be performed on the boat or in a test tank.*

1. If the engine has been operated in salt water, the cooling system should be flushed with fresh water prior to storage. Run the engine in fresh water or use a flushing adaptor which is available commercially. This is not necessary on the air-cooled 3.5 and 3.6 hp models.

Prop No.	*Dia. x Pitch (in.)*	*No. of Blades*	*Material*	*Horsepower*	*Model Year*	*Application*
P19 *	7½ x 4½	2	Al.	3.5, 3.6	All	Medium Load
P73	8 x 3½	2	Al.	4.4, 5, 6	68–72	Sailboat
P317	7 x 4¾	2	Al.	4.4, 5	68–70	Medium Load
P409	8 x 5	2	Al.	6	72	Medium Load
P50 *	7½ x 7½	2	Al.	6	Thru 67	Medium Load
P75	8 x 5	2	Al.	6.6, 7, 8	68–72	Sailboat
P410	7½ x 6½	2	Al.	6.6, 7, 8	68–72	Medium Load
P61 *	8 x 8	2	Al.	9.2	Thru 67	Medium Load
P396	8¼ x 4½	3	Al.	9.9, 12.9	68–72	Sailboat
P395	8¼ x 6	3	Al.	9.9, 12.9	68–72	Heavy Load
P330	8 x 8	3	Al.	9.9	68–72	Medium Load
P286	8¼ x 8¼	2	Al.	9.9	68–72	Medium Load
P408	8¼ x 8¼	3	Al.	12.9	72	Medium Load
P70	8¼ x 8¾	2	Al.	9.9, 12.9	68–72	Light Load
P77 *	8½ x 8½	3	Al.	20	Thru 67	Medium Load
P315	8½ x 6	3	Al.	20	68–72	Houseboat & Sailing
P102	8½ x 7½	3	Al.	20	68–72	Heavy Load
P324	8½ x 8½	3	Al.	20	68–72	Medium Load
P346	8½ x 10	3	Al.	20	68–72	Light Load
P326	8½ x 11	2	Br.	20	68–72	Light Load

*—Pin drive; all others spline drive.

2. Run the engine until it is thoroughly warmed.

3. Place the gear shift in Neutral and allow it to run at fast idle. Remove the fuel line from the engine and rapidly inject rust preventive oil into the air intakes for approximately 10–20 seconds until the engine stops.

4. Remove the motor from the boat or test tank and turn the starter several times to expel any water from the cooling system (except 3.5 and 3.6 hp models).

5. Drain all fuel from the lines and carburetor.

6. Remove the spark plugs, pour an ounce or two of SAE 30 engine oil into the cylinders, and manually turn the engine over several times to distribute the oil. Clean, regap, and install the spark plugs.

7. Drain all grease from the lower housing and refill the gear housing as described under "Lubrication."

8. Lubricate all moving parts as described under "Lubrication."

9. Wipe off the engine with a clean rag and apply an automotive-type wax to the exterior.

10. Remove the propeller and lubricate the propeller shaft. Reinstall the propeller shaft.

11. Store the engine upright in a dry, well-ventilated area.

12. This is an excellent time to have the propeller reconditioned and to perform any maintenance.

PREPARATION FOR USE AFTER STORAGE

1. Remove the spark plugs and replace them as necessary.

2. Check the lubricant level in the lower unit.

3. Lubricate all moving parts described under "Lubrication."

4. Clean the exterior of the engine and apply an automotive wax to protect the finish (especially in salt water areas).

5. Check the condition of the battery.

6. Start the motor in a test tank (or on the boat) and be sure that it is operating correctly. Replace any parts as necessary.

STEERING FRICTION ADJUSTMENT

The steering friction can be adjusted to the desired tension by one of the following methods.

3.5 and 3.6 HP

The steering friction is controlled by a friction clamp and springs attached to the swivel bracket. Adjust it by tightening or loosening the hex nut.

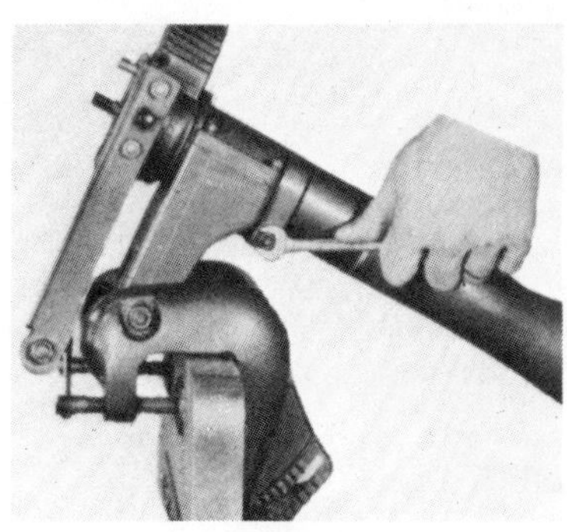

Steering friction adjustment—3.5 and 3.6 HP (© Chrysler Outboard Corporation)

4.4, 5.0, 6.0, 6.6, 7.0, 8.0, 9.2, and 9.9 HP

The steering friction is controlled by a setscrew in the top, port side of the swivel bracket. Tighten or loosen the swivel screw as desired.

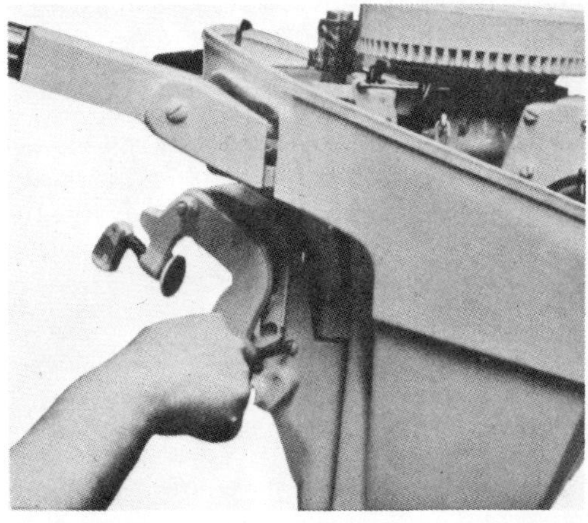

Steering friction adjustment—4.4, 5.0, 6.0, 6.6, 7.0, 8.0, 9.2, and 9.9 HP. (© Chrysler Outboard Corporation)

12.9 and 20.0 HP

The steering friction is adjusted by means of a friction plate attached to the swivel bracket. Adjust the nut to obtain the desired steering friction.

NOTE: *The illustration shows the powerhead removed. This is not necessary to perform the adjustment.*

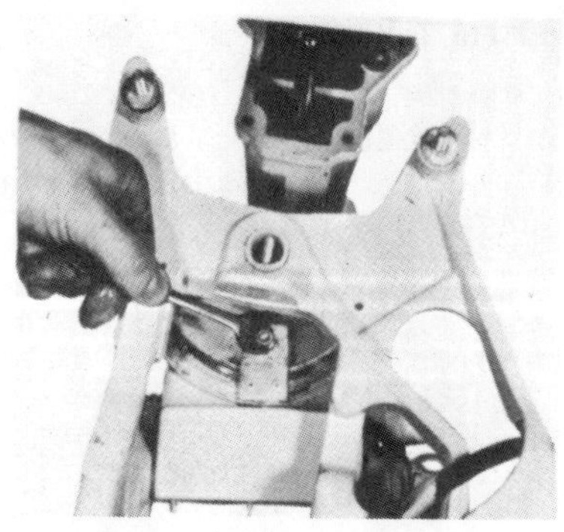

Steering friction adjustment—12.9 and 20.0 HP. (© Chrysler Outboard Corporation)

THRUST PIN (SHEAR PIN) REPLACEMENT

1. To prevent accidental starting, disconnect the negative battery cable or the spark plug wires.
2. Remove the cotter pin from the propeller shaft nut and remove the seal.
3. Pull the propeller from the shaft to gain access to the shear pin. A light tap with a block of wood should be sufficient to remove the propeller should it be "frozen" on the shaft.
4. Remove a damaged or broken shear pin by driving it out with a new pin.
5. Install a new thrust pin, propeller nut seal, propeller nut, and cotter pin, and then reinstall the propeller.
6. It is wise to always carry a spare cotter pin, propeller nut, propeller nut seal, and thrust pin, for use in emergencies. In an emergency of this type, one quite often also needs a spare propeller.

COOLING SYSTEM

Chrysler outboards (except the 3.5 and 3.6 hp models) are water-cooled by the intake of water through holes in the side of the lower unit. A water pump distributes the water, acting as a positive displacement pump at low speeds and a centrifugal pump at high speeds. The pump, located in the lower leg, picks up water from the underside of the cavitation plate, just ahead of the propeller, and is discharged after circulation along with the exhaust gases.

The 3.5 and 3.6 hp models are air-cooled and require no water pump. Engine heat is dissipated to the air through cooling fins on the cylinder and on the exhaust portion of the lower leg. A fan on the flywheel blows an air stream over the fins to accelerate cooling. A cooling tube picks up water from below the slipstream to cool the exhaust portion of the lower leg.

Checking Water Pump Operation

All Except 20 HP

Normal water pump operation is indicated by a spray of water from the idle exhaust relief port on the back of the motor leg. When running the motor at Wide Open Throttle, however, little or no water will be visible; water should be clearly visible at all other speeds.

20 HP

Normal operation is indicated by a spray of water from the idle exhaust relief port on the rear of the motor leg, *at all times.*

All Models

If water is not visible, stop the motor immediately. Check the water intake passages on the side of the motor leg gear housing to make sure that they are not obstructed by weeds and foreign material. If trouble persists, check the water pump impeller.

Operation of the water pump is necessary to avoid internal damage due to overheating.

TILT PIN ADJUSTMENT

Location

The tilt pin is located on the bottom of the mounting bracket. It consists of a long pin which can be moved into different holes to change the angle of the motor relative to the transom.

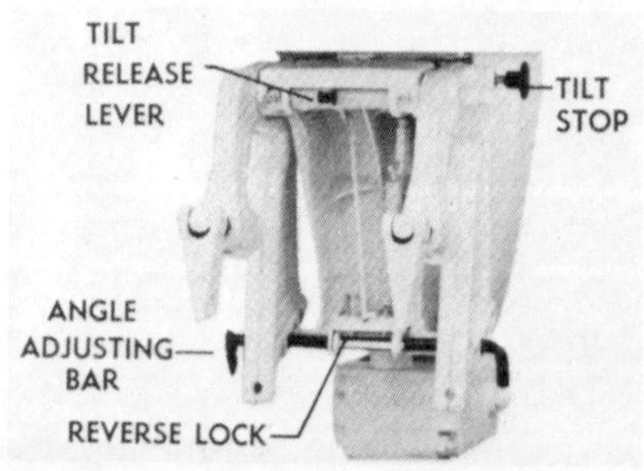

Tilt angle adjusting bar location. (© Chrysler Outboard Corporation)

Adjustment

See the introductory chapter of this book for the method of adjusting the tilt pin setting.

Lubrication

GENERAL

The lubrication system of Chrysler outboards is the standard type used on almost all two-stroke engine designs. Oil is mixed with the fuel in the recommended proportion and, as the fuel is distributed, the oil in the fuel lubricates the pistons, cylinder walls, bearings, rings, and other moving parts, except the lower unit. The lower unit is lubricated by a self-contained supply of special lubricant.

It is worthy to note that in many cases, Chrysler recommends a greater amount of oil if you are not using Chrysler Outboard Oil.

BREAKING IN A NEW MOTOR

The following recommendations should be used when breaking in a new motor or when breaking in a motor which has been overhauled. Consult the following chart for oil ratio recommendations.

Chrysler Outboard Oil should be used in a Chrysler outboard motor but several other oils are acceptable for use when Chrysler Outboard Oil is not available. Oil which is certified TC—W by the Boating Industry Association may be used as well as high-quality SAE 30 or 40 Heavy Duty Outboard Oil, as a limited substitute for Chrysler Outboard Oil.

FUEL RECOMMENDATIONS

1966–68

Marine white or regular-grade automotive gasoline (approximately 85 octane) is recommended. Avoid the use of premium fuel (approximately 95 octane) with anti-knock additives. Gasolines and oils containing TCP, phosphorus additives, friction-reducing compounds, and break-in oils are unnecessary and not recommended for use in Chrysler outboards.

1969–70

Non-leaded (or low lead) high-octane gasolines such as marine white, automotive, or light aircraft are highly recommended for Chrysler outboards.

Regular grade automotive gasolines of 90 octane minimum can be used and are considered acceptable.

The use of premium fuels which contain phosphorus compounds and other additives should be avoided.

1971–72

Unleaded marine white gas, unleaded automotive gas, and light aircraft gas are preferred fuels. These low-lead fuels should be of at least 87 octane.

Regular grade automotive gas, premium grade automotive gas (containing no phosphorus), and automotive gasoline of at least 85 octane are considered acceptable.

Do not use low-octane white fuel (lamp gas), motor fuel containing phosphorus or excessive lead, or any fuel not intended for use in modern automotive engines.

Fuel Mixing Procedure

The following procedure will make sure that the oil and fuel are completely mixed and that a minimum of contaminants are allowed to enter the fuel system. Obviously, it is not wise to smoke while filling the gas tank or to fill the tank in an unventilated area where a chance spark could ignite the fumes.

1. Always maintain a clean fuel tank.
2. If possible, strain all fuel through a clean mesh filter.
3. Pour one gallon of fresh gasoline into an empty tank.
4. Add the proper amount of Chrysler Outboard Oil, SAE 30 or SAE 40 Heavy Duty Outboard Oil to the tank.
5. Add the balance of the gasoline and mix the oil and fuel thoroughly.
6. It cannot be stressed too thoroughly to add the recommended amount of oil to the fuel. This is the method of lubricating your outboard and nothing will cause it to wear out faster than using too little oil. Nothing will foul the engine faster than using too much oil.

Fuel Ratio Conversion Table

Fuel/Oil Ratio	*Gasoline Quantity*	*Oil Quantity*	
16/1 6 percent oil	1 gallon	½ pt	8 oz
	6 gallon	3 pt	48 oz
	12 gallon	6 pt	96 oz
24/1 4 percent oil	1 gallon	⅓ pt	5.3 oz
	6 gallon	2 pt	32 oz
	12 gallon	4 pt	64 oz
50/1 2 percent oil	1 gallon	⅙ pt	2.6 oz
	6 gallon	1 pt	16 oz
	12 gallon	2 pt	32 oz

Fuel Oil Mixture Requirements

Year	*Model (hp)*	*Break-In Period*				*Minimum Hrs Prior to Continuous WOT Operation*	*Oil Ratio After Break-In*			
		Oil Ratio		*Minimum Hours Req'd*	*Special Run-in Period (hrs)*		*Pleasure*		*HD or Racing*	
		Chrysler Outboard Oil	*Other Oils*				*Chrysler Outboard Oil*	*Other Oils*	*Chrysler Outboard Oil*	*Other Oils*
1966–	3.5	16/1	16/1	4①	NA	4	16/1	16/1	16/1	16/1
1967	6.0	24/1	24/1	1②	NA	1	24/1	24/1	24/1	24/1
	9.2									
	20.0	24/1	24/1	1②	10③	1	50/1	50/1	24/1	24/1
1968	3.5	16/1	16/1	4①	NA	4	16/1	16/1	16/1	16/1
	4.4	24/1	24/1	1②	10③	1	50/1	50/1	24/1	24/1
	6.6									
	9.9	24/1	24/1	1②	10③	1	50/1	50/1	24/1	24/1
	20.0	24/1	24/1	1②	10③	1	50/1	50/1	24/1	24/1
1969–	3.5	16/1	16/1	3	NA	3	16/1	16/1	16/1	16/1
1970	3.6									
	5.0	24/1	24/1	3①	1④	3	50/1	50/1	50/1	24/1
	7.0									
	9.9	24/1	24/1	3①	1④	3	50/1	50/1	50/1	24/1
	20.0	24/1	24/1	3①	1④	3	50/1	50/1	50/1	24/1
1971–	All									
1972	Models	25/1	25/1	3	1⑤	3	50/1	50/1	50/1	25/1

NA—Not applicable.

①—During the first four hours, the engine must be operated with the magneto control lever advanced to within 1 in. of the wide open throttle position. Do not run the engine below this speed except for brief periods during docking.

②—During the break-in period, operate the motor between Idle and Start positions only.

③—During the first ten hours of operation, use 24/1 fuel/oil ratio. Do not use the 50/1 ratio until after the first ten hours.

④—Momentary burst at wide open throttle.

⑤—Advance to full throttle for a few seconds and return to moderate speed for a few minutes. Repeat this process gradually increasing the full throttle operation time until five minutes of full throttle operation is attained. For the first tank of fuel, use a good commercial break-in additive.

OIL SELECTION

3.5 and 3.6 HP

Most outboard oils are designed for use in water-cooled outboards. If these air-cooled outboards seem to run sluggishly or hot when operated for extended periods of time at low speeds, try using a SAE 30 MM or MS (designated SE after 1971–72) automotive oil.

All Other Models

Chrysler Outboard Motor Oil is recommended for use in Chrysler outboards. This is a high-quality, heat-resistant base oil with a non-metallic additive. If this oil is not available, use SAE 30 engine oil (up to and including 1968) or SAE 40 engine oil (after 1968).

20.0 HP

UPPER AND LOWER GEAR HOUSINGS—Check after every thirty hours of operation and replace after every 100 hours with a non-corrosive leaded outboard gear oil—Texaco Outboard Gear Oil—EP90 or equivalent. Do not use corrosive hypoid oil under any circumstances.

CONTROL LINKAGE—Lubricate all moving parts and control linkage with Rykon no. 2EP, part no. K—65, twice each season or more often if required.

STERN BRACKET—Lubricate stern bracket and associated parts with Rykon no. 2EP, part no. K—65, twice each season or more often if required.

GREASE FITTINGS—Grease fittings are provided at critical points where bearing surfaces are not exposed externally. Using an automotive-type grease gun and lubricant, grease twice each season or more often if required.

STARTER PINION GEAR—Lubricate with Rykon no. 2EP, part no. K—65, twice each season or more often if required.

External Lubrication

3.5 and 3.6 HP

Part Name	*Type of Lubricant*	*Frequency*
Throttle shaft	SAE 30 Motor Oil	Twice each season
Clamp screws	SAE 30 Motor Oil	Twice each season
Join in steering handle	SAE 30 Motor Oil	Twice each season
Swivel bracket bearing	Graphite Grease	Twice each season
Contact surface between magneto stator plate and upper bearing cage	EP—All Purpose Chassis Lubricant	If magneto control lever becomes hard to move
Gear housing	Underwater Grease	Every 30 hours, more often if required

4.4, 5.0, 6.0, 6.6, 7.0, 8.0, 9.2, 9.9, and 12.9 HP

Part Name	*Type of Lubricant*	*Frequency*
Starter pinion gear	SAE 30 Motor Oil	If starter operation becomes sluggish
Starter spool bearings	SAE 30 Motor Oil	If starter operation becomes sluggish
Throttle cam follower	SAE 30 Motor Oil	Twice each season, more often if required
Magneto control shaft bearings	SAE 30 Motor Oil	Twice each season, more often if required
Steering handle pinion gear	EP—All Purpose Chassis Lubricant	Twice each season, more often if required
Steering handle bevel gear	EP—All Purpose Chassis Lubricant	Twice each season, more often if required
Reverse lock	SAE 30 Motor Oil	Twice each season, more often if required
Clamp screws	SAE 30 Motor Oil	Twice each season, more often if required
Stern bracket pivot bolt	SAE 30 Motor Oil	Twice each season, more often if required
Gear housing	Non-Corrosive Leaded Outboard Gear Oil—EP90 Chrysler Outboard Gear Lube	Every 30 hours, more often if required
Fuel line coupler release ring	SAE 30 Motor Oil	Twice each season, more often if required

GREASE FITTINGS—Grease fittings are provided at critical points where bearing surfaces are not exposed externally. Using an automotive type grease gun and lubricant, grease twice each season or more often if required.

LOWER UNIT LUBRICATION

The lubricant in the lower unit (gear housing) should be checked every 30 hours of operation and should be replaced every 100 hours (6 months) or at least once each season (prior to storage). The recommended gear lube is Chrysler Outboard Gear Lube. If this is not available, use a non-corrosive, leaded EP 90 outboard gear lube. Do not use corrosive, hypoid gear lubricants.

Inspection

1. Loosen, but do not remove, the gear-housing drain screw and allow a small amount of lubricant to drain. If water is present, it will drain out, prior to the actual lubricant.

2. Should water be present in the lower unit lubricant, the cause of the entry of water must be found and corrected. The propeller seal is an excellent place to begin.

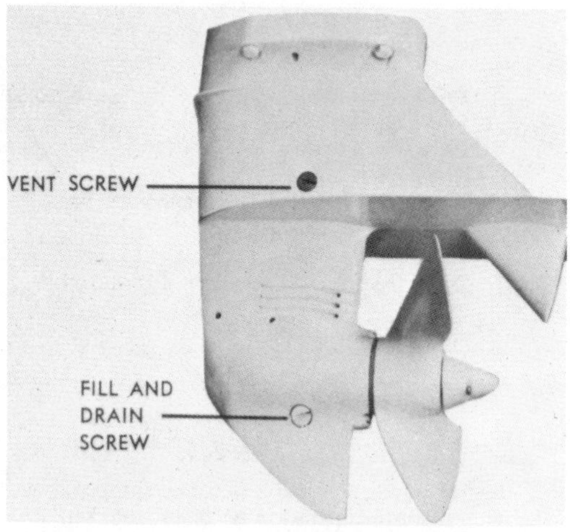

Drain and vent screw location for lubricating the lower unit. (© Chrysler Outboard Corporation)

Lubricant Replacement

1. With the engine in an upright position, remove the upper and lower plug screws and allow the lubricant to drain.

2. Insert the tube into the lower drain hole and fill the gear housing with gear lube until it appears at the top vent hole.

3. Install the top plug and washer.

4. Remove the tube of lubricant and install the lower plug screw and washer. Tighten the screw securely.

5. Allow the engine to stand in an upright position for at least one-half hour with the upper screw removed. This will allow the gear lube to completely fill all of the cavities in the gear housing.

6. Recheck the gear lube level. Add lubricant as necessary, using the procedure above.

Tune-Up

1966–69 3.5 HP

Spark Plugs

1. Remove the spark plug.

2. Inspect the condition of the spark plug, referring to the introductory chapter.

3. If the spark plug is deemed serviceable, clean and regap the plug to specification.

4. Reinstall the plug and torque it to specification.

5. If a new plug is installed, set it to the proper gap and install it, using a new gasket. Be sure to clean the seat before installation.

Flywheel

Removal

NOTE: *The flywheel must be removed to adjust the breaker points.*

1. Remove the fuel tank as outlined in the section on the fuel system.

2. Remove the flywheel bolt securing the starter rewind cup to the flywheel and crankshaft.

3. Use a large screwdriver between the flywheel and top of the powerhead to pry off the flywheel, after removing the starter rewind cup. Carefully pry the flywheel from the crankshaft taper. Striking the top of the crankshaft lightly with a brass mallet or brass drift may aid in breaking the flywheel loose.

CAUTION: *Do not strike the crankshaft hard as this may damage the crankshaft and bearings.*

4. Lift the flywheel from the crankshaft and inspect the flywheel.

Inspection

1. Inspect carefully for chips or cracks in the flywheel. Flywheels in this condi-

tion could fly apart at high rpm, causing severe bodily harm.

2. Inspect the tapered bore of the flywheel for fretting or chatter marks. If this condition is evident or the engine has twenty-five or more hours of operation, the flywheel should be lapped.

3. To lap the flywheel, proceed as follows.

4. Remove the flywheel key from the crankshaft.

5. Apply a light coating of valve grinding compound on the crankshaft taper.

6. Lightly install the flywheel on the crankshaft and rotate the crankshaft gently about one-quarter turn. Do not spin the flywheel. Rotate the flywheel 90° and repeat the operation.

7. Remove the flywheel and clean the crankshaft taper and flywheel. The taper in the bore should contact the crankshaft taper on a minimum of 90 percent of the surface.

8. Reinstall the flywheel key and flywheel.

Installation

1. Install the flywheel key, flywheel, starter cup, and bolt. Be sure to locate the shoulder of the flywheel bolt in the hole in the starter cup by lifting the starter cup against the bolt head. Torque the bolt to 25 ft lbs.

2. Reinstall the fuel tank.

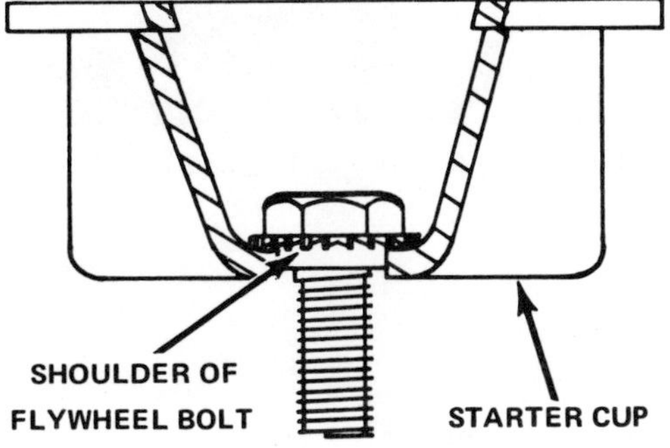

Installed position of the flywheel bolt—3.5 HP (© Chrysler Outboard Corporation)

Breaker Point Adjustment

1. Remove the flywheel.

2. Check the points for burning or pitting. Clean or replace them as necessary.

3. Check the breaker arm spring tension at right angles to the center of the contact surfaces. Spring tension should be 14–28 oz.

4. Squeeze the cam wiper felt to be sure it is sufficiently lubricated. If it appears dry, work a small amount of cam grease into the felt with your fingers.

5. Reinstall the flywheel bolt into the crankshaft and turn the crankshaft with an open-end wrench until the follower arm of the breaker points is aligned with the index mark.

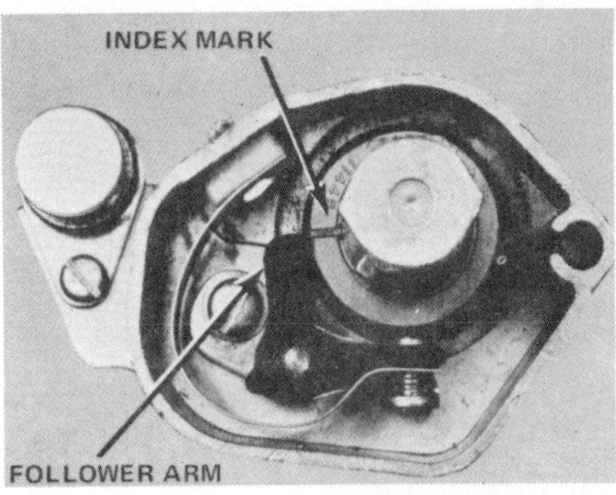

Correct position of breaker cam for point adjustment—3.5 HP (© Chrysler Outboard Corporation)

6. With a feeler gauge, adjust the points to specification.

7. After setting the points, rotate the engine and recheck the adjustment.

8. Reinstall the flywheel.

Condenser

1. Remove the flywheel.

2. Remove the condenser.

3. Check the condenser as outlined in the first chapter. Replace it if it is defective.

4. Install the condenser.

5. Install the flywheel.

Carburetor

Throttle Pick-up Adjustment

1. Align the magneto control lever with the idle adjustment screw on the carburetor.

2. Check the position of the throttle link location in the throttle lever. It should be in the hole nearest the throttle shaft.

3. Loosen the throttle bellcrank swivel and push the throttle swivel against the throttle cam on the stator.

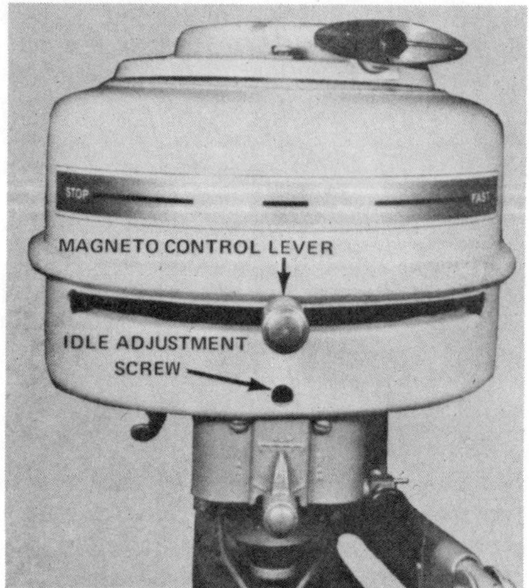

Magneto control lever aligned with idle adjustment screw—3.5 HP (© Chrysler Outboard Corporation)

4. Push down on the brass throttle link lightly to take up all play. Do not push hard enough to move the throttle lever.
5. While holding pressure on the link, tighten the swivel screw.
6. Check the throttle pick-up point by retarding the magneto control lever and slowly advance the lever until movement of the throttle shaft is detected. At this point, the magneto control lever should be aligned with the idle adjustment screw.
7. Correct any maladjustment by moving the swivel down on the brass link (if the pick-up is too early) or up (if the pick-up is too late).

HIGH- AND LOW-SPEED ADJUSTMENT

1. Turn the idle adjustment screw to seat it lightly in the carburetor. Do not overtighten it.
2. Back out the idle adjustment screw one turn.
3. Seat the high-speed adjusting needle lightly in the carburetor; do not force it.
4. Back out the high-speed needle one turn. Disregard the position of the high-speed knob at this point.
5. Start the motor and warm it thoroughly.
6. Set the throttle control lever to the lowest reliable setting.
7. Turn the idle adjustment screw (clockwise) until the motor begins to stall from a lean mixture.
8. Note the position of the slot in the adjustment screw.
9. Turn the idle adjustment screw (counterclockwise) until the motor begins to "roll" from a rich fuel mixture.
10. Set the idle screw at the midpoint between the two settings in steps 7 and 9.
11. Advance the magneto control lever to wide open throttle.
12. Perform the same adjustment (steps 7–10) for the high-speed needle.
13. Remove the high-speed adjusting knob (do not disturb the position of the needle) and reposition the high-speed knob so that it is vertical on the needle. The adjusting knob should be vertical when the high-speed needle is at the maximum rpm setting.

Positioning the high-speed adjusting knob (© Chrysler Outboard Corporation)

1970–72 3.6 HP

Spark Plug

1. See "1966–69 3.5 HP."

Flywheel

REMOVAL

NOTE: *The flywheel must be removed to adjust the breaker points.*

1. Remove the front and rear engine cover screws (1970) or the rear cover screw (1971–72).

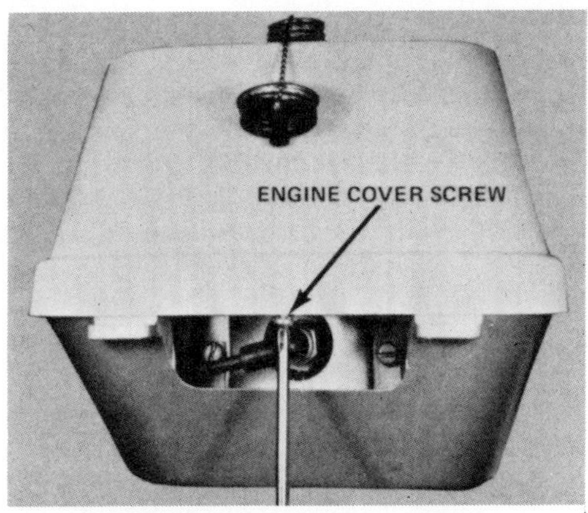

Location of engine cover screw—3.6 HP (© Chrysler Outboard Corporation)

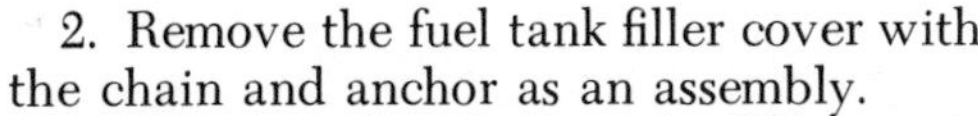

2. Remove the fuel tank filler cover with the chain and anchor as an assembly.
3. Remove the fuel tank filler neck grommet.
4. Lift the engine cover part-way off and tie a knot in the starter rope between the cover eyelet and the rewind starter. This will allow removal of the rope handle.

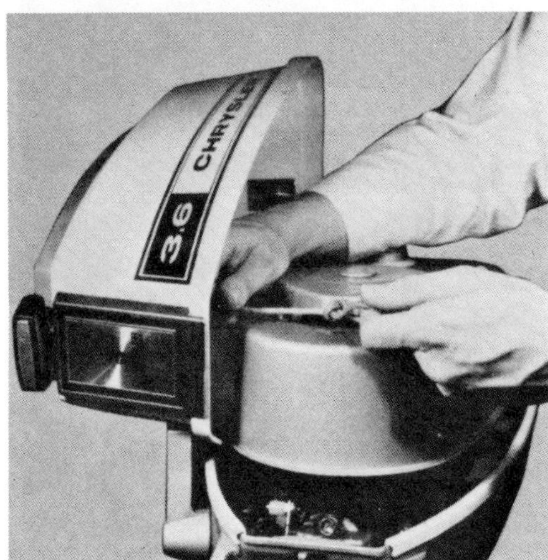

Tying knot in starter rope—3.6 HP (© Chrysler Outboard Corporation)

5. Pry the starter rope from the starter handle and remove the rope from the handle.
6. Completely remove the engine cover.
7. Remove the fuel tank as outlined in "Fuel System."
8. Perform steps 2–5 under "1966–69 3.5 HP."

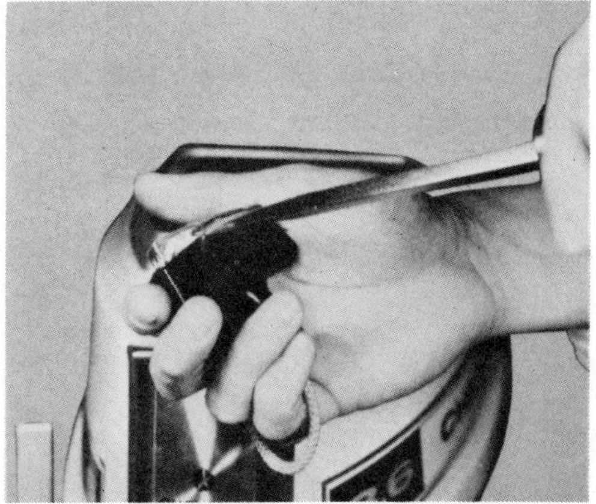

Removing starter rope and retainer from handle —3.6 HP (© Chrysler Outboard Corporation)

Inspection

1. See "1966–69 3.5 HP."

Installation

1. Install the flywheel key, flywheel, starter cup, and bolt. Locate the shoulder of the flywheel bolt in the hole in the starter cup by lifting the starter cup against the bolt head. Torque the nut to 25 ft lbs.
2. Install the fuel tank as outlined in "Fuel System."
3. Center the starter rewind and thread the starter rope through the starter handle and retainer.
4. Untie the knot in the starter rope and locate the cover on the support plate.
5. Install the front and rear engine cover screws (1970) or the rear cover screw (1970–72).
6. Install the fuel tank filler neck grommet and the fuel tank filler cover with chain and anchor.

Breaker Point Adjustment

1. Remove the flywheel.
2. The breaker points on these models are adjusted in the same manner as those on 1966–69 3.5 hp models.
3. Reinstall the flywheel.

Condenser

1. Remove the condenser and test it as outlined in the introductory chapter.
2. If the condenser is defective, replace it with a new one.

Carburetor

THROTTLE PICK-UP ADJUSTMENT

1. Rotate the throttle cam forward to contact the roller on the throttle shaft lever.

2. If the index mark does not appear through the center of the roller, bend the throttle shaft as necessary. Do not bend this lever too much, as excessive bending will loosen the lever on the throttle shaft.

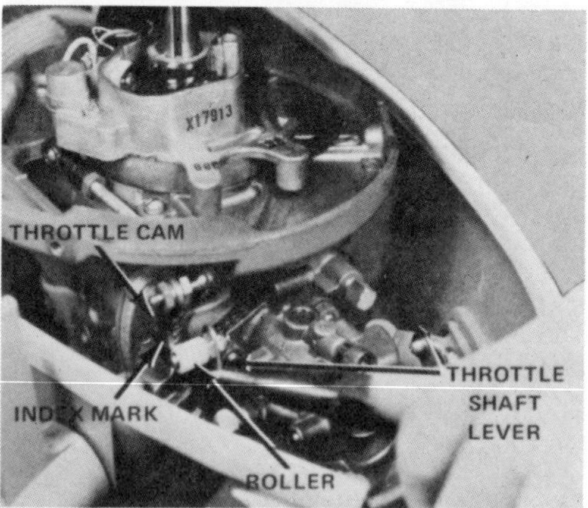

Adjusting throttle pick-up point—3.6 HP (© Chrysler Outboard Corporation)

3. At the point of initial contact, the index mark must appear to pass through the center of the roller.

4. With the throttle cam against the roller at the pick-up point, check the position of the ball stud on the stator in relation to the index marks on the bearing cage. The ball stud must be centered on the index marks. Adjust the length of the stator control rod link by snapping off the ball stud connector; adjust the length of the rod by turning the connector. Tighten the locknuts after the proper length is achieved.

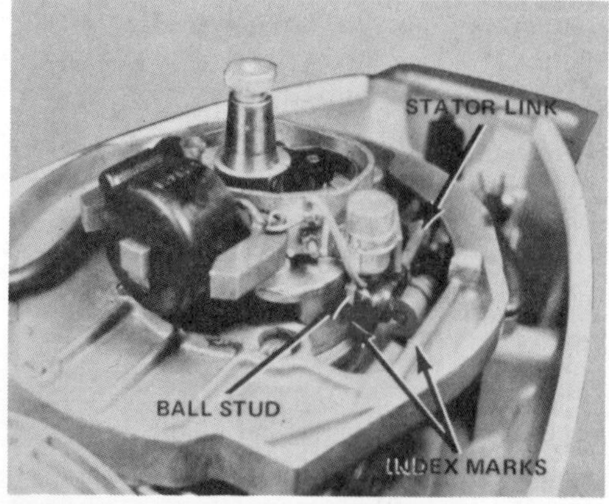

Adjusting the length of the stator link—3.6 HP (© Chrysler Outboard Corporation)

5. Rotate the magneto control lever to wide open throttle and check the throttle shutter. It should be horizontal. The cam should be on the throttle roller away from the roller end. If not, it is possible that step 2 was not performed properly. Recheck the bending of the throttle shaft lever.

IDLE SCREW ADJUSTMENT

1. Lightly seat the idle adjustment screw in the carburetor. Do not force the needle.

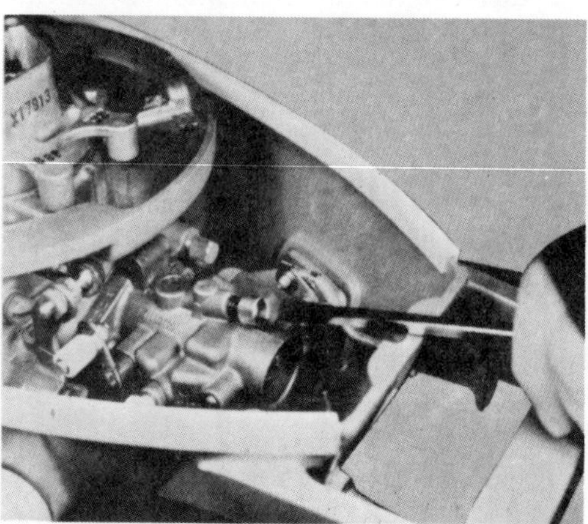

Location of idle adjustment screw (© Chrysler Outboard Corporation)

2. Open the idle adjustment screw one turn counterclockwise.

3. Start the motor and allow it to reach operating temperature.

4. Turn the idle screw clockwise until the motor begins to stall from a lean mixture. Note the position of the slot on the adjustment screw.

5. Turn the idle screw counterclockwise until the motor begins to "roll" from a rich mixture.

6. Set the idle adjustment screw at the midpoint between steps 4 and 5.

1968–72 4.4, 5.0, 6.0, 6.6, 7.0, AND 8.0 HP

Spark Plugs

1. See "Spark Plugs" under "1966–69 3.5 HP."

Flywheel

NOTE: *The flywheel must be removed to adjust the breaker points.*

REMOVAL

1. Remove the nut securing the flywheel to the crankshaft.
2. Insert a strong screwdriver approximately one-half inch under the flywheel. Avoid contact with the stator ring. Pry the flywheel off the crankshaft. Tapping lightly on the crankshaft with a brass mallet or brass drift may aid flywheel removal.
3. Lift the flywheel from the crankshaft and inspect it.

INSPECTION

1. Inspection and lapping are identical to the procedure for the 1966–69, 3.5 hp model.

INSTALLATION

1. Install the flywheel key, flywheel, emergency start collar, and nut. Torque the nut to 35–40 ft lbs.

Breaker Point Adjustment

1. Remove the flywheel.
2. Check the points for pitting or burning and replace them as necessary.
3. Install the nut on the crankshaft and turn the crankshaft clockwise until the breaker point follower arm is approximately 10° past the top of the ramp on the cam. The top of the ramp is the point at which further cam rotation produces no further point opening. Once the correct point on the cam is found, mark the spot for adjusting the other set of points.
4. Adjust the breaker point gap to specification.
5. Repeat the procedure for the other set of points.
6. Rotate the crankshaft and recheck the adjustment.
7. Install the flywheel, emergency start collar, and nut.

Condenser

1. Check the condenser as outlined in the introductory chapter and replace it if it is defective.

Carburetor

THROTTLE PICK-UP ADJUSTMENT

1. Back off the idle stop screw until the throttle pick-up mark on the throttle cam is on the starboard side of the roller on the carburetor follower.
2. Advance the throttle cam until it contacts the roller on the follower arm.
3. Slowly advance the throttle cam until the throttle shaft just begins to move. Check the position of the roller in relation to the mark on the throttle cam. The roller

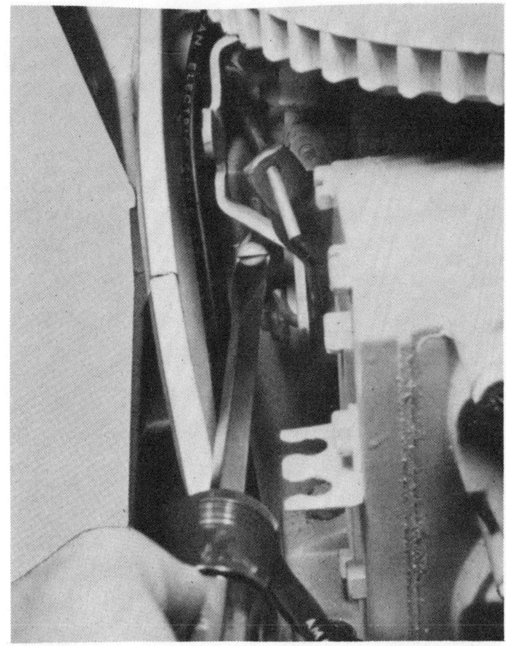

Idle stop screw on 4.4–8.0 HP (© Chrysler Outboard Corporation)

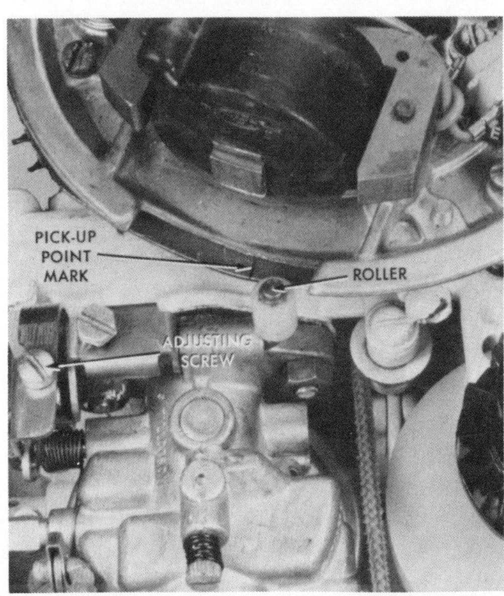

Pick-up point adjustment—4.4–8.0 HP (© Chrysler Outboard Corporation)

should be at, or within, 1/32 in. of the mark. If the roller is not positioned this way, turn the adjusting screw on the carburetor follower until this is achieved.

IDLE SCREW ADJUSTMENT

1. Seat the idle adjustment screw lightly in the carburetor. Do not force the needle into the seat.

Idle adjustment screw—4.4–8.0 HP (© Chrysler Outboard Corporation)

2. Open the idle adjustment screw one turn counterclockwise. Shift the engine to Neutral and turn the throttle twist grip to "start."

3. Start the motor and allow it to reach operating temperature.

4. Shift to Forward and set the throttle twist grip at the lowest reliable throttle setting.

5. Turn the idle adjustment screw clockwise until the engine begins to stall from an overly lean mixture. Note the position of the slot in the screw.

6. Turn the idle adjustment screw counterclockwise until the motor begins to "roll" from a rich mixture. Note the setting.

7. Turn the idle adjustment screw to the midpoint between the settings in steps 5 and 6.

8. Adjust the setting of the idle stop screw so that the motor idles at 700 rpm in Forward gear.

1966–67 6.0 AND 9.2 HP

Spark Plugs

1. See "1966–69 3.5 HP" for spark plug service.

Flywheel

REMOVAL

NOTE: *The flywheel must be removed to adjust the breaker points.*

1. Remove the flywheel nut.

2. Pry up on the edge of the flywheel and lightly tap the end of the crankshaft with a brass mallet or brass drift. Do not tap too hard.

3. Remove the flywheel and inspect it.

INSPECTION

1. Inspection and lapping are identical to those procedures listed under "Flywheel Inspection" for 1966–69 3.5 hp models.

INSTALLATION

1. Installation is the reverse of removal. Torque the nut to specification.

Breaker Point Adjustment

1. Check the breaker points for burning or pitting. If they are excessively burnt or pitted, replace them with new ones. Check the condenser as this is a likely cause of excessively burnt points.

2. The points can be cleaned (if serviceable) in the following manner. Use a small strip of 320 grit emery cloth, folded and inserted between the points. Rotate the emery cloth using the points as a pivot and holding the points closed.

3. Use a piece of hard surface cardboard, inserted between the points and rotated, to clean oxide and other foreign material from the points.

4. Set the throttle at wide open throttle to establish a common stationary point for adjustment.

5. Install the flywheel nut on the crankshaft and rotate the crankshaft in the direction of engine rotation until the breaker point follower arm of no. 1 set of points is aligned with the mark on the cam. The mark on the cam is the point at which further crankshaft rotation produces no further point opening.

6. Set the breaker points to specification with a feeler gauge.

7. Perform the same adjustment for the second set of points.

Carburetor

POINT OF THROTTLE
OPENING ADJUSTMENT

1. Set the throttle cam follower so that the throttle shutter will be closed and all

slack will be removed from the linkage. The throttle cam follower should be on the adjusting mark on the throttle cam plate.

Idle Speed—Preliminary Adjustment

1. Loosen the screw which retains the idle adjustment arm to the idle shaft on the carburetor and remove the adjustment arm.
2. Turn the idle screw in until it seats lightly. Do not force it into the seat.
3. Back the needle out one full turn.
4. Install the adjustment arm on the shaft so that it abuts the shoulder. The hole in the arm must point to the starboard side of the engine. Lock the arm on the shaft with the setscrew so that arm points forward and is horizontal in relation to the engine.
5. Install the link to the hole in the idle adjustment arm.
6. Assemble the arm to the shaft in the control panel. Position the arm so that it is horizontal while pointing to the starboard side of the engine.
7. Turn the knob so that the idle adjustment shaft in the control panel is horizontal. Lock the arm with the setscrew and take up all end-play.

Idle Speed—Final Adjustment

1. Start the motor and warm it thoroughly.
2. Shift the engine to Forward and advance the throttle to the wide open position.
3. Turn the high-speed adjustment screw counterclockwise until the motor begins to "roll" from an overly rich mixture. Turn the high-speed screw clockwise until the motor begins to stall from an overly lean mixture. Set the high-speed needle midway between the two points, favoring the rich mixture.
4. Retard the throttle and shift the motor to Neutral. Turn the idle adjustment needle as necessary to obtain a smooth idle. It is better to have too rich a mixture, rather than too lean a mixture.

1968–72 9.9 HP AND 1971–72 12.9 HP

Spark Plugs

1. Refer to the spark plug section under "1966–69 3.5 HP."

Flywheel

Removal

NOTE: *The flywheel must be removed to adjust the breaker points.*

1. Refer to the procedure under "Flywheel Removal" for "1968–72 4.4, 5.0, 6.0, 6.6, 7.0, and 8.0 HP."

Inspection

1. Inspection and flywheel lapping procedures are identical to those under "1966–69 3.5 HP."

Installation

1. Installation procedures are the same as those for "1968–72 4.4, 5.0, 6.0, 6.6, 7.0, and 8.0 HP."

Breaker Point Adjustment

1. See the procedure under "Breaker Point Adjustment" for "1968–72 4.4, 5.0, 6.0, 6.6, 7.0, and 8.0 HP."

Carburetor

Throttle Pick-up Adjustment

1. See the procedure under "1968–72 4.4, 5.0, 6.0, 6.6, 7.0, and 8.0 HP."

Idle Screw Adjustment

1. See this procedure under "1968–72 4.4, 5.0, 6.0, 6.6, 7.0, and 8.0 HP." The only difference is that the idle adjustment screw is opened $1\frac{1}{4}$ turns on 1968–72 9.9 hp models and on 1971–72 12.9 hp models.

1966–72 20.0 HP

Spark Plugs

1. See spark plug service under "1966–69 3.5 HP."

Flywheel

NOTE: *The flywheel must be removed to adjust the breaker points.*

Removal

1. Flywheel removal is identical to those procedures for "1966–67 6.0 and 9.2 HP."

Inspection

1. See the procedures listed under "1966–69 3.5 HP" for flywheel inspection and lapping.

INSTALLATION

1. Installation is the reverse of removal. Torque the nut to specification.

Breaker Point Adjustment

1. The procedure is identical to that listed under "1968–72 4.4, 5.0, 6.0, 6.6, 7.0, and 8.0 HP."

IDLE STOP SWITCH

1. All manual-start 20.0 hp motors have an idle stop switch which shorts out the ignition when the magneto is retarded. This will not happen if the idle stop screw is used.
2. Check the adjustment of the idle stop switch as follows.
3. Remove the flywheel.
4. Position the magneto stator so that the centerline of the idle stop switch aligns with the indent line on the switch cam.
5. The plunger on the switch must be touching the brass contact from the breaker point terminal screw when the switch is aligned with indent mark on the cam.

Idle stop switch—20.0 HP (© Chrysler Outboard Corporation)

6. Adjust the cam by loosening the two screws holding the cam to the transfer port covers and adjusting the cam to obtain the conditions in step 5.
7. Tighten the retaining screws and install the flywheel.

Carburetor

THROTTLE PICK-UP ADJUSTMENT

1. Retard the throttle until the pick-up mark on the cam is aligned with the starboard side of the roller on the carburetor follower.
2. Advance the throttle cam until it contacts the roller on the follower arm. Slowly advance the throttle cam until the throttle shaft arm just starts to move. Check the position of the roller in relation to the mark on the throttle cam. The roller should contact the cam at or within 1/32 in. of the mark. If the roller is not at this point, loosen the screw on the carburetor follower and adjust the follower arm position.
3. Tighten the screw and recheck the adjustment.

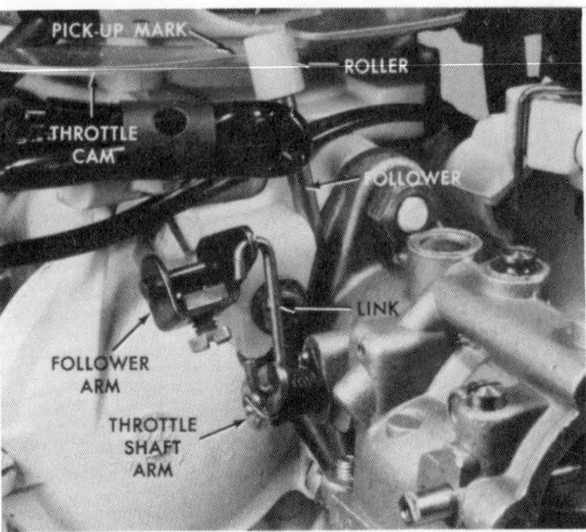

Throttle pick-up adjustment—20.0 HP (© Chrysler Outboard Corporation)

IDLE SCREW ADJUSTMENT

1. Lightly seat the idle needle in the carburetor. Do not force the needle.
2. Open the idle adjustment screw 1¼ turns.
3. Shift the motor to Neutral and turn the twist grip throttle to the "start" position.
4. Start the motor and allow it to warm to operating temperature.
5. Shift into Forward and set the throttle to the lowest reliable throttle setting.
6. Turn the idle adjustment screw clockwise until the engine begins to stall from an overly lean mixture. Note the position of the slot in the screw.

7. Turn the idle adjustment screw counterclockwise until the engine begins to "roll" from an overly rich mixture. Note the setting.

8. Set the idle adjustment screw at a point midway between the settings in steps 6 and 7.

9. Adjust the idle stop screw until the engine idles at 700 rpm in Forward gear.

NOTE: *Setting of the idle stop screw is required for motors using a single lever remote control.*

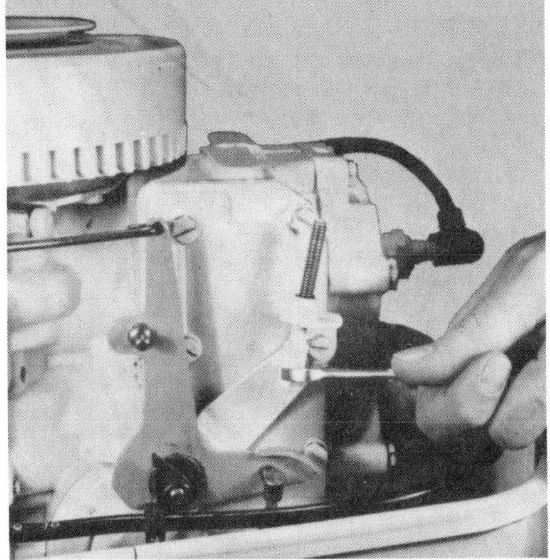

Idle stop screw—20.0 HP (© Chrysler Outboard Corporation)

Fuel System

Chrysler outboards are equipped with Tillotson carburetors. All carburetors are basically alike, differing only in minor components. Some are equipped with fixed, high-speed jets and some are not. Service procedures are given for a typical example; it must be realized that minor differences will exist.

CARBURETORS

Removal

3.5 HP

1. Using hose-clamp pliers, slide the fuel line clamp down the fuel line approximately one inch. Pull the fuel line from the fuel valve, and plug the fuel line. Do not use pliers to remove the fuel line.

2. Remove the two nuts holding the carburetor to the adaptor plate.

3. Remove the carburetor from the adaptor plate.

4. Loosen the swivel screw on the throttle bellcrank and remove the brass throttle link.

3.6 HP

1. Remove the engine cover as outlined in the tune-up section.

2. Remove the fuel tank. See "Fuel Tank Removal" in the fuel system section.

3. Remove the choke rod retaining clip from the choke rod. Disconnect the choke rod from the arm of the carburetor.

4. Position the throttle control handle at full retard and remove the two nuts securing the carburetor to the adaptor plate. Remove the carburetor from the adaptor plate.

5. Slide the hose clamp down the fuel line approximately one inch and pull the carburetor free of the fuel line. Be sure to plug the fuel line.

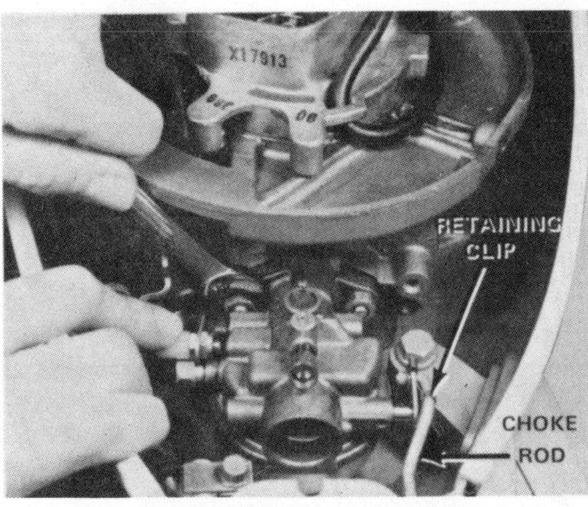

Removing the carburetor—3.6 HP (© Chrysler Outboard Corporation)

4.4, 5.0, 6.0, 6.6, 7.0, 8.0, 9.9, AND 12.9 HP

1. Remove the flywheel as outlined under "Tune-Up."

2. Remove the choke rod retaining clip from the choke rod. Disconnect the choke rod from the carburetor arm.

3. Loosen the screw that holds the throttle cam follower arm to the follower.

4. Slide the follower out and disconnect the follower arm from the carburetor.

5. Unbolt and remove the carburetor from the adaptor plate.

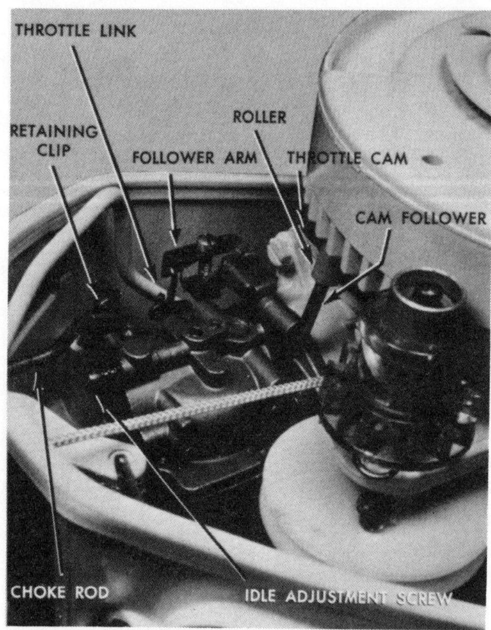

The throttle linkage must be disconnected before removing the carburetor (© Chrysler Outboard Corporation)

6. Using hose-clamp pliers, slide the fuel line clamp down the fuel line approximately one inch. Pull the carburetor from the fuel line and plug the fuel line.

6.0 and 9.2 HP

1. When disconnecting the throttle link from the carburetor, be careful not to bend the link out of shape. If the link is bent during removal, it is recommended that it be replaced with a new one at installation.
2. Disconnect the fuel line from the carburetor and plug the line.
3. Remove the idle adjustment arm from the idle adjustment needle.
4. Remove the choke rod from the carburetor shaft.
5. Unbolt the carburetor and remove it from the adaptor.

20.0 HP

1. Disconnect the choke rod from the choke shaft.
2. Remove the screw holding the cam follower to the retainer on the cylinder.
3. Disconnect the throttle link from the throttle shaft on the carburetor.
4. Remove the starter spool.
5. Using hose-clamp pliers, slide the fuel line clamp down the fuel line approximately one inch.
6. Pull the fuel line free from the carburetor and plug the line.
7. Unbolt the carburetor and remove it from the adaptor flange.

Installation

3.5 HP

1. Install the carburetor on the adaptor plate and secure it with the nuts.
2. Connect the hose to the valve and position the hose clamp to seal the union.
3. Install the brass throttle link in the inner hole of the carburetor shaft arm and through the bellcrank swivel. The open end of the link at the arm should face away from the carburetor.
4. Adjust the throttle pick-up as outlined in "Tune-Up."
5. Adjust the idle setting as detailed in the "Tune-Up" section.
6. Adjust the high-speed setting as outlined under "Tune-Up."

3.6 HP

1. Connect the fuel line to the carburetor and secure it with the hose clamp.
2. Install the carburetor on the adaptor plate and secure it with nuts.
3. Position the choke rod retaining clip on the carburetor choke shaft lever and install the choke rod.
4. Snap the retaining clip on the choke rod.
5. Adjust the throttle pick-up and idle setting as outlined in the "Tune-Up" section.
6. Install the engine cover as detailed under "Tune-Up."

4.4, 5.0, 6.0, 6.6, 7.0, 8.0, 9.9, and 12.9 HP

1. Connect the hose to the carburetor and secure it with the hose clamp.

NOTE: *On MD-type carburetors, the fuel hose must be routed under the shift linkage.*

2. Install the carburetor on the adaptor and secure it with nuts.
3. Facing the front of the engine, install the throttle cam follower through the right side on the boss of the carburetor.
4. Install the brass throttle link in the hole of the carburetor throttle shaft arm and the inner hole on the cam follower arm for CO-type carburetors (outer hole of the cam follower arm for MD-type carburetors).

5. Slide the follower arm on the cam follower.

6. Position the throttle cam with the pick-up mark on the cam approximately one-quarter inch to the left of the roller when facing the front of the engine. Press the roller against the cam at that point and tighten the retaining screw of the follower arm 1/16 of a turn beyond finger-tight.

7. Adjust the throttle pick-up point as outlined under "Tune-Up."

8. Install the flywheel.

9. Adjust the idle as detailed under "Tune-Up."

6.0 AND 9.2 HP

1. Installation is the reverse of removal.

2. Adjust the throttle pick-up and idle setting as detailed under "Tune-Up."

20.0 HP

1. Install the carburetor and gasket on the adaptor flange and secure them with nuts.

2. Install the fuel hose on the carburetor and secure it with the hose clamp.

3. Install the starter spool.

4. Install the brass throttle link in the inner hole of the carburetor throttle shaft. The link ends should face toward the carburetor.

5. Install the throttle cam follower and cam.

6. Adjust the throttle pick-up as outlined under "Tune-Up."

7. Connect the choke rod to the choke shaft on the carburetor.

Overhaul

NOTE: *Service procedures are given for two basic carburetors. Small differences may exist between these procedures and any given Chrysler carburetor.*

MD TYPE

1. Remove the carburetor from the motor.

2. Remove the screw retaining the throttle plate to the shaft.

3. Position the throttle shutter in the wide open throttle position and pull the throttle plate out with a minimum of force.

4. Disconnect the throttle return spring from the pin.

5. Pull the throttle shaft from the carburetor body.

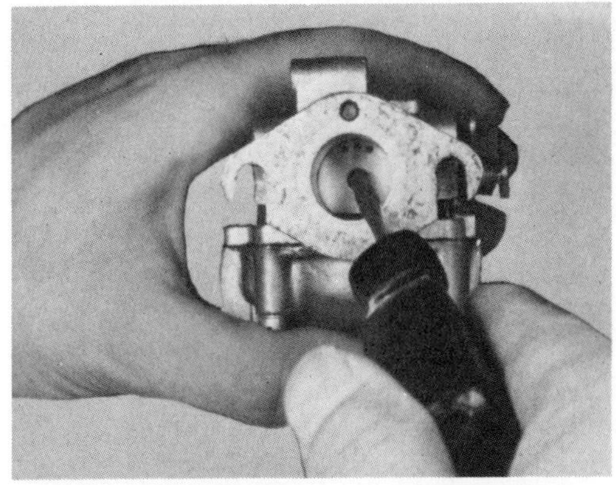

Removing throttle plate screw—MD-type (© Chrysler Outboard Corporation)

6. Remove the choke friction screw, friction spring, and friction plunger from the carburetor body.

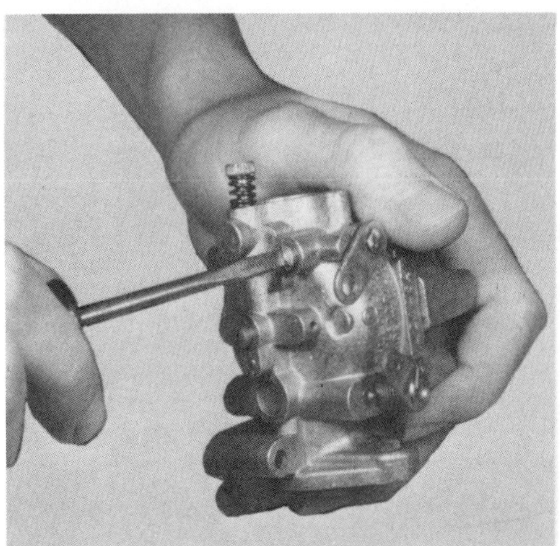

Removing the choke friction screw—MD-type (© Chrysler Outboard Corporation)

7. Remove the choke plate from the choke shaft.

8. Pull the choke shaft from the carburetor.

9. Remove the idle adjustment needle by turning the needle counterclockwise. Pull the needle and spring from the carburetor.

10. Examine the needle for deep grooves around the tapered portion. If any grooves are present, the needle must be replaced.

11. Remove the screws holding the fuel bowl to the carburetor. Remove the fuel bowl.

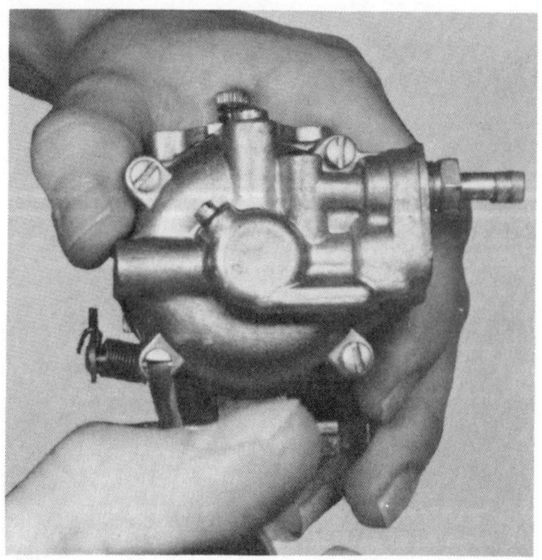

Removing the fuel bowl retaining screws—MD-type (© Chrysler Outboard Corporation)

12. Remove the fuel bowl gasket and clean any traces of gasket material from the carburetor body and fuel bowl.

13. Remove the main fuel jet from the carburetor body.

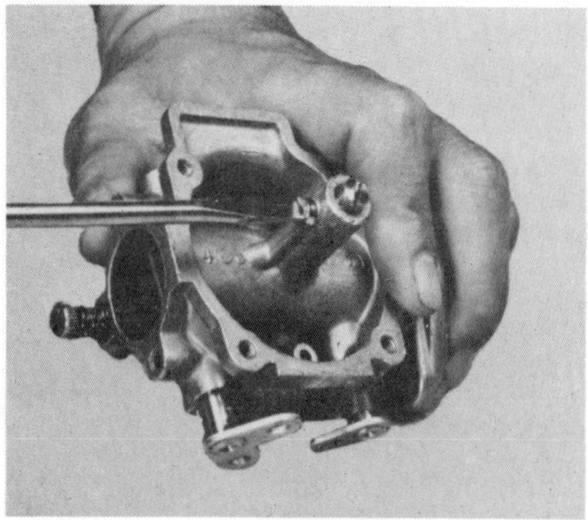

Removing the main fuel jet—MD-type (© Chrysler Outboard Corporation)

14. Remove the by-pass tube from the carburetor.

15. Remove the main nozzle.

16. Remove the float lever pin from the fuel bowl and lift out the float.

17. Remove the plug screw from the fuel bowl. Slide the intake needle out of the seat.

18. Remove the intake needle seat and gasket.

Removing the main nozzle—MD-type (© Chrysler Outboard Corporation)

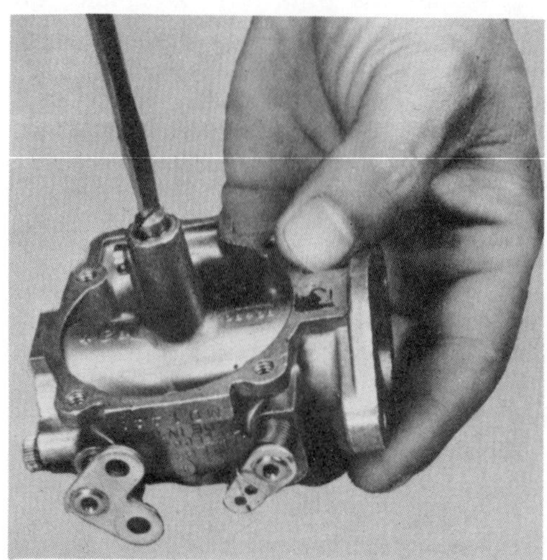

Removing the by-pass tube—MD-type (© Chrysler Outboard Corporation)

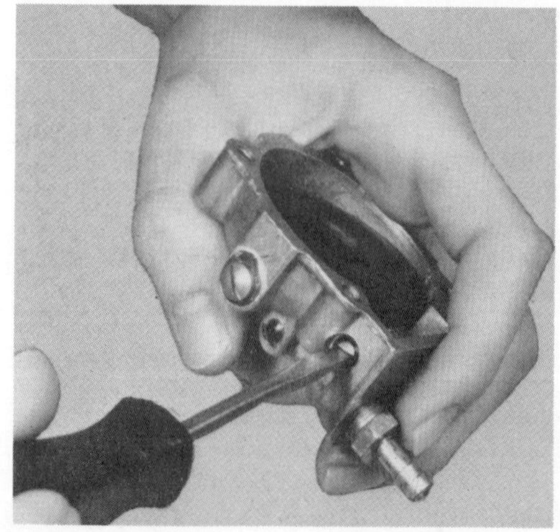

Removing float lever pin—MD-type (© Chrysler Outboard Corporation)

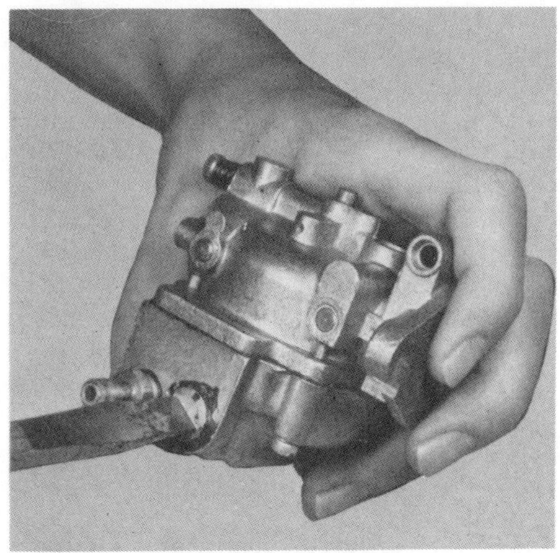

Removing the plug screw—MD-type (© Chrysler Outboard Corporation)

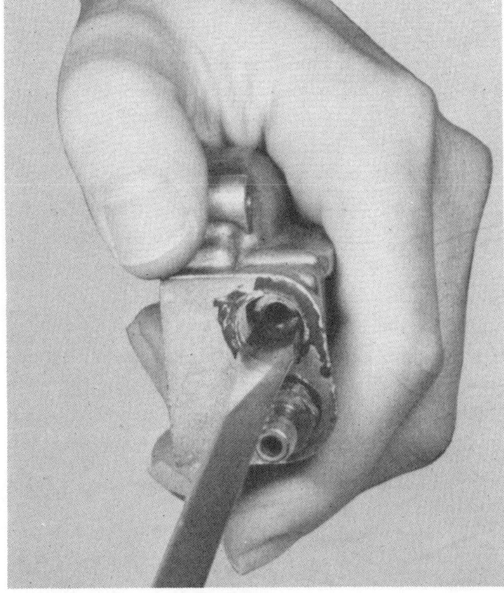

Removing the intake needle seat—MD-type (© Chrysler Outboard Corporation)

19. The carburetor and all parts (excluding gaskets and floats) should be cleaned in carburetor solvent and examined for wear. Replace all worn or defective parts. Carburetor rebuilding kits are recommended for each overhaul.

20. Air-dry all components before assembling.

21. Begin assembly by installing the intake needle seat and gasket in the fuel bowl.

22. Slide the intake needle into position with the pointed end in.

23. Install the float in the bowl and align the slot in the metal tab of the float with the notch on the intake needle.

24. Apply a light coat of sealant to the threads of the float lever pin and secure the float with the float lever pin.

25. Hold the fuel bowl upside down and check the float level. See "Float Level Specifications" in this section.

26. Thread the by-pass tube into the carburetor body.

27. Thread the main nozzle into the carburetor.

28. Install the main fuel jet in the carburetor body.

29. Install the fuel bowl gasket on the carburetor body with the outer contour of the gasket matching that of the carburetor body.

30. Assemble the fuel bowl to the carburetor with four screws.

31. Install the spring on the idle adjustment needle.

32. Thread the screw and spring into the carburetor until the needle seats lightly. Do not force the needle into the seat.

33. Facing the front of the carburetor, install the choke shaft from the left side.

34. Position the choke shaft with the flat side facing the front of the carburetor.

35. Install the choke plate with the flat on the plate down.

36. Apply a light coat of sealant to the choke plate screws and install the screws.

37. Install the choke friction spring, friction plunger, and friction screw.

38. Place the throttle return spring on the shaft with the large loop toward the shaft arm. Hook the large loop end of the spring on the shaft arm.

39. Facing the rear of the carburetor, insert the throttle shaft from the right side.

40. Hook the loop end of the throttle return spring over the pin on the carburetor. Hook the other end over the throttle lever.

41. Rotate the throttle shaft clockwise approximately one-half turn until the flat on the shaft faces the rear of the carburetor.

42. Install the throttle plate with the pointed edge down, toward the carburetor bowl. Place the plate against the flat side of the shaft.

43. Apply a light coat of sealant to the screws and install them in the throttle plate and shaft.

44. Check the throttle plate action by activating the plate. There must be no binding or sticking.

45. Install the carburetor on the motor and perform all carburetor adjustments listed under "Tune-Up."

CO Type

NOTE: *The illustrations for the CO type are basically identical to those for the MD type.*

1. Remove the carburetor from the motor.
2. Remove the screw holding the throttle plate to the shaft.
3. Place the throttle plate in the wide open throttle position and pull the plate out with needle-nosed pliers. Do not use excessive force.
4. Lift the large hook end of the spring off the boss for the intake fitting and pull the throttle shaft out of the carburetor body.
5. Remove the choke plate from the choke shaft and remove the bottom half of the choke plate.
6. Pull the choke shaft out from the carburetor body.

NOTE: *There is a detent ball and spring at the opposite end from the choke lever arm, which must be kept track of.*

7. Remove the choke plate spring and top half of the choke plate.
8. Remove the fuel bowl and fuel bowl gasket from the carburetor. Remove the gasket for the bowl screw which is located in the boss on the carburetor.
9. Remove the main fuel jet.

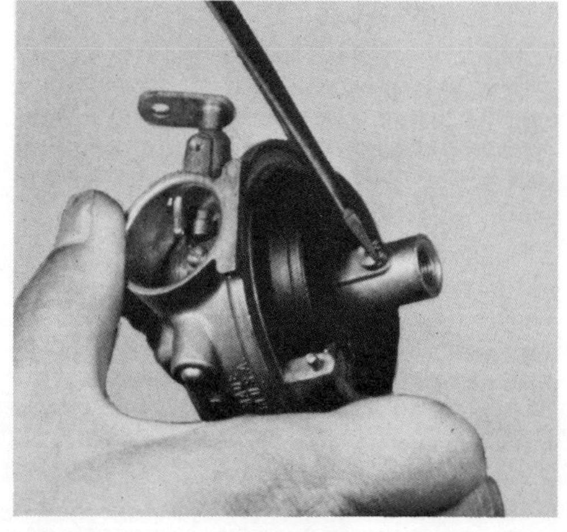

Removing fuel jet—CO-type (© Chrysler Outboard Corporation)

10. Drive the groove pin (securing the float to the carburetor) out from the pin end.
11. Remove the float from the carburetor body.
12. Remove the intake needle from the seat.
13. Remove the intake needle seat and gasket.
14. Remove the idle adjustment screw by turning it counterclockwise.
15. Remove the spring from the needle.
16. Examine the needle for grooves around the tapered portion. If such grooves are present, the needle should be replaced.
17. The carburetor body and all parts (except the float and gaskets) should be washed thoroughly in carburetor cleaner and examined for wear. Replace all worn or defective parts. Carburetor rebuilding kits are recommended for each overhaul.
18. Air-dry all components before assembling.
19. Begin assembly by installing the spring on the adjusting idle screw and installing the spring and needle in the carburetor. Screw the needle in until it seats lightly. Do not force the adjustment.
20. Install the intake needle seat and gasket, and tighten them securely.
21. Install the intake needle in the seat. Install the float in the carburetor and secure it with the groove pin. Adjust the float height, referring to the specifications concerning float level in this section. Adjustment is made by bending the tab on the float.
22. Install the main fuel jet.
23. Install a new fuel bowl gasket in the groove of the carburetor body and a new bowl screw gasket in the counterbore in the boss of the carburetor.
24. Install the fuel bowl, positioning the indented portion of the bowl toward the front of the carburetor.
25. Install a new gasket under the head of the bowl screw and secure the bowl to the carburetor.
26. Start the choke shaft into the bore of the carburetor from the starboard side of the carburetor, until the shaft extends into the air horn.
27. Install the top half of the choke plate on the end of the shaft with the open ends of the plate pivot toward the front of the carburetor.

Float Level Specifications

Model (hp)	*Carburetor Type*	*Float Level*	*Method of Adjustment*
3.5	MD	Top of the float parallel to top of fuel bowl	Bend metal tab attached to intake needle
3.5, 3.6	CO	13⁄32 in.	Bend tab on the float
4.4, 5.0, 6.0, 6.6, 7.0, 8.0	MD	Top of the float parallel to top of fuel bowl	Bend metal tab attached to intake needle
4.4, 5.0, 6.0, 6.6, 7.0, 8.0	CO	13⁄32 in.	Bend tab on the float
6.0, 9.2	MT	17⁄64 ± 1⁄64 in. from flange of cover with gasket removed to edge of float	Bend tab on the float
9.9, 12.9	MD	Top of float parallel to top of fuel bowl	Bend metal tab attached to intake needle
9.9, 12.9	CO	13⁄32 in.	Bend tab on the float
20.0	MD	Top of float parallel to top of fuel bowl	Bend metal tab attached to intake needle

3.5 and 3.6 HP float level adjustment (CO-type carburetor) (© Chrysler Outboard Corporation)

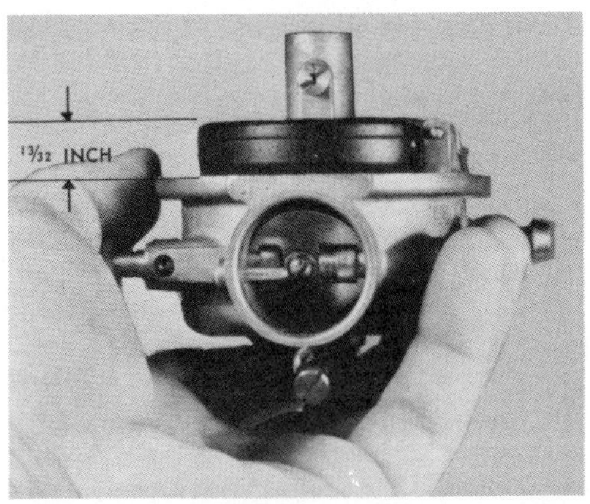

4.4, 5.0, 6.0, 7.0, and 8.0 HP float level adjustment (CO-type carburetor) (© Chrysler Outboard Corporation)

28. Install the plate spring with the spring ends pointing inside the carburetor and straddling the top half of the choke plate.

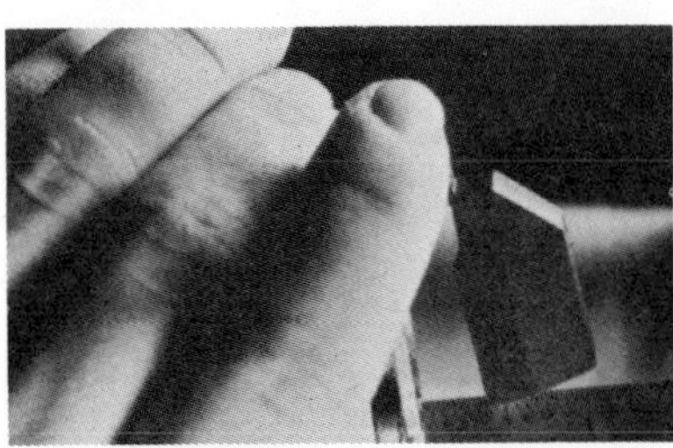

6.0 and 9.2 HP float level adjustment (MT-type carburetor) (© Chrysler Outboard Corporation)

9.9 and 12.9 float level adjustment (CO-type carburetor) (© Chrysler Outboard Corporation)

29. Slide the choke shaft through the pivots of the top half of the choke plate.

30. Install the detent ball and spring in the bore located on the port side of the carburetor near the end of the choke shaft bore.

31. Using a punch, depress the ball against the spring and slide the choke

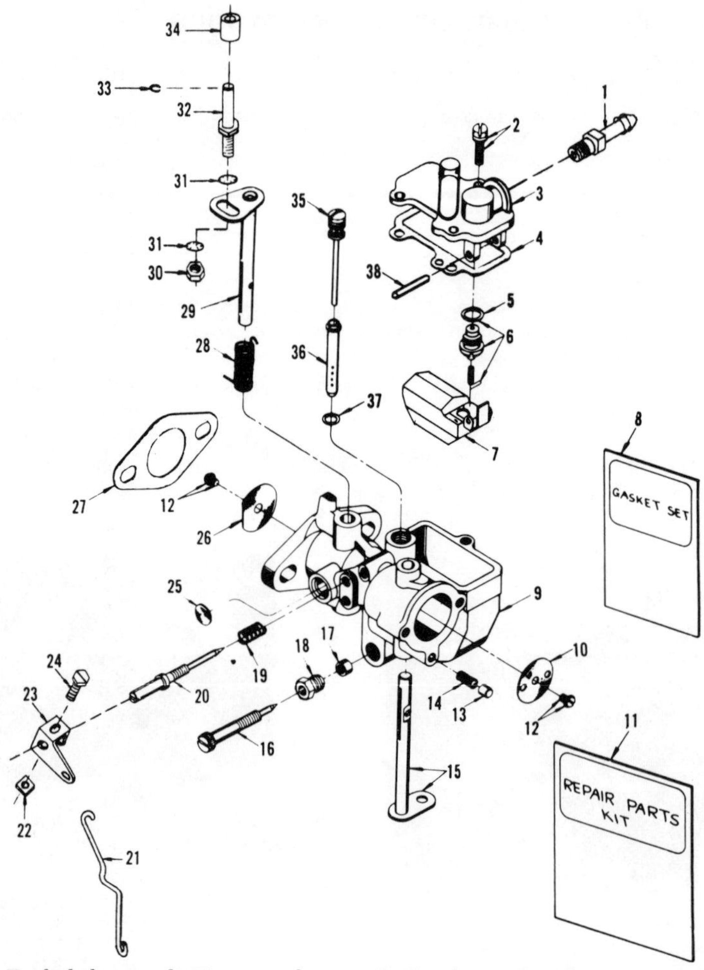

Exploded view of MT-type carburetor (© Chrysler Outboard Corporation)

1. Fuel line connector
2. Bowl cover screw
3. Bowl cover
4. Bowl cover gasket
5. Intake seat gasket
6. Intake needle seat and gasket
7. Float
8. Gasket set
9. Body
10. Choke plate
11. Rebuilding kit
12. Choke and throttle plate screw
13. Choke friction pin
14. Choke friction spring
15. Choke shaft and lever
16. Main adjustment screw
17. Main adjustment screw packing
18. Main adjustment screw packing nut
19. Idle adjustment screw spring
20. Idle adjustment screw
21. Idle adjustment link
22. Nut
23. Idle adjustment arm
24. Screw
25. Body channel plug
26. Throttle plate
27. Carburetor gasket
28. Throttle shaft return spring
29. Throttle shaft and lever
30. Nut
31. Lockwasher
32. Throttle cam follower
33. Retaining ring
34. Throttle cam follower roller
35. Idle tube
36. Main nozzle
37. Main nozzle gasket
38. Float lever pin

shaft the remainder of the way through the bore until the detent ball seats in the groove of the choke shaft.

32. Position the choke plate spring on the left side next to the flat on the choke shaft (when facing the front of the carburetor).

33. Install the bottom half of the choke plate, positioning the end of the spring, which is in front of the top half of the choke plate, behind the top half of the choke plate.

34. The extended portion of the bottom half above the screw hole must be in front of the top half of the plate.

35. Secure the bottom half of the choke plate to the choke shaft.

36. Slide the throttle return spring onto

the throttle shaft with the small hook end toward the lever portion of the shaft.

37. Facing the rear of the carburetor, install the throttle shaft into the carburetor from the right side.

38. Install the large hook of the return spring on the boss for the intake fitting and the small hook on the throttle shaft lever. Rotate the throttle shaft approximately one-half turn until the flat side of the shaft is facing the rear of the carburetor.

39. When installing the throttle plate, position the pointed edge side toward the bowl of the carburetor and the shutter half containing the holes installed first. Install the plate against the flat on the throttle shaft.

40. Apply a light coat of sealant to the threads of the throttle plate screws and install the screws.

41. Check the action of the shutter by activating the plate slowly. There should be no binding or sticking. A properly positioned throttle plate will show no light between the edge of the plate and the carburetor bore.

42. Install the carburetor and perform the carburetor adjustments listed under "Tune-Up."

MT Type

Service procedures for the MT-type carburetors are basically the same as those for MD-type carburetors. See "Float Level Specifications" for float level adjustment.

FUEL VALVE

3.5 and 3.6 HP

Removal

1. Remove the engine cover.
2. Slide the fuel clamp approximately one inch down the fuel line. This line is located on the center fitting of the fuel valve.
3. Remove the fuel line from the valve and plug the line.
4. Slide the fuel line clamp back on the carburetor.
5. Remove the hose from the carburetor to the fuel valve.
6. Remove the fuel valve knob from the fuel valve.
7. Remove the screw holding the fuel valve and retainer.
8. Remove the fuel valve through the hole in the support plate.

Installation

1. Install the fuel valve through the hole in the support plate and locate the side fitting on the valve toward the port side of the support plate.
2. Install the fuel valve retainer and screw.
3. Thread the knob onto the valve and tighten it.
4. Disconnect the fuel line from the tank and install the line on the center fitting on the fuel valve. Route the fuel line between the throttle lever friction screw boss and the support plate, then under the carburetor to the valve hose. Secure it with a clamp.
5. Install the engine cover.

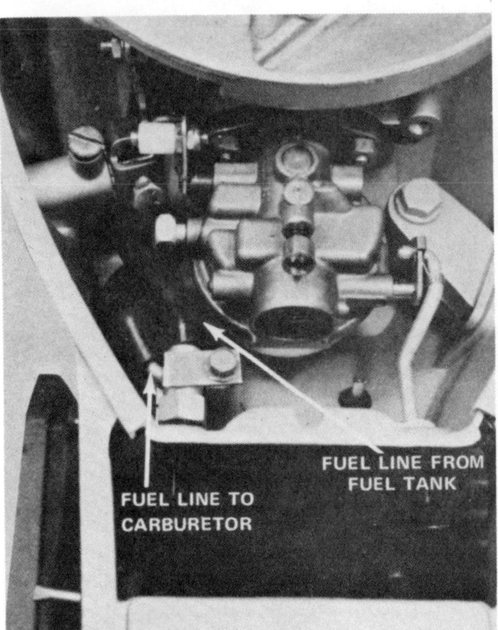

Fuel line routing for installation of fuel valve (© Chrysler Outboard Corporation)

FUEL PUMP

The fuel pump is attached to the side of the transfer port cover or the side of the powerhead; it consists of a diaphragm, reed plate with two reeds, and a cover with gaskets. Because of the relatively small volume displaced by the flexing of the diaphragm, there must be no leaks in the fuel system and no restrictions in the fuel supply.

4.4, 5.0, 6.0, 6.6, 7.0, 8.0, 9.2, 9.9, 12.9, and 20.0 HP

Fuel Pump Cover

Removal

1. Slide the hose clamps down from the fuel line fittings. Disconnect the fuel lines and plug them.
2. Remove the screws holding the cover to the powerhead, including the screw holding the stator ground wire.
3. Remove the fuel pump cover.

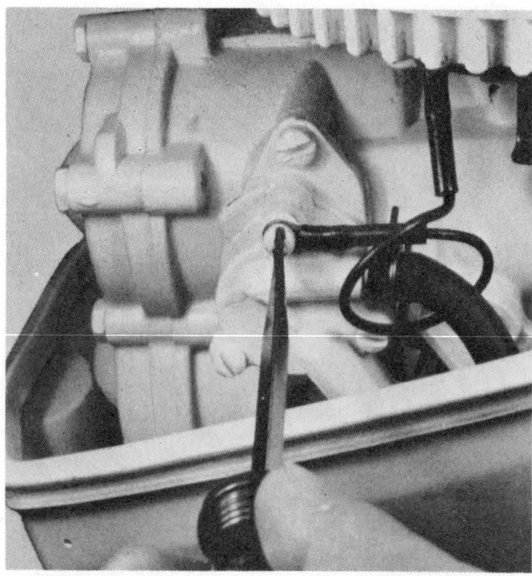

Fuel pump mounting screws (© Chrysler Outboard Corporation)

Installation

1. Connect the fuel line (bushing on support plate to fuel pump cover) to the lower fitting on the fuel pump cover.
2. Connect the fuel line (fuel pump cover to carburetor) to the upper fitting on the fuel pump cover.
3. Place a new gasket on the fuel pump cover and secure the cover with screws.

Fuel Pump Diaphragm

Removal

1. Remove the pump cover.
2. Remove the fuel pump reed plate and diaphragm from the powerhead or transfer port cover.

Installation

1. Place a gasket on both sides of the fuel pump diaphragm and install it on the recessed side of the reed plate.

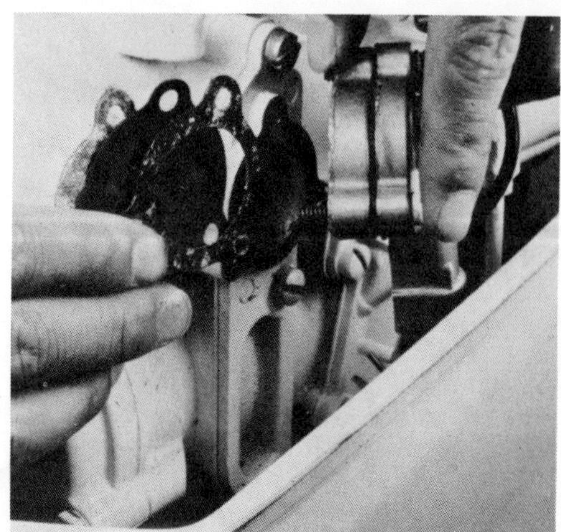

Fuel pump diaphragm (© Chrysler Outboard Corporation)

2. Install the fuel pump cover and gasket on the flat side of the reed plate.
3. Install the cover on the powerhead or transfer port cover.

Fuel Pump Reed Valves

Removal

1. Remove the fuel pump cover.
2. Remove the reed plate from the powerhead or transfer port covers.
3. Remove the screw holding the reed to the reed plate.

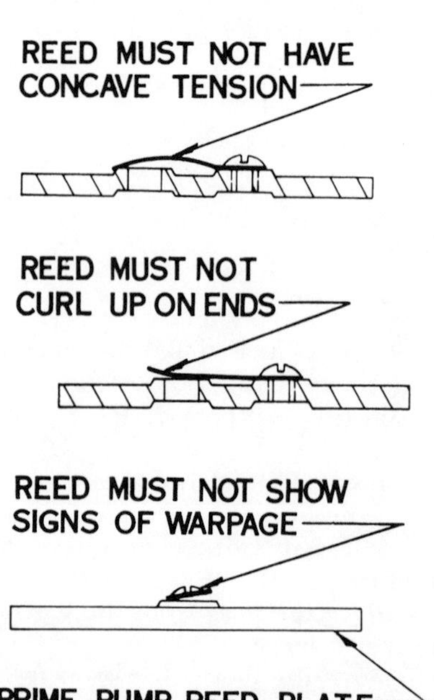

Proper reed installation (© Chrysler Outboard Corporation)

Installation

1. Check the reed for warpage. The reed must like flat on the reed surface without any tension. Reeds which must be forced flat will restrict fuel flow. The ends of the reeds must not stand open from the reed plate more than 0.003 in. Any reeds not meeting these specifications must be replaced.

2. Secure the reed to the reed plate and recheck for flatness.

3. Install the reed plate assembly on the fuel pump cover.

4. Install the fuel pump cover.

FUEL PUMP FILTER

Removal

1. Remove the fuel line (from the fuel bushing) to the fuel pump cover.

2. Remove the lower fitting from the fuel pump cover. The filter is attached to this fitting.

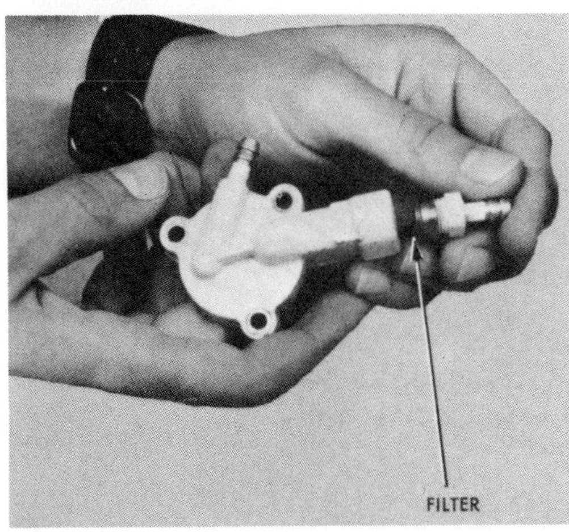

Removing fuel pump filter (© Chrysler Outboard Corporation)

Installation

1. Install the fitting with the filter in the fuel pump cover.

2. Connect the fuel line from the fuel pump bushing in the support plate to the fuel pump cover and secure it.

FUEL TANK

3.5 HP

REMOVAL

1. Loosen the jam nut on the magneto control lever.

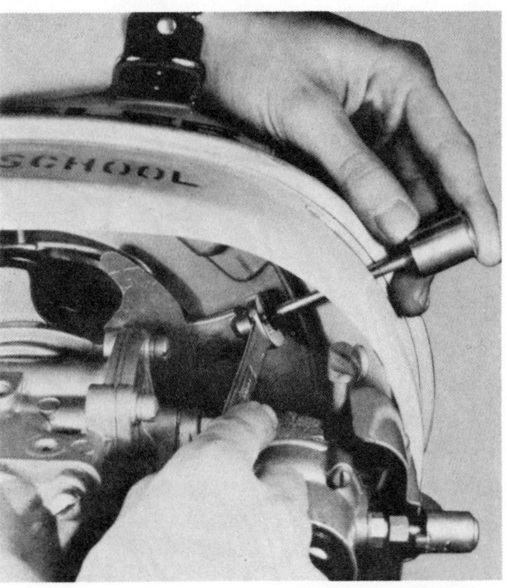

Loosen the jam nut on the magneto control lever —3.5 HP (© Chrysler Outboard Corporation)

2. Thread the control lever counterclockwise and remove it from the motor.

3. Disconnect the fuel line from the fuel shut-off valve which is located on the port side of the carburetor. Plug the end of the line.

4. Remove the four screws securing the fuel tank to the support plate.

5. Lift the tank off the engine.

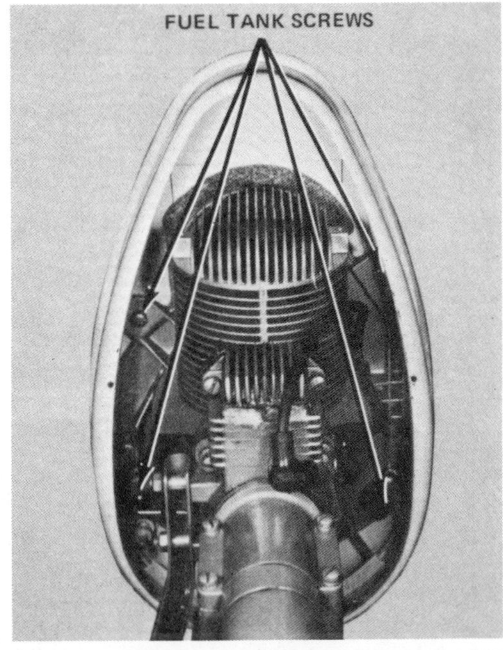

Location of fuel tank attaching screws—3.5 HP (© Chrysler Outboard Corporation)

INSTALLATION

1. Place the fuel tank on the motor and install the four securing screws in the support plate.

2. Thread the magneto control lever into the magneto control lever bracket. Tighten the jam nut.

3. Connect the fuel line to the fuel shut-off valve.

3.6 HP

REMOVAL

1. Remove the engine cover as detailed in the "Tune-Up" section.

2. Remove the starter assembly. See "Engine Electrical."

3. Disconnect the fuel line from the center fitting on the fuel valve. Plug the fuel line.

4. Remove the spark plug.

5. Remove the screws that secure the front of the fuel tank to the bearing cage.

6. Remove the screws securing the rear of the fuel tank to the brackets.

NOTE: *Later model motors have a mounting bracket on the port side only.*

7. Lift the fuel tank off the motor.

INSTALLATION

1. Place the fuel tank on the motor.

2. Install the screws securing the rear of the fuel tank to the brackets (or bracket).

3. Install the screws that secure the front of fuel tank to the bearing cage.

4. Connect the fuel line to the center fitting on the fuel valve.

5. Install the starter assembly. See "Engine Electrical."

6. Install the spark plug.

7. Install the engine cover as detailed in the "Tune-Up" section.

PUDDLE DRAIN SYSTEM

The puddle drain system is located just forward of the transfer port covers on the starboard side of the engine.

The puddle drain system on Chrysler outboards performs the very important function of keeping the crankcase free of raw fuel which accumulates in the lower portions. These puddles of raw fuel are formed by condensation of fuel on the cylinder walls while the fuel charge is present in the crankcase. The lower rpm ranges accompany the greatest severity of puddle accumulation when the engine is operated for extended periods of time in the low rpm ranges. This is due to the fact that the fuel charge is delayed in the crankcase for a longer period of time.

If these puddles of raw fuel were allowed to remain, they would tend to enrich the fuel mixture and force the engine to display characteristics of an overly rich mixture. An engine which has a faulty puddle drain system will stutter and falter during acceleration and generally run roughly.

Reed Adjustment

1. The puddle drain reeds must not stand open and the reed stop must be set so that they are open 0.017–0.023 in. at the top. Be sure that the screens for the puddle drain reed plate are in place.

Puddle drain reed plate (© Chrysler Outboard Corporation)

Engine Electrical

All Chrysler outboards use a color-coded wiring system. An understanding of the color coding will greatly facilitate the repair and maintenance of the motor.

Check the color of the insulation on the wire itself. If it has a distinctive color (other than black), such as red, orange, yellow, or blue, then this is the color code of the wire. If the wires are black or gray, check the color of the protective sleeve over the terminal end of the wire. The color of the sleeve indicates the color of the wire code.

The following colors are assigned to each of the electrical circuits in the motor.

Black—Whenever a black wire appears,

it indicates that the wire is attached to the negative terminal of the battery and is, therefore, ground.

Red—All wires coded red are connected to the battery positive post and are "hot."

Blue—All blue color-coded wires are part of the ignition primary circuit and are "hot" when the ignition is on.

Yellow—All yellow coded wires are part of the electric start circuit and are "hot" when the ignition switch is in the "start" position.

White—Any wire color-coded white is part of the tachometer control circuit.

Orange—All wires color-coded orange are part of the temperature indicator circuit. This circuit is only operative after the heat indicator switch is installed on the engine and the indicator light or gauge is installed.

Green—All wires coded green are part of the choke circuit and "hot" only when the choke is activated.

Purple—All purple color-coded wires are part of the charge indicator circuit and are "hot" when the engine is running.

3.5 HP

Flywheel

Removal

1. Flywheel removal, lapping, and installation are covered in the "Tune-Up" section of this chapter.

Stator Plate

Removal

1. Remove the fuel tank.
2. Remove the flywheel.
3. Remove the screws holding the throttle cam and magneto control lever bracket to the stator plate.
4. Remove the spark plug lead from the stator plate.
5. Remove the spark plug wire from the spark plug.
6. Lift the friction shoe assembly approximately one-quarter inch.
7. Lift the stator plate off the support plate.

Installation

1. Route the spark plug wire around the throttle cam bosses before installing the stator plate on the support plate.
2. Install the stator plate on the support plate.

Spark plug wire routing—3.5 HP (© Chrysler Outboard Corporation)

3. Position the stator plate at full retard (throttle cam bosses facing starboard).
4. Install the throttle cam and lever bracket on the starboard-side boss of the stator.
5. Do not fully tighten the starboard-side screw until the port-side screw is installed.
6. Position the stator at full advance and install the port-side screw to secure the throttle cam and magneto lever bracket. Tighten the port-side screw.

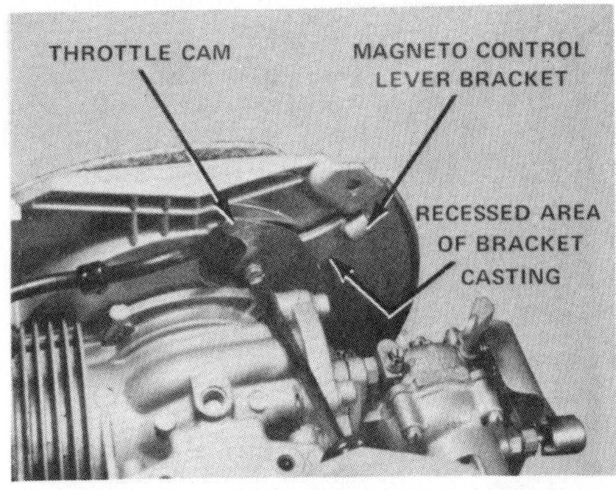

Install throttle cam and lever bracket—3.5 HP (© Chrysler Outboard Corporation)

7. Position the stator at full retard and tighten the starboard-side screw.
8. Install the clamp on the spark plug wire. Fully advance the stator and secure the clamp to the support plate.
9. Adjust the stator friction by turning the friction shoe assembly. A definite drag must be felt when the stator is moved.
10. Adjust the breaker points. See "Tune-Up."

11. Install the flywheel.
12. Install the fuel tank.
13. Connect the spark plug wire to the plug.

Breaker Cam

REMOVAL

1. Remove the flywheel and flywheel key.
2. Pull the cam up and off the crankshaft.

INSTALLATION

1. Slide the cam on the crankshaft with the letters and arrow pointing up.
2. Place the follower arm of the breaker points and wiper wick to clear the cam. Push the cam down until it seats on the shoulder of the crankshaft.
3. Adjust the breaker points. See "Tune-Up."
4. Install the flywheel key and flywheel.

Breaker Points

REMOVAL

1. Remove the flywheel.
2. Loosen the nut holding the coil and condenser wires to the terminal block on the stator. Slip the end of the breaker point spring from under the terminal block screw.
3. Remove the breaker point assembly from the stator.

INSTALLATION

1. Install the breaker point on the stator, aligning the breaker point pivot hole with the hole in the stator.
2. Install the end of the spring under the terminal block screw and tighten the screw.
3. Install the screw holding the breaker point assembly to the stator plate. Do not tighten this screw until after the points have been adjusted.
4. Adjust the breaker point gap. See "Tune-Up."
5. Install the flywheel.

Ignition Coil

REMOVAL

1. Remove the flywheel.
2. Remove the stator plate.
3. Disconnect both coil lead wires from the terminal block on the stator.
4. Straighten the coil lamination which retains the coil. This can be accomplished with pliers, if they are used carefully.
5. Use a piece of stiff wire, small enough to fit between the coil laminations and stator wall, to push the coil wedge spring down and pry the coil out.
6. Pull the coil from the laminations. Note the routing of the spark plug lead.
7. Remove the insulation and contact from the end of the spark plug wire and pull the wire through the stator. Remove the coil.

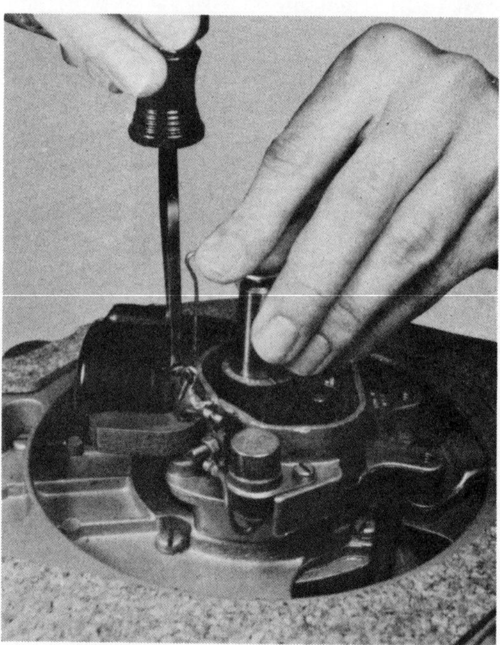

Removing ignition coil—3.5 HP (© Chrysler Outboard Corporation)

INSTALLATION

1. Place a new coil at the coil lamination of the stator plate so that the spark plug lead extends from the upper left.
2. Install the coil wedge spring in the coil so that the small lip of the spring faces up.
3. Install the coil with the wedge spring onto the laminations approximately half-way.
4. Route the spark plug wire as it was originally.
5. Push the coil down the rest of the way until the wedge spring snaps into place at the rear of the coil.
6. The large lip of the wedge spring must be over the front of the coil. Bend the top coil lamination to retain the coil.

7. Slip the coil ground wire between the insulating block and the stator wall.
NOTE: *The bent tabs on the ground wire must be against the insulating block or shorts will occur.*
8. Connect the insulated wire to the stator terminal screw.
9. Reinstall the contact and insulating boot on the end of the spark plug wire. Be sure the contact completes the circuit by contacting the spark plug wire.
10. Install the stator plate.
11. Install the flywheel.

3.6 HP

Flywheel

Removal

1. Flywheel removal, lapping, and installation are covered in the "Tune-Up" section of this chapter.

Stator Plate

Removal

1. Remove the flywheel.
2. Disconnect the throttle link end from the ball pivot on the stator.
3. Disconnect the spark plug wire from the plug.
4. Lift the friction shoe up approximately ¼ in.
5. Lift the stator plate off the support plate.

Installation

1. Route the spark plug lead wire as it was originally installed.

Spark plug wire routing—3.6 HP (© Chrysler Outboard Corporation)

2. Install the stator plate on the support plate.
3. Adjust the stator friction by turning the friction shoe assembly. A definite drag must be felt when moving the stator plate.
4. Connect the throttle end link to the ball pivot on the stator.
5. Adjust the breaker point gap. See "Tune-Up."
6. Install the flywheel and connect the spark plug wire to the plug.

Breaker Cam

Removal

1. See "Breaker Cam Removal" for the 3.5 hp model.

Breaker Points

Removal

1. This procedure is identical to the one for 3.5 hp models.

Breaker point removed—3.5, 3.6 HP (© Chrysler Outboard Corporation)

Ignition Coil

Removal

1. Removal and installation procedures for the ignition coil are identical to those for the 3.5 hp model.

Ignition coil wedge spring—3.5, 3.6 HP (© Chrysler Outboard Corporation)

4.4, 5.0, 6.0 (1971–72), 6.6 7.0, 8.0, 9.9, AND 12.9 HP

Flywheel

Removal

1. Removal, lapping, and installation procedures are covered in the "Tune-Up" section of this chapter.

Stator Plate

Removal

1. Remove the flywheel. See "Tune-Up."
2. Remove the screw holding the ground lead to the fuel pump.
3. Disconnect the spark plug wires from the spark plugs and from the clips on the exhaust port cover.
4. Unscrew the magneto stator plate from the stator ring.
5. Lift the stator plate up and to the port-side to disconnect the stator ring from the throttle cam link.
6. Turn the stator over and remove the screws securing the throttle cam. Bend the tab on the cam to remove the spark plug leads and ground wire.

Installation

1. Install the throttle cam and stator plate and place the spark plug wires and ground wires on the retaining tab on the throttle cam.
2. Attach the throttle cam to the stator plate. The magneto ground wire is attached to the rear starboard screw.
3. Hold the throttle cam link in the hole of the throttle cam on the port side.
4. Install the stator plate over the crankshaft and secure it to the magneto stator ring with four screws.
5. Before tightening the screws, be sure that the follower roller is not under the throttle cam.

Stator hold-down screw locations—4.4–12.9 HP (© Chrysler Outboard Corporation)

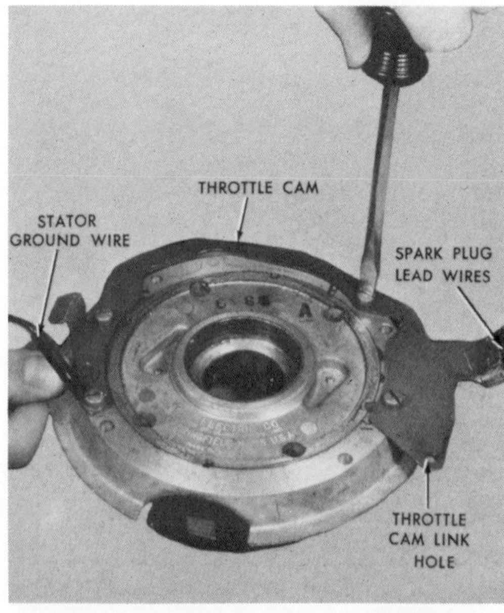

Assembling the throttle cam to the stator—4.4–12.9 HP (© Chrysler Outboard Corporation)

6. Connect the magneto ground wire to the top screw of the fuel pump.

7. Route the spark plug wires along the powerhead and install the wires in the clip on the exhaust port cover. The spark plug wire with the sleeve is the one that goes to the top (no. 1) cylinder. Attach the leads to the spark plugs.

8. Adjust the breaker point gap and the throttle pick-up.

9. Reinstall the flywheel.

Breaker Cam

Removal

1. Remove the flywheel.
2. Remove the flywheel key from the crankshaft.
3. Slide the cam up and off the crankshaft.

Installation

1. Slide the cam on the crankshaft with the letters and arrow facing up.
2. Position the breaker points follower arm and wiper wick to clear the cam.
3. Push the cam down to seat it on the crankshaft shoulder and align the keyways.
4. Install the flywheel key.
5. Adjust the breaker point gap.
6. Install the flywheel.

Breaker Points

Removal

1. Remove the flywheel.
2. Remove the screws holding the breaker points to the stator plate.

Location of breaker point securing screws—4.4–12.9 HP (© Chrysler Outboard Corporation)

3. Disconnect the lead wires from the coil and condenser from the breaker points.
4. Remove the breaker points from the stator.

Installation

1. Install the breaker point assembly on the stator. Do not tighten the mounting screws at this time.
2. Connect the leads from the coil and condenser to the breaker points.
3. Adjust the breaker points and tighten the mounting screws. See "Tune-Up" for breaker point adjustment.

Ignition Coil

Removal

1. Remove the flywheel. See "Tune-Up."
2. Remove the stator plate.
3. Disconnect the coil lead wire from the terminal block at the breaker points.

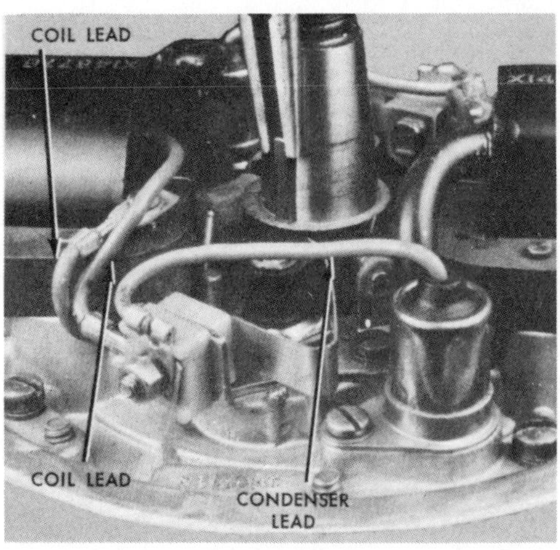

Coil lead wires—4.4–12.9 HP (© Chrysler Outboard Corporation)

4. Disconnect the coil lead wire that attaches to the coil laminations.
5. Straighten the coil lamination which retains the coil.
6. Pry the lip of the coil wedge spring up from the coil laminations.
7. Pull the coil away from the laminations. Note the routing of the spark plug wire for future reference.
8. Remove the insulating boot and contact spring from the spark plug lead.
9. Pull the spark plug wire through the stator plate and remove the coil.

INSTALLATION

1. Position the new coil at the coil lamination of the stator plate so that the spark plug lead extends from the upper left.
2. Install the coil wedge spring so that the small lip of the spring is facing down.

Ignition coil wedge spring—4.4–12.9 HP (© Chrysler Outboard Corporation)

3. Install the coil with the wedge spring onto the laminations approximately halfway. Route the spark plug lead as it was originally installed.
4. Push the coil down the remainder of the way until the wedge spring snaps into place at the rear of the laminations. The large lip on the spring must be seated on the front of the coil. Bend the bottom coil lamination to retain the coil.
5. Connect the coil ground wire from the bottom of the coil to the lamination.
6. Connect the lead from the top of the coil to the insulated terminal on the breaker point.
7. Install the contact spring and insulated boot on the spark plug wire and be sure of a good contact inside the insulation.
8. Install the stator plate.
9. Install the flywheel.

6.0 (1966–67) AND 9.2 HP

NOTE: *Service procedures for the flywheel, stator plate, breaker cam, breaker points, and ignition coil are the same as the corresponding procedures in the preceding section (4.4–12.9 hp)*

20.0 HP

Flywheel

REMOVAL AND INSTALLATION

1. Flywheel removal, lapping, and installation procedures are covered in the "Tune-Up" section of this chapter.

Stator Plate

REMOVAL AND INSTALLATION

1. Removal and installation of the stator plate is similar to 4.4 through 12.9 hp models. The only difference is that the magneto shorting wire clip must be removed from the carburetor adaptor flange before removing the stator plate.

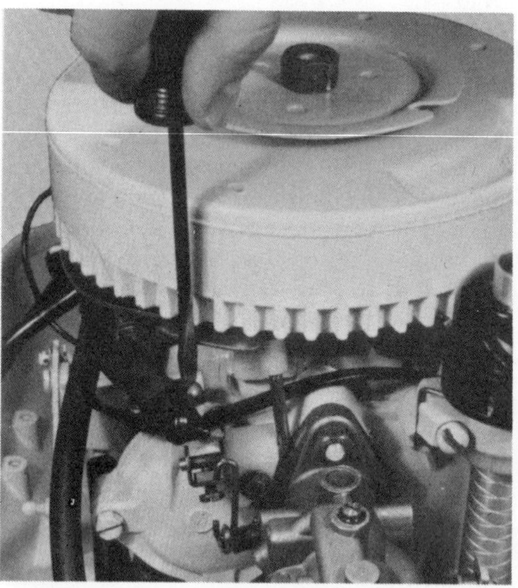

Removal of shorting wire—20.0 HP (© Chrysler Outboard Corporation)

Breaker Cam

REMOVAL AND INSTALLATION

1. Breaker cam removal and installation on these models is identical to the procedure for 4.4 through 12.9 hp models.

Breaker Points

REMOVAL AND INSTALLATION

1. Breaker point removal and installation is identical to the procedures for 4.4 through 12.9 hp models.

Ignition Coil

REMOVAL AND INSTALLATION

1. Ignition coil removal and installation for these models is identical to that for 4.4 through 12.9 hp models.

AUTOELECTRIC MODELS—ALL

Troubleshooting With A Test Light

Before plunging into electrical troubleshooting, two checks must be made. The mechanical condition of the motor should be checked by turning the motor over several times by hand to be sure that nothing is binding or seized. Second, visually check the condition of the battery. Be sure that the terminals are not loose. The battery must be a 30 amp hour unit and must be at full charge.

1. Check the test light by connecting one lead to one battery terminal and the other lead to the other battery terminal. The light should come on. If not, check the test light for loose terminals or replace the test light bulb. Refer to the troubleshooting chart and perform checks in the order listed.

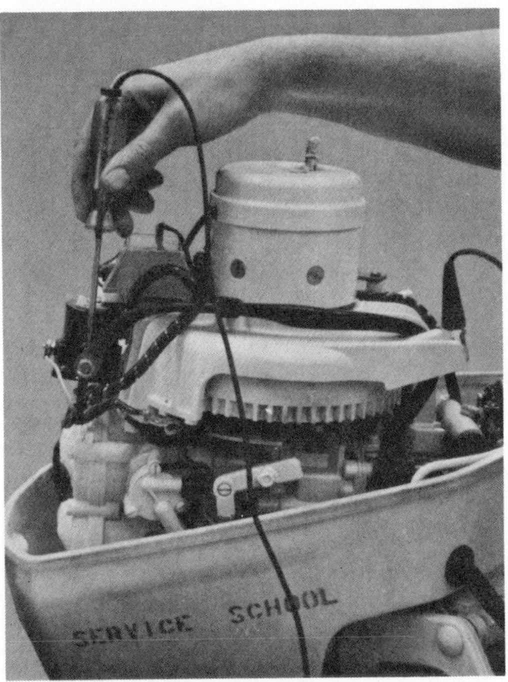

Checking input side of starter relay—Autoelectrics (© Chrysler Outboard Corporation)

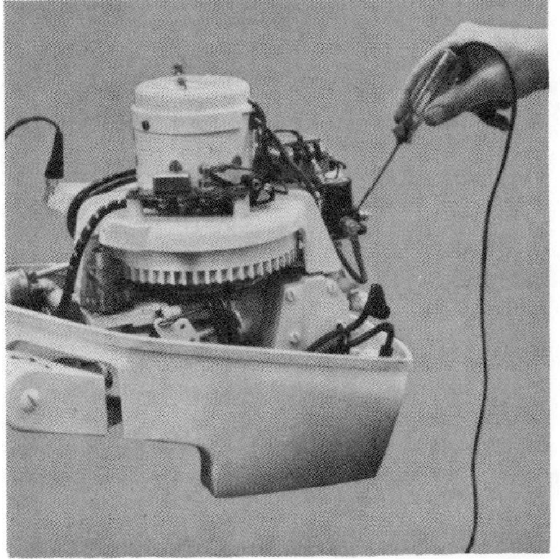

Checking output side of starter relay—Autoelectrics (© Chrysler Outboard Corporation)

Checking start terminal of starter relay—Autoelectrics (© Chrysler Outboard Corporation)

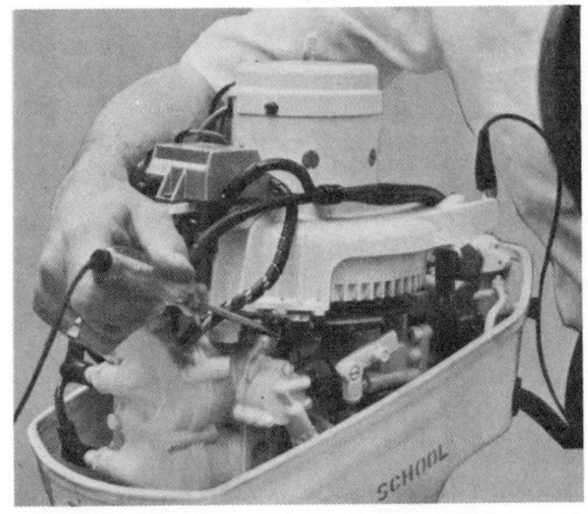

Checking interlock switch—Autoelectrics (© Chrysler Outboard Corporation)

Autoelectric Troubleshooting and Diagnosis

NOTE: *All checks are performed with test light lead grounded (e.g.—cylinder block to support plate ground strap.)*

Test	*Reaction of Test Light*	*Problem*	*Remedy*
1. Place the twist grip at Stop. Place the probe of the test light on the input side of the starter relay.	The light should come on.	If no light appears, the battery cable is defective, or the terminal clamp is loose.	Replace the battery cable or tighten the clamp.
2. Place the probe of the test light on the starter relay output terminal.	The light should come on and the motor should turn over. If the light does not come on, proceed to the next step.	If the light comes on, but the engine does not turn over, or turns over slowly, the starter should be removed.	Replace the starter or have it checked and overhauled.
3. Place the test light probe on the small terminal (yellow lead) of the starter relay. Place the ignition switch at Start.	The light should remain off. Proceed to next step.	If the light comes on, the starter relay is defective.	Replace the starter relay.
4. Place the test probe on the outside terminal of the starter interlock switch.	The light should remain off. Proceed to the next step.	If the light comes on, the interlock switch and starter relay are defective or open.	Tighten connections or replace components.
5. Move the test probe to the inside terminal of the interlock switch.	The light should remain off. Proceed to next step.	If the light comes on, the interlock switch is open or defective.	Replace the interlock switch.
6. Place the test light probe on the S (yellow lead) terminal of the ignition switch. Place the ignition switch at Start.	The light should remain off. Proceed to the next step.	If the light comes on, the wire between ignition switch and interlock switch is defective.	Replace or repair the wire.
7. Place the test light probe on the B (battery) terminal (red wire) of the ignition switch. Place the ignition switch at Start.	The light should remain off. Proceed to the next step.	If the light comes on, the ignition switch is defective.	Replace the ignition switch.
8. Place the test probe on the long terminal of the circuit breaker.	The light should remain off. Proceed to the next step.	If the light comes on, the wire from the circuit breaker to the ignition switch is defective.	Replace or repair the wire.
9. Move the test probe to the short terminal of the circuit breaker.	The light should remain off. Proceed to the next step.	If the light comes on, the circuit breaker is defective.	Replace the circuit breaker.
10. Place the test probe on the choke terminal of the choke solenoid. Place the ignition switch at on and push the key in to activate the choke solenoid.	The light should remain off. Proceed to the next step.	If the light comes on, the choke solenoid is defective.	Replace the choke solenoid.
11. Move the test probe to the choke terminal of the ignition switch (green wire).	The light should come on. Proceed to the next step.	If light comes on, the lead wire between the switch and choke solenoid is defective or the ignition switch is defective.	Replace the switch or replace or repair the wire.
12. Connect a tachometer to the motor. Place the test probe at the gray lead of the voltage regulator. Operate the motor until the test light comes on.	The light should come on below 3700 rpm.	If the light comes on above 3700 rpm, proceed to the next step.	Proceed to the next step.
13. Disconnect red lead from the ignition terminal of the voltage regulator and the gray lead of the starter frame assembly. Connect the red and gray leads and place the test probe at the connection. Run the engine to full throttle.	See Problem column.	If the light stays off, the problem is in the generator. If the light comes on, the problem is in the voltage regulator.	Remove the generator on the voltage regulator and replace as necessary.

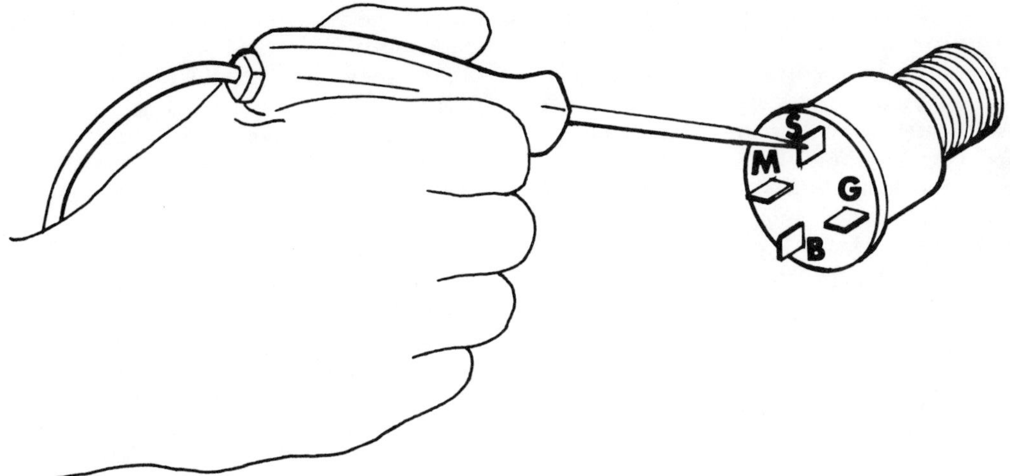

Checking start terminal of ignition switch—Autoelectrics (© Chrysler Outboard Corporation)

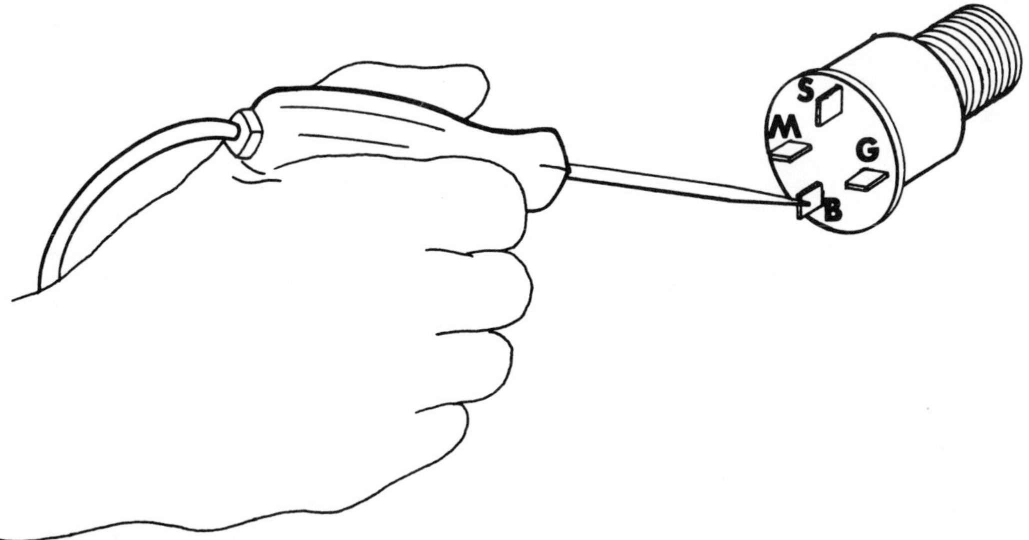

Checking battery terminal of ignition switch—Autoelectrics (© Chrysler Outboard Corporation)

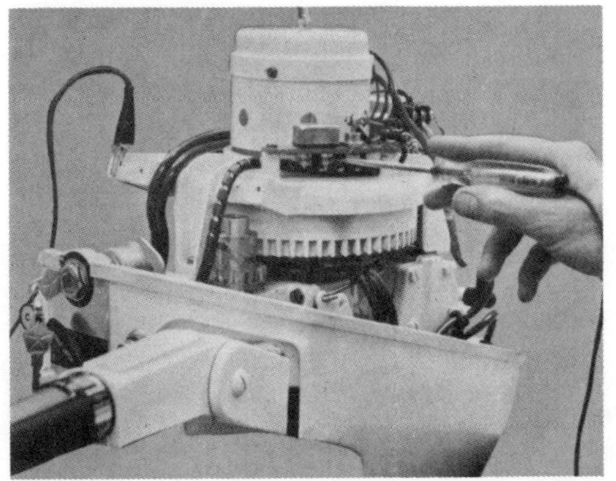

Checking circuit breaker—Autoelectrics (© Chrysler Outboard Corporation)

Troubleshooting the Autoelectric System with Ammeter and Voltmeter

Perform the tests in the order listed and refer to the accompanying chart to diagnose problems in the starter. Before performing any of the following tests, disconnect the spark plug wires to prevent accidental starting of the motor. Connect the voltmeter/ammeter (or separate instruments) in accordance with the manufacturer's instructions.

1. Operate the starter with the ignition key and observe the starter current draw. The indicator on the tester should stabilize before taking a reading. The current draw

should be 65–75 amps. If the starter meets these specifications, the problem is not in the starter. Proceed to the next step.

2. Place the motor in Neutral. Connect a tachometer and measure the no-load rpm and current draw of the starter. The no-load rpm should be 700–900; current draw, approximately 40 amps. Refer to the accompanying charts if the readings do not fall within the specifications.

Test Indication (Problem)	*Cause*
1. No-load rpm is low and current draw is high.	A. Loose pole shoes B. Grounded Armature C. Shorted armature
2. Very high current draw and no armature rotation.	A. Direct ground at ignition key switch B. Direct ground at starter brushes C. Direct ground at field connections
3. No current draw and the starter fails to operate.	A. Defective ignition switch B. Open circuit breaker C. Defective starter relay D. Broken or loose wire connections E. Defective interlock switch F. Incorrectly adjusted remote control G. Dirty brushes or dirty commutator
4. Low no-load speed and low current draw (indicates high resistance).	A. Dirty or loose connections B. Dirty brushes C. Dirty commutator and brush spring
5. High no-load rpm and high current draw.	A. Shorted fields

3. To test the generator, replace the spark plug leads and start the engine. Accelerate slowly, until approximately one amp reading is obtained on the meter. The cut-in speed should be below 3700 rpm.

4. Accelerate the engine to wide open throttle. The reading on the ammeter should be a minimum of six amps.

5. Check the voltage regulator. Connect a voltmeter to ground of the engine and the other lead to the long terminal of the circuit breaker. Start the engine and accelerate to 4000 rpm. Disconnect the positive battery cable. The voltmeter reading should not exceed 16 volts. If the reading is above 16 volts, replace the voltage regulator.

6. If no reading is obtained in test 5, disconnect the red lead from the ignition side of the voltage regulator and the gray lead from the field side of the voltage regulator, then connect the two leads. Connect the plus (+) terminal of the voltmeter to the connection and accelerate the motor until the voltmeter reads 14.5 volts. If no reading is obtained, remove the starter generator for testing or replacement. If the 14.5 volt reading is obtained, the voltage regulator is defective and should be replaced.

7. If all of the checks have been made and the generator still fails to recharge the battery, the problem is due to prolonged trolling, improper operation of the motor, or operation of the generator below cut-in speed.

Autoelectric Components

Removal

1. Disconnect both battery cables.

2. Remove the starter generator cover, lift up the cover, and disconnect the ground wire for the light.

3. Disconnect the wire between the light and the resistor at the resistor end. Remove the starter cover.

4. Remove the red lead from the starter generator and the starter relay. Remove the small red lead from the blocking diode of the terminal board.

5. Remove the gray lead of the starter generator from the voltage regulator.

6. Remove the screws which retain the starter generator to the generator support. Remove the generator.

7. Remove the hex bolt and washer which retain the armature to the crankshaft. Remove the armature from the engine with a suitable puller.

8. Remove the ignition switch from the support plate. Remove the five screws retaining the wires to the ignition switch and remove the ignition switch from the engine.

9. Remove the light switch from the support plate and disconnect the wires from it. Remove the switch from the engine.

10. Remove the terminal board and components from the bracket.

11. Remove the red wire from the wiring harness to the voltage regulator.

12. Remove the voltage regulator from the support plate.

13. Disconnect the positive battery

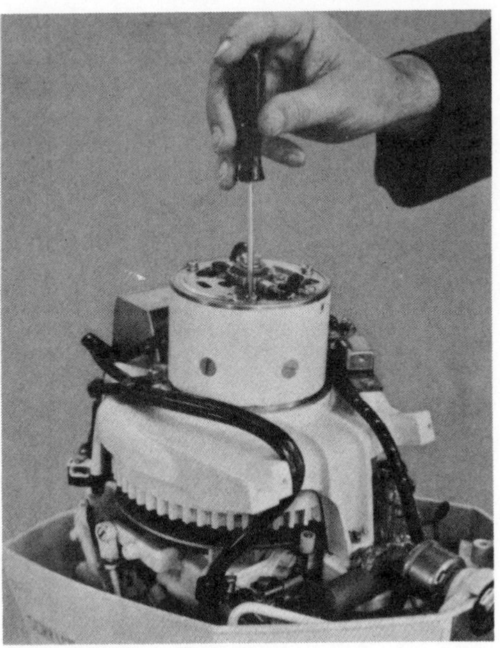

Removing starter generator frame—Autoelectrics (© Chrysler Outboard Corporation)

cable from the starter relay. Remove the small red lead from the same terminal of the starter relay. Remove the yellow lead from the starter relay. Remove the starter relay from the engine.

14. Disconnect the wires from the starter interlock switch and remove the switch.

15. All components are now free from the engine. The wiring harness and components can be separated for individual replacement or testing.

16. Remove the starter generator bracket from the powerhead.

17. The flywheel can now be removed for further component service. Refer to the particular model under "Tune-Up."

Installation

1. If the flywheel was removed, reinstall it.

2. Install and seat the starter support on the crankshaft.

3. Lightly tap the starter support until it seats firmly against the mounting points on the powerhead.

4. Tighten the two rear screws first to properly position the starter support.

5. Install the small spacer on the crankshaft.

6. Install the crankshaft key in the keyway.

7. Install the armature on the crankshaft, making sure that the keyways align. Tighten the armature retaining bolt to specifications.

8. Slide the brushes back until they are locked in position by the rear brush spring.

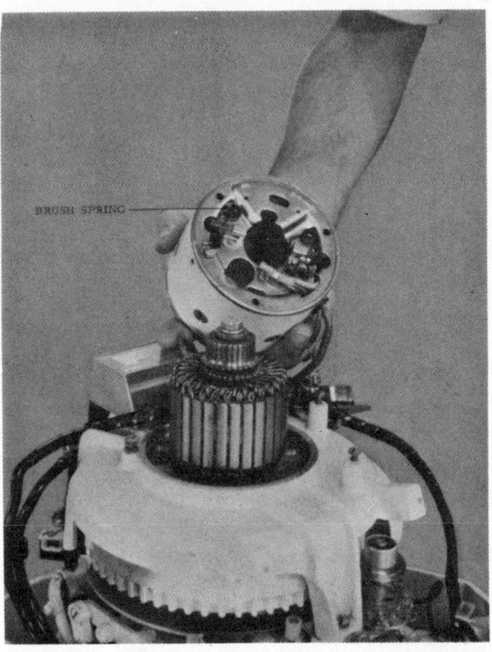

Locking the brushes in position—Autoelectrics (© Chrysler Outboard Corporation)

9. Install the starter frame assembly (the starter lead from the frame assembly should come out on the rear, port side of the engine). Secure it with five screws.

10. Release the pressure from the brush spring and slide the brush forward against the armature.

11. Install the ground lead, of the light in the starter cover, to the starter field assembly with the ground screw of the ground brush.

12. Install the starter cover on the starter frame assembly and secure it with screws.

13. Install the starter relay with the securing screws. Place the battery ground lead under the forward screw.

14. Install the voltage regulator.

15. Install the terminal board. Assemble the component parts on the terminal board and place the terminal board on the mounting bracket.

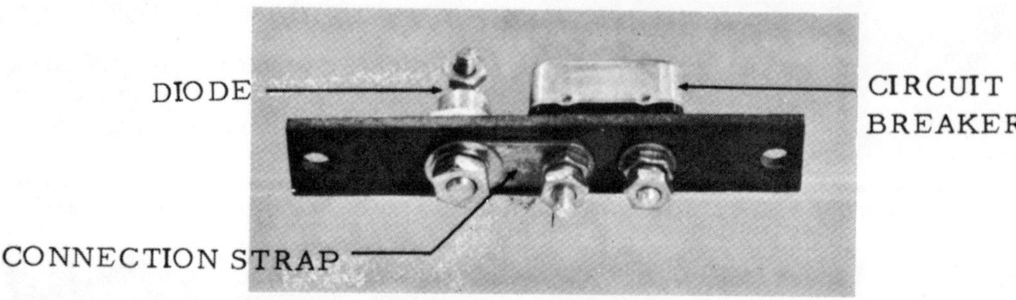

Terminal board components—Autoelectrics (© Chrysler Outboard Corporation)

16. Install the neutral interlock switch.

17. Install the wiring harness. Attach the component parts to the wiring harness in the same positions from which they were removed. (The wiring diagrams at the beginning of the chapter may be of some help in this respect.)

18. Install the ignition switch. After all components have been properly placed and attached to the ignition switch, place the switch in the proper position with the S terminal upward, so that when the switch is in the "off" position, the key slot is vertical. Secure it to the support plate with a washer and retaining nut.

MANUAL STARTER

All Models—Except 3.5 and 3.6 HP

PINION GEAR REMOVAL

1. Remove the flywheel.
2. Remove the screw from the top of the starter spring arbor in the spool shaft.
3. To accomplish anything further on the rewind starter, it is best to have a special tool. This is a rewind key which is inserted in place of the screw that was just removed.
4. Remove the pin from the slot of the pinion gear. Before entirely removing the pin, grasp the rewind key firmly so that the starter spring will not abruptly unwind. Remove the pin and let the spring slowly unwind.
5. Remove the rewind key and lift the pinion gear from the spool shaft.
6. Remove the starter pinion spring from the pinion gear.

PINION GEAR INSTALLATION

1. Apply grease to the inner diameter and groove of the pinion gear.
2. Install the spring in the groove of the pinion gear.

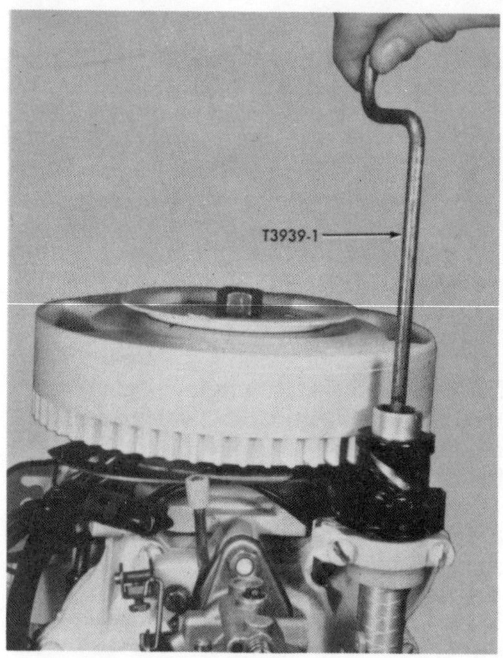

Removing the starter spring with rewind key (© Chrysler Outboard Corporation)

3. Install the pinion gear on the spool shaft with the spring end in the hole of the upper starter bracket.
4. Install the rewind key in the starter spring arbor.
5. Align the pin hole in the pinion gear with the holes in the spool shaft and starter spring arbor. Partially insert the pin. Hold the end of the pin and tighten the rewind key.
6. Remove the pinion pin starter spring by turning the rewind key 3½–4 turns, in a counterclockwise direction.
7. Align the pin holes of the spool shaft, arbor, and pinion gear. Partially insert the pin and, holding the end, remove the rewind key.
8. Drive the pinion pin in the rest of the

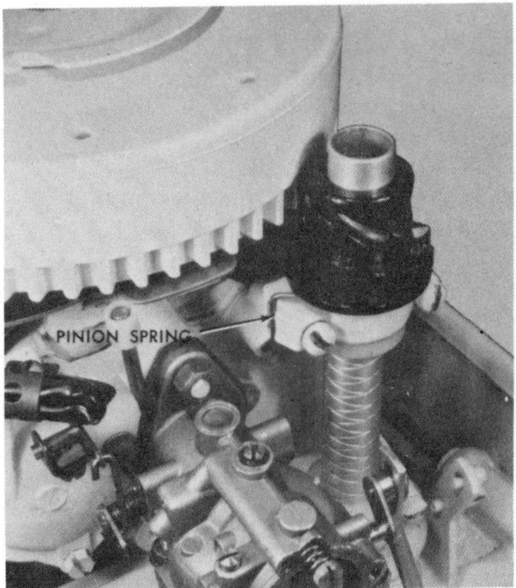

Proper installation of starter pinion spring (© Chrysler Outboard Corporation)

way and install the screw to retain the pin in the top of the arbor.

9. Install the flywheel.

Starter Rope Removal

1. Remove the starter rope handle by removing the retainer.

2. Firmly grasp the rope from inside the support plate and let the spring slowly unwind.

3. Remove the pinion gear and starter spring.

4. Remove the upper starter bracket.

5. Remove the spool and rope assembly from the lower starter bracket.

6. Unwind the rope and remove it from the spool.

Starter Rope Installation

1. Install the rope in the spool with the knot of the rope outside the spool. Wind the rope in a counterclockwise direction as viewed from the top of the spool.

2. Install the spool with the rope in the lower starter bracket.

3. Route the rope around the starter rope pulley on the carburetor or adaptor flange and through the support plate.

4. Feed the rope through the handle and route the rope through the grooves in the handle as shown in the illustrations. NOTE: *There are two types of handles.*

5. Pull the retainer onto the handle and take up all slack.

6. Install the upper starter bracket.

7. Install the starter spring.

8. Install the starter pinion gear.

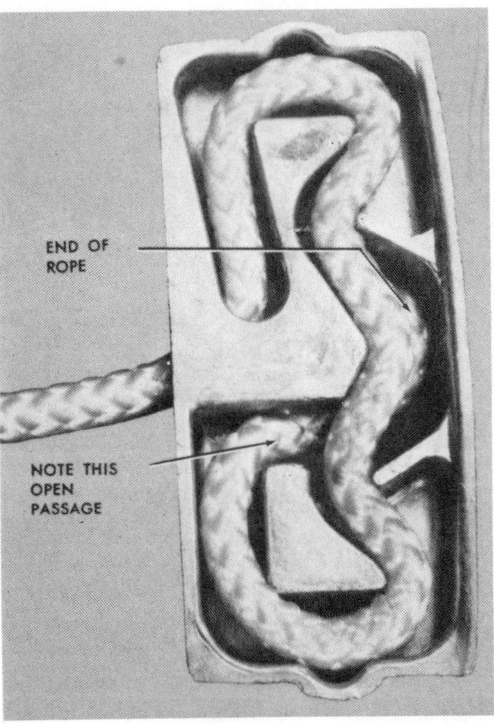

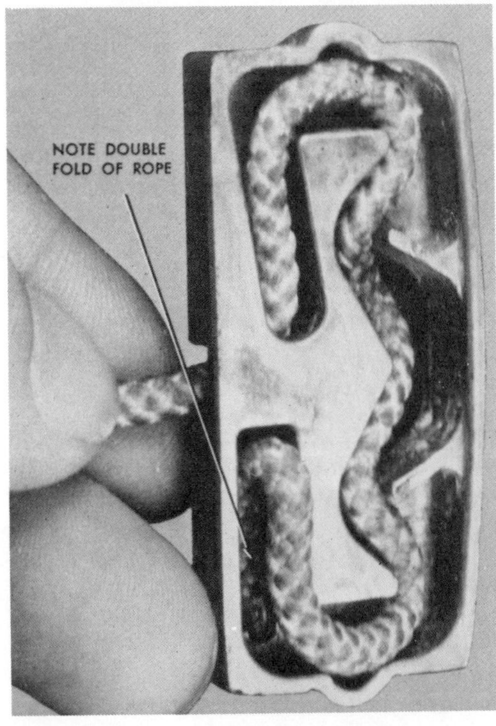

Assembly of starter rope in retainer (© Chrysler Outboard Corporation)

3.5 and 3.6 HP

Starter Removal

1. Remove the screws securing the starter to the fuel tank.
2. Lift the starter from the fuel tank.

Starter Installation

1. Install the starter on the fuel tank.
2. Install the attaching screws, but do not tighten them.
3. Engage the friction shoe plates against the starter cup and tighten the screws.

Rotor and Starter Rope Removal

1. Remove the starter.
2. Pull out the rope and tie a knot in the rope to keep it from retracting.
3. Remove the plug in the rope handle.
4. Pull the rope from the handle and remove the handle.
5. Untie the knot and allow the rotor to unwind slowly.
6. Remove the retaining ring from the end of the rotor shaft.
7. Remove the brake retainer washer, spring, and fiber washer. Lift the brake lever assembly from the rotor shaft.
8. Remove the other fiber washer and lift the rotor and rope from the housing.
9. Unwind the rope from the groove and remove the rope from the rotor.

Rotor and Starter Rope Installation

1. Thread in the end of the rope, without the metal clamp, first, and fold the end of the rope with the clamp over and lock it in the rotor.
2. Viewing the rotor from the bottom, when in the housing, wind the rope in the rotor counterclockwise.
3. Lubricate the bore of the rotor and install the rotor in the starter cobet aligning the hooked end of the spring with the slot in the rotor.
4. Position the loose end of the rope in the slot provided in the rotor.
5. Rewind the starter by turning it in a clockwise direction three full turns.
6. Thread the rope through the guide holes in the starter cover. Tie a slip knot in the rope to prevent the spring from rewinding.
7. Pull the rope out as far as it will go and turn the rotor an additional one-quarter turn. If the rotor cannot be turned an additional one-quarter turn, the spring is bottomed out. Check the length of the rope, which should be forty-eight inches.
8. Install the fiber washer on the rotor shaft.
9. Install the brake lever assembly on the shaft. It can only be installed one way.
10. Install the other fiber washer.
11. Install the spring and the brake retainer spring. Secure them to the shaft with the retaining ring.
12. Install the rope in the rope handle. Install a washer and tie a knot in the rope end. Pull the knot into the cavity in the starter handle.
13. Install the plug on the starter handle.
14. Install the starter.

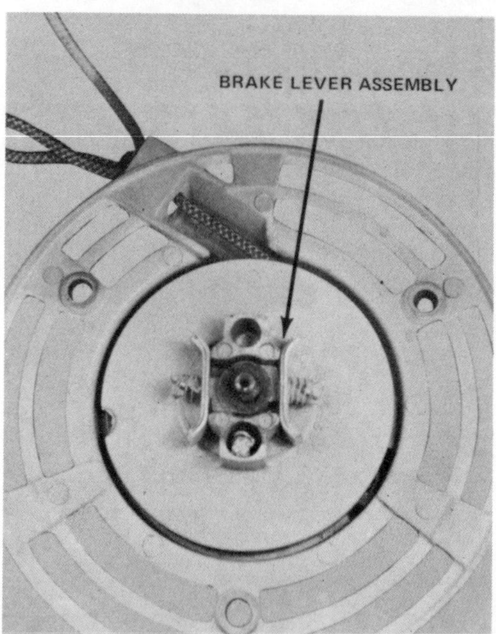

Proper position of brake lever assembly (© Chrysler Outboard Corporation)

Powerhead

Two types of powerhead are used on Chrysler outboards. The 3.5 and 3.6 hp models use a single-cylinder, air-cooled powerhead while all others use either a single or two-cylinder, water-cooled type. All powerheads on Chrysler outboards are two-strokes. Removal and installation procedures for all models are given separately (where there are differences) but service procedures are broken down into air-cooled and water-cooled types for model groupings. Small differences may exist between various models of any given type, but basic service procedures are similar for all water-cooled models and similar for all air-cooled models.

3.5 AND 3.6 HP

Crankshaft Bearing Cage

REMOVAL

1. Remove the fuel tank.
2. Remove the flywheel.
3. Remove the stator plate, flywheel key, and breaker cam.
4. Remove the screws securing the bearing cage to the powerhead.
5. Lift the bearing cage from the powerhead.

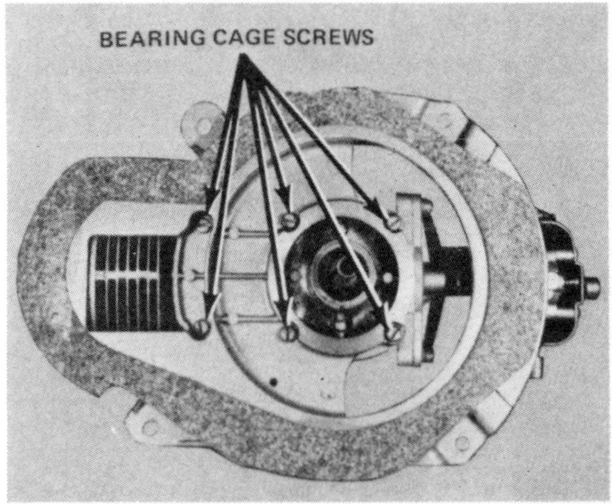

Bearing cage screw locations—3.5 and 3.6 HP (© Chrysler Outboard Corporation)

INSTALLATION

1. Glue the large cork gasket to the bearing cage.
2. Clean the gasket surface on the cylinder and install the bearing cage on the cylinder.
3. Install the six retaining screws and torque them to 30 in. lbs.
4. Install the stator, breaker cam, flywheel key, flywheel, and fuel tank.

Crankshaft Bearing Seal

REMOVAL

1. Remove the bearing cage. (See previous section.)
2. Drive the seal out from the bearing side of the bore.

INSTALLATION

1. Install the seal in the bearing cage bore with the sealing lip down (toward the bearing).
2. Press the seal down to within one-eighth inch of the bearing.
3. Install the bearing cage. See "Crankshaft Bearing Cage Installation."

Reed Plate and Reeds

REMOVAL

1. Remove the carburetor.
2. Remove the screws securing the reed plate assembly to the powerhead and remove the reed plate assembly.
3. Remove the three screws retaining the reed stop and reeds to the reed plate.

INSTALLATION

1. Center each reed over the reed opening.
2. Check to be sure that each reed lies flat. If reeds are curved more than $1/64$ in., the reeds should be replaced.
3. Install the reed stop and secure it with three screws.
4. Check again to be sure that the reeds are not curved.
5. Check the reed stop gap. The tip of the reed stop must be $0.160 \pm .010$ in. from the reed plate.
6. Install the reed plate in the reverse order of removal.

Short Block

REMOVAL

1. Remove the fuel tank.
2. Remove the flywheel.
3. Remove the complete stator.
4. Remove the crankshaft bearing cage assembly.
5. Remove the carburetor and reed plate assembly by removing the screws securing the reed plate to the cylinder.
6. Remove six screws securing the powerhead to the motor leg and remove the powerhead from the motor leg.

INSTALLATION

1. Install the short block on the motor leg, aligning the driveshaft splines with the crankshaft splines.

2. Secure the powerhead to the motor leg with six screws.
3. Install the reed plate and carburetor assembly.
4. Install the crankshaft bearing cage.
5. Install the complete stator.
6. Install the flywheel and fuel tank.

Crankshaft and Connecting Rods

Removal

1. Remove the short block. (See the preceding procedure.)
2. Remove the connecting rod caps by bending back the locktabs of each rod screw.
3. Push the connecting rod and piston down the cylinder toward the spark plug.
4. Remove the snap-ring from the bottom of the crankshaft, using snap-ring pliers.
5. Remove the crankshaft spacer from the bottom of the crankshaft.
6. Position the counterweights of the crankshaft to clear the connecting rod and pull the crankshaft from the cylinder.

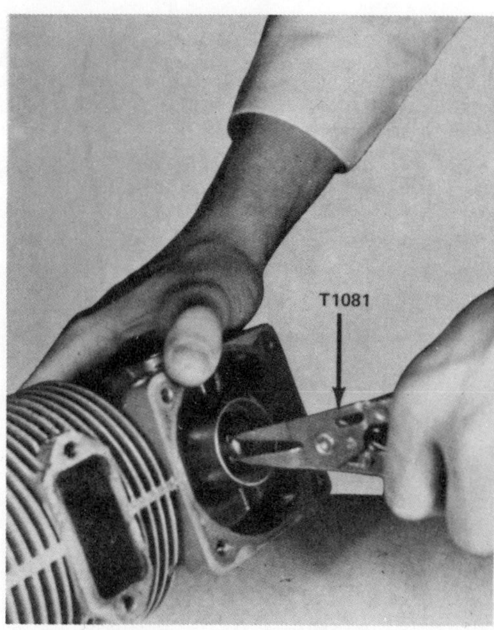

Removing the retaining ring from bottom of the crankshaft—3.5 and 3.6 HP (© Chrysler Outboard Corporation)

Installation

1. Install the crankshaft in the cylinder with the thrust washer between the crankshaft and lower bearing. Position the chamfer on the inner diameter of the washer up, toward the counterweights. Note the difference between the thrust washer and the spacer. The thrust washer is thicker.
2. Install the crankshaft spacer and secure the crankshaft with the retaining ring.
3. Slide the connecting rod and piston up to the crankshaft and install the rod cap. Align the matchmark as illustrated. Torque the connecting rod screws to specifications.
4. Bend up the locking tabs against the connecting rod screw heads.
5. Install the short block.

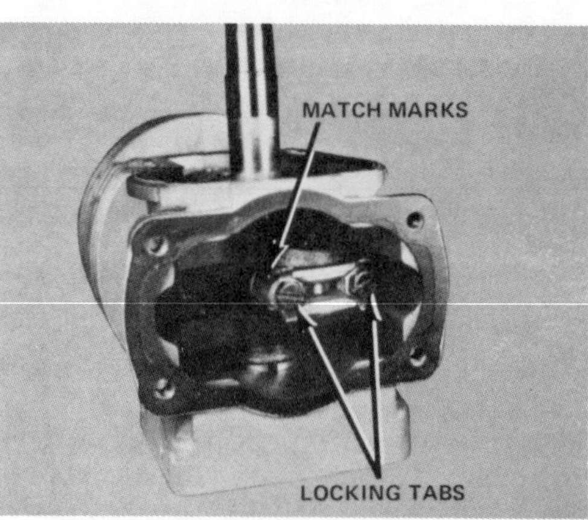

Connecting rod bearing cap matchmarks—3.5 and 3.6 HP (© Chrysler Outboard Corporation)

Connecting Rods, Pistons, and Rings

Removal

1. Remove the short block.
2. Remove the crankshaft. (See the previous procedure.)
3. Pull the piston assembly from the cylinder and matchmark the bearing caps, and the front of the piston, to facilitate correct and original installation.
4. Remove the piston rings from the pistons, using a ring expander. The piston rings can be removed by hand, provided great care is used, as the rings are very brittle.
5. Remove the retaining rings from the wrist pin using snap-ring pliers.
6. Remove the piston pin by driving it out with a one-quarter inch diameter drift.
7. Remove the connecting rod from the piston.

Installation

1. Heat the piston before assembling it to the connecting rod. Drive the wrist pin

partially in with the open end of the wrist pin toward the exhaust side of the piston. Drive the wrist pin in approximately one-eighth inch beyond the inside boss in the piston.

3. Install the connecting rod in the piston with the matchmark on the same side as the intake baffle.

4. Drive in the wrist pin the rest of the way and install the retaining snap-rings.

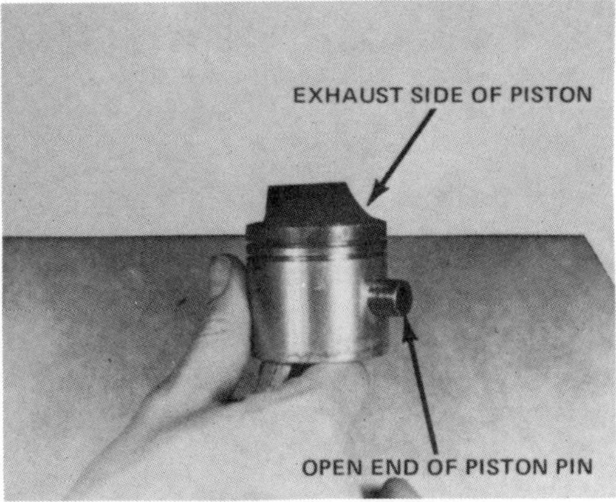

Installing the wrist pin in the piston—3.5 and 3.6 HP (© Chrysler Outboard Corporation)

5. Install the piston rings to the piston with the inside bevel toward the top of the piston. Lubricate the piston and rings with light oil.

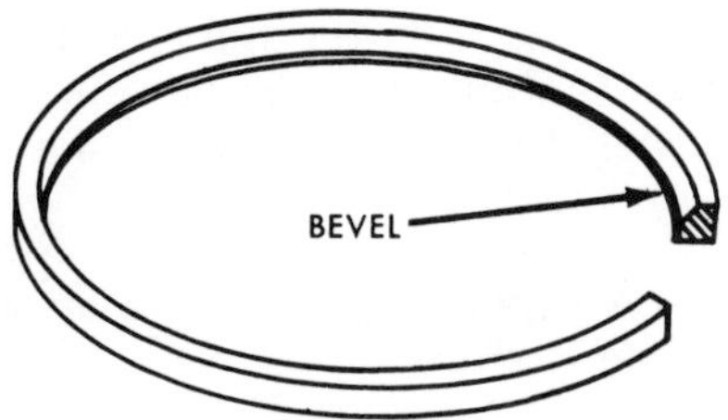

The piston ring bevel should face up when installed (© Chrysler Outboard Corporation)

6. Align the ring gaps to straddle the anchor pin on the piston and install the piston in the cylinder with the sloping side of the piston dome toward the exhaust ports of the cylinder. The bottom of the cylinder sleeve is designed to act as a ring compressor. Carefully press the piston into the cylinder while gently rocking the piston.

CAUTION: *If the rings were not aligned properly, they will break when compressed.*

7. Push the piston into the cylinder as far as it will go (do not force it) to align the connecting rod for crankshaft installation.

8. Install the crankshaft.

9. Install the short block on the motor leg.

4.4, 5.0, 6.0 (all), 6.6, 7.0, 8.0, 9.9, and 12.9 HP

Powerhead Removal— 4.4, 5.0, 6.0 (1970–72), 6.6, 7.0, and 8.0 HP

1. Disconnect the choke link from the carburetor.

2. Remove the starter rope handle and grasp the rope from inside the support plate. Tie a knot in the end and wedge it against the starter rope pulley.

3. Disconnect the fuel line from the bushing, using hose-clamp pliers.

4. Loosen the magneto shaft retainer setscrew. With the tiller handle up, pull the magneto control shaft with the gear out from the boss in the steering arm. Slip the magneto control link from the magneto control shaft.

Removing magneto control shaft link—4.4–8.0 HP (© Chrysler Outboard Corporation)

5. On models with an MD-type carburetor, the carburetor must be removed.

6. Remove the six screws from the base of the cylinder and the powerhead from the support plate.

Powerhead Installation— 4.4, 5.0, 6.0 (1970–72), 6.6, 7.0, and 8.0 HP

1. Clean all gasket surfaces and install a new gasket on the support plate.

2. Install the powerhead with the driveshaft splines engaged with the crankshaft splines. Rotate the propeller to engage the splines and ease the powerhead into position.

3. Install the screws securing the powerhead and torque them to 150–170 ft lbs.

4. Connect the magneto control rod link to the magneto control shaft. Seat the magneto control gear on the boss on the tiller handle. Position the shaft retainer against the opposite end of the boss.

5. Untie the slip knot in the rope and insert the rope through the support plate. Reinstall the handle.

6. On models with MD-type carburetors, install the carburetor.

7. Connect the choke link to the choke lever.

Powerhead Removal—6.0 and 9.2 HP (1966–67)

1. Remove the magneto, carburetor, and related linkage. It is not necessary to disassemble the starter. Simply pull out the starter rope and tie a knot in the rope to prevent it from rewinding.

2. Remove the fuel line from the bushing.

3. Disconnect the throttle control by removing the magneto control lever assembly from the exhaust port plate. By doing it this way, the throttle settings will remain undisturbed.

4. Remove the spark plugs and cylinder head.

5. If the cylinder block is to be replaced, remove as many components as possible to provide greater leverage. Remove the eight powerhead attaching screws and remove the powerhead.

Powerhead Installation—6.0 and 9.2 HP (1966–67)

1. Installation is the reverse of removal. Be sure to engage the driveshaft and crankshaft splines, by slowly rotating the propeller. Always install new gaskets and always clean the mounting surfaces.

Powerhead Removal—9.9 and 12.9 HP

1. Remove the starter handle and insert. From inside the support plate, grasp the rope and tie a slip knot, allowing the knot to jam against the starter pulley.

2. Disconnect the choke link from the carburetor.

3. Disconnect the fuel line from the bushing.

4. Remove the stop nut on the magneto control lever. Remove the control lever from the pivot stud and disconnect the links from the throttle cam and the magneto control shaft. Remove the lever and links.

5. Disconnect the interlock link from the interlock lever.

6. Remove the attaching screws at the base of the powerhead and remove the powerhead.

Powerhead Installation—9.9 and 12.9 HP

1. Clean all gasket surfaces and install a new gasket on the motor leg.

2. Install the powerhead on the support plate and rotate the propeller shaft slowly to engage the crankshaft and driveshaft splines. Do not fold over the rubber seal on the support plate.

3. Install the attaching screws and torque them to 150–170 ft lbs.

4. Install the neutral interlock lever on the swivel and bearing.

5. Install the magneto control lever on the pivot stud on the powerhead by connecting the magneto control lever to the throttle cam link (longer link) and the magneto control lever to the magneto control shaft link (shorter link). Swing the magneto control lever on the pivot stud and install the bearing washer and stop nut.

6. Untie the knot in the starter rope and insert the rope through the support plate. Install the starter rope handle.

7. Connect the choke link to the choke lever on the carburetor.

Crankshaft Bearing Cage—4.4–12.9 HP

Removal

1. Remove the flywheel.

2. Remove the stator plate.

3. Remove the four screws securing the bearing cage to the powerhead. Remove the bearing cage and stator ring.

4. Remove the bearing cage gasket and discard it. Clean the gasket surface of the powerhead.

INSTALLATION

1. Install a new bearing cage gasket.
2. Apply a coat of grease to the lips of a new seal.
3. Install the bearing cage in the counterbore of the stator ring and install this assembly on the crankshaft.
4. Align the holes in the bearing cage with the tapped holes in the powerhead. Apply sealant to the threads of the screws and install the four screws. Torque them to 70 in. lbs.
5. Install the stator plate.
6. Install the flywheel.

Crankshaft Bearing Cage Seal—4.4–12.9 HP

REMOVAL

1. Remove the crankshaft bearing cage. (See the previous procedure.)
2. Press the seal out of the bore in the bearing cage. If a pressing tool is not available, it may be carefully pried out. Do not scratch the seal bore.

INSTALLATION

1. Press the seal into the bearing cage with the large lip of the seal toward the powerhead.
2. Install the bearing cage in the powerhead.

Magneto Control Lever and Links—4.4–12.9 HP

REMOVAL

1. Remove the stop nut securing the magneto control lever to the powerhead. Remove the washer.
2. Set the magneto at full advance. (Be sure the motor is in gear or the magneto will not fully advance.)
3. Swing the control lever off the pivot stud and disconnect the magneto control shaft link from the magneto control shaft.
4. Remove the magneto control lever off the support plate and disconnect the throttle cam link.

INSTALLATION

1. Install the throttle cam link on the magneto control shaft so that the end of the link is on the support plate side of the lever. The link can only be installed one way.

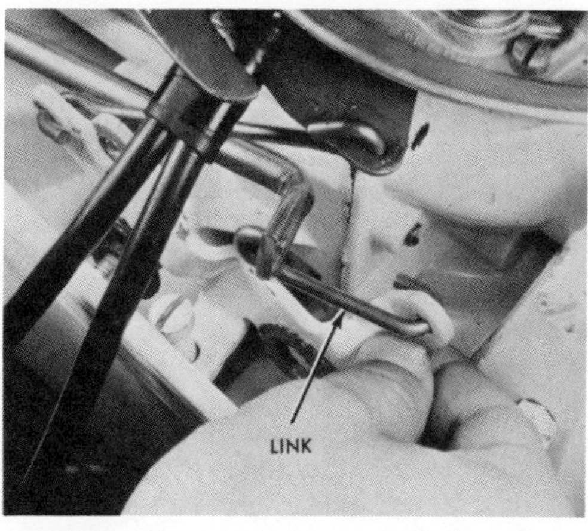

Disconnecting the magneto control link—4.4–12.9 HP (© Chrysler Outboard Corporation)

2. Install the magneto control shaft link on the lever so that the link is on the powerhead side of the lever.
3. Connect the throttle cam link on the throttle cam.
4. Swing the lever assembly under the spark plug lead and install it in the support plate area.
5. Connect the magneto control link to the magneto control shaft.
6. Install the magneto control lever on the pivot stud. Install the nylon washer and stop nut. Tighten the nut enough that the friction will keep the lever from moving when the engine is running.

Cylinder Head—4.4–12.9 HP

REMOVAL

1. Remove the powerhead.
2. Unbolt and remove the cylinder head, after disconnecting the spark plug.

INSTALLATION

1. Install a new cylinder head gasket.
2. Install the cylinder head and torque the attaching bolts to specification in the specified sequence.
3. Install the powerhead.

Exhaust Port Cover, Transfer Port Cover, and Cylinder Drain Cover—4.4–12.9 HP

REMOVAL

1. Unscrew and remove the exhaust port cover, plate, and gaskets.
2. Remove the fuel pump if applicable.

3. Unscrew and remove the transfer port cover and gaskets.
4. Disconnect the neutral interlock link, if applicable. Swing the link away from the cylinder drain cover.
5. Release the hose from the clamp on the drain cover.
6. Remove the fuel pump and swing it out of the way.
7. Unscrew and remove the cylinder drain cover.

INSTALLATION

1. Installation is the reverse of removal. Be sure that the screens are in place covering the check valves.

Reed Plate and Reeds—4.4–12.9 HP

REMOVAL

1. Remove the powerhead.
2. Remove the carburetor adaptor flange.
3. Remove the reed plate and gasket from the powerhead behind the carburetor adaptor.
4. Remove the two reeds from the V portion of the plate.
5. Remove the screws securing the reed stops and reeds to the plate.

INSTALLATION

1. Lay the reeds flat on the reed plate and check for flatness. If the reeds are bowed more than 1/64 in., they should be replaced.
2. Install the reeds and secure them to the reed plate. Check the reeds for flatness again. The maximum allowable opening is 0.005 in. The tip of the reed stop must be 0.265±0.010 in. from the reed plate.
3. Install the reed plate assembly.
4. Install the carburetor adaptor flange.
5. Install the powerhead.

Crankshaft and Center Main Rollers—4.4–12.9 HP

REMOVAL

1. Remove the flywheel.
2. Remove the stator plate.
3. Remove the crankshaft bearing cage assembly.
4. Remove the powerhead.
5. Remove the carburetor, carburetor adaptor flange, and reed plate assembly.
6. Remove the starter assembly and the mounting brackets.
7. Remove the cylinder head.
8. Remove the eight screws securing the crankcase cover to the cylinder block.
9. Using a suitable size drift, drive out the two locating pins.

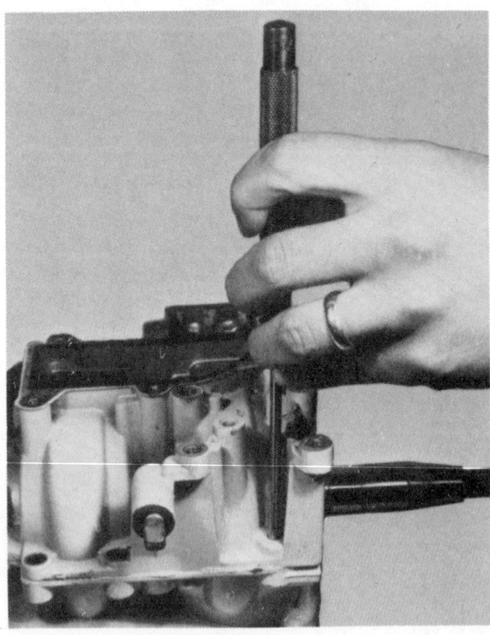

Drive out the locating pins—4.4–12.9 HP (© Chrysler Outboard Corporation)

10. Pry the crankcase cover from the cylinder block using a screwdriver at the pry points.

Pry the crankcase cover from the cylinder block—4.4–12.9 HP (© Chrysler Outboard Corporation)

11. Matchmark the bearing caps and connecting rods so that the connecting rod caps can be installed on the rod from which each was removed.

12. Remove the connecting rod screws.

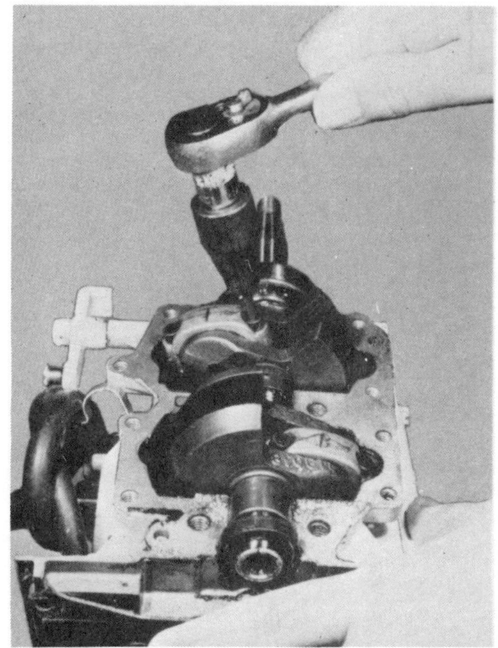

Remove the connecting rod screws—4.4–12.9 HP (© Chrysler Outboard Corporation)

13. Remove the connecting rod caps from the connecting rods. Remove the rod bearing rollers.

NOTE: *When removing the rod cap, hold each end of the connecting rod flange at the joint line to prevent the bearing rollers from falling into the crankcase. If a roller should fall into the crankcase, remove it immediately with a magnet or screwdriver magnetized by the flywheel magnet.*

14. Remove the exposed half of the center main bearing liner and remove all exposed rollers.

15. Lift the crankshaft from the cylinder. Remove the center main bearing rollers from the cylinder block. The other half of the center main bearing liner can remain in the block.

16. Remove the lower main bearing and seal from the crankshaft.

INSTALLATION

1. Clean the joint faces of the cylinder block and crankcase. Remove the peened metal from around the seal bore.

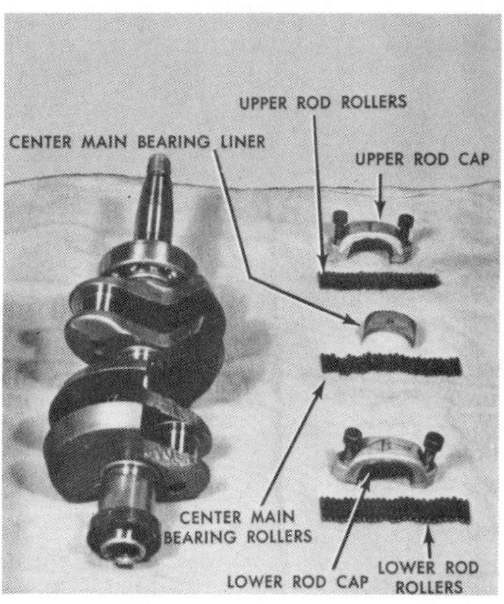

Exploded view of crankshaft connecting rod caps and roller bearing—4.4–12.9 HP (© Chrysler Outboard Corporation)

2. Clean the outside casing on the lower main bearing. Lubricate the rollers inside the casing with SAE 30 oil prior to assembly. Install the bearing on the crankshaft.

3. Coat the center main bearing liner with grease to retain the rollers.

4. Install twelve rollers on the liner half in the cylinder block. Install the crankshaft in the cylinder. Coat the center main bearing journal lightly with grease and install the remaining fourteen rollers. Install the other half of the center main bearing liner.

5. Install the rod caps and rollers as outlined later. Position the lower main bearing in the bore of the cylinder block $1/8 \pm 1/16$ in. from the floor of the bottom cylinder.

6. Apply Permatex no. 2 sealant to the sealing faces of the cylinder block and crankcase. Do not apply excess sealant, and be sure that sealant reaches the lower main bearing seal case and the upper main bearing race.

7. Install the crankcase cover on the cylinder block and drive in the two locating pins with an appropriate punch. Install four screws retaining the crankcase cover at the main bearing locations and torque the screws to specifications.

8. Install the screws retaining the crankcase cover to the cylinder block.

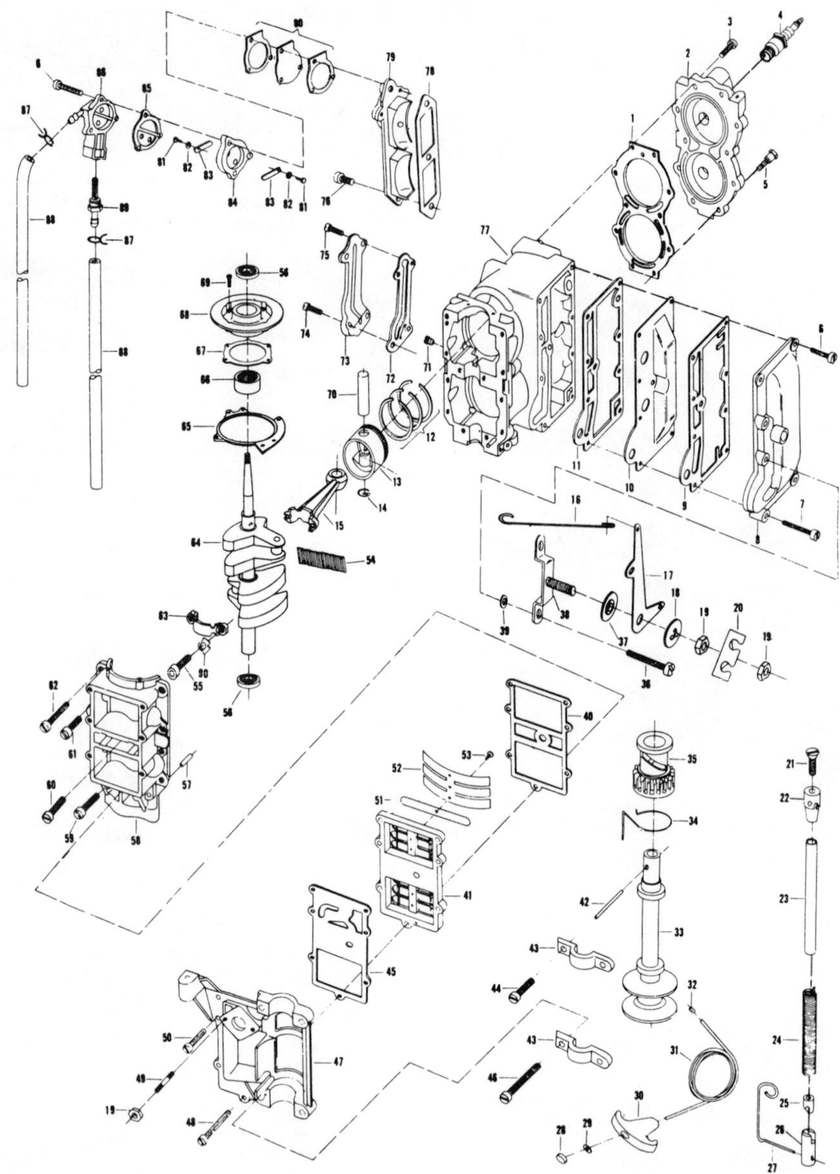

Exploded view of typical 2 cylinder powerhead—all models (© Chrysler Outboard Corporation)

1. Cylinder head gasket
2. Cylinder head
3. Fill head screw
4. Spark plug
5. Cylinder head screw
6. Fill head screw
7. Fill head screw
8. Exhaust port cover
9. Gasket, exhaust port cover
10. Exhaust port plate
11. Gasket, exhaust port plate
12. Piston ring
13. Piston
14. Lock ring
15. Connecting rod
16. Link, magneto control lever
17. Lever, magneto control
18. Washer, magneto control lever
19. Hex nut
20. Lead wire clip
21. Flat head screw
22. Starter rewind spring drive
23. Starter rewind spring guide post
24. Starter rewind spring
25. Starter spring retainer
26. Starter retainer extension
27. Starter rope guide
28. Starter rope handle plug
29. Plain washer
30. Starter rope handle
31. Starter rope
32. Starter rope end
33. Starter spool
34. Starter pinion spring
35. Starter pinion gear
36. Fill head screw
37. Bearing, magneto control lever
38. Pivot pin
39. Plain washer
40. Gasket, reed plate
41. Reed plate
42. Starter pinion pin
43. Starter bearing cap
44. Fill head screw
45. Carburetor adapter plate
46. Fill head screw
47. Carburetor adapter flange
48. Fill head screw
49. Carburetor stud
50. Fill head screw
51. Reed

Apply sealant to the screw located inside the crankcase at the reed plate area.

9. Install the lower main bearing seal as outlined in the following procedure.
10. Install the cylinder head.
11. Install the starter and mounting brackets.
12 Install the carburetor adaptor flange, reed plate assembly, and carburetor.
13. Install the crankshaft bearing cage and stator ring.
14. Install the stator plate assembly.
15. Install the powerhead.
16. Install the flywheel.

Stake the lower main seal in place—4.4–12.9 HP (© Chrysler Outboard Corporation)

Lower Main Bearing and Seal— 4.4–12.9 HP

Removal

1. Follow the disassembly procedures in the preceding procedure (steps 1–10).
2. Remove the center main liner half and the exposed rollers.
3. Lift the crankshaft slightly at the lower main journal and slide the seal and lower main bearing from the crankshaft.

Installation

1. Clean the outside case of the bearing and lubricate the rollers inside the casing with SAE 30 oil.
2. Follow steps 2 and 5–16 of the preceding installation procedure. When the seal is fully seated, stake the bottom of the cylinder block at two places (180° apart) and 1/16 in. from the seal bore.

Connecting Rod Roller Bearings— 4.4–12.9 HP

Removal

1. Follow the disassembly procedures in the removal section for "Crankshaft and Center Main Rollers." The crankshaft and center main bearing rollers do not have to be removed.
2. Remove the rollers from the connecting rods.

Installation

1. Lightly coat the connecting rod bearing liner with grease to retain the rollers. Install twelve rollers in the bearing liner.
2. Slide the connecting rod and rollers under the crankshaft journal.
3. Coat the crankshaft journal with grease and install fourteen rollers on the journal. Remember to align the matchmarks.
4. Install the rod cap with the liner on the connecting rod, aligning the matchmarks.
5. Install the connecting rod screws and torque to specifications.
6. Complete the assembly as outlined in the installation procedure for "Crankshaft and Center Main Rollers."

52. Reed stop
53. Reed head screw
54. Connecting rod needle bearing, not used on 5 and 6 H.P.
55. Connecting rod screw
56. Seal
57. Dowel pin
58. Crankcase cover (order cylinder)
59. Fill head cap screw
60. Fill head screw
61. Fill head screw
62. Fill head screw
63. Connecting rod cap (order connecting rod)
64. Crankshaft
65. Magneto stator ring
66. Bearing, crankshaft upper
67. Gasket, crankshaft bearing cage
68. Crankshaft bearing cage
69. Fill head screw
70. Piston pin
71. Cylinder drain valve
72. Gasket, cylinder drain cover
73. Cylinder drain cover
74. Fill head screw
75. Fill head screw
76. Fill head screw
77. Cylinder
78. Gasket transfer port cover
79. Transfer port cover
80. Fuel pump diaphragm
81. Pan head screw
82. Plain washer
83. Reed
84. Fuel pump feed plate
85. Gasket, fuel pump
86. Fuel pump cover
87. Fuel line clamp
88. Fuel line
89. Fuel pump filter
90. Tab lock, not used on 8 and 9 H.P.

Connecting rod and bearing cap matchmarks—4.4–12.9 HP (© Chrysler Outboard Corporation)

Connecting Rods, Pistons, and Rings—4.4–12.9 HP

Removal

1. Remove the crankshaft as outlined previously.
2. Matchmark the connecting rod, connecting rod caps, and cylinder (including front of piston and block) so that all parts may be returned to their original locations.
3. Remove the connecting rods and pistons from the cylinder bores.
4. Remove the piston rings from the piston with a ring expander. This can be done by hand if great care is used.
5. Remove the snap-rings retaining the wrist pins.
6. Drive the wrist pin out with a suitable size drift.
7. Remove the connecting rod from the piston.

Installation

1. Heat the pistons prior to assembling the connecting rod to the piston.
2. Drive the wrist pin into the piston.
3. Install the retaining rings to hold the wrist pin in place.
4. Install the rings on the piston with the bevel toward the top of the piston.
5. Oil the rings with SAE 30 oil and install the piston in the cylinder, noting the

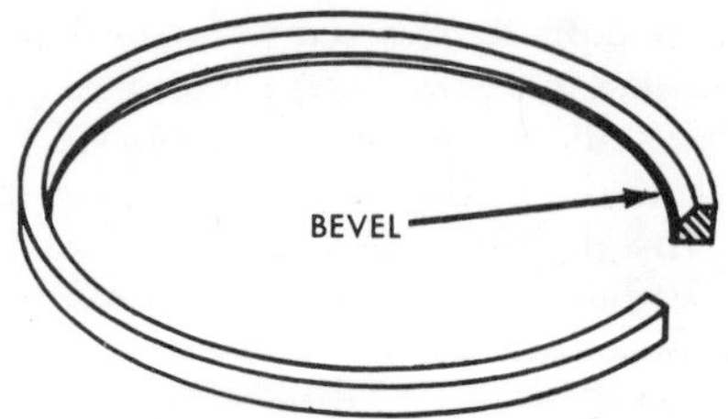

Piston ring showing beveled edge—4.4–20.0 HP (© Chrysler Outboard Corporation)

Correct installation of pistons in cylinder—4.4–20.0 HP (© Chrysler Outboard Corporation)

matchmarks made at disassembly. Position the piston so that the intake baffle on the piston is toward the intake ports or transfer cover.

6. Install the connecting rod bearings and complete assembly as detailed previously.

20.0 HP

Removal

1. Disconnect the choke rod from the lever on the carburetor.
2. Disconnect the magneto control connector from the magneto control connector.
3. Remove the starter handle insert and starter handle. Grasp the rope from inside the support plate and pull it out. Tie a knot in the end of the rope and wedge the knot against the starter rope guide.

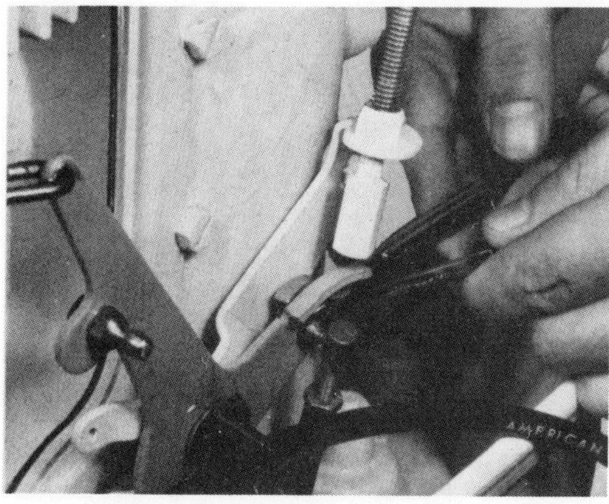

Disconnect magneto control connector—20.0 HP (© Chrysler Outboard Corporation)

4. Slide the hose clamp off the fitting on the fuel pump and disconnect the fuel hose. Plug the hose.

5. Remove the cotter pin from the end of the gearshift rod.

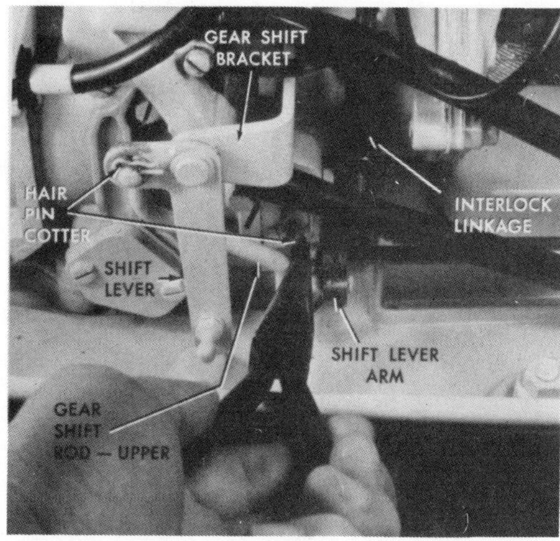

Remove the cotter pin from the gearshift rod—20.0 HP (© Chrysler Outboard Corporation)

6. Disconnect the interlock linkage from the gearshift lever arm. Pull the gearshift from the shift rod bracket.

7. Disconnect the upper gearshift rod from the lever arm of the gearshift bracket.

8. Remove the motor leg covers.

9. Remove the six mounting screws and lift the powerhead from the motor leg and support plate.

Installation

1. Clean the gasket surfaces of the powerhead and support plate. Install a new gasket on the spacer plate.

2. Install the powerhead on the support plate. Engage the crankshaft splines with the driveshaft splines by rotating the propeller with the lower unit in gear.

3. Install the six mounting screws and torque them to 65–75 ft lbs.

4. Install the motor leg covers. See "Lower Unit."

5. Insert the end of the upper shift rod in the hole in the gearshift lever arm. Secure it with a cotter pin.

6. Insert the end of the shift rod through the hole in the gearshift bracket, aligning the elongated hole in the lever arm with the short projection of the upper shift rod. Secure it with a cotter pin.

7. Install the pivot screw to secure the interlock linkage to the gearshift lever arm.

8. Connect the fuel hose to the bottom fitting on the fuel pump.

9. Untie the slip knot in the starter rope and feed the rope through the support plate. Install the handle and insert.

10. Install the magneto control connector to the magneto control lever.

11. Connect the choke rod to the choke lever on the carburetor.

Crankshaft Bearing Cage

Removal and Installation

1. Removal and installation procedures are identical to the 4.4–12.9 hp models.

Crankshaft Upper Seal

Removal and Installation

1. These removal and installation procedures are identical to those for the 4.4–12.9 hp models. Press the seal in so that the seal is flush to 1/64 in. depressed from the top of the seal bore.

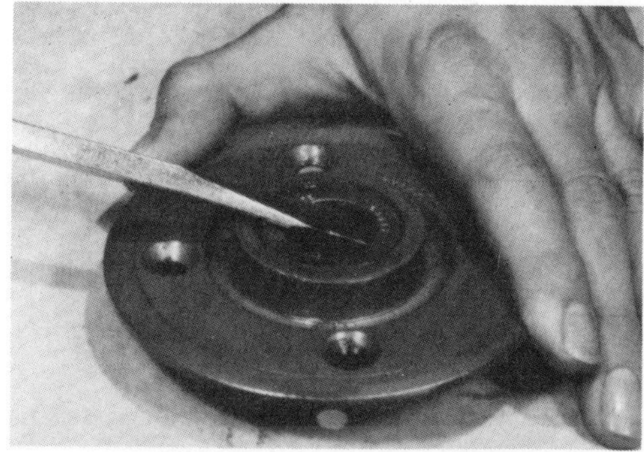

Removing the upper seal—20.0 HP (© Chrysler Outboard Corporation)

Cylinder Head

REMOVAL

1. Remove the spark plugs from the cylinder head.
2. Remove the ten bolts securing the cylinder head and gasket to the powerhead.
3. Remove the cylinder head and gasket by inserting a screwdriver at the pry points. Discard the gasket.

INSTALLATION

1. Install a new cylinder head gasket. Be sure to align the holes in the gasket with those in the powerhead.
2. Install the cylinder head, matching the intake side of the cylinder head with the intake side of the powerhead.

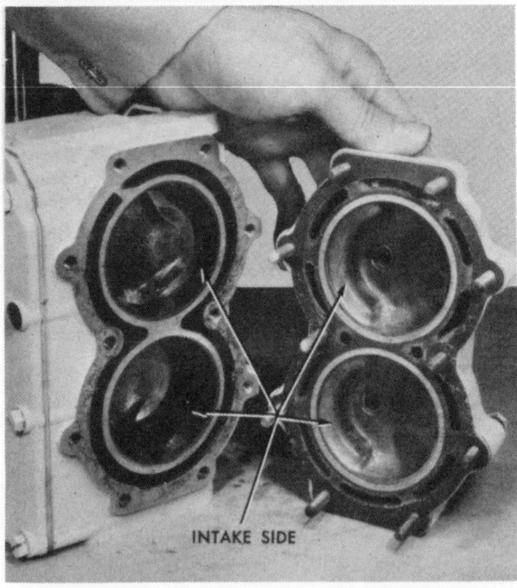

Intake sides of cylinder block and cylinder head —20.0 HP (© Chrysler Outboard Corporation)

3. Apply sealant to the threads of five cylinder head bolts as shown on the torque sequence illustration in the specifications section.
4. Torque the cylinder head bolts, as shown in the specifications, to the proper torque figure.

Exhaust Port Cover and Plate

REMOVAL

1. Disconnect the magneto control connector from the magneto control lever.
2. Remove the magneto control bracket assembly. Disconnect the bracket assembly from the magneto control link.
3. Remove the cover plate and gasket from the powerhead.

INSTALLATION

1. Clean the gasket surfaces on the plate and powerhead.
2. Install one gasket between the powerhead and the exhaust port plate. Install the other gasket between the exhaust plate and cover.
3. Install all of the securing screws except two (the bottom forward screw and the one at the rear, second from the top). These screws secure the magneto control bracket.
4. Connect the magneto control bracket to the magneto control link. Install the bracket assembly to the exhaust port cover. Make sure that spacers are used between the bracket and the exhaust port cover.
5. Install the connector stud on the magneto control lever.

Transfer Port Cover

REMOVAL

1. Remove the screws securing the transfer port covers and idle stop switch to the powerhead.
2. Remove the transfer port cover, idle stop switch cam, and gasket.

INSTALLATION

1. Installation is the reverse of removal.

Reed Plate and Reeds

REMOVAL AND INSTALLATION

1. Reed plate and reed service is identical to that for the 4.4–12.9 hp models.

NOTE: *Some models require removal of the powerhead while others do not.*

Water Outlet Tube

REMOVAL AND INSTALLATION

1. The water tube may be removed after the powerhead is removed. Remove it by twisting it loose with a pair of pliers.
2. The water tube can be installed by pushing into the hole provided after coating the end liberally with sealant.

Removing water outlet take—20.0 HP (© Chrysler Outboard Corporation)

Gearshift Bracket

REMOVAL

Disconnect the gearshift knob rod from the shift lever arm.

2. Disconnect the upper gearshift rod from the lever of the gearshift bracket.
3. Disconnect the neutral interlock linkage from the shift lever arm.
4. Unbolt and remove the bracket from the crankcase cover.
5. Remove the shift interlock lever with the interlock linkage from the bracket assembly.

INSTALLATION

1. Install the interlock lever and linkage on the pivot stud of the shift bracket. Secure this assembly with a washer and retaining ring.
2. Install the bracket on the crankcase cover with the interlock lever positioned up. Align the holes in the bracket with the second and fourth holes from the top of the cylinder block on the starboard side. Secure the bracket.
3. Connect the upper gearshift rod to the shift bracket lever and secure it with a cotter pin.
4. Connect the gearshift knob rod to the shift lever arm.
5. Connect the interlock lever and linkage to the shift lever arm.

Crankshaft and Center Main Rollers

REMOVAL AND INSTALLATION

1. Removal and installation procedures are the same as for the 4.4–12.9 hp models.

Lower Main Bearing and Seal

REMOVAL AND INSTALLATION

1. Removal and installation are the same as for the 4.4–12.9 hp models.

Connecting Rod Roller Bearings

REMOVAL AND INSTALLATION

1. See this procedure in the section on 4.4–12.9 hp models.

Connecting Rods, Pistons, and Rings

REMOVAL AND INSTALLATION

1. This procedure is the same as for the 4.4–12.9 hp models.

Motor Leg and Water Pump

The gear housing is located immediately below the motor leg, which supports the powerhead. The motor leg consists of the motor leg covers and tilt bracket, and houses the driveshaft and water tubing (water-cooled models only).

3.5 AND 3.6 HP

Gear Housing

REMOVAL

1. Remove the propeller nut, cotter pin, propeller, and shear pin from the end of the propeller shaft.
2. Remove the vent screw from the port side of the gear housing.
3. Remove the drain screw from the port side of the gear housing. Drain the lubricant.
4. Remove the nut from the stud on the upper front part of the gear housing.
5. Remove the motor leg clip from the front of the gear housing.
6. Remove the screw from the upper rear edge of the gear housing.
7. Tilt the motor leg and pull the gear housing free.

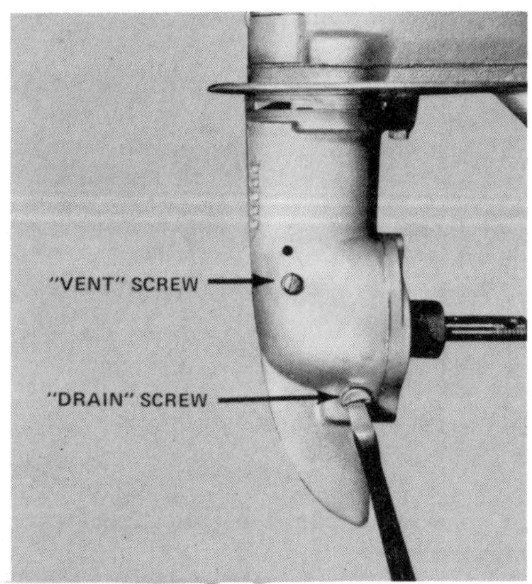

Remove the vent and drain screws—3.5 and 3.6 HP (© Chrysler Outboard Corporation)

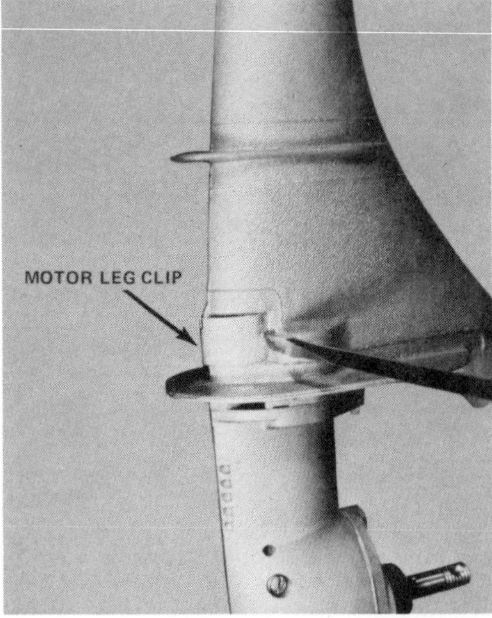

Removing motor leg clip—3.5 and 3.6 HP (© Chrysler Outboard Corporation)

INSTALLATION

1. Tilt up the motor leg.
2. Slide the driveshaft up into the motor leg until it contacts the crankshaft. Align the driveshaft with the crankshaft.
3. Turn the propeller shaft until the splines of the driveshaft engage the splines on the crankshaft.
4. Install the end of the water line into the rubber end of the water line seal on the water pump.
5. Push the driveshaft up until the gear housing contacts the motor leg.
6. Install the screw in the rear edge of the gear housing and torque it to 65–75 in. lbs.
7. Install the nut on the stud on the upper front edge of the gear housing. Torque the nut to 65–75 in. lbs.
8. Gently tap the motor leg clip until it snaps into place.
9. Fill the gear housing with Chrysler Outboard Gear Lubricant and install the vent screw and drain screw.

Bearing Cage

REMOVAL

1. Remove the propeller from the shaft.
2. Drain the gear housing.
3. Remove the screws retaining the bearing cage to the gear housing.
4. Remove the bearing cage by gently tapping it with a leather mallet.
5. Pull the bearing cage from the shaft and remove and discard the old gasket.

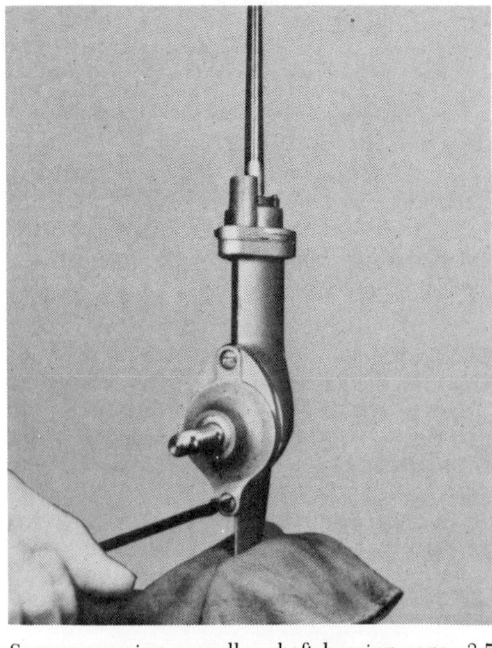

Screws securing propeller shaft bearing cage—3.5 and 3.6 HP (© Chrysler Outboard Corporation)

INSTALLATION

1. Position the cage gasket on the gear housing.
2. Install the bearing cage over the pro-

peller shaft and secure it to the gear housing. Torque the screws to 65–75 in. lbs.

3. Fill the gear housing with Chrysler Outboard Gear Lubricant and install the vent and drain screws.

4. Install the shear pin, propeller, nut, and cotter pin.

Propeller Shaft Seal

REMOVAL

1. Remove the bearing cage as outlined previously.

2. Pry the old seal out of the retainer and cage. Discard the old seal and retainer.

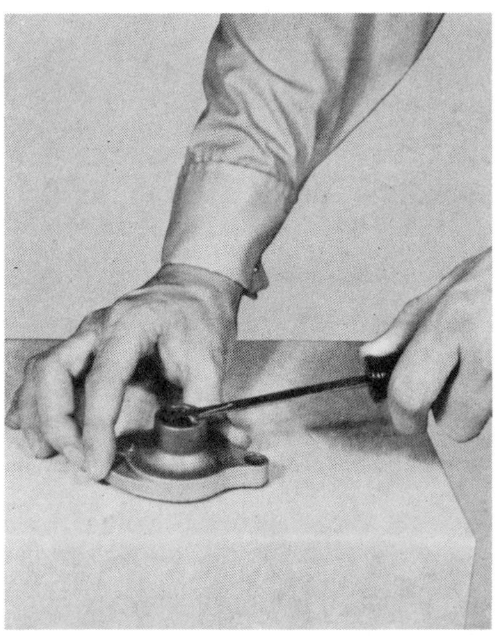

Removing propeller shaft seal—3.5 and 3.6 HP (© Chrysler Outboard Corporation)

INSTALLATION

1. Install a new seal in the bearing cage with the lip of the seal facing the bottom of the bore.

2. Install a new seal retainer with the curved side facing the bottom of the bore.

3. Install the bearing cage. (See the previous procedure.)

Water Pump Body and Impeller

REMOVAL

1. Remove the gear housing.

2. Remove the nut securing the water pump body to the front stud on the gear housing.

3. Slide the pump body up the driveshaft.

4. Remove the water pump impeller.

5. Remove the water pump pin from the driveshaft.

6. Remove the water pump backing plate.

INSTALLATION

1. Lubricate the bore of the water pump body with waterproof grease.

2. Push the water pump impeller into the bore of the pump body, while rotating the impeller counterclockwise.

3. The slots in the bushing of the impeller must face the bottom of the pump body.

4. Install the backing plate on the pump body with the hole in the backing plate aligned with the detent.

5. Insert the impeller drive pin through the hole in the driveshaft.

6. Slide the pump body and backing plate onto the driveshaft and turn the driveshaft until the drive pin engages the slot in the impeller.

7. Install the nut on the gear housing front stud and tighten it finger-tight.

8. Install the 1/4—20 bolt through the rear gear housing mounting hole. This aligns the holes in the gear housing and pump body.

9. Torque the nut on the front stud to 65–75 in. lbs. Remove the 1/4—20 bolt from the rear gear housing mounting hole.

10. Install the gear housing and fill the housing with Chrysler Outboard Gear Lubricant.

4.4 HP–20.0 HP

Gear Housing

REMOVAL—4.4, 5.0, 6.0 (ALL), 6.6, 7.0, 8.0, 9.2, 9.9, AND 12.9 HP

1. Shift the engine into Reverse gear (Forward gear on 9.9 and 12.9 hp models).

2. When shifting the engine, rotate either the propeller or flywheel to avoid damaging the clutch dogs and gears.

3. Remove the four screws from the base of the motor leg.

4. Pull the lower unit down to expose the screw connecting the upper gear shift rod to the lower gear shift rod.

5. Remove the screw (step 4) and pull the lower unit free.

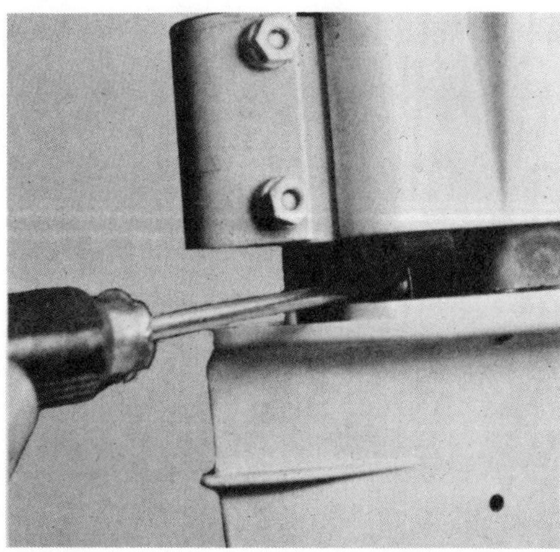

Removing gearshift rod screw—4.4–12.9 HP (© Chrysler Outboard Corporation)

Installation—4.4, 5.0, 6.0 (All), 6.6, 7.0, 8.0, 9.2, 9.9, and 12.9 HP

1. Check the lower gearshift rod adjustment. The centerline of the hole in the gearshift rod should be $3/16 \pm 3/64$ in. below the mounting surface of either the motor leg-to-gear housing (standard-shaft models) or the motor leg extension (long-shaft models). The motor must be in Neutral.

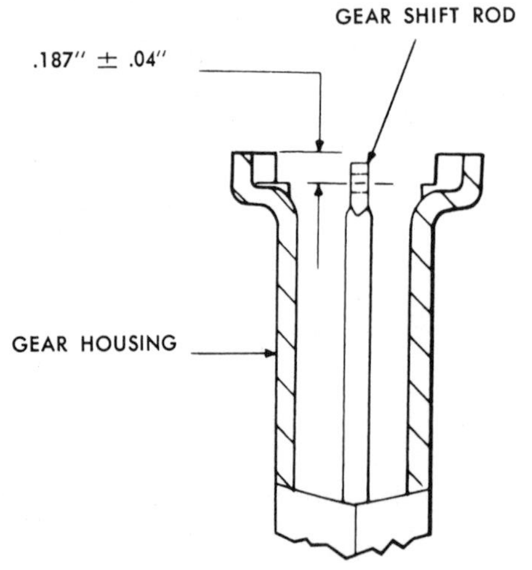

Gearshift rod adjustment—4.4–12.9 HP (© Chrysler Outboard Corporation)

2. Shift the lower unit into Reverse (Forward for 9.9 and 12.9 hp models) by pulling up on the lower gearshift rod to position the hole in the lower shift rod for assembly to the upper shift rod.

3. Coat the splines on the driveshaft liberally with silicone rubber sealant and install the lower unit on the motor leg. Engage the driveshaft splines in the crankshaft.

4. Align the upper and lower gearshift rods as shown. Connect the rods with a screw.

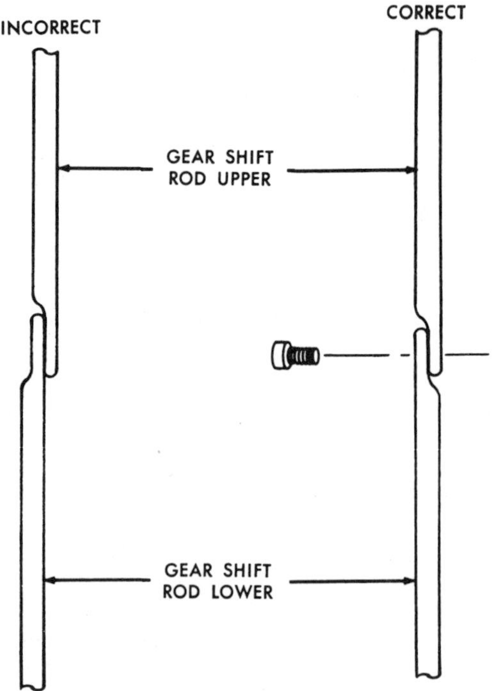

Gearshift rod assembly—4.4–12.9 HP (© Chrysler Outboard Corporation)

5. Check to be sure that the waterline seal is seated in the seal of the water pump body.

6. Attach the lower unit gear housing to the motor leg with four screws.

Removal—20.0 HP

1. Remove the motor leg covers as outlined later.

2. Loosen the jam nut above the shift rod coupling.

3. Shift the motor into Reverse. Turn the coupling clockwise until the lower shift rod separates from the upper shift rod.

4. Remove the four bolts securing the gear housing to the motor leg (or motor leg extension in the case of long-shaft models).

5. Pull the gear housing from the motor leg.

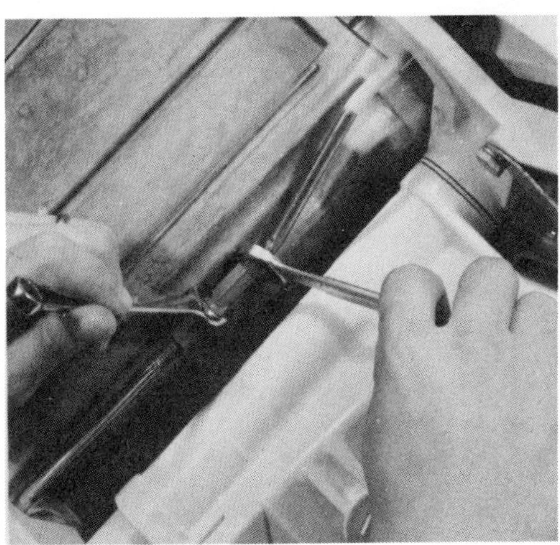

Loosen the jam nut on the shift rod coupling—20.0 HP (© Chrysler Outboard Corporation)

INSTALLATION—20.0 HP

1. Thread the shift rod into the shift cam until it bottoms in the cam. Back the shift rod out until the bend in the rod is centered over the front water pump mounting screw on the starboard side.
2. Slide the gear housing into place on the motor leg or motor leg extension. Be sure that the water pick-up tube seats in the rubber seal on the water pump and that the lower shift rod is aligned with the hole in the front of the motor leg.

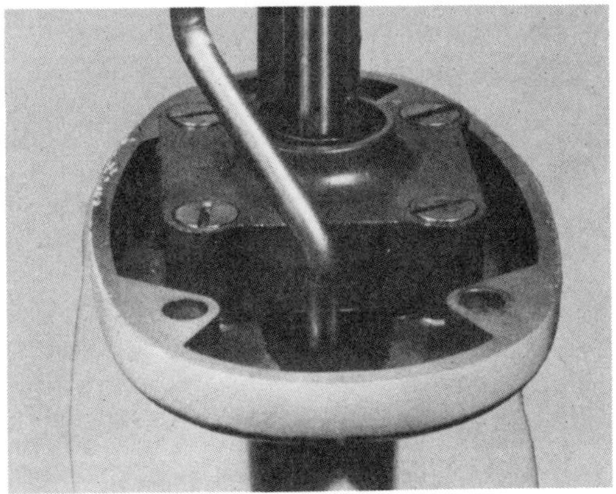

Correct installed position of lower shift rod—4.4–20.0 HP (© Chrysler Outboard Corporation)

3. Push up the lower unit until the driveshaft splines engage the crankshaft splines.
4. Secure the gear housing to the motor leg, or extension, with four screws.
5. Shift the motor into Neutral.
6. Thread the upper shift rod coupler until the lower end of the coupler engages the lower shift rod. Thread the coupler on the shift rods until the shift knob on the support plate is centered in the Neutral position (shift knob vertical).
7. Tighten the jam nut against the coupler.
8. Install the motor leg covers.

Water Pump Body Impeller and Plates—4.4–20.0 HP

REMOVAL

1. Remove the gear housing.
2. Remove the screws securing the water pump body to the upper gear housing and slide the water pump body off the driveshaft.
3. Remove the impeller by sliding it up the driveshaft.
4. Remove the impeller pin from the driveshaft.
5. Slide the bottom plate up the driveshaft.
6. Remove the top plate from the cavity in the water pump body.

INSTALLATION

1. Install the water pump backing plate on the upper gear housing by sliding it over the driveshaft. Align all of the screw holes.
2. Install the drive pin in the driveshaft.
3. Install the water pump top plate in the water pump body.

   NOTE: *The top plate is used on pumps with three screw holes. Pumps with four screw holes do not use a top plate.*

4. Install the impeller in the water pump body with the slot facing the bottom plate.

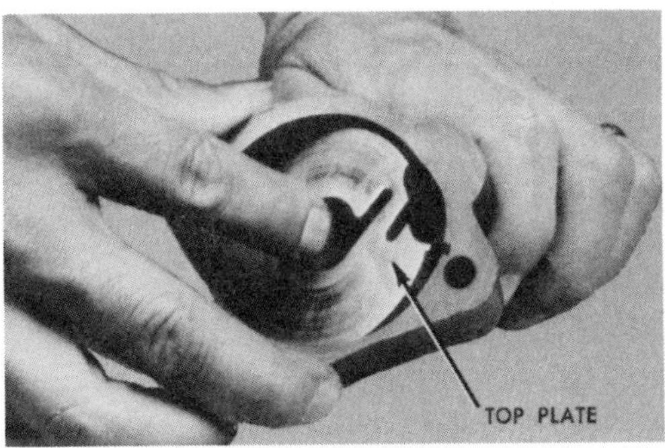

Water pump top plate installed—4.4–20.0 HP (© Chrysler Outboard Corporation)

5. Slide the water pump body assembly down the driveshaft, aligning the slot with the impeller drive pin.

6. Apply Lockite to the water pump body screws and secure the water pump body to the upper gear housing.

NOTE: *On models with three screws, the longest screw is installed next to the waterline seal.*

7. Install the gear housing.

Intake Waterline Seal

Removal

1. Remove the gear housing.
2. Depress the tabs on the seal and pull the seal from the water pump body.

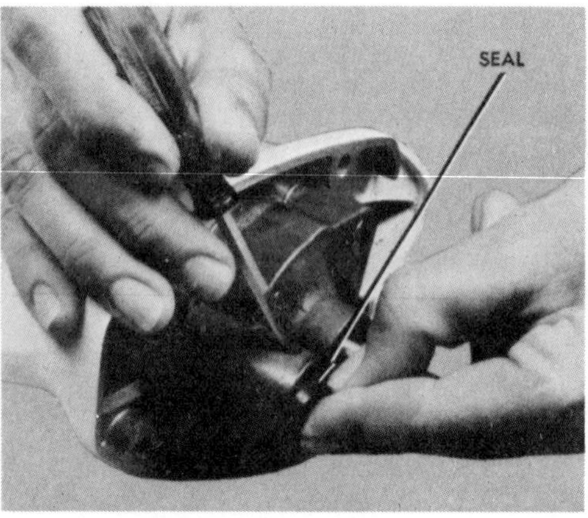

Removing the intake water line seal—4.4–20.0 HP (© Chrysler Outboard Corporation)

Installation

1. Install a new seal in the pump body and seat the tabs in the bores of the pump body.
2. Install the gear housing.

Water Pump Body Driveshaft Seal

Removal

1. Remove the gear housing.
2. Remove the water pump body.
3. Using a screwdriver, pry the seal out of the pump body. Make sure that the bore for the seal is not scratched.

Installation

1. Grease the lips of a new seal.
2. Install the seal in the pump body with the sealing lip pointing upward.
3. Install the water pump body.
4. Install the gear housing.

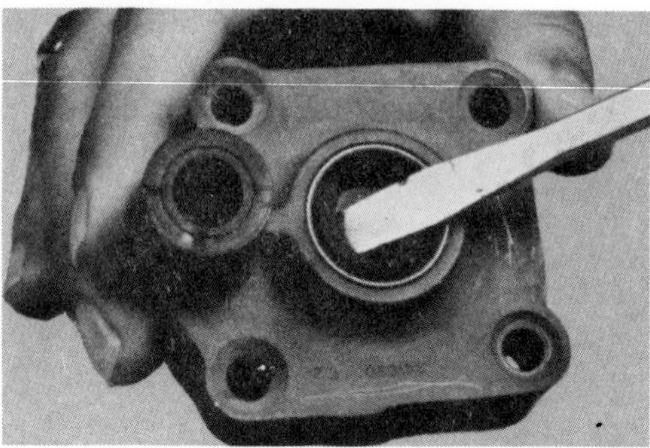

Removing the water pump body driveshaft seal—4.4–20.0 HP (© Chrysler Outboard Corporation)

3 · Kiekhaefer Mercury

Introduction

In the under 30 horsepower range, Kiekhaefer Mercury has six models; Merc 39, 40, 60, 75, 110, and 200. As with the larger-horsepower models, Mercury has continually improved its motors during its thirty-two years of production. The Glide-Angle design of the leading edge of the lower unit allows it to slide over underwater obstructions. Should fishing line wind around the propeller shaft, tiny concealed blades shear the line so that it does not damage the grease seal.

All Mercury outboards produced since 1971 are equipped with Thunderbolt ignition, for a hotter spark, and surface gap spark plugs, for long plug life. Other notable Mercury features include a patented Cross-Flow fuel induction system, a Jet-Prop exhaust, which discharges exhaust gases into a slipstream vacuum, and the use of anti-corrosion alloys. The drive train is protected against damage from impact by a live rubber safety clutch.

Engine Serial Number

The engine serial numbers are stamped on plates which are located on the swivel bracket and also on the powerhead. The number is the manufacturer's key to many engineering details and should be included in any correspondence with a dealer or the manufacturer.

Model Identification

Year	*Model*	*No. of Cyls*	*Horsepower*	*Displacement (cu in.)*
1966	39	1	3.9	5.5
	60	2	6.0	7.2
	110	2	9.8	11.0
	200 (Gear Shift)	2	20.0	22.0
1967	39	1	3.9	5.5
	60	2	6.0	7.2
	110	2	9.8	11.0
	200	2	20.0	22.0
1968	39	1	3.9	5.5
	60	2	6.0	7.2
	110	2	9.8	11.0
	200	2	20.0	22.0
1969	40	1	4.0	5.5
	75	2	7.5	11.0
	110	2	9.8	11.0
	200	2	20.0	22.0
1970	40	1	4.0	5.5
	75	2	7.5	10.9
	110	2	9.8	16.7
	200	2	20.0	21.9
1971	40	1	4.0	5.5
	75	2	7.5	10.9
	110	2	9.8	16.7
	200	2	20.0	21.9

1971 Merc 40 (1 cylinder) (© Kiekhaefer Mercury)

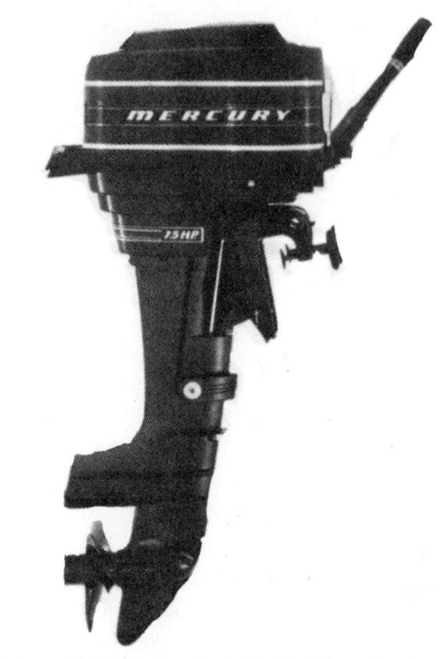

1971 Merc 75 (2 cylinder) (© Kiekhaefer Mercury)

1971 Merc 110 (2 cylinder) (© Kiekhaefer Mercury)

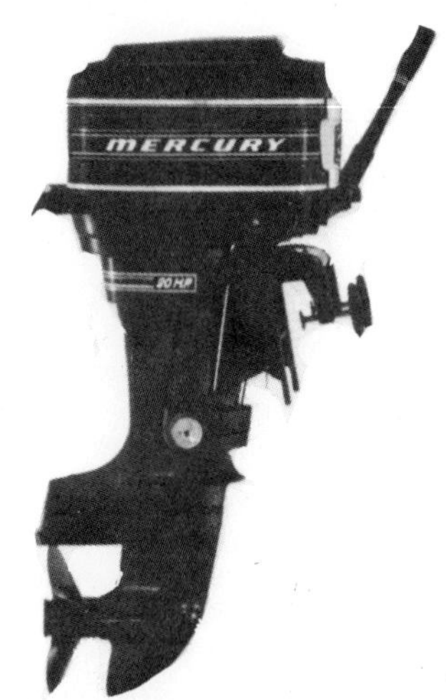

1971 Merc 200 (2 cylinder) (© Kiekhaefer Mercury)

General Engine Specifications

Year	*Model*	*Displacement (cu in.)*	*Horsepower (OBC)*	*Full Throttle Range (rpm)*	*Bore (in.)*	*Stroke (in.)*
1966	39	5.5	3.9	5000–5400	2.000	1.750
	60	7.2	6.0	5000–5400	1.750	1.500
	110	11.0	9.8	5000–5400	2.000	1.750
	200	22.0	20.0	5000–5400	2.562	2.125
1967	39	5.5	3.9	5000–5400	2.000	1.750
	60	7.2	6.0	5000–5400	1.750	1.500
	110	11.0	9.8	5000–5400	2.000	1.750
	200	22.0	20.0	5000–5400	2.562	2.125
1968	39	5.5	3.9	5000–5400	2.000	1.750
	60	7.2	6.0	5000–5400	1.750	1.500
	110	11.0	9.8	5000–5400	2.000	1.750
	200	22.0	20.0	5000–5400	2.562	2.125

General Engine Specifications (cont.)

Year	Model	Displacement (cu in.)	Horsepower (OBC)	Full Throttle Range (rpm)	Bore (in.)	Stroke (in.)
1969	40	5.5	4.0	4500–5500	2.000	1.750
	75	11.0	7.5	4500–5500	2.000	1.750
	110	11.0	9.8	5000–5400	2.000	1.750
	200	22.0	20.0	5000–5400	2.562	2.125
1970	40	5.5	4.0	4500–5500	2.000	1.750
	75	10.9	7.5	4500–5500	2.000	1.750
	110	16.7	9.8	4500–5500	2.000	1.750
	200	21.9	20.0	4800–5500	2.562	2.125
1971	40	5.5	4.0	4500–5500	2.000	1.750
	75	10.9	7.5	4500–5500	2.000	1.750
	110	16.7	9.8	4500–5500	2.000	1.750
	200	21.9	20.0	4800–5500	2.562	2.125

Tune-Up Specifications

NOTE: *When analyzing compression test results, look for uniformity among cylinders, rather than specific pressure. Variation between cylinders should not exceed 15 psi.*

Year	Model	Spark Plugs Type	Spark Plugs Gap (in.)	Firing Order	Ignition Timing (in.) @ Max Advance	Ignition Timing (deg) @ Max Advance	Breaker Point Gap (in.)	Idle Speed (rpm)
1966	39	Ch—J8J	0.025	Single-Cyl	④	④	0.020	500–550
	60	Ch—J7J	0.025	Alternate	④	④	0.020	500–550
	110	Ch—J6J	0.025	Alternate	④	④	0.020	500–550
	200	Ch—J6J	0.025	Alternate	0.275 B	——	0.020	500
1967	39	Ch—L9J	0.030	Single-Cyl	④	④	0.020	500–550
	60	Ch—L7J	0.030	Alternate	④	④	0.020	500–550
	110	Ch—L4J	0.030	Alternate	④	④	0.020	500–550
	200	Ch—L4J	0.030	Alternate	⑤	——	0.020	500
1968	39	Ch—L9J	0.030	Single-Cyl	④	④	0.020	500–550
	60	Ch—L7J	0.030	Alternate	④	④	0.020	500–550
	110	Ch—L4J	0.030	Alternate	④	④	0.020	500–550
	200	Ch—L4J	0.030	Alternate	⑤	——	0.020	500
1969	40	Ch—L9J	0.030	Single-Cyl	④	④	0.020	500–550
	75	Ch—L7J	0.030	Alternate	④	④	0.020	500–550
	110	Ch—L4J	0.030	Alternate	④	④	0.020	500–550
	200	Ch—L4J	0.030	Alternate	⑤	——	0.020	500
1970	40	AC—V40FFK	①	Single-Cyl	④	④	0.020	650–700
	75	AC—V40FFK	①	Alternate	0.193 B	——	0.020	500–550③
	110	AC—V40FFK	①	Alternate	0.193 B	——	0.020	500–550③
	200	AC—V40FFK	①	Alternate	0.196 B	33	0.020	550–600③
1971	40	AC—V40FFK	①	Single-Cyl	④	④	②	650–700
	75	AC—V40FFK	①	Alternate	0.193 B	——	②	500–550③
	110	AC—V40FFK	①	Alternate	0.193 B	——	②	500–550③
	200	AC—V40FFK	①	Alternate	0.196 B	33	②	550–600③

① Spark plug gap not adjustable
② Thunderbolt ignition—uses no breaker points
③ In Forward gear
④ Not adjustable
⑤ To serial number 2432535, 0.375 in. B
Above serial number 2432535, 0.300 in. B
—— Not available
B—Before Top Dead Center

Carburetor Specifications

NOTE: *Because Mercury has used many carburetors over the years, it is necessary to positively identify the carburetor before attempting to use the specifications charts. The carburetor manufacturing number is the only positive identification; it is stamped on the front of the carburetor. The numbers following the engine model number in the chart are beginning serial numbers for the particular model.*

Merc 39, 40, and 60

Merc Model	*60-4-5-6-7*	*60J*	*40*	*39-1-2*	*39-3-4*
Carburetor mfg no.	KB6B	KB6B	KB10A	KB7A	KB7B
High-speed system					
Nozzle ID	32	32	30	31	30
Nozzle cross holes	72① 58①	58(2) Lo 72(4) Up	65(4)① 55(4)②	60① 60	55(2)
Nozzle air bleed	0.054	0.0537	0.060	53	0.060
Fixed jet	0.045	0.045	0.036	0.043	0.036
Idle system—pick-up tube					
Bottom—ID or restriction	74	74	0.053	70	70
Top—ID or restriction	74			70	
Air bleed—body or tube	43	43	65	50③	43
Idle adjustment					
Restriction—orifice	42	42	50	40	40
Discharge holes—in tube			60(2)		
By-pass holes					
1st under welch plug	74	60	62(2)	70	60
2nd under welch plug	60	74	70	60	70
Inlet seat	52	52	52	52	52
Shutter valve—hole (cutoff) side	Bottom	Bottom	By-Pass		Float
Air relief to bore	46	46			

①—4 holes, upper ②—4 holes, lower ③—1 hole, front of venturi

Merc 60, 75, and 110

Merc Model	*110-1-2-3-4-5-6-7*	*110-8*	*110*	*75*	*75*	*60-2 60-3*
Carburetor mfg no.	KB5A	KB8A	KB11A	KB9A	KB12A	KB6A
High-speed system						
Nozzle ID	31	⅛	⅛	32	32	32
Nozzle cross holes	60	60(4)	60(2) 60(2)	58(2)	58(2)	72① 65①
Nozzle air bleed	0.054	60	0.060	65	65	68
Fixed jet	0.049	0.049	0.047	0.034	0.035	0.045
Idle system—pick-up tube						
Bottom—ID or restriction	55	0.053–0.056	0.053–0.056	0.053–0.056	0.053–0.056	55
Top—ID or restriction	70					74
Air bleed—body or tube	50	65	67	65	65	50②
Idle adjustment						
Restriction—orifice	42	52	52	56	56	42
Discharge holes—in tube		65(2)	65(2)	65(2)	65(2)	65(2)
By-pass holes						
1st under welch plug	70	66(2)	60	68(2)	68	74
2nd under welch plug	62	56	60	68	68	60
Throttle bore—top	72					
Miscellaneous						
Inlet seat	52	52	52	52	52	52
Shutter valve—hole (cutoff) side	Bottom	By-Pass		By-Pass		
Air relief to bore						46

①—4 holes, upper ②—1 hole, front of venturi

Carburetor Specifications (cont.)

Merc 200

Merc Model	*200-1-2 Shift*	*200-3*	*200-4 200-5*	*200-6*	*200*
Carburetor mfg no.	KA20A	KA22A	KA22B	KA23A	KA25A
High-speed system					
Nozzle ID	28	28	28	28	0.1405
Nozzle cross holes	60	60	60(2)	60(2)	60(6)
Nozzle air bleed	60	60	56	56	66
Fixed jet	0.061	0.059	0.063	0.063	0.057
Idle system—pick-up tube					
Bottom—ID or restriction	52	50	0.065	0.065	0.053–0.056
Top—ID or restriction	50	50		50	
Air bleed—body or tube	68	68	60	60	60
Idle adjustment					
Restriction—orifice	50	50	50	50	50
Discharge holes—in tube					68(2)
By-pass holes					
1st under welch plug	56	56	50	50	60–62
2nd under welch plug	56	56	68	68	55
3rd under welch plug	47	47	55	55	
Throttle bore—top	65	65			
Miscellaneous					
Inlet seat	42	42	3/32	3/32	3/32
Shutter valve—hole (cutoff) side			By-Pass	By-Pass	

Jet Changes for Elevation

Engine Model	*Jet Sizes for Elevations* Up to 4000 ft	*4000–7000 ft*	*7000–10000 ft*	*Up to 2500 ft*	*2500–5000 ft*	*5000–7500 ft*	*7500–10000 ft*
Merc 200 (1967–68)	0.063 in.	0.061 in.	0.059 in.	——	——	——	——
Merc 200 (Thunderbolt)	0.059 in.	0.057 in.	0.055 in.	——	——	——	——
Merc 200 (gear shift)	0.061 in.	0.059 in.	0.057 in.	——	——	——	——
Merc 110 (Thunderbolt)	——	——	——	0.047 in.	0.045 in.	0.043 in.	0.043 in.
Merc 110	——	——	——	0.049 in.	0.047 in.	0.045 in.	0.043 in.
Merc 75 (Thunderbolt)	——	——	——	0.035 in.	0.033 in.	0.031 in.	0.031 in.
Merc 60	0.045 in.	0.043 in.	0.041 in.	——	——	——	——
Merc 40 (Thunderbolt)	——	——	——	0.039 in.	0.034 in.	0.032 in.	0.032 in.
Merc 39 (1967–68)	0.036 in.	0.034 in.	0.032 in.	——	——	——	——
Merc 39	0.043 in.	0.041 in.	0.039 in.	——	——	——	——

NOTE: *Jet sizes are intended as a guide. Try a size smaller or larger if you are in doubt. No change in spark advance is recommended for elevation. Propellers of lower pitch should be used at high elevation to allow proper engine rpm.*

Reed Stop Openings

Engine Model	*Reed Stop Opening (in.)*
39	NA
40 (Thunderbolt)	NA
60	0.109
75 (Thunderbolt)	0.093
110	0.156
200	0.156

Cylinder Block Finish Hone Diameter

Model	*Cylinder Block Finish Hone Diameter (in.)*
60	1.753
110, 75, 40, 39	2.001
200 (gear shift, 1966)	2.573
200 (198–71)	2.563①

①—Serial Number 2432536 and up is 2.556

Torque Specifications

Model	*39, 40*	*60*	*110, 75*	*200 (1966)*	*200 (1967–71)*
Connecting rod (in. lbs)	180	180	180	180	180
Flywheel-to-crankshaft (ft lbs)	35	35	35	65	—
Water pump cover (ft lbs)	—	65	—	—	—
Water pump—plastic (in. lbs)	25–30	—	25–30	35–40	—
Spark plugs (ft lbs)	20	20	20	20	20
Center main bearing lockscrew (in. lbs)	—	30–35	40–45	150	120
Center main bearing reed stop screw (in. lbs)	—	20–25	20–25	35–40	35–40
Exhaust outer cover (in. lbs)	70	70	70	200	200
Cylinder block cover (in. lbs)	70①	70	70①	90	70
Crankcase-to-cylinder block (in. lbs)	90	90	90	185	185
Upper and lower end-caps (in. lbs)	150	150	150	150	150
Distributor shaft nut (in. lbs)	—	—	65–75	65–75	—

NOTE: *Due to the extensive use of white metal and aluminum to resist corrosion, torque specifications must be adhered to strictly.*

①—¼ in. bolt and nut—90 in. lbs.

Torque Sequences

Crankcase

NOTE: *For one- and two-cylinder engines, start with the center bolts and work to the top, then from the center to the bottom. It is advisable, when tightening two or more screws on the same part, to tighten all screws (in the proper sequence) to one-third of the specified torque, then to two-thirds of the specified torque, then torque down completely.*

Wiring Diagrams

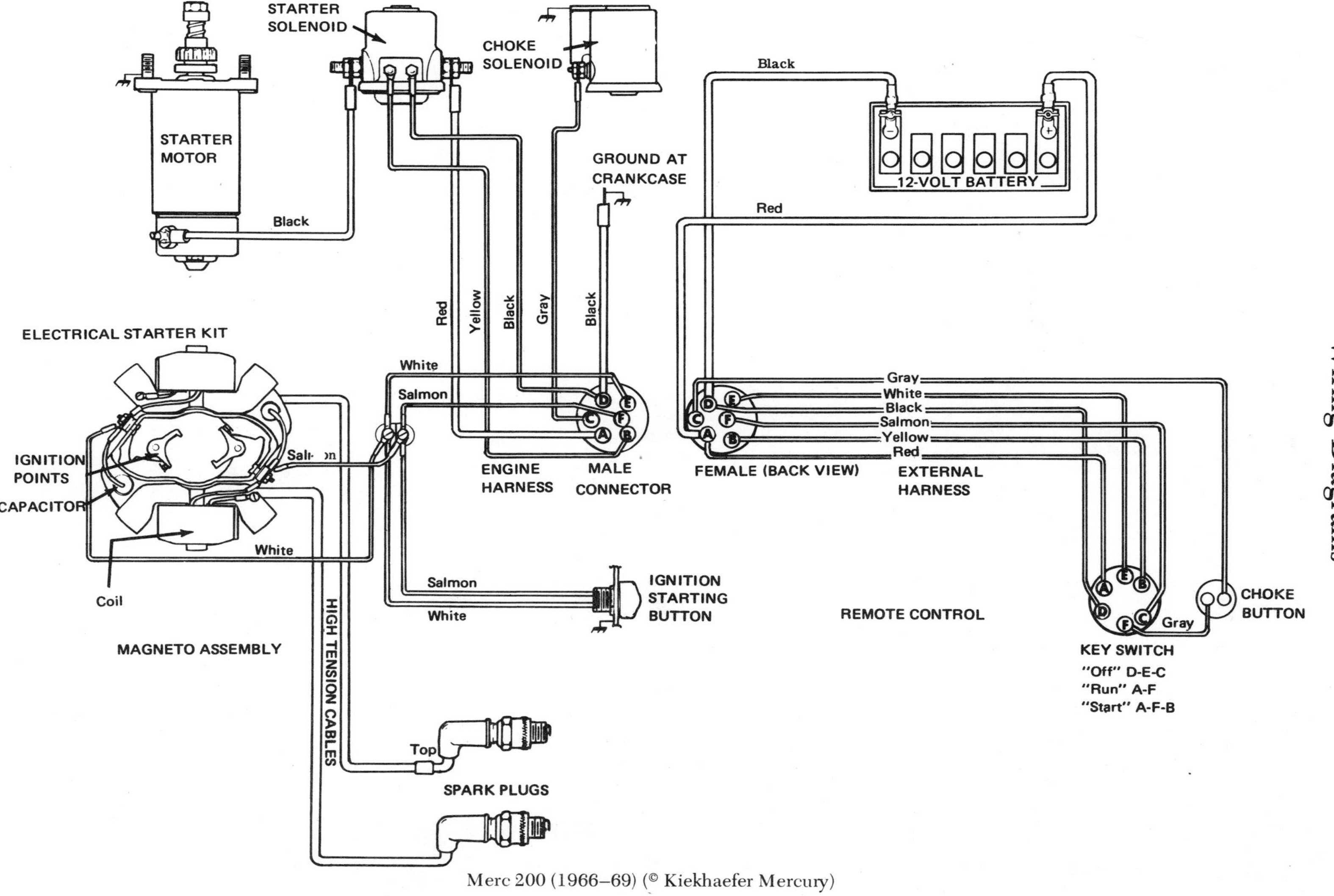

Merc 200 (1966–69) (© Kiekhaefer Mercury)

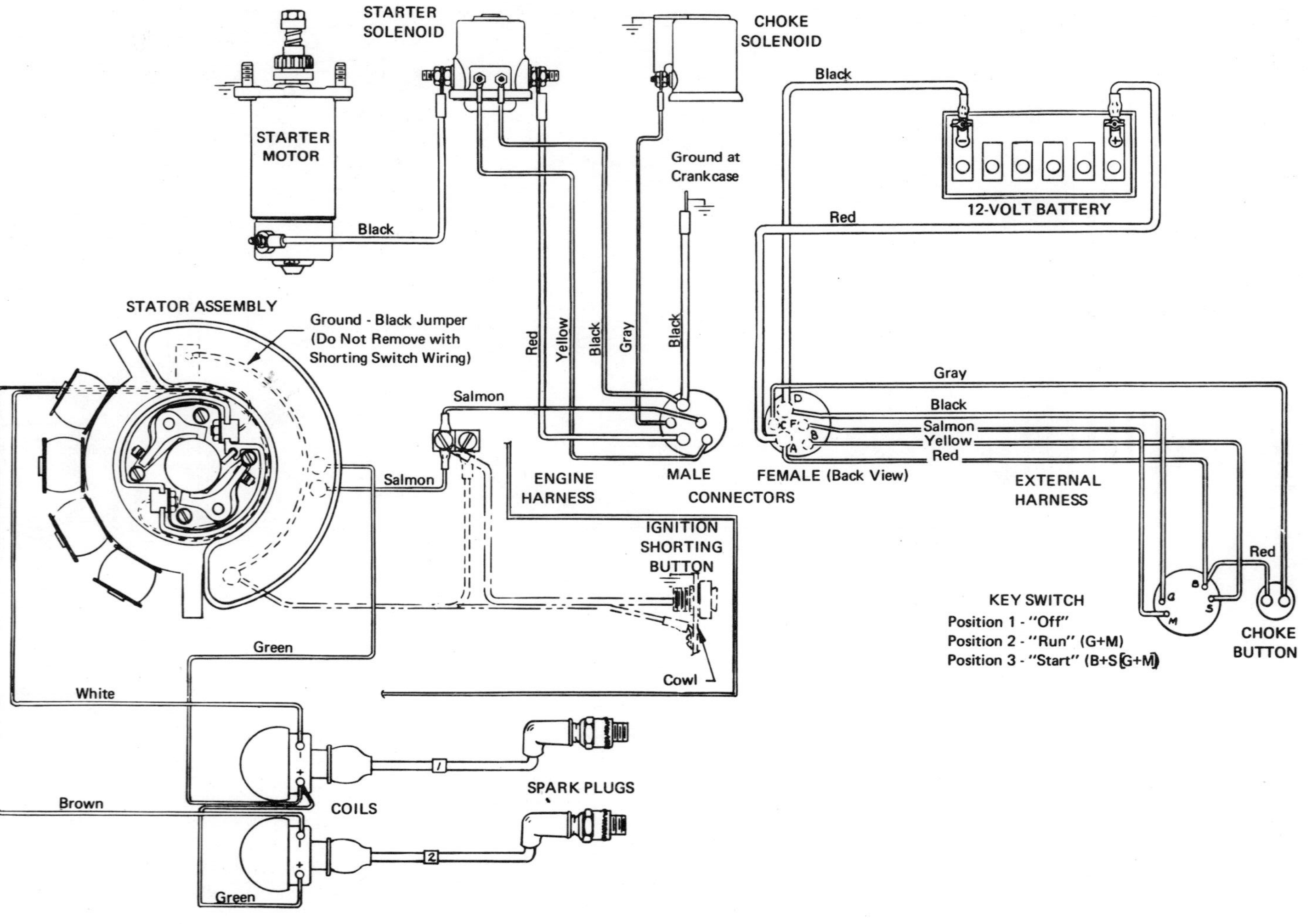

Merc 200 (1970–71) (© Kiekhaefer Mercury)

General Care and Maintenance

FLUSHING THE MOTOR

Motors which are operated primarily in salt water should be flushed periodically to remove deposits of salt which build up in the passages and inhibit cooling. Ideally, motors should be flushed after every use; however, flushing the motor thoroughly at least two or three times a season should be adequate for motors in normal use. One of the following flushing kits should be used.

Engine Model	*Mercury Kit Part No.*
200 from ser no. 2432536	C—48755A—1
All 2 cylinder except those listed above and prior to 1966.	C—24789A—1

1. Remove the plug marked "Flush" and the washer from the flushing intake.
2. Connect the flushing attachment and couple a garden hose to the attachment.
3. Turn on the water, but *do not operate* the motor. Water pressure from the tap is sufficient to flush the motor and does not even need to be at maximum pressure.

CAUTION: *If the motor must be operated while flushing, to prevent damage to the impeller, it is imperative that a Flush-Test device be used, which attaches directly over the intake holes in the gear housing strut. Do not operate the motor above idle speed, while flushing, or engine rpm will be uncontrollable. When flushing, it is advisable to remove the propeller as a precautionary measure.*

4. During and after flushing, keep the motor in an upright position, resting on the skeg, until all water has drained from the driveshaft housing.

PREVENTIVE MAINTENANCE AND PERIODIC SERVICE

Periodic maintenance as recommended by the manufacturer, is designed to keep your motor running in peak condition and to assure a long motor life with a minimum of service time. The following recommendations apply to all Mercury outboards.

25 Hour Service

The following service should be completed approximately every twenty-five hours.

1. Remove the engine cover and thoroughly clean all accessible parts.
2. Lubricate the lower unit as detailed in the following section.
3. Lubricate the Ride-Guide steering tube.

Lubricate the Ride-Guide steering tube. (© Kiekhaefer Mercury)

4. Lubricate the throttle linkage and upper shift shaft.
5. Lubricate the reverse lock lever and swivel bracket.

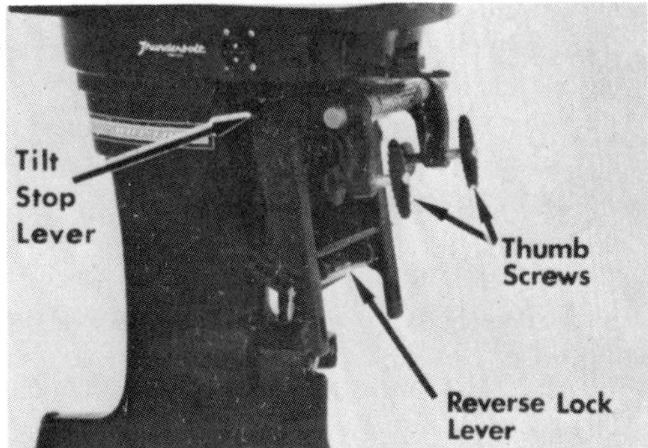

Lubricate the reverse lock lever and swivel bracket (© Kiekhaefer Mercury)

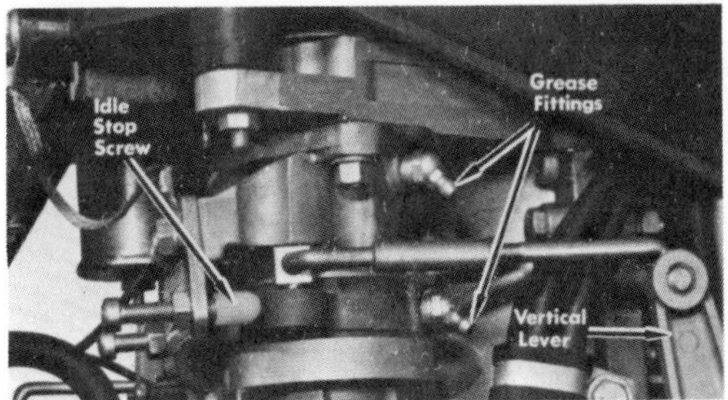

Lubricate the distributor adaptor fittings (if equipped) (© Kiekhaefer Mercury)

6. Lubricate the distributor adaptor fittings and control handle (if equipped).
7. Remove and inspect the propeller. Trim any nicks with a file, but do not remove more metal than is necessary. Lubricate the propeller shaft with graphite grease or Quicksilver Anti-Corrosion Grease. Install the propeller.

Lubricate the throttle shaft and upper shift shaft (© Kiekhaefer Mercury)

8. Service the spark plugs. See the tune-up section in the front of this book.

9. Inspect the spark plug leads for deterioration, particularly where insulation contacts metal.

10. Inspect the fuel lines (including tank) for deterioration.

11. Inspect the entire surface for corroded areas; these may be cleaned thoroughly and repainted with matching paint.

12. Check the entire motor for loose parts, tightening where necessary.

13. Service the fuel filter on the remote tank after every 100 hours (or at least once a season) or whenever performance conditions warrant.

14. Check to be sure that all control fittings are securely attached and properly adjusted.

15. Other than those models with the Thunderbolt ignition, the breaker points should not be disturbed as long as the engine is operating satisfactorily. If the points are cleaned and adjusted at the mid-season check, they should not normally require service for at least another 100 hours.

16. Check the condition of the starter cable and replace it if it is cracked or broken.

17. Replace the engine hood.

LOWER UNIT LUBRICATION

NOTE: *Use only Quicksilver Super-Duty Gear Lubricant in the lower unit; regular automotive grease is not acceptable. In an absolute emergency, extreme pressure marine gear lubricant may be used.*

1. Remove the lubricant filler plug which is located on the right side of the gear housing, just above the skeg.

2. Remove the air vent screw, located just above the cavitation plate.

CAUTION: *Never apply lubricant to the lower unit without first removing the air vent screw. The injected lubricant will displace air which must escape, so that the lower unit will be entirely filled.*

3. Inject lubricant through the filler plug hole until the lubricant begins to flow from the air vent hole. This indicates that the housing is filled.

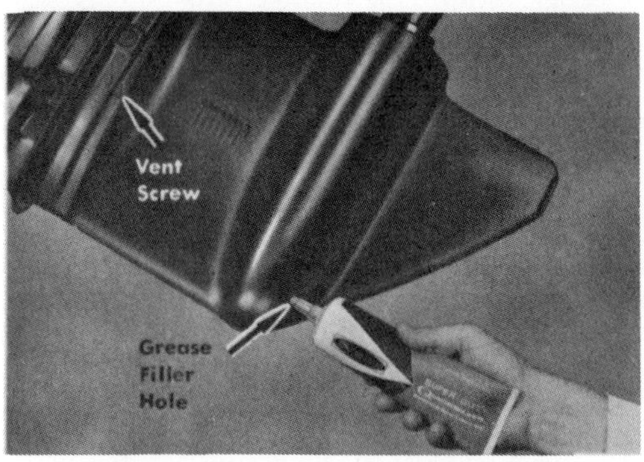

Lubricate the lower unit (© Kiekhaefer Mercury)

4. Replace the air vent screw first, then the grease plug, making sure that the washer is located under each, to prevent the entry of water into the gear housing.

Gear Housing Capacities

Model	*Capacity (fl oz)*
Merc 110, 75, 60, 40, and 39	3
Merc 200	6

TRIM TAB

The trim tab is an anodic tab and is self-sacrificing to help combat galvanic corrosion on Mercury 200, and larger, models. Inspect the trim tab periodically for corrosion. If the trim tab is being eaten away, it should be replaced.

NOTE: *Do not paint or coat the trim tab, or its inhibiting value will be lost.*

Removal and Replacement

1. Before removing the trim tab, mark the location of the trailing edge on the cavitation plate.

2. Remove the plug which is located directly above the trim tab.

3. Through the hole in the drive housing, loosen the screw which holds the trim tab.

4. Remove the trim tab and clean the recessed area, to assure good metal contact

between the drive housing and the trim tab.

5. Install the trim tab by reversing the removal procedure.

6. Test the boat and motor, and adjust the trim tab if necessary.

Adjustment

1. Operate the boat at the best throttle setting.

2. Adjust the tilt pin setting or trim the boat with Power-Trim.

3. Turn the steering wheel to the left and right, noting which direction is easier. With the boat at rest, remove the plug in the driveshaft housing and loosen the trim tab retaining screw.

4. If the steering wheel turns more easily to the right, position the trailing edge of the trim tab to the right, and vice versa. Tighten the retaining screw and replace the plug.

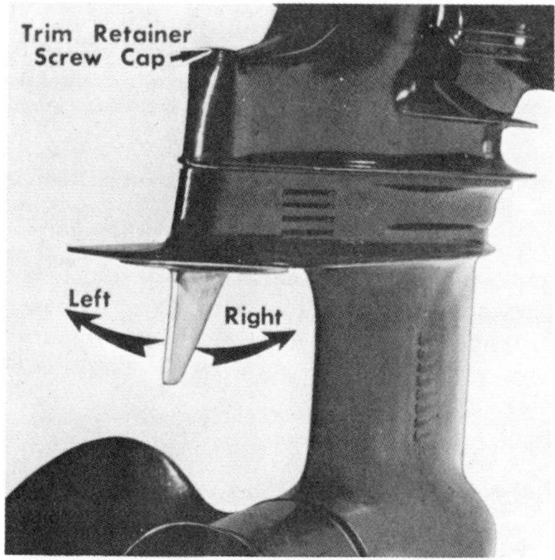

Trim tab adjustment (© Kiekhaefer Mercury)

5. Operate the boat to check the setting. Readjust the trim tab if necessary.

NOTE: *Steering torque may increase even though the trim tab has been adjusted properly. The trim tab will be most effective at the boat speed and trim setting for which it was adjusted.*

WINTERIZING

Because outboard motors are so susceptible to corrosion, care must be taken to properly store the motor when not in use. The motor should always be stored upright in a clean, cool, dry place. The following procedure is recommended by the manufacturer for winterizing.

1. Operate the motor on the boat or in a test tank. Disconnect the fuel line and allow the engine to run at idle.

2. Inject approximately four oz of Quicksilver Storage Seal into each carburetor and allow the engine to stall out. This indicates that the carburetors have run dry.

3. Drain the fuel tank and fuel lines.

4. Remove the engine hood.

Fuel Tank Filter

1. Remove the fuel line from the fuel tank and remove the fuel pick-up tube by removing the screws in the top connector housing.

2. The fine mesh wire filter can be cleaned by rinsing it in clean benzine.

Motor Fuel Filter

1. Remove the front bracket by removing the screws which hold it to the front of the bottom cowling.

2. Remove the screw from the top of the filter covers on the carburetors.

3. Remove the fuel filter covers.

4. Inspect the fuel filters, lines, and fittings for signs of wear or leakage.

5. Drain and clean the filters.

6. Replace the filter covers and tighten the screws.

7. Replace the front bracket and cowlings.

Power Head

1. Lubricate the lower unit. (See "25 Hour Service.")

2. Lubricate the control linkage. (See "25 Hour Service.")

3. Lubricate the distributor adaptor. (See "25 Hour Service.")

4. Thoroughly clean the motor and spray it with Corrosion and Rust Preventive.

5. Install the cowling and apply a thin film of clean, fresh engine oil to all of the painted surfaces.

6. Remove the propeller and apply Anti-Corrosion grease or waterproof-type grease to the propeller shaft. Install the propeller.

7. Lubricate the swivel bracket. (See "25 Hour Service.")

BATTERY STORAGE

1. Remove the battery from its installation as soon as possible. Remove all grease and sulphate from the top surface. A diluted ammonia or soda solution will neutralize any acid present, and may be flushed away with clean water. Care must be taken to keep the vent plugs tight so that neutralizing solution does not enter the cells.
2. Cover the plates with distilled water, but not over 3/16 in. above the perforated baffles.
3. Lubricate the terminals with cup grease or petroleum jelly.
4. With the battery at full charge (specific gravity 1.260–1.275), store it in a dry place where the temperature will not fall below freezing.
5. Remove the battery from storage every forty-five days. Check the water level and charge the battery for 5–6 hours at 6 amps. Do not fast-charge the battery.
6. When you are ready to return the battery to service, remove all excess grease from the terminals (leaving a film on), charge as necessary, and reinstall it.

MOTOR STORAGE

When storing outboard motors for the winter, be sure that all water drain holes in the gear housing are free and open, and that the flushing plug is removed so that all of the water will drain out. Trapped water may freeze and expand, and crack the gear housing or water pump housing. Be sure that the lower unit is full of grease to protect against water leakage into the gear housing, caused by a loose air vent plug or loose filler plug. Be careful to replace the gaskets under the screws and flush plug, renewing any damaged gaskets.

PROPELLER SELECTION

The following charts contain all propellers available from Mercury for the models contained in this book. Before attempting to use these charts to select a different propeller, it is absolutely imperative that the information in the first chapter under "Boat Performance and Propeller Selection" be read and followed.

Select a trial propeller from the chart using the approximate boat length and load (if known). Establish the exact transom height and tilt pin setting by test. Make a trial run using an accurate tachometer. It is extremely important that the engine rpm fall within the recommended full throttle rpm range. Make the trial run with a light load (one person). Under these conditions, the engine rpm should be near the top of the full throttle rpm range so that, under a heavy load, the engine rpm will not fall below the full throttle rpm range. If the engine speed is too high, try a propeller of a higher pitch or a cupped propeller of the same pitch. If the engine speed is too low, try a lower-pitched propeller. There is a difference in this chart of approximately 300–500 rpm between propeller pitches.

Propeller Chart (Right-Hand Rotation—Facing Bow)

Motor Model	Clockwise RH Rotation	Propeller Dia (in.)	Pitch (in.)	No. Bl	Material	Approx Gross Load ①	Approx Boat Length (ft)	Transom Height Std Length (in.)	Long Shaft (in.)	Speed Range (mph)
Merc 39 RPM Range: 5000–5400	A—48—31214A1	8¼	6	2	Alum.	All Purpose	All Purpose	15½	20½	All Purpose
Merc 40 Merc 39 (1968) RPM Range: 5000–5500	A—48—47940A1	8¼	6	2	Alum.	All Purpose	All Purpose	15½	20½	All Purpose
Merc 60	A—48—34398A1	8	8	2	Bronze	Up to 500	8–13	All	All	8–18
Full Throttle	A—48—31105A1	7⅞	8	2	Alum.	Up to 500	8–13			8–18
RPM Range: 5000–5400	A—48—45890A1	8⅞	5	3	Alum.	All Purpose	All Purpose	15½	20½	3–12

Propeller Chart (Right-Hand Rotation—Facing Bow) (cont.)

Motor Model	Clockwise RH Rotation	Propeller Dia (in.)	Pitch (in.)	No. Bl	Material	Approx Gross Load ①	Approx Boat Length (ft)	Transom Height Std Length (in.)	Long Shaft (in.)	Speed Range (mph)
Merc 60 (1968)	A—48—47920A1	8	8	2	Bronze	Up to 500	8–13	All	All	8–18
Full Throttle	A—48—47938A1	7⅞	8	2	Alum.	Up to 500	8–13			8–18
RPM Range: 5000–5400	A—48—47944A1	8⅞	5	3	Alum.	All Purpose	All Purpose	15½	20½	3–12
Merc 75	A—48—47922A1	9	9	2	Alum.	Up to 450	8–13			16–20
RPM Range: 4500–5500	A—48—47670A1	9	7	3	Alum.	All Purpose	All Purpose	15½	20½	3–16
Merc 100 Full Throttle										
RPM Range:	A—48—26608A1	9½	9½	2	Alum.	400–750	12–14	15½	16½	17–26
5000–5400	A—48—27787A1	9	7½	3	Alum.	600–1200	14–16	15½	16½	12–19
Merc 110 (Early)	A—48—34400A1	9	10	2	Bronze	Up to 750	11–14	All	All	15–26
Full Throttle	A—48—31504A1	9	10	2	Alum.	Up to 750	11–14			15–26
RPM Range:	A—48—32364A1	9	9	2	Alum.	600–Plus	14–16			10–18
5000–5400	A—48—37318A1	9	7	3	Alum.	Aux Power or Work Boat		15½	20½	1–11
Merc 110										
(1968–69–70–71)	A—48—47924A1	9	10	2	Bronze	Up to 750	11–14	All	All	15–26
Full Throttle	A—48—47926A1	9	10	2	Alum.	Up to 750	11–14			15–26
RPM Range:	A—48—47922A1	9	9	2	Alum.	600–Plus	14–16	15½	20½	10–18
4500–5500	A—48—47670A1	9	7	3	Alum.	Aux Power or Work Boat				1–10
Merc 200 FGS	A—48—34402A1	9⅞	11	2	Bronze	Up to 1000	12–15	All	All	22–33
Full Throttle	A—48—33480A1	9⅞	11	2	Alum.	Up to 1000	12–15			22–33
RPM Range:	A—48—33482A1	9⅞	9	3	Alum.	850–1600	15–Plus	15½	20½	13–24
4800–5500	A—48—37316A1	9⅞	7	3	Alum.	Aux Power or Work Boat				1–14

①—Gross loads are approximate—include weight of boat, motor, fuel, passengers, and gear.

NOTES:
(a)—The selection procedure for dual installations is the same, but use the next higher pitch propellers on the chart.
(b)—For water skiing, use the next lower pitch propeller on the chart.
(c)—CAUTION: *When using a low-pitch propeller on a boat for water skiing, do not operate the motor at full throttle when not pulling skis. Over-revving of the engine and possible damage will result.*
(d)—Use the next lower pitch propeller for each additional 2500 feet of elevation.
(e)—For commercial operation, use the lower listed rpm.

Lubrication and Fuel Recommendations

FUEL

The manufacturer recommends that regular leaded automotive gasolines be used in Mercury outboards equipped with Thunderbolt (CD) ignition systems and surface gap spark plugs. Some marine white gasolines have been known to cause trouble because of their very low octane rating. Detonation, ring sticking, and port plugging are common complaints resulting from the use of low-octane marine white fuel. Regular gasolines are of a more uniform quality and are readily available from most service stations or marinas.

Mercury outboards with conventional ignition systems and conventional spark plugs operate with much higher plug temperatures than those with the Thunderbolt ignition. Do not operate Mercury outboards with new lead-free or no-lead fuels, other than those approved by Kiekhaefer Mercury. To be certain as to the quality of a particular fuel, consult an authorized Mercury dealer. Some oil companies have for years manufactured high-grade, lead-free fuels which contain no phosphorus (major cause of piston failure) and is designed for use in two-cycle engines, either directly or as a pre-mixed fuel. Such fuels, if known to be of good quality, may be used.

NOTE: *Kiekhaefer Mercury reserves the right to refuse warranty on parts which are damaged when using improper fuels.*

INTERNAL LUBRICATION

Kiekhaefer Mercury specifically recommends that only FORMULA 50 Quicksilver 2 Cycle Super Outboard Motor Oil or Formula 2 Quicksilver 2 Cycle Outboard Motor Oil be used in their outboard motors. In an absolute emergency, when FORMULA 50 or Formula 2 Quicksilver Oil are not available, a high-grade two-cycle oil, intended for use in outboards, may be substituted.

WARNING: *Do not, under any circumstances, use multigrade or other detergent automotive oils or oils which contain metallic additives. This type of oil may result in piston scoring, bearing failure, or both.*

When using FORMULA 50 Quicksilver Super 2 Cycle Outboard Motor Oil, thoroughly mix twelve ounces with each five gallons of gasoline (eight ounces with each three gallons), in your remote fuel tank.

When using Formula 2 Quicksilver 2 Cycle Motor Oil, thoroughly mix thirty ounces with each six gallons of gasoline (fifteen ounces with each three gallons), in the remote fuel tank.

For operation in Canada, use fifteen ounces of FORMULA 50 Quicksilver 2 Cycle Super Outboard Motor Oil to each five Imperial gallons of gasoline, or thirty-five ounces of Formula 2 Quicksilver 2 Cycle Outboard Motor Oil to five Imperial gallons of gasoline in the remote fuel tank.

WARNING TO MERCURY OUTBOARD OWNERS: *The use of any other oil than Kiekhaefer Quicksilver FORMULA 50 in the 50 : 1 ratio may cause piston scoring, bearing failure, or both. The motor warranty may be voided if failure should occur with the use of any other oils in the 50 : 1 fuel/oil mixture.*

Examinations of those outboard motors with scored pistons which have been returned to Mercury Service Department, show that the use of certain so-called "outboard motor oils" has caused piston scoring.

BREAK-IN FUEL/OIL MIXTURE

FORMULA 50 Quicksilver Super

For the first two tankfulls, thoroughly mix twenty-four ounces with each six-gallon tank of fuel (or twelve ounces with each three-gallon tank of fuel). After break-in, refer to "Internal Lubrication."

Operate the new motor at one-half throttle (2500–3500 rpm) for the first two hours. After the first two hours, the motor may be run at any speed, but sustained operation at full throttle should be avoided for an additional eight hours of running time.

Formula 2 Quicksilver

For the first two tankfulls, thoroughly mix thirty ounces to each six-gallon tank of fuel (or fifteen ounces to each three-gallon tank of fuel). After break-in refer to "Internal Lubrication."

Operate the new motor at one-half throttle (2500–3500 rpm) for the first two hours. After the first two hours, the motor may be run at any speed, but sustained operation at full throttle should be avoided for an additional eight hours of running time.

Fuel Mixing Procedure

Observe all fire prevention rules, particularly regarding smoking. Mix fuel in a well-ventilated area and mix it directly in the remote tank.

Measure accurately the required amounts of oil and fuel. Pour a small amount of gasoline into the tank and add a small amount of oil (about the same amount as gas). Mix thoroughly by shaking vigorously. Add the balance of oil and fuel (oil first). Cleanliness is of prime importance in mixing fuel, since even a small particle of dirt can clog the jets and calibrated passages in the carburetor. Fresh gasoline should always be used, since gasoline contains gum and varnish deposits which, when left in a tank for a length of time, may cause carburetor and spark plug fouling.

Carburetor idle adjustment is sensitive to fuel mixture variations. Careless or inaccurate mixing will necessitate frequent adjustment. Be consistent and prepare each batch of fuel in exactly the same way. Using less than the recommended proportion of oil will result in serious motor damage; using more than the recommended proportion will cause spark plug fouling, erratic carburetion, excessive smoking, and faster-than-normal carbon accumulation.

EXTERNAL LUBRICATION AND MAINTENANCE

For best operation and performance, the following maintenance and lubrication charts should be followed in great detail. It is also recommended that the stated lubricant be used.

Lubrication Frequency

Model	*Location*	*Lubricant*	*Frequency* Every 30 Days	Every 60 Days	Once in Season	Twice in Season
		Super-duty gear lubricant				
All	Lower drive unit	(C—92—52650)	●			
All	Propeller shaft splines	Anti-corrosion grease	●			
All	Swivel pin	(C—92—45134A1)	★	●		
		New multipurpose lubri-				
If equipped	Ride-guide tube and cable	cant (C—92—49588)	★	●		
If equipped	Ride-guide pivot/ball joint		★	●		
All	Throttle/shift linkage		★	●		
All	Upper shift shaft		★	●		
All	Thumb screws	Anti-corrosion oil	★	●		
All	Reverse lock lever	(C—92—39928A1)	★	●		
All	Tilt stop lever		★	●		
200, 110, 75, and 40	Stator plate clamps				●	★
110, 75, and 40	Tiller handle pivot/gears		★	●		
Electric-start	Starter motor pinion gear	SAE no. 10 oil		★	●	
		Formula 4 oil				
If equipped	Power trim pump oil level	(C—92—33157)		●		

★—Units operated in salt water

Lubrication and Maintenance

Locations ▲	*Every 30 Days*	*Every 60 Days*	*Once in Season*	*Twice in Season*
Check lubricant level in lower drive unit	A			
Lubricate propeller shaft splines		C-Each prop installation		
Lubricate swivel pin	①	C		
Lubricate magneto/distributor adaptor *			D	①
Lubricate ride-guide steering tube	①	D		
Lubricate ride-guide steering cable	①	D		
Lubricate ride-guide steering pivot/ball joint	①	E		
Lubricate throttle/shift linkage	①	E		
Lubricate thumb screws	①	E		
Lubricate upper shift shaft	①	E		
Lubricate reverse lock lever *	①	E		
Lubricate reverse locking cams	①	C		
Lubricate tilt stop lever	①	E		
Lubricate starter motor pinion gear		①	J	
Lubricate tiller handle knuckle pivot/gears *	①	E		
Lubricate stator plate clamps			E	①
Check lubricant level in power trim pump		I		
Check condition of battery/terminals	①			●
Inspect spark plug leads/all electrical connections			●	

Lubrication and Maintenance (cont.)

Locations ▲	Every 30 Days	Every 60 Days	Once in Season	Twice in Season
Clean fuel filter(s)			●	
Clean fuel tank filter			●	
Inspect all fuel lines/connections				●
Check entire unit/loose, damaged or missing parts			●	
Check condition of spark plugs			●	
Inspect breaker points			●	
Inspect propeller for possible damage				●
Inspect and clean entire unit/touch-up paint			L-M	①

▲—Complete list of maintenance is not applicable to all models
①—Units operated in salt water
★—Includes all pivot points and sliding surfaces unless stated elsewhere
A—Super Duty Quicksilver Gear Lubricant (C–92–52650)
C—Anti-Corrosion Grease (C–92–45134A1)
D—New Multipurpose Quicksilver Lubricant (C–92–49588)
E—Anti-Corrosion Oil (C–92–39928A1)
L—Quicksilver Marine Cleaner (C–92–32172)
M—Quicksilver Spray Paint
I—Quicksilver Formula 4 Oil (C–92–55573–24) or SAE 20–20W Specification MS
J—SAE No. 10 oil

Lubricant and Sealer Application Chart

Lubrication Point	Merc Model 39–40	75–60	110	200
Gear housing	A	A	A	A
Drive shaft splines	C	C	C	C
Shift shaft coupling	B	B	B	B
Magneto bushing	C	C	C	C
Swivel pin grease fitting	B	B	B	B
Tilt-to-swivel bracket	D	D	D	D
Tilt tube inside diameter (ID)	D	D	D	D
Propeller shaft splines	D	D	D	D
Reverse lock cams	—	—	—	C
Thumb screws	D	D	D	D
Tilt stop levers	B	B	B	B
Reverse lock latch in swivel bracket	E	E	E	—
Throttle linkage ★	D	D	D	D
Shift linkage ★	D	D	D	D
Tiller handle knuckle pivot	D	D	D	D
Tiller handle knuckle gears	D	D	D	D
Tiller handle universal joint	D	D	D	D
Choke shutter stud	D	D	D	D
Choke shaft in bottom cowl	—	—	—	D
Starter sheave pawls	C	C	C	C
Piston rod and crank needles	C	C	C	C
Top cowl mounts	B	B	B	—
Piston rings	E	E	E	E
Bearing carrier spool—gear housing	C	C	C	C
Water pump base and housing	C	C	C	C
Shift shaft threaded bushing—gear housing	C	C	C	C
End caps—crankshaft	E	E	E	E
Impeller pin and drive shaft	C	C	C	C
Screws—exhaust cover	D	D	D	D
Crankcase-to-block split line	J	J	J	J

★—Includes all pivot points and sliding surfaces unless stated elsewhere.
A—Super-Duty Quicksilver Gear Lubricant (C—92—52645—1)
B—Anti-Corrosion Grease (C—92—45134A1)
C—New Multipurpose Quicksilver Lubricant (C—92—49588—12)
D—Anti-Corrosion Oil (C—92—39928A1)
E—Formula 50 Quicksilver 2 Cycle Motor Oil (C—92—39607—1)
J—Gasket Sealer (C—92—28804—1)

MOTOR INSTALLATION

Very special attention should be given to mounting the motor on the transom. The clamp bracket must not only support the weight of the motor, but must also accept the stress of thrust, impact, inertia, and steering. These forces are transferred directly to the transom through the clamp bracket.

The motor is designed for a recommended transom height. To avoid damage to the motor it is important that the clamp screws be tightened securely and equally. Clamp screws should be tightened and positioned near a horizontal plane to allow full tilt and turn of the motor. If this is not observed, damage to the steering may result. It is also advisable to consult the general section, "Mounting the Motor on the Boat," for general instructions.

CAUTION: Before operating your motor, refer to instructions on the red "caution" tag attached to a new motor. Upper mounting bolts must be installed if the transom has an extremely hard, smooth surface. Occasionally check the clamp screws to be sure that they are tight. Failure to bolt the motor to the transom may result in damage to or loss of motor.

Transom Mounting Specifications

These specifications apply only to Mercury outboards. The specifications given in "Transom and Motor Well Dimensions," in the front of the book, are intended to apply to all motors in general.

Model	*Dim. A*	*Dim. B*	*Dim. C ★*	*Dim. D*	*Dim. E*	*Dim. F Short Shaft*	*Dim. F Long Shaft*	*Dim. G*	*Dim. H ▲*	*Dim. J*
Merc 200 (1966–71)	39¼	21	18¼	16¾	23⅜	15½	20½	19⅝ ①	4⅜	1⅞
Merc 110, 75, 60 (1966–71)	35¼	21¾	13½	14⅜	20⅛	15½	20½	19⅝ ①	2⅞	1⅞
Merc 40, 39 (1966–71)	35¼	21¾	13½	12¾	18¼	15½	20½	18¾ ①	2⅞	1⅞

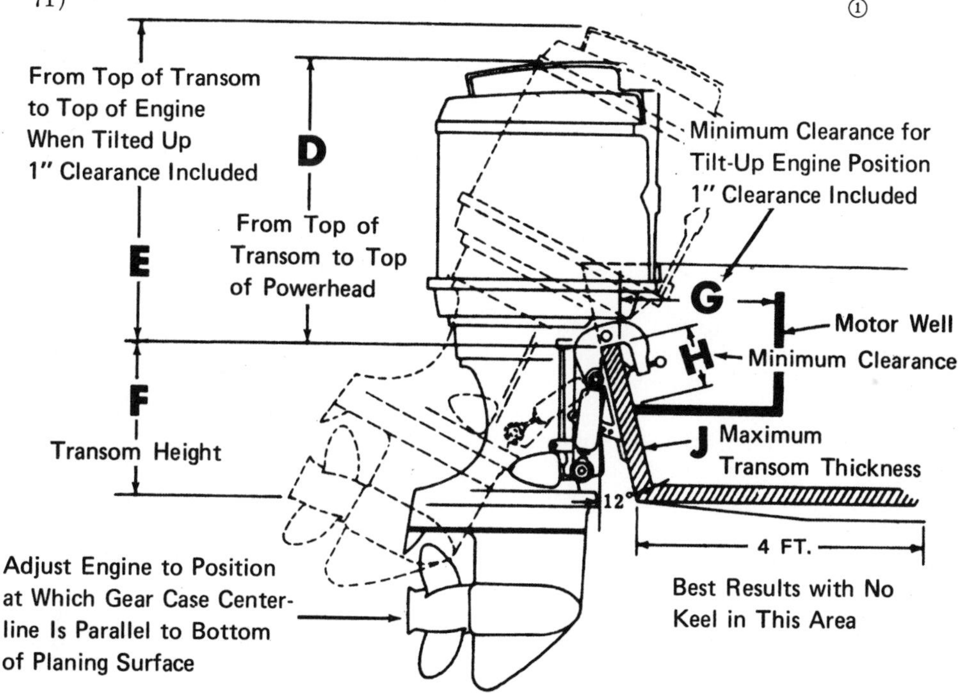

Motor well dimensions (© Kiekhaefer Mercury)

▲—This allows sufficient clearance for Ride-Guide steering unit. For rope steering, add to this figure according to type of bracket used
★—Variable on deep V-type hulls
①—End of throttle-shift steering handle
NOTE: *All dimensions are given in inches with 1/16 in. tolerance.*

TILT PIN ADJUSTMENT

Holes are provided in the clamp bracket to permit changing the location of the tilt lock pin for proper adjustment of tilt angle. See "Tilt Pin Adjustment" in the general section at the front of this book.

Fuel System

Mercury outboards are equipped with pressure-type carburetors, remote fuel tanks, and either vacuum-type or diaphragm-type fuel pumps. Most models are also equipped with a fuel filter at the tank or the carburetor.

CARBURETORS

All Mercury pressure-type carburetors are serviced in an identical manner.

Removal

1. Detach the choke and throttle linkage at the carburetor.
2. Remove the fuel line from the carburetor.
3. If necessary, remove the starter motor.
4. Remove the two nuts attaching the carburetor to the crankcase and remove the carburetor.

Disassembly

1. Remove the cap screw and gasket from the fuel filter cover.
2. Detach the filter housing, gasket, filter element, and filter element gasket.
3. Unscrew the idle adjustment screw and remove the spring.
4. Unscrew the idle restriction tube which extends inside the main discharge nozzle of the top carburetor. Do not lose the small restriction tube gasket.
5. Remove the discharge jet plug screw. Using a screwdriver of exact size, unscrew the high-speed discharge nozzle.
6. Remove the brass, hex-head plug and gasket from the carburetor body with a 3/8 in. wrench.
7. Remove the fixed jet and gasket with a screwdriver of exact size.
8. Remove the two screws which hold the float bowl cover and gasket to the carburetor body. Lift off the cover and gasket.

Remove the idle restriction tube (© Kiekhaefer Mercury)

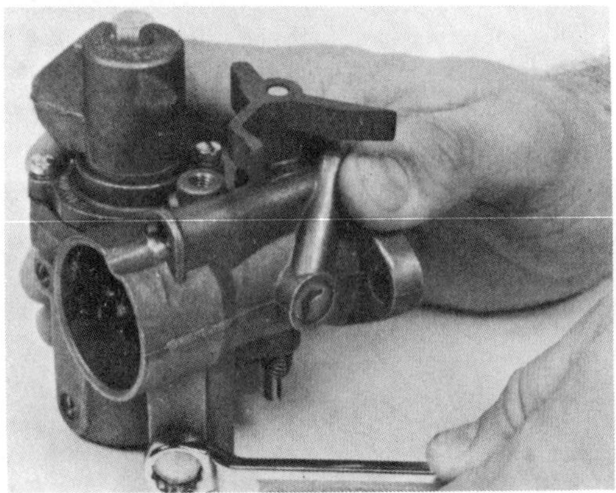

Remove the brass plug and gasket (© Kiekhaefer Mercury)

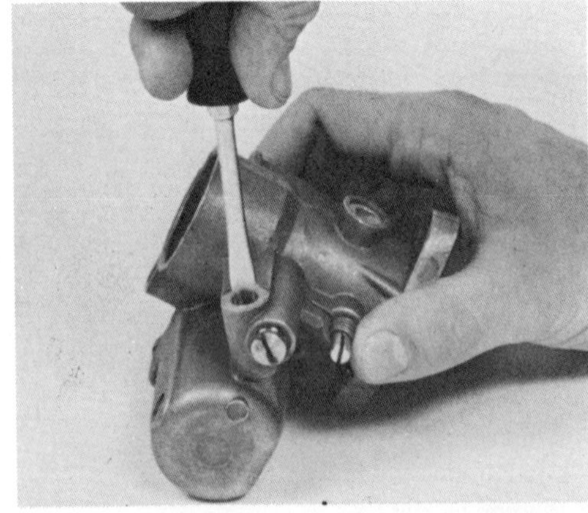

Remove the fixed jet (© Kiekhaefer Mercury)

9. Remove the lower float lever pin and lever, allowing the upper lever to pivot back. This will expose the inlet needle.
10. Remove the inlet needle.

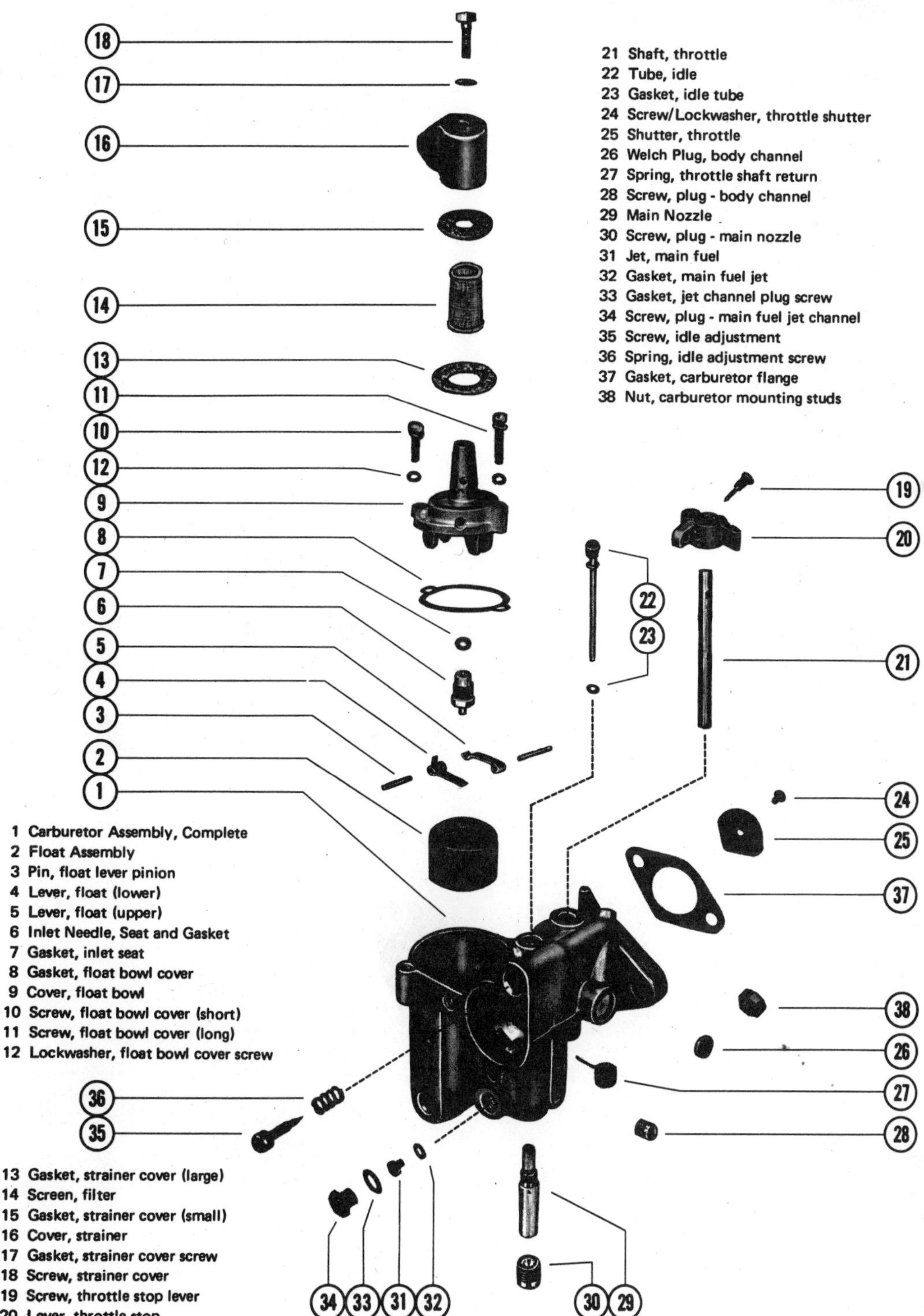
21 Shaft, throttle
22 Tube, idle
23 Gasket, idle tube
24 Screw/Lockwasher, throttle shutter
25 Shutter, throttle
26 Welch Plug, body channel
27 Spring, throttle shaft return
28 Screw, plug - body channel
29 Main Nozzle
30 Screw, plug - main nozzle
31 Jet, main fuel
32 Gasket, main fuel jet
33 Gasket, jet channel plug screw
34 Screw, plug - main fuel jet channel
35 Screw, idle adjustment
36 Spring, idle adjustment screw
37 Gasket, carburetor flange
38 Nut, carburetor mounting studs
1 Carburetor Assembly, Complete
2 Float Assembly
3 Pin, float lever pinion
4 Lever, float (lower)
5 Lever, float (upper)
6 Inlet Needle, Seat and Gasket
7 Gasket, inlet seat
8 Gasket, float bowl cover
9 Cover, float bowl
10 Screw, float bowl cover (short)
11 Screw, float bowl cover (long)
12 Lockwasher, float bowl cover screw
13 Gasket, strainer cover (large)
14 Screen, filter
15 Gasket, strainer cover (small)
16 Cover, strainer
17 Gasket, strainer cover screw
18 Screw, strainer cover
19 Screw, throttle stop lever
20 Lever, throttle stop

Exploded view of typical Mercury carburetors (© Kiekhaefer Mercury)

11. Remove the inlet needle seat which has a right-hand thread. (A ⅜ in. socket will do this nicely.) Do not lose the small gasket behind the inlet needle seat.

12. Remove the float by tipping the carburetor upside down.

13. Tap the welch plug, which covers the idle bypass chamber, with a center punch and pry it off.

14. Remove the throttle plate from the throttle shaft.

15. Remove the throttle shaft from the top of the carburetor.

16. Remove the throttle plate return spring from the carburetor body.

17. Remove the lead plugs with a sharp punch.

18. Unscrew the two nuts and remove the choke plate and screen.

19. If applicable, remove the choke linkage from the plate.

Cleaning and Inspection

1. Insert the proper size drills in the passages. See "Carburetor Specifications" for the proper size of drill. Be sure that the passages are clear and free of restrictions.

2. Immerse the carburetor body in carburetor solvent for a short period of time (long enough to remove all dirt and varnish which has accumulated).

3. Rinse the carburetor thoroughly in clean solvent and blow it dry with compressed air. If compressed air is not available, shake the carburetor body to remove most of the solvent and allow it to air-dry.

4. Check the fuel filter for chips or cracks.

Assembly

1. Check the float for deterioration.

2. Check the float spring adjustment.

3. Check to make sure that the spring has not been stretched.

4. Place the float in the bowl on the float needle.

5. Place the inlet needle seat gasket in the float bowl cover and thread the inlet needle seat securely into place. Do not overtighten it.

6. Set the inlet needle into the neoprene seat.

7. Place the upper float lever in position and insert the float lever pin.

8. Install the lower float lever and pin.

9. Install the float bowl cover. Bend the secondary lever as necessary to obtain

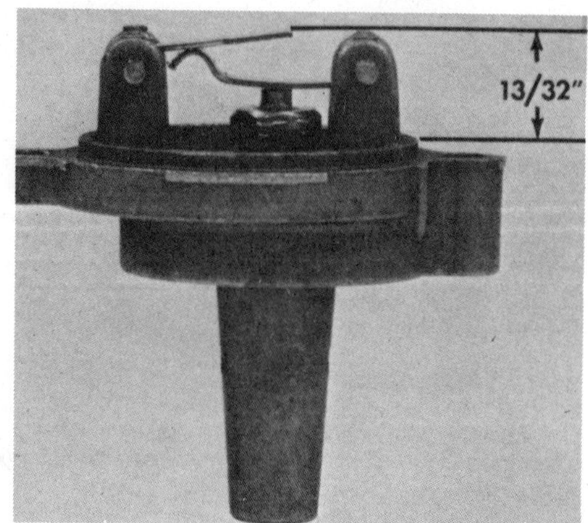

Adjusting the primary lever (© Kiekhaefer Mercury)

a distance of $^{13}/_{32} \pm {}^{1}/_{64}$ in. from the face of the shoulder in the primary lever.

10. Be sure that the needle does not stick in the seat. Tip the assembly upright and the needle should move freely on the primary lever.

11. Hold the float bowl cover in an upright position. The distance between the levers as illustrated, should be one-quarter inch. Bend the tab on the secondary lever as required to obtain this dimension.

Clearance adjustment between levers (© Kiekhaefer Mercury)

12. Check to make sure that the float spring measures approximately $^{3}/_{32}$ in. from the top of the float to the end of the exposed spring.

13. Install a new gasket on the end of

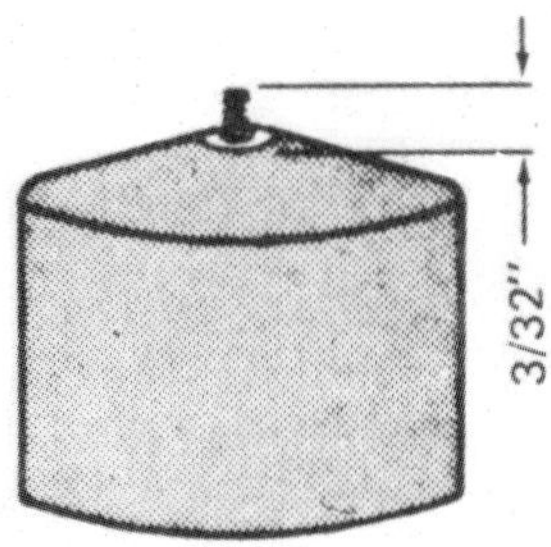

Carburetor float adjustment (© Kiekhaefer Mercury)

the float bowl cover and install on the carburetor float bowl. Secure the cover with two screws and lockwashers.

14. Install the fuel filter gasket and fuel filter element with another gasket and the filter bowl cover.

15. Replace the filter bowl cover gasket and install the filter on the carburetor.

16. Assemble the choke plate and screen on the carburetor throat studs. Install the choke linkage on the choke plate.

17. Install the throttle shaft return spring in the recess at the lower end of the carburetor.

18. Insert the throttle shaft into the top of the carburetor and into the return spring slot. Be sure to have one coil of the spring turned to allow sufficient return of the throttle plate to the closed position from spring tension.

19. Secure the throttle plate to the throttle shaft.

20. Insert the main discharge nozzle into the receptacle at the bottom of the carburetor. Tighten it securely but do not overtighten it. Be sure to use a screwdriver of the exact size.

21. Thread the discharge plug into the carburetor.

22. Where applicable, place the gasket on the correct fixed jet and insert the jet (see "Specifications") into the carburetor.

23. Place the gasket on the ⅜ in. brass hex-head plug and secure the plug.

24. Where applicable, place the gasket on the idle restriction tube and install the idle restriction tube into the carburetor.

25. Insert a new welch plug over the idle by-pass chamber and tap the center of the plug lightly to hold the plug in place.

26. Seal with Liquid Neoprene.

27. Place the spring on the idle adjustment screw and thread the idle adjustment screw into the carburetor.

Installation

1. Installation is the reverse of removal.

Adjustments

High-Speed Jet

The high-speed jet is fixed and no adjustment is possible. To alter the high-speed jet, it must be replaced with a jet of a different size. Consult the "Jet Changes for Elevation" chart in the specifications section, for alternate jet sizes or "Carburetor Specifications" for the standard jet size.

1. Jet size recommendations are intended as a guide. Try a size larger or smaller if in doubt.

2. The manufacturer does not recommend altering the spark advance for operation in higher altitudes. Use a propeller of lower pitch in higher elevations to allow the engine to operate at the recommended rpm.

3. Test the engine in a test tank with a propeller or test wheel.

Idle Speed

1. The idle speed is set at the factory for optimum performance. Due to ambient conditions, however, it may be necessary to adjust the idle speed periodically.

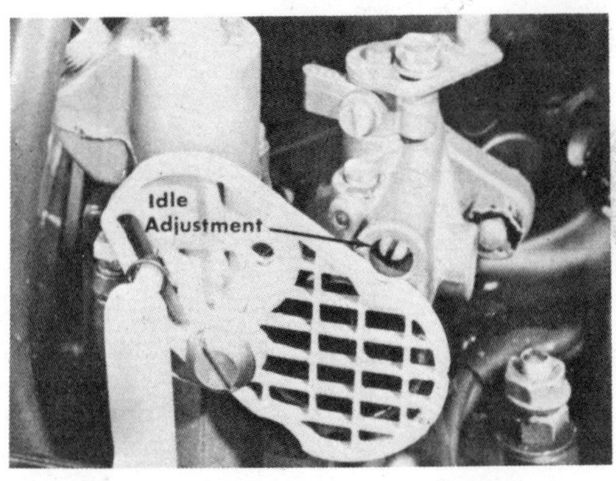

Idle speed adjustment (© Kiekhaefer Mercury)

2. If adjustment is necessary, it can be done with a test wheel or regular propeller in a test tank, or on the boat. For optimum low-speed performance, adjust the idle mixture and idle speed under actual operating conditions.

3. Warm the engine thoroughly before attempting any adjustment.

4. Start with all idle needles one turn open and adjust for maximum rpm with

the magneto retarded to give about 600–700 rpm.

5. With the engine idling in Forward gear, turn the low-speed mixture adjustment needle counterclockwise until the cylinders fire unevenly. This will indicate an overly rich mixture.

6. Slowly turn the needle clockwise until the engine fires evenly and picks up speed.

7. Continue turning the needle clockwise until the motor begins to slow down and fire unevenly. This will indicate a mixture which is too lean.

8. Set the adjustment screw ½–¾ turn counterclockwise from the too-lean position. This is the approximate true setting. Do not lean the mixture any more than is necessary to obtain a reasonably smooth idle. When in doubt, it is preferable to have a slightly rich mixture rather than a mixture which is too lean.

9. If the motor hesitates during acceleration, after adjusting the idle mixture, the mixture is too lean and should be enriched slightly to produce smooth acceleration.

10. Run the engine at idle and adjust the idle stop screw on the stop bracket until the engine idles at the recommended rpm (see "Tune-Up Specifications") in Forward gear.

11. Run the engine at full throttle to clear the cylinders and recheck the idle stop adjustment.

12. It may be necessary to adjust the idle screw up to one-quarter turn with each change in brand of gasoline to account for differences in volatility and refining process.

Float Level and Float Drop

1. (See steps no. 9–12 of the carburetor "Assembly" procedure.)

Hard Starting

Hard starting is often traced to the improper operation of the choke plate. Adjust the choke linkage and choke return spring for fast, positive action of the choke plate. Be sure that it moves freely and quickly.

1. Clearance between the choke plate and carburetor body must not be more than 0.015 in. when the choke is closed, or else the motor will be hard to start.

Fuel Pressure

Fuel pressure at the top carburetor should be checked whenever insufficient fuel supply is suspected or if a fuel tank of other than Kiekhaefer Mercury manufacture is being used. Check fuel tanks (other than Mercury) for the following:

a. Adequate air vent in the fuel cap.

b. Adequate fuel line diameter. The fuel line must be 5/16–3/8 in. in diameter.

c. A clogged or too-small filter on the end of the pick-up, or too-small pick-up tube. A fuel pick-up assembly (A—32—33909A4) may be used as a comparison.

An insufficient fuel supply will cause the motor to run lean, lose rpm, or cause piston scoring.

1. Connect a pressure gauge into the fuel line that leads to the upper carburetor. The fuel pressure must be at least two psi at full throttle.

Throttle Pick-up

Because this adjustment is so closely related to the other adjustments made to the electrical system, the throttle pick-up adjustment is included in the "Electrical System" adjustments.

Throttle Stop

This adjustment is also included among the adjustments in the "Electrical System."

FUEL PUMP

Diaphragm-type fuel pumps are used on most Mercury outboards. Crankcase pulsating pressure is transferred to the fuel pump diaphragm which draws fuel from the fuel tank. Before servicing the fuel pump, obtain replacement parts from a Mercury dealer.

Removal

1. Remove the fuel tank line from the adaptor.

2. Remove the fuel lines from the fuel pump.

3. Remove the screws securing the fuel pump to the crankcase and remove the fuel pump from the motor.

Disassembly

1. Separate the fuel pump components, referring to the illustrations.

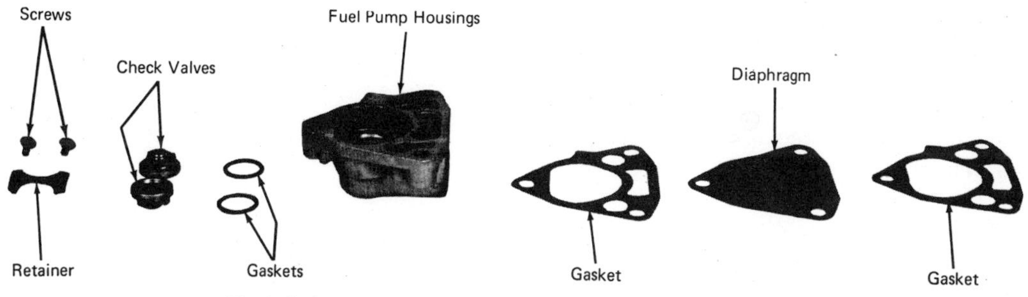

Exploded view of type A—53238A3 (© Kiekhaefer Mercury)

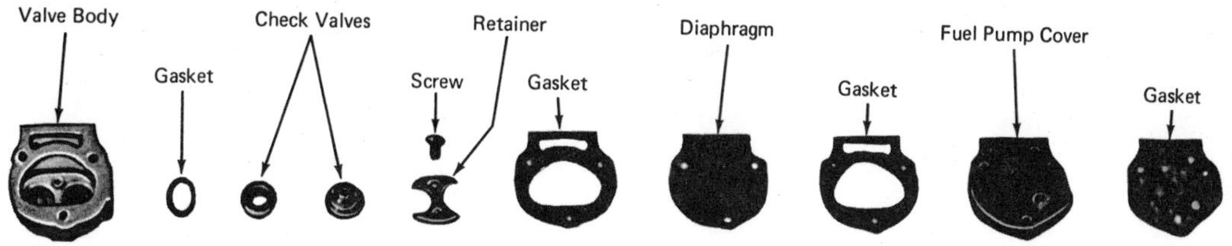

Exploded view of type A—30269A2 and A—23009A1 fuel pump (© Kiekhaefer Mercury)

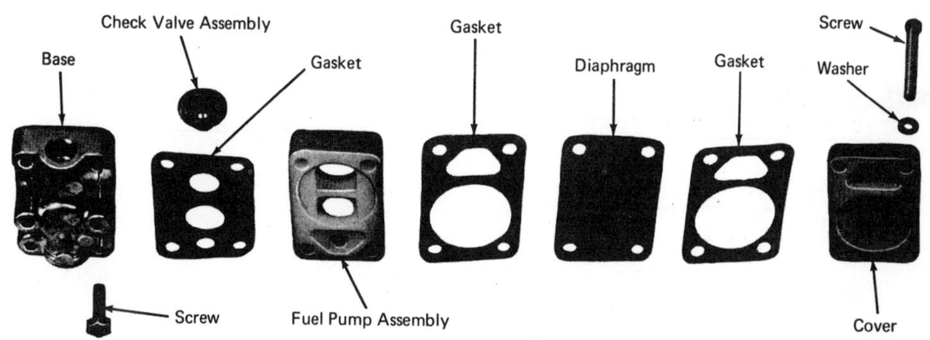

Exploded view of type A—55156A5 fuel pump (© Kiekhaefer Mercury)

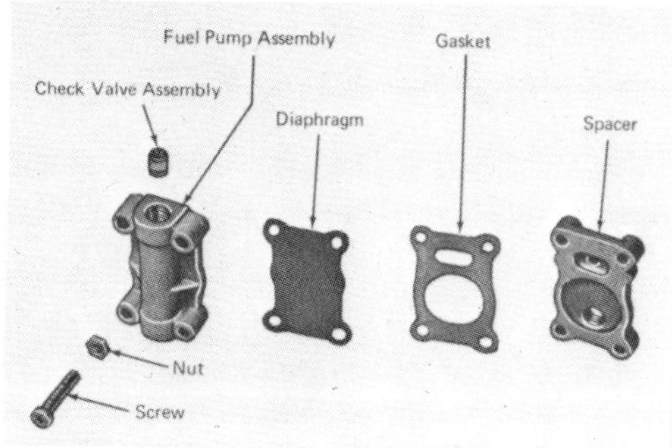

Exploded view of type A—39082Ar fuel pump (© Kiekhaefer Mercury)

2. Remove the gaskets, diaphragm, and check valve retainer screw.

NOTE: *The fuel pumps on small, one- and two-cylinder motors in 1966–68 had check valves pressed into the pump housing. These may be replaced individually or with the housing.*

Cleaning and Inspection

1. Wash all parts thoroughly and allow them to air-dry.
2. Inspect each part for wear or damage.
3. Replace the pulsator diaphragm and gaskets with new parts.
4. Be sure that the valve seats provide good contact area for the valve disc.
5. Tighten elbows and check valve connections firmly when installing.
6. Do not use Permatex on the valve retainer gasket.
7. Reassemble the fuel pump cover and inspect the check valves. Blow through the

outlet hole. Air should be drawn through the valve, but it should close immediately when attempting to blow through it.

8. Check the inlet valve by reversing the procedure in step no. 7. If leakage exists, check for free operation and accurate setting of the valves.

9. A worn or slightly warped valve will cause leakage. Replace worn or slightly warped valves with new ones.

CHECK VALVE REPLACEMENT
(PRESSED-IN TYPE)

1. Remove the check valves by presssing them out with a 9/32 in. drift, from the intake side through the outside. Once these check valves are removed, they should be replaced with new ones.

2. Press the new check valves into the fuel pump housing from the intake side.

3. Press the first check valve in until the top of the valve housing is 1⅜ in. from the face of the intake side.

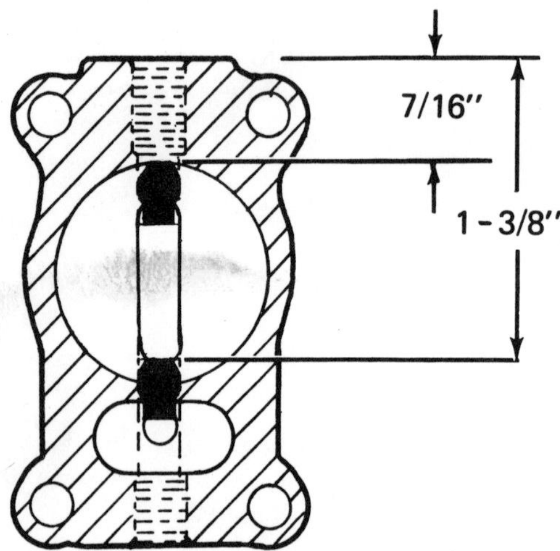

Check valve replacement (pressed-in type) (© Kiekhaefer Mercury)

4. Press the second check valve in until the top of the valve housing is 7/16 in. from the face of the intake side.

Assembly

1. Inspect all parts, making sure that they are usable and ready for assembly.

2. Install new check valve gaskets in the seats and set the check valve discs in position. The inlet check valve seat is identified by its tip which protrudes into the casting.

3. The flat side of the check valve fits

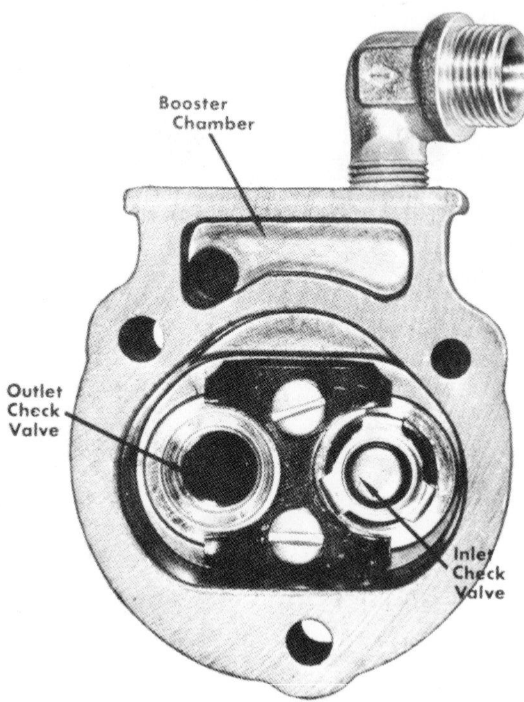

Install new check valve gaskets (© Kiekhaefer Mercury)

over this tip. The outlet check valve is installed opposite (flat end up) so that tension is against the valves.

4. Place the retainer on the check valves in the housing and secure it with two screws.

5. Place the new gasket on the pump body, followed by the neoprene diaphragm, another gasket, and the fuel pump cover.

VACUUM FUEL TANK AND FUEL LINE

Because the fuel pump on the motor pumps fuel from the tank to the carburetor, only one fuel line is necessary between the tank and motor.

NOTE: *Under law, all gasoline containers must be colored red.*

Priming

1. Prior to starting the motor, the fuel tank must be primed by squeezing the primer bulb on the fuel line.

2. Slowly squeeze the primer bulb by hand. This will draw fuel from the tank to the carburetor bowl.

3. When the bowl on the carburetor is filled, pressure will be felt on the bulb.

Primer Bulb Replacement

1. Remove the damaged or inoperative primer bulb by cutting the fuel line as close to the bulb as possible. Do not damage the check valve assembly.

2. Place a small clamp over the end of the long fuel line (fuel tank-to-primer bulb) and install the small end of the check valve assembly into the end of the fuel line.

3. Place a large clamp over the end of the primer bulb and fit the primer bulb over the large end of the check valve assembly.

4. Position the clamps on the primer bulb and fuel line as shown (do not pinch the check ball) and pinch the sides of the clamp with a pair of end-cutter pliers. Do not pinch the clamp any more than is necessary to obtain a good seal.

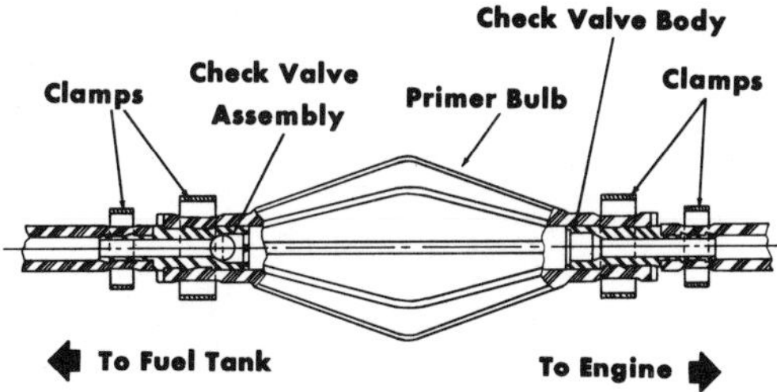

Primer bulb replacement (© Kiekhaefer Mercury)

5. Repeat this procedure with the primer bulb-to-engine end of the fuel line, being careful to install the check valve body into the primer bulb.

6. Squeeze the primer bulb several times to be sure that there are no leaks and that the bulb is pumping fuel.

Repairing Fuel Tank Leaks

1. Remove the filler cap and fuel tank cover assembly.

2. If the spot of the leak is known, circle the hole with a pencil, drain the tank completely, and flush it with carbon tetrachloride or trichlorethylene.

CAUTION: *Do no use either of these solvents in an unventilated space.*

3. If the spot of the leak is not known, drain and flush the tank, as in step no. 2.

4. Submerge the tank in water and look for bubbles arising from the hole in the tank.

5. Leaks in the tank sheet metal may be repaired by welding, according to recommended procedures. It is best to leave this type of work to a shop, where proper facilities are available.

Custom Fuel Tanks

If a tank other than Kiekhaefer Mercury is used, an air vent is the only requirement. Check all "foreign" tanks for the following:

a. Adequate air vent in fuel cap.

b. A large enough diameter fuel line. The fuel line should be 5/16–3/8 in. inside diameter.

c. Adequate filter on the end of the pick-up, or an adequate pick-up tube.

Electrical System

STARTER

The electric starter motor (available on Merc 200) operates under great load and produces a great deal of horsepower for its size. Under no circumstances should the starter motor be operated for more than fifteen seconds at a time. Cranking should not be repeated without a pause of at least two minutes to allow the heat to escape.

Motors equipped with electric-start are distinguished by the letter E following the model number. The electric start system is a twelve volt type, especially designed for outboard use. There are no adjustments to be made.

Maintenance

The cranking motor and solenoid are encased to prevent the entry of dirt and moisture. Preventive maintenance, however, should be performed as follows.

1. Inspect the terminals for corrosion and loose connections.

2. Inspect the wiring for worn or frayed insulation.

3. Check the mounting bolts to be sure that they are tight.

Removal

NOTE: *The Delco-Remy starter motor replaces the Bosch unit on later electric-start models and is completely interchangeable as a unit.*

1. Be sure that the battery is discon-

nected before working on the electrical system.

2. Remove the electrical connections from the starter motor.

3. Remove the mounting bolts from the flange and remove the starter motor and drive.

Removing the mounting bolts from the starter motor (© Kiekhaefer Mercury)

Brush Replacement

Replacement brush sets are available and contain insulated brushes and ground brushes, along with necessary screws, nuts, and washers.

1. Cut off the old brush leads where they attach to the field coils.

2. Clean the ends of the coils by filing or grinding the old brush lead connections. Remove varnish only as far as is necessary to make solder connections.

3. Using resin flux, solder the leads to the field coils, making sure that they are in the correct position to reach the brush holders. It is recommended that the leads be soldered to the back sides of the coils so that excessive solder will not rub the armature. Do not overheat the leads as excessive solder will run onto the leads and it will no longer be flexible.

4. Remove the old ground brush holders and attach the new assemblies to the frame with screws, washers, and nuts. Peen the ends of the screws so that they do not vibrate loose.

5. Be sure that none of the soldered connections are touching the frame and grounding the fields.

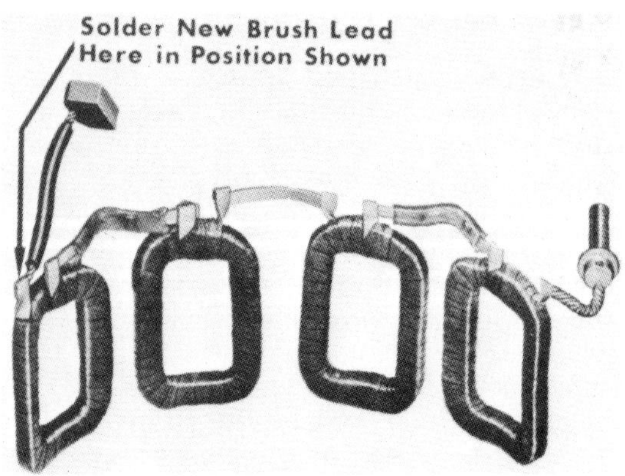

Replacing the brush lead to the car field coil on 2 cylinder models (© Kiekhaefer Mercury)

IGNITION SYSTEM

Merc models 39 through 200 use either a Phelon magneto or a Thunderbolt capacitor discharge ignition system, with maker points. The following chart identifies the motor model and ignition type.

Ignition Identification

Year	*Model*	*Ignition Type*
1966	39	Phelon Magneto
	60	Phelon Magneto
	110	Phelon Magneto
	200	Phelon Magneto
1967	39	Phelon Magneto
	60	Phelon Magneto
	110	Phelon Magneto
	200	Phelon Magneto
1968	39	Phelon Magneto
	60	Phelon Magneto
	110	Phelon Magneto
	200	Phelon Magneto
1969	40	Phelon Magneto
	75	Phelon Magneto
	110	Phelon Magneto
	200	Phelon Magneto
1970	40	Thunderbolt C.D. w/points
	75	Thunderbolt C.D. w/points
	110	Thunderbolt C.D. w/points
	200	Thunderbolt C.D. w/points
1971	40	Thunderbolt C.D. w/points
	75	Thunderbolt C.D. w/points
	110	Thunderbolt C.D. w/points
	200	Thunderbolt C.D. w/points

NOTE: Refer to the specific section for service procedures.

Precautions

The following precautions should be observed for the appropriate ignition system.

Standard Ignition System

1. Do not touch or disconnect any ignition system component with the engine running or the battery connected.
2. When checking for spark, do not hold the wire far away from the plug. Only make this test for a brief instant because this puts a strain on the coil and might break down a perfectly good coil.
3. Avoid using spark plug testers with a hypodermic needle type of probe. This punctures the leads and protectors, causing electrical leakage and allows moisture to enter the system.
4. When assembling spark plug protectors to cables, be sure that the prong of the spring goes through the center of the cable and makes solid contact with the ignition wire. This will prevent the possibility of a weak spark.
5. Do not use a plated gauge in checking point gap, as the plating may come off.
6. Do not use pliers to bend the maker point springs. These will make a sharp bend and impair efficiency.
7. Remove ignition components from the powerhead prior to cleaning. The solvent may damage the ignition components.

Capacitor Discharge System

1. Do not reverse the battery leads.
2. Do not spark the battery lead wires.
3. Use only recommended spark plugs. Do not use resistor spark plugs or resistor spark plug wires.
4. Do not disconnect any wires while the engine is running.
5. Do not ground any wires to the engine block for checking spark. Ground only to the bottom cowl or front cover plate.
6. Use only approved Mercury tachometers.
7. Due to the high degree of sophistication on Mercury outboards, only a good-quality, transistorized DC timing light should be used. If the cylinder to which the timing light is connected is shorting out (but fires normally, without the light connected), the probability is that the timing light is of insufficient quality.

CAUTION: *When servicing the ignition system, do not touch or disconnect any ignition components while the engine is running, or with the battery connected. Extremely high voltage is present in this type of system.*

Phelon Magneto

This magneto-type ignition consists of coil(s), condenser(s), laminated core(s), and one or two sets of breaker points. The system is self-energizing and requires no battery. All 1966–69 Merc 39, 40, 60, 75, 110, and 200 models use the Phelon magneto ignition system.

Removal

1. Remove the flywheel. (See "Powerhead.")
2. Remove the high-tension leads from the spark plugs.
3. On some models, remove the clamp screws which hold the high-tension leads to the cylinder block.
4. Rotate the stator plate clockwise and lift off the stator plate.

NOTE: *The magneto unit is an integral part of the flywheel. It is assembled and machined with the flywheel and should never be removed or recharged. Attempts at either of the above will result in the necessity of magneto replacement.*

Disassembly

1. Remove the primary connection and spark plug wire.
2. Bend down the clip which holds the coil on the core and remove the coil from the core.
3. Remove the condenser mounting screws and the condenser.
4. Remove the breaker points mounting screws and the breaker points.

Cleaning and Inspection

1. Wash all parts, except the coil and condenser, in cleaning solvent.
2. Check the lead wire to be sure that spark is not leaking through at some point.
3. If the points are pitted severely, replace them with a new set.
4. Inspect the coil for insulation leakage or for evidence that the spark is leaking to a ground.

Assembly

1. Replace the cam breaker (on engines equipped with cam) on the crankshaft with the word "top" facing up. Install the key into the crankshaft keyway.
2. Replace the thrust washer or flywheel key, whichever is used.
3. Set the magneto on the upper end cap and rotate it to seat it properly.

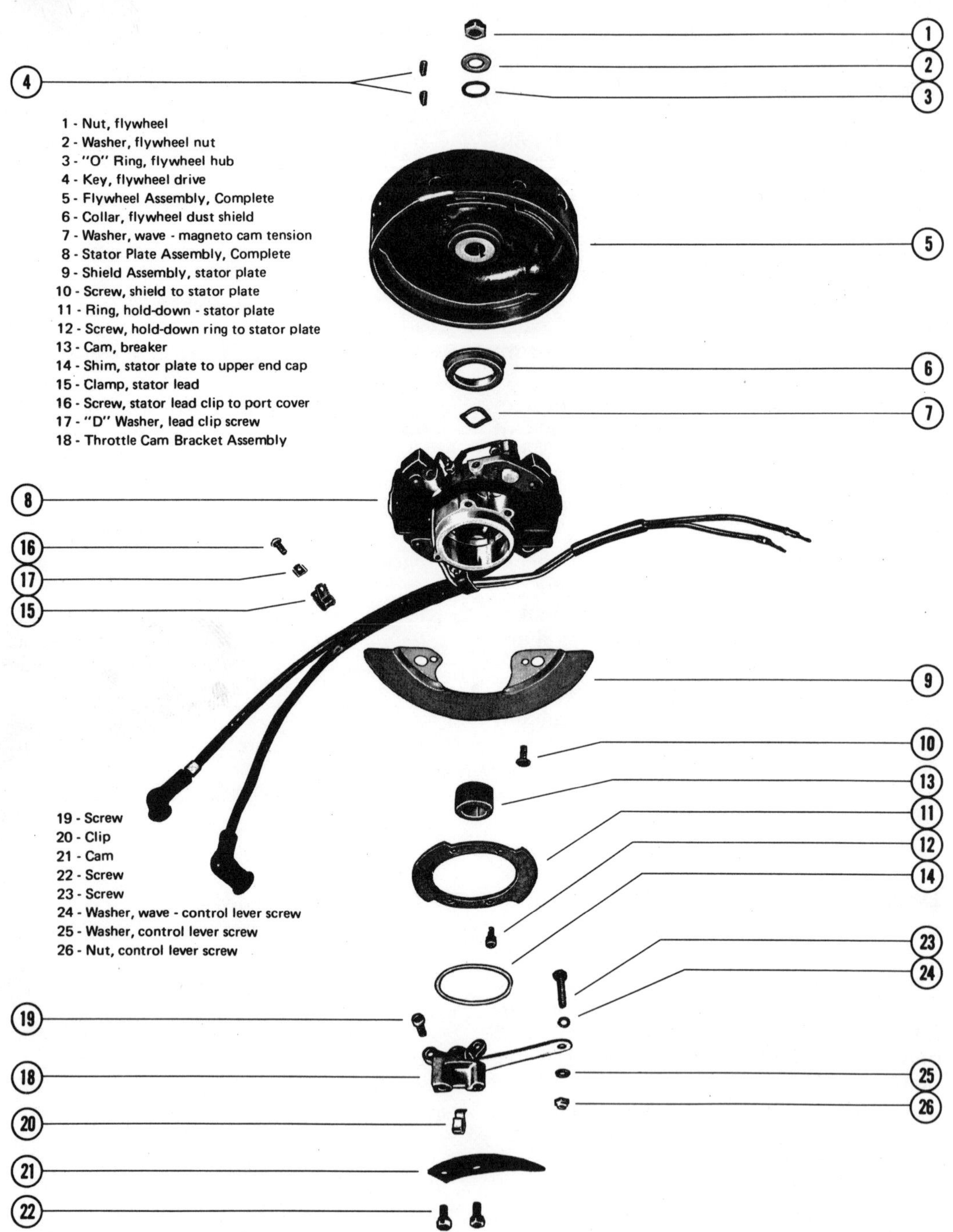

Exploded view of Phelon magneto (© Kiekhaefer Mercury)

4. When replacing the coil on the core, be careful not to bend the laminated core. Be sure that the coil is fully seated before bending the core.

5. Check the ground connection for a good contact under the screw.

6. Check the insulation at the breaker point connection to be sure that the lead does not ground against the fixed contact or the spring.

7. If the cam wick becomes dry, it should be replaced. Do not oil the wick. If the breaker arm pivot dries out, lubricate it lightly with New Multipurpose Lubri-

cant. Avoid excessive lubrication at this spot.

Thunderbolt C.D. (w/Maker points)

Merc 40, 75, 110, and 200 models, in 1970–71, use a Thunderbolt capacitor discharge ignition system. The conventional breaker points have been replaced with maker points. When servicing this system (or any other C.D. system), refer to the precautions listed at the beginning of the section.

REMOVAL

1. Remove the top cowl.
2. Remove the retaining screws from the rewind starter. Loosen the coil retaining screws and nuts, and remove the rewind starter.
3. Using an automotive-type flywheel

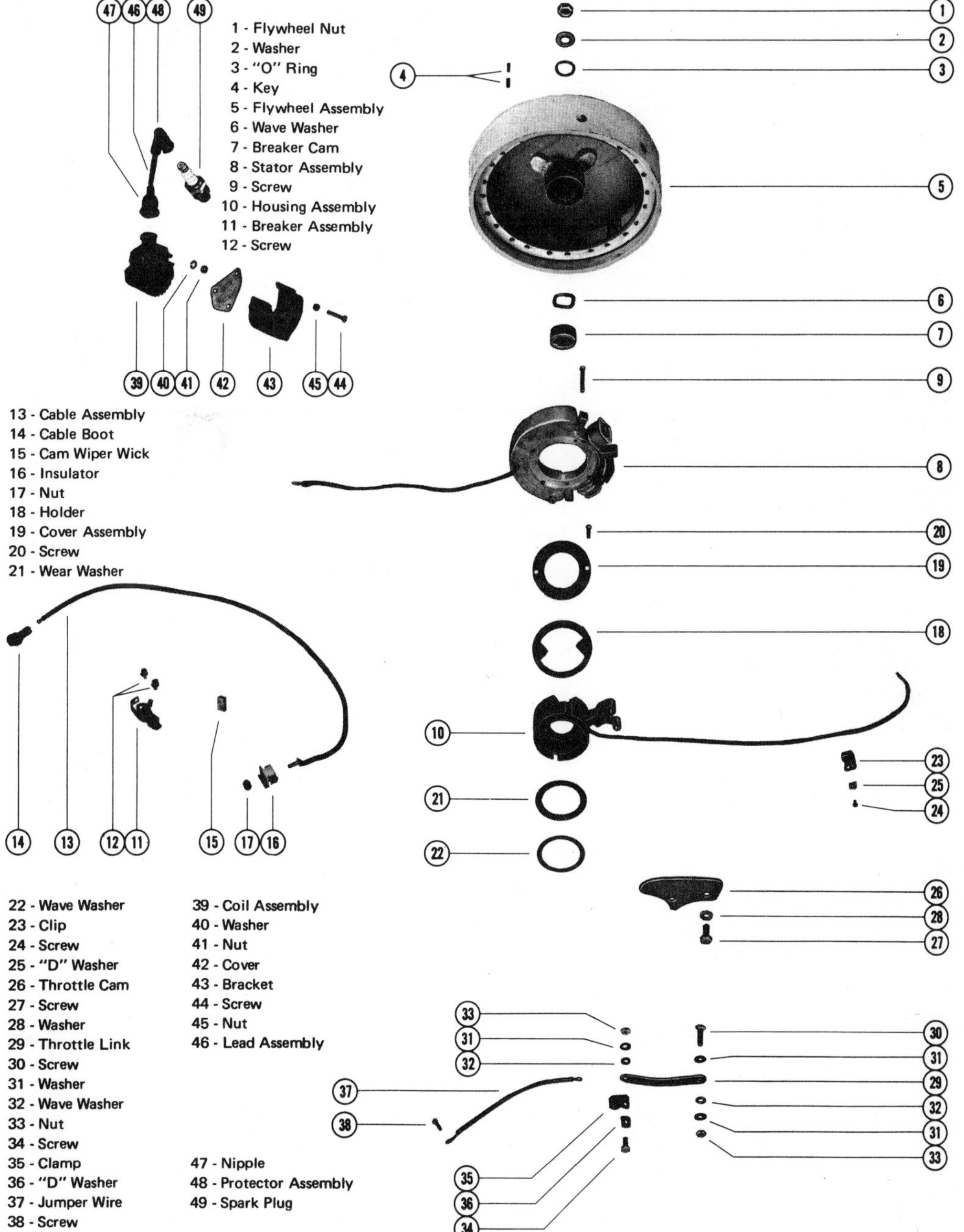

Exploded view of ignition components (© Kiekhaefer Mercury)

holder, remove the flywheel nut and washer.

4. Remove the flywheel with a flywheel puller.

Stator and Housing Removal

1. Remove the screw from the stator advance arm.

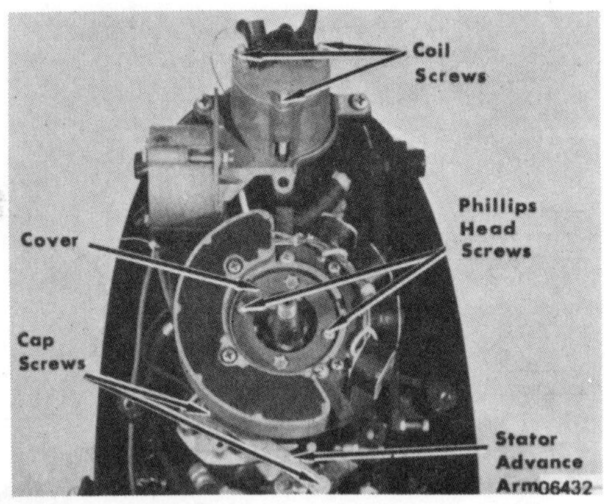

Removing the stator advance arm (© Kiekhaefer Mercury)

2. Disconnect the wires from the stop switch and coil.

3. Remove the screws and D washer from the wire clamp.

4. Remove the screw and stator ground strap.

5. Remove the stator and housing.

Component Removal

1. Remove the screws from the cover assembly.

NOTE: *To replace the maker points, the stator assembly must be removed.*

2. Remove the phillips screws and the stator assembly.

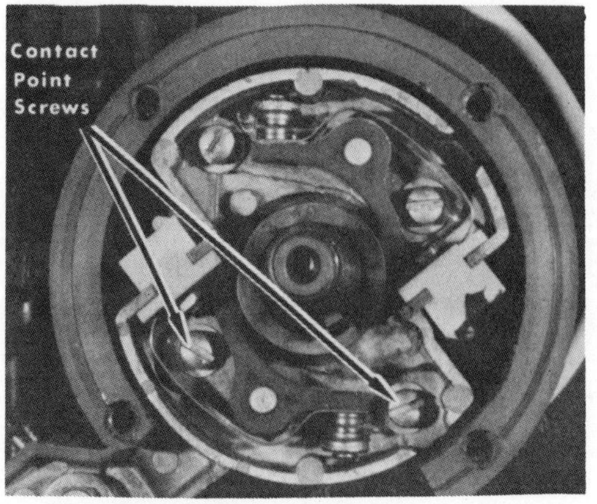

Location of contact point screws (© Kiekhaefer Mercury)

Removal of the contact points (© Kiekhaefer Mercury)

3. Remove the contact housing holder.

4. Remove the screws and nut from each set of points and remove the maker points.

5. Replace the oiler wick, if necessary.

6. Remove the coils by removing the nuts and screws from the bracket.

Cleaning and Inspection

1. Check the condition of the maker points. The high primary voltage in the Thunderbolt ignition system will darken and roughen the points in very short order. While conventional points will not operate in this condition, it is perfectly normal for the points in the Thunderbolt system to appear this way. Do not replace the Thunderbolt ignition points unless an obvious malfunction exists, or the points are loose or burned away. In general, the cam follower will have worn away before the points go bad.

2. Check the stator.

Installation

1. Install the points and set the points to 0.020 in. (See the adjustments, following.)

2. Install the contact housing holder.

3. Install the stator assembly with the phillips screws.

4. Install the cover assembly.

5. Connect all wires.

6. Install the flywheel, washer, and nut.

7. Install the rewind starter and cowl.

Contact Point Replacement

See the appropriate section concerning ignition system service.

Contact Point Adjustment—All Models

1. The flywheel must be removed to adjust the points.

2. Care must be taken when adjusting the points gap. The high point of the cam is not the keyway.

3. Adjust the contact points so that the cam follower arm is at the high point of the cam. This is approximately one-quarter inch after the points open.

4. A degree plate should be used to set the points, but if it is not available, set the breaker arms at the highest point of the cam lobe.

5. Using a feeler gauge, between the open faces of the points, set the gap at 0.020 in. by loosening the screw on the base plate.

6. Rotate the crankshaft 180° and set the other set of points in the same manner.

7. Check the breaker cam for looseness due to wear. It should be tight on the crankshaft and installed with the arrow or part number to the top. If this is loose, it will probably cause misfiring at idle.

NOTE: *Some models have the breaker cam cut into the crankshaft as a one-piece assembly.*

8. Reinstall the flywheel.

Timing and Additional Adjustments

MERC 39, 40, 60, 75, AND 110 (1966–69)

Timing

The timing on these models is fixed and cannot be adjusted.

Pick-up Adjustment

1. With the engine running in Forward, turn the twist grip throttle to obtain 1000–1100 rpm, as indicated by a tachometer.

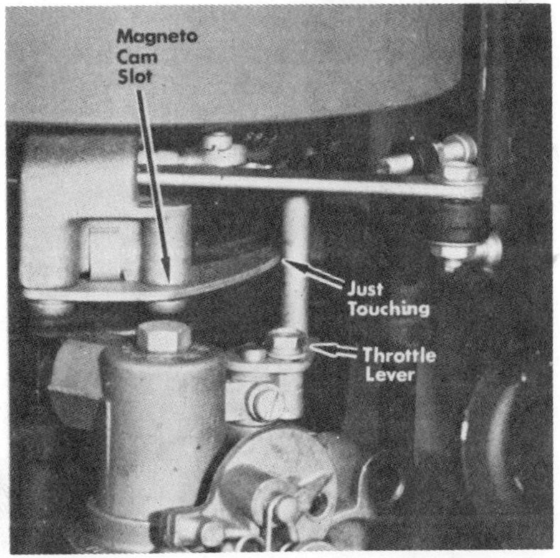

Throttle pick-up adjustment (Merc 39, 40, 60, 75, and 110—1966–69) (© Kiekhaefer Mercury)

2. At this point, the magneto cam should just touch the throttle lever on the carburetor.

3. If the recommended rpm is not obtained, loosen the screws securing the throttle lever to the carburetor and adjust the slotted throttle lever. On later 1968 models, the magneto cam is also slotted for finer adjustment of the pick-up plate.

Throttle Stop Adjustment—Merc 60 (ser no. 1610265 and above)

1. Adjust the throttle stop screw so that the threaded end of the screw extends 5/16 in. through the throttle lever control.

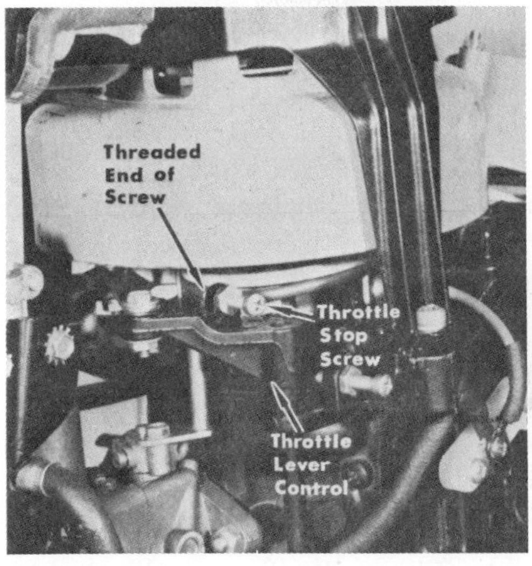

Throttle stop adjustment (Merc 39, 40, 60, 75, and 110—1966–69) (© Kiekhaefer Mercury)

Throttle Stop Adjustment—Merc 110 (ser no. 1580203 and above)

1. Adjust the throttle stop so that the threaded end of the screw extends a quarter-inch through the throttle lever control.

Maximum Neutral RPM—Merc 110 (ser no. 1492282 and above)

1. Shift the motor into Neutral.

2. Adjust the Neutral speed limiter stop to obtain a maximum speed of 2400–2700 rpm.

Tiller Handle Adjustment

1. With the engine running in Neutral, turn the twist grip to obtain 2400–2700

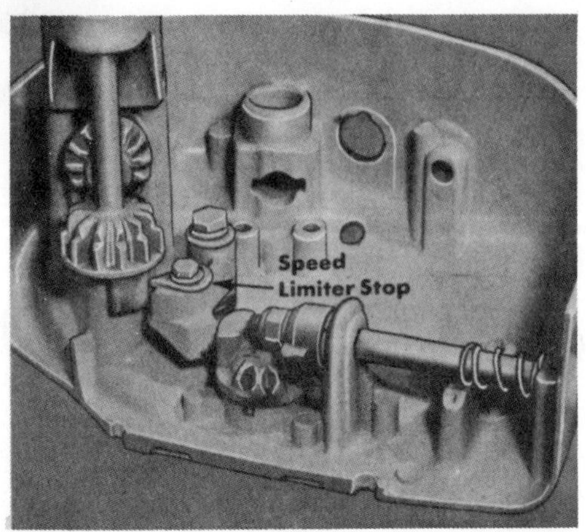

Maximum neutral rpm adjustment (Merc 39, 40, 60, 75, and 110—1966–69) (© Kiekhaefer Mercury)

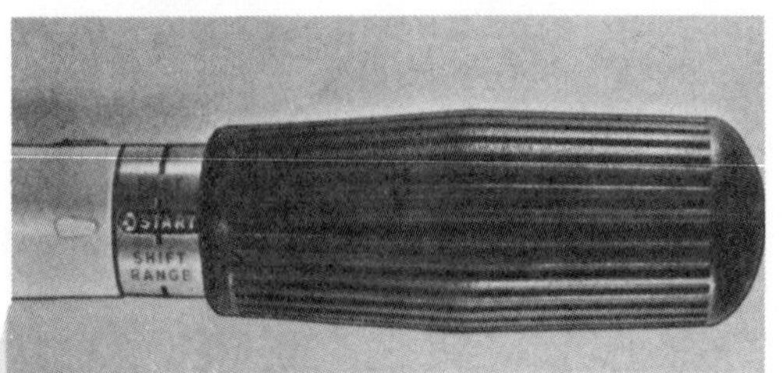
Tiller handle adjustment (Merc 39, 40, 60, 75, and 110—1966–69) (© Kiekhaefer Mercury)

rpm as indicated by a tachometer. At this point, the start position on the twist grip should align with the indicator arrow on the tiller handle.

2. If the twist grip is improperly aligned, loosen the allen screw at the bottom of the twist grip and align it properly.

3. Recheck the adjustment by returning to idle and advancing to the "start" position. This will eliminate possible error on the throttle linkage, caused by play.

NOTE: *This adjustment must be accurate to ensure easy starting with a cold motor.*

Merc 40, 75, and 110 w/ Thunderbolt Ignition (1970)

Timing and Pick-up Adjustment—Merc 40

1. Shift the motor into Forward.

2. Remove the flywheel (see "Powerhead") to expose the points.

3. Rotate the crankshaft to position the contact point cam follower at the high

Checking point gap (Merc 40, 75, and 110—1970) (© Kiekhaefer Mercury)

point of the cam. Adjust the point gap to 0.020 in. and reinstall the flywheel.

4. Turn the twist grip to obtain the maximum stator plate advance. Merc 40 maximum spark advance is not adjustable.

5. Adjust the throttle lever to allow approximately 0.050 in. play between the throttle lever and throttle cam.

6. Remove the spark plug and install a dial indicator or timing tool in the spark plug hole. Timing gauges are available at any well-stocked marine or snowmobile

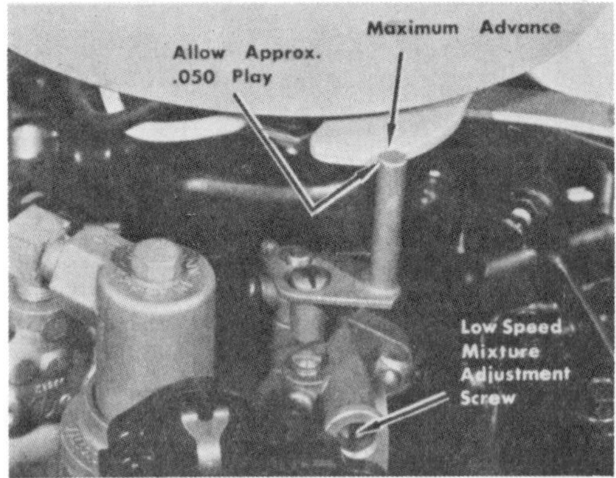

Maximum stator plate advance (Merc 40—1970) (© Kiekhaefer Mercury)

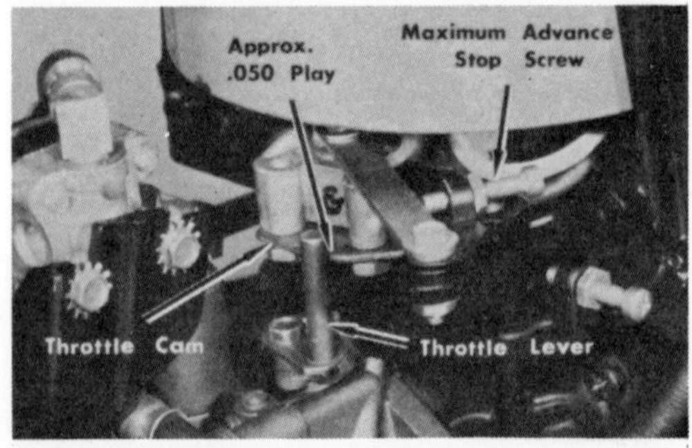

Maximum spark advance (Merc 75 and 110—1970 (© Kiekhaefer Mercury)

outlet; these consist of a barrel which is screwed into the hole and a graduated plunger which moves in the barrel showing the position of the piston, relative to Top Dead Center.

7. Connect a test light to the points. See the introductory chapter for the use of the test light.

8. Rotate the crankshaft clockwise to find TDC, and zero the dial indicator or timing gauge.

9. Rotate the crankshaft to locate the piston at 0.005 in. ATDC. Close the throttle with the twist grip until the test light indicates that the points are just open (light goes out).

10. Adjust the throttle cam to just touch the lever.

11. Remove the test light and dial indicator or timing gauge. Reinstall the spark plug.

Timing and Pick-up Adjustment—Merc 75 and 110

1. Perform steps 1–3 of the preceding procedure.

2. Remove no. 1 (top) spark plug and install a dial indicator or timing gauge in the spark plug hole. Timing gauges are available from any well-stocked marine or snowmobile outlet, and consist of a barrel, which is screwed into the hole, and a graduated plunger, which moves in the barrel showing the position of the piston, relative to Top Dead Center.

3. Rotate the crankshaft clockwise to determine TDC and zero the dial indicator or timing gauge.

Dial indicator installed (© Kiekhaefer Mercury)

4. Rotate the crankshaft counterclockwise to place the piston at 0.193 in. BTDC.

5. Turn the twist grip to open the throttle to the point of maximum spark advance.

6. Connect a test light to the contact points. See the introductory chapter for the use of the test light.

7. Adjust the maximum spark advance screw so that the test light indicates that the points just open (light goes out) when the piston is at 0.193 in. BTDC. Tighten the stop screw locknut.

8. Adjust the throttle lever to allow approximately 0.050 in. play between the throttle lever and throttle cam.

9. Rotate the crankshaft until the piston is placed at 0.002 in. ATDC, as indicated by the dial indicator or timing gauge.

10. With the twist grip, close the throttle until the test light indicates that the points are just open (light goes out). Adjust the throttle cam to just touch the throttle lever.

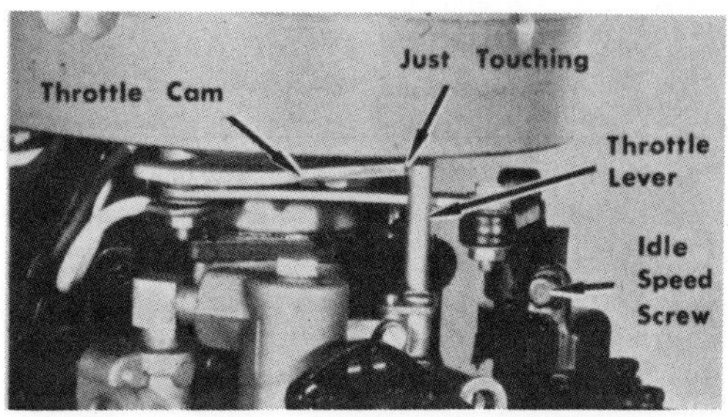

Throttle pick-up adjustment (Merc 40—1970) (© Kiekhaefer Mercury)

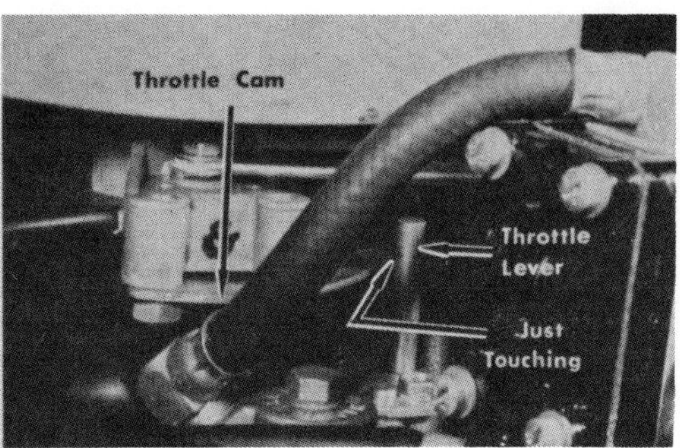

Throttle pick-up adjustment (Merc 75 and 110—1970) (© Kiekhaefer Mercury)

11. Remove the test light and dial indicator or timing gauge. Reinstall the spark plugs.

Maximum Neutral RPM and Tiller Handle Adjustment

NOTE: *Steps 1 and 2 apply to Merc 75 and 110 only.*

1. Shift the motor into Neutral.

2. Adjust the neutral speed limiter stop to obtain a maximum speed of 2400–2700 rpm as indicated on a tachometer.

Maximum neutral rpm adjustment (Merc 75 and 110—1970) (© Kiekhaefer Mercury)

3. With the engine running in Neutral, turn the twist grip to obtain 2400–2700 rpm. At this point the Start position on the twist grip should be aligned with the arrow on the tiller handle.

4. If the twist grip is not properly aligned, loosen the allen screw at the bottom of the tiller handle and properly align the Start position.

5. Recheck the adjustment by returning to idle and advancing the throttle to the Start position. This will eliminate any possible error in the throttle linkage, caused by play.

NOTE: *This adjustment is very important to ensure easy starting with a cold motor.*

Merc 200 w/ Full Gear Shift (1966)

Linkage Adjustment

1. Shift the engine into Neutral and turn the twist grip throttle to the maximum throttle position (in Neutral).

2. Set the throttle lever, on the vertical shaft, until the fore and aft position is obtained. Lock the screw.

Timing and Maximum Spark Advance

1. The flywheel must be removed to set the maximum spark advance.

2. For this operation it is best to spend

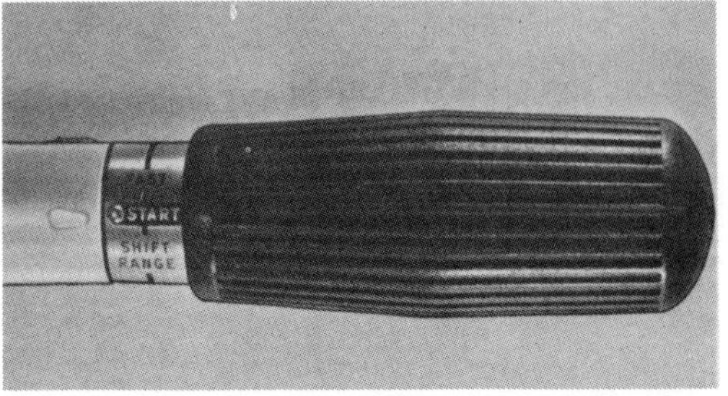

Tiller handle adjustment (Merc 40, 75, and 110—1970) (© Kiekhaefer Mercury)

a few dollars to obtain a timing gauge which threads into the spark plug hole after the plug is removed. This will take the place of the special tool used by dealers to position the piston relative to TDC. These timing gauges are available from any well-stocked marine or snowmobile outlet (with complete instructions).

3. Remove the spark plug from no. 1 (top) cylinder.

4. Install the timing gauge into the spark plug hole.

5. Rotate the crankshaft clockwise until the piston is positioned at 0.275 in. BTDC. Do not move the tool or piston once the setting is established, or else the procedure must be repeated.

6. Connect a test light (see introductory chapter) between the terminal of one set of points and the stator plate (ground).

7. Advance the magneto slowly until the points just break (light goes out).

8. Hold the magneto in this position and adjust the magneto advance stop screw to just touch the magneto stop and tighten the locknut.

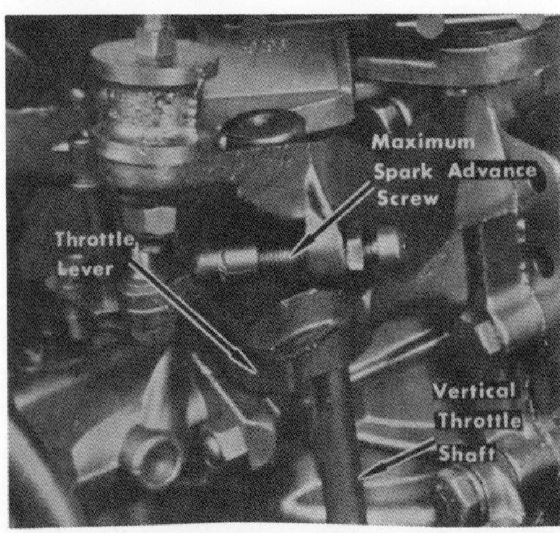

Maximum spark advance (Merc 200—1966) (© Kiekhaefer Mercury)

9. Recheck the magneto advance to ensure proper adjustment.
10. Install the flywheel.

PICK-UP ADJUSTMENT

1. No pick-up adjustment is necessary on this model.

MAXIMUM NEUTRAL RPM ADJUSTMENT

1. Shift the motor into Neutral.
2. Adjust the maximum Neutral speed by loosening the lockscrew and rotating the throttle lever to obtain 2400 rpm with the twist grip rotated against the Neutral stop.
3. Tighten the lockscrew and check the adjustment.

TILLER HANDLE ADJUSTMENT

1. This adjustment is performed in the same manner as on the 1966–69 Merc 110.
2. Turn the twist grip to obtain 2200–2400 rpm as indicated by a tachometer.

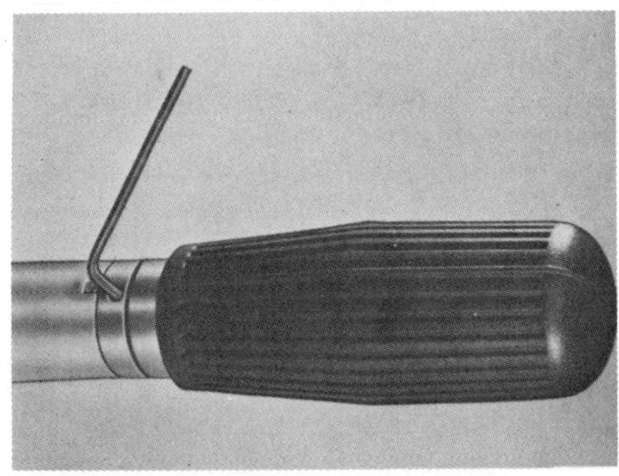

Tiller handle adjustment (Merc 200—1966) (© Kiekhaefer Mercury)

Merc 200 w / Full Gear Shift (1967–69)

MAXIMUM SPARK ADVANCE

1. Remove the flywheel.
2. Obtain a timing gauge described under the section for the 1966 Merc 200.
3. Remove the spark plug from no. 1 (top) cylinder.
4. Install the timing gauge in no. 1 spark plug hole. Set no. 1 piston at 0.375 in. BTDC (to ser no. 2432535) or 0.300 in. BTDC (from ser no. 2432535) by rotating the crankshaft in a clockwise direction.
5. Connect one lead of a test light (see introductory chapter) to no. 1 set of points and the other lead to the stator plate (ground).
6. Shift the motor into Forward.
7. Advance the throttle until the pin on the intermediate magneto lever is positioned as illustrated.

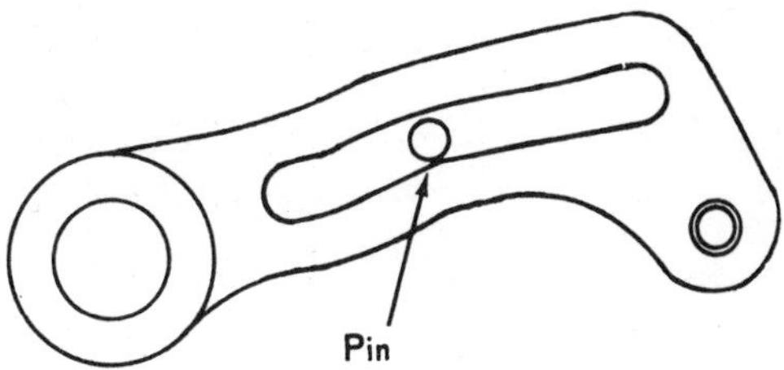

Intermediate magneto lever and pen position (Merc 200—1967–69) (© Kiekhaefer Mercury)

8. No. 1 set of points should open as indicated by the test light when the intermediate magneto lever is positioned as illustrated.

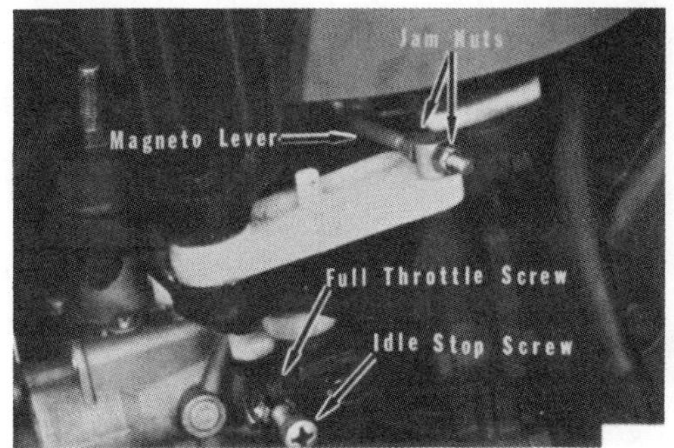

Jam nut location (Merc 200—1967–69) (© Kiekhaefer Mercury)

9. If the points do not open, at this time, loosen the jam nuts on the magneto lever and adjust the lever until the points break. Tighten the jam nuts.
10. Install the flywheel.

FULL THROTTLE SPARK ADVANCE

1. Perform steps 1–5 of the preceding procedure.
2. Back off the full throttle screw.
3. Advance the throttle to the full throttle position.
4. While applying slight pressure to the twist grip, to hold it in the full throttle position, turn in the full throttle screw until the points break as indicated by the test light.
5. Tighten the nut.

6. Advance the throttle against the full throttle stop. The carburetor shutter should be in the full throttle position.

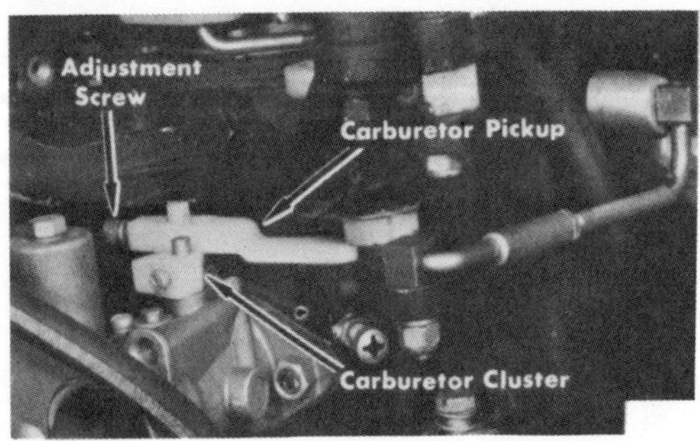

Carburetor pick-up and cluster (Merc 200—1967–69) (© Kiekhaefer Mercury)

7. Adjust the screw in or out to obtain the correct setting.

8. Allow 0.005–0.015 in. play in the carburetor cluster to prevent jamming.

9. Idle the engine and adjust the idle stop screw to obtain 500 rpm in Forward gear.

TILLER HANDLE ADJUSTMENT

1. See the procedure for the 1966–69 Merc 110.

PICK-UP ADJUSTMENT

1. No pick-up adjustment is necessary on this model.

Merc 200 w/ Thunderbolt Ignition (1970–71)

TIMING AND PICK-UP ADJUSTMENT—ENGINE STOPPED

1. Shift the motor into Forward gear.

2. Remove the flywheel to expose the maker points.

3. Rotate the crankshaft to position the cam follower at the high point of the cam. Adjust the point gap to 0.020 in. Repeat the procedure for the second set of points.

4. Reinstall the flywheel.

5. Remove no. 1 spark plug and install a dial indicator or timing gauge as described previously.

6. Rotate the crankshaft clockwise and set no. 1 piston at TDC.

7. Zero the dial indicator or timing gauge.

8. Rotate the crankshaft counterclockwise and set no. 1 piston at 0.196 in. BTDC.

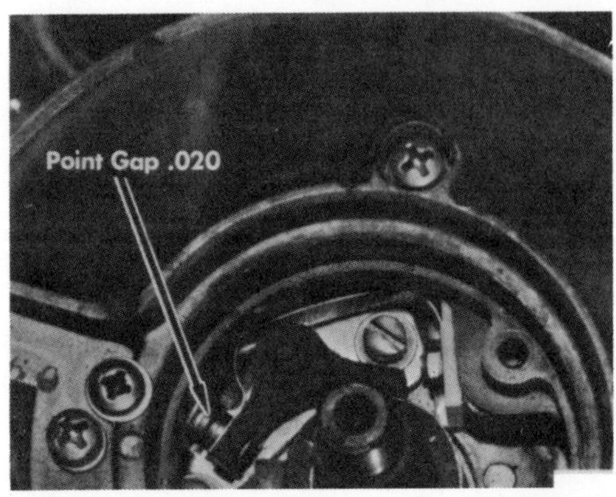

Point gap adjustment (Merc 200—1970–71) (© Kiekhaefer Mercury)

Dial indicator installed (© Kiekhaefer Mercury)

Maximum spark advance (Merc 200—1970–71) (© Kiekhaefer Mercury)

9. Turn the twist grip to open the throttle to maximum spark advance.

10. Connect one lead of a test light (see introductory chapter) to the contact housing arm and the other lead to ground.

11. Adjust the two elastic stop-nuts on the throttle control link rod so that the

light indicates that the points just close when no. 1 piston is at 0.196 in. BTDC.

12. Continue rotating the crankshaft until the dial indicator or timing gauge indicates that no. 1 piston is 0.002 in. BTDC.

13. Close the throttle with the twist grip until the test light indicates that the points just open.

14. Adjust the carburetor pick-up screw until the screw just touches.

Carburetor pick-up screw adjustment (Merc 200—1970–71) (© Kiekhaefer Mercury)

15. Open the twist grip to full throttle.

16. Adjust the upper screw in the vertical shaft while moving the carburetor cluster to obtain 0.035–0.048 in. play between the pick-up screw and the carburetor cluster.

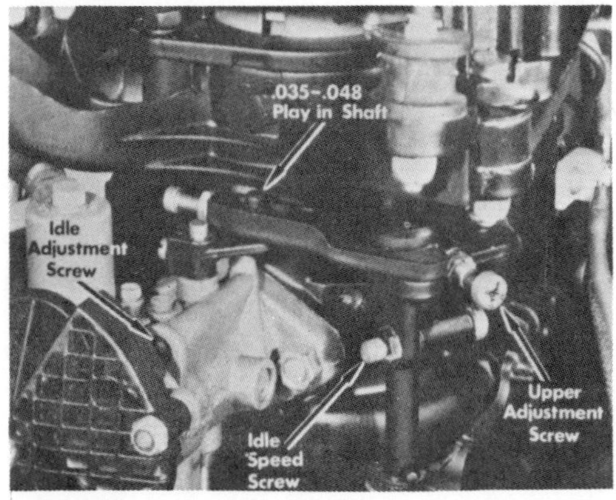

Carburetor cluster adjustment (Merc 200—1970–71) (© Kiekhaefer Mercury)

17. Remove the dial indicator, test light, or timing gauge. Reinstall the spark plugs.

Timing and Pick-up Adjustment—Engine Running

1. Adjust the maker points as described in the preceding procedure.

2. Place the engine in a test tank (or on a boat) and connect the fuel line.

3. Connect a good quality DC timing light to the motor, following the manufacturer's instructions.

4. Start the engine and shine the timing light at the degree markings on the top cowl support frame.

5. Open the throttle with the twist grip to align the timing marks on the flywheel with the 33° BTDC mark on the cowl frame and adjust the two elastic stop nuts on the throttle link rod.

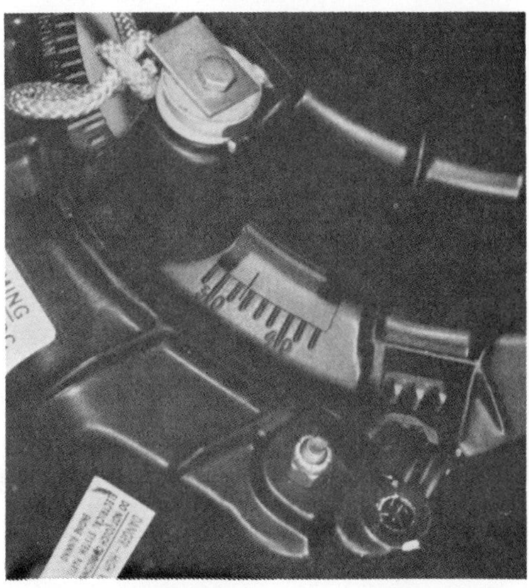

Timing at 33° BTDC (Merc 200—1970–71) (© Kiekhaefer Mercury)

6. Whole holding the timing light in line with the degree markings, close the throttle with the twist grip until the timing mark on the flywheel falls between 1° BTDC and 4° ATDC. Adjust the carburetor pick-up screw until the screw just touches.

Timing mark alignment at 1° BTDC–4° ATDC (Merc 200—1970–71) (© Kiekhaefer Mercury)

7. Stop the engine and remove the timing light.
8. Turn the twist grip to full throttle.
9. Adjust the upper screw in the vertical shaft while moving the carburetor cluster until there is 0.035–0.048 in. play between the pick-up screw and carburetor.

Maximum Neutral RPM and Tiller Handle Adjustment

1. See this adjustment for the 1966–69 Merc 110.

BATTERY MAINTENANCE

Precautions

When charging batteries, an explosive gas forms in each cell. Part of this gas escapes through the vent plugs and may form an explosive atmosphere around the battery in poorly ventilated areas, which may linger for several hours. The following precautions should be observed:

a. Do not smoke near batteries being charged.

b. Do not break live circuits at the battery terminals. Sparks may be caused and ignite the surrounding explosive atmosphere of batteries under charge.

c. Do not reverse the connections to the battery on Thunderbolt ignitions, since the components can be severely damaged.

d. If battery acid contacts the skin, wash immediately with mild soap. If battery acid contacts the eyes, flush immediately with water and see a doctor.

Specific Gravity

See the first chapter of this book for battery procedures relating to specific gravity.

Electrolyte Level

The electrolyte level in the battery should be checked regularly. In hot weather, check it more frequently. If the electrolyte level is found to be low, distilled (or colorless, in an emergency) water should be added to bring the level to about 3/16 in. above the level of the plates. The electrolyte level should never be allowed to fall below the level of the plates.

MANUAL STARTING

Automatic Rewind Starters

Removal

1. Remove the cowling from the motor.
2. Unbolt the three screws securing the automatic rewind housing and remove it from the motor.

Disassembly

1. Pull the handle out of the housing (fully extended) and pry the end cap out of the rubber handle. Tie a knot in the rope to prevent its return into the housing.
2. Remove the cable from the rubber handle and release the cable so that the spring unwinds.
3. Bend down the locktabs on the nut and place a screwdriver in the sheave shaft slot to hold the shaft while removing the nut (left-hand thread).
4. Remove the nut securing the internal parts to the top of the housing.

CAUTION: *When removing the following parts, be sure that the rewind spring does not fly out of the sheave, causing bodily injury. The best practice is to wrap a large heavy cloth around the hand (or wear a heavy glove) and pull the spring out, allowing it to uncoil slowly.*

5. Remove the retainer plate, shaft, starter pawls, wave washers, bushings, spring guide, retainer spring, sheave shaft spacer, wave washer, and wave washer retainer.
6. Remove the cable from the sheave by unwinding and twisting the end near the anchor one-half turn.

Assembly

1. Replace the starter cable in the starter sheave by attaching the anchor end of the cable in the slot. Slide in sideways and twist one-half turn after the anchor is in the hole.
2. Wind the cable on the sheave (clockwise) working from the bottom of the sheave. Leave enough free end to insert through the starter housing opening.
3. Place the sheave in a vise and engage the outer loop of the spring in the slot of the spring recess in the sheave.
4. Wind counterclockwise until the spring is in place.
5. Install the spring guide bushing on the sheave hub, with the chamfered end toward the sheave.
6. Install the spring retainer on top of the spring and engage the inner loop in the anchor pin of the spring retainer plate.
7. Lubricate the spring and spring guide bushing.

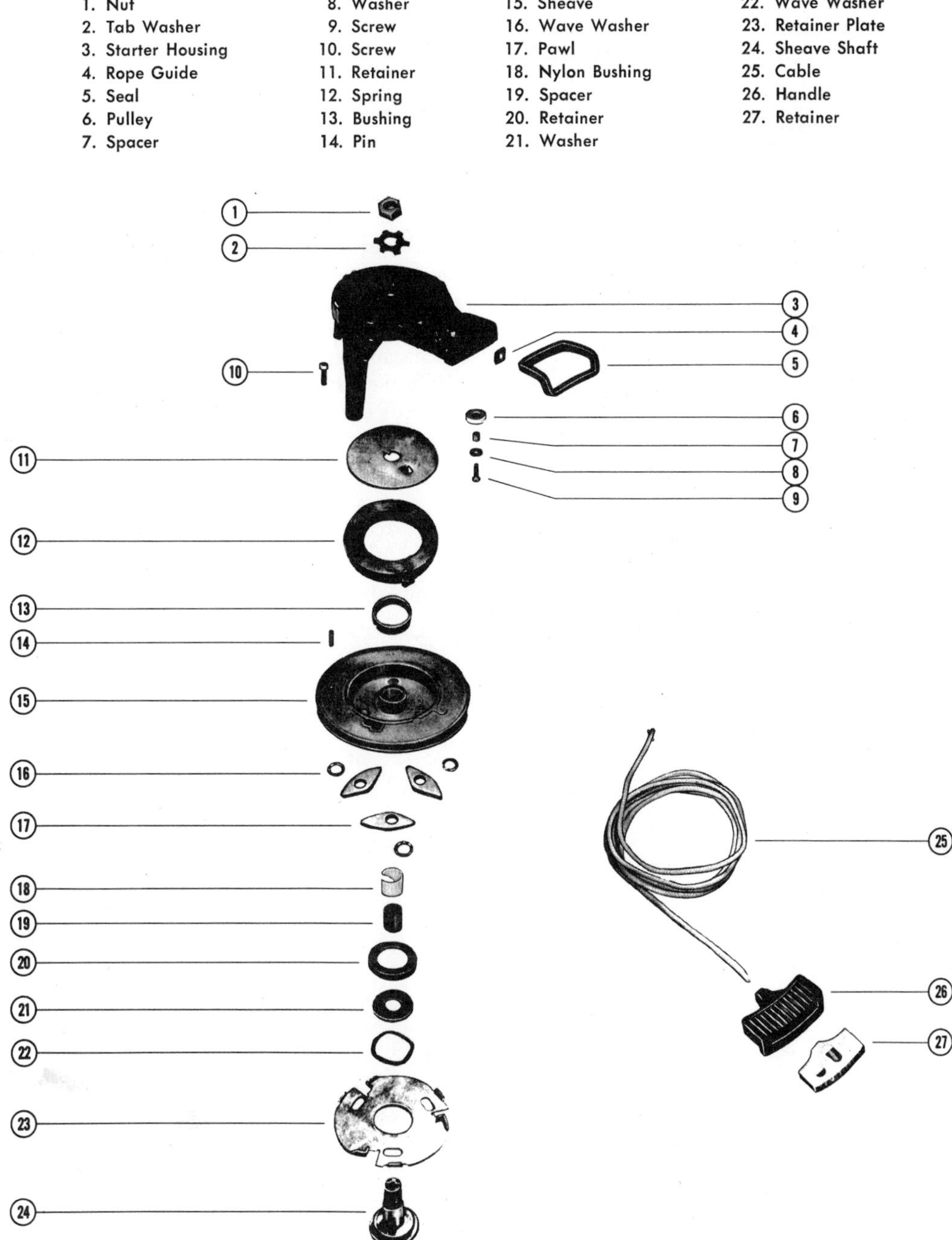

Exploded view of automatic rewind starter mechanism (© Kiekhaefer Mercury)

8. Assemble the starter pawl to the sheave with the identification mark side toward the rim of the sheaves.

9. Mount the three starter pawl wave washers on the anchor pins and place the starter pawls on top of the pins. Lubricate all parts as they are being installed. Be careful when installing the pawls; they are all installed the same way. The radii of the pawls are to follow the radius of the pawl retainer plate.

10. Install the sheave shaft spacer on the sheave shaft.

11. Install the wave washer retainer with the cupped end up.

12. Place the washer equalizer ring into the cup and set the wave washer and pawl retainer plate in position.

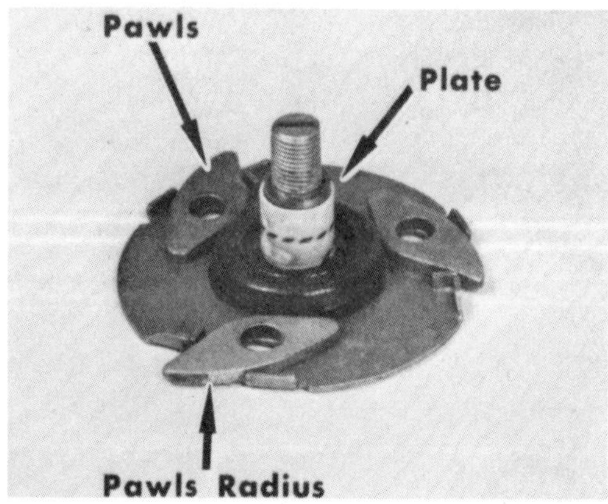

Installing the starter pawls (© Kiekhaefer Mercury)

13. Be sure that the pawls extend through the slots in the sides and insert the sheave shaft so that the keyway goes through the spring retainer notch.

14. Insert the sheave shaft through the pawl retainer plate assembly and sheave.

15. Insert the free end of the starter cable through the outlet in the starter housing and tie a temporary knot about one foot from the end of the cable.

16. Place the sheave assembly (sheave shaft up) into the starter housing.

17. Install the lockwasher and nut (left-hand thread) on the sheave shaft.

18. Untie the temporary knot and insert the cable through the starter handle end cap.

19. Install the cable into the starter handle as illustrated.

20. Pull the cable and end cap into the handle.

21. Turn the sheave shaft counterclockwise with a screwdriver until the handle is against the guide bushing. Turn an additional $1\frac{1}{4}$ turns to wind the spring to the correct tension.

22. Tighten the nut on the sheave shaft while keeping the screwdriver in the slot to prevent the spring from unwinding.

23. Lock the nut in place with the lockwasher tabs (bend one up and one down).

24. Replace the cover and secure it with a small screw.

25. Pull the cord several times to be sure that the mechanism operates correctly. Pull the cord out to full length to be sure that it will not stick.

Installation

1. Installation is the reverse of removal.

Powerhead

Specific repair procedures vary between individual models, but basic repair instructions are similar for all Mercury outboard powerheads. The powerhead consists of cylinder block and crankcase, crankshaft and center main bearing, connecting rod and piston, crankcase end caps, manifold covers, and cylinder block covers.

Cleanliness is of the utmost importance when working on the powerhead. All components must be inspected and cleaned before assembly. Refer often to the lubrication and torque charts.

ALL MODELS (1 AND 2 CYLINDER)

Removal

1. Remove the front panel (if applicable). Remove the cowling.

2. Pull out the starter rope and tie a knot to hold it. Remove the rope handle.

Removing the starter rope handle (© Kiekhaefer Mercury)

3. Remove the three nuts and top cowl on the Merc 200.

4. Remove the two nuts holding the fuel line adaptor to the bottom cowl.

5. Remove the bolts securing the mounting bracket to the bottom cowl.

6. Remove the water discharge hose from the bottom cowl outlet.

7. Remove three screws and the driveshaft housing cover.

8. Remove the nuts holding the powerhead to the driveshaft housing.

9. Loosen the powerhead from the bottom cowl.

10. Remove the powerhead from the driveshaft housing.

Installation

1. Install new gaskets on the driveshaft housing and adaptor and install the powerhead on the bottom cowl and driveshaft housing. Torque to specifications.

2. Install the discharge hose, magneto actuator linkage mounting bracket, and fuel line adaptor.

3. Connect the shut-off switch wires and magneto ground wires to the terminal block.

4. Install the driveshaft cowling, top cowl, and side cowl.

Flywheel

Removal

1. With the powerhead mounted on a stand, remove the flywheel nut and washer.

2. Attach a puller to the flywheel, using the screwholes in the top of the flywheel to secure the puller.

3. If the flywheel is exceptionally tight, tap on the center screw with a hammer.

4. Remove the flywheel key from the crankshaft.

Installation

1. With the stator in place on the powerhead, install the flywheel key on the crankshaft. Tap to seat it.

2. Install the flywheel, aligning the key and keyway.

3. Install the washer and flywheel nut. Torque to specifications.

Upper and Lower End Cap Assemblies

Removal

1. Remove the screws securing the end caps to the crankcase and cylinder block.

2. Remove the end cap lockscrews and tab washers.

3. Using a suitable puller, remove the end cap with even pressure.

4. Pry the end cap oil seals out with a screwdriver.

5. Remove the ball bearing and roller bearing from the end cap with a ball bearing puller.

Cleaning and Inspection

1. Needle bearings should be replaced when rusted or at each overhaul. Caged needle bearings should also be replaced at each overhaul, or when they become wet or rusted.

2. Clean and air-dry the ball bearings before checking them. Do not use compressed air to dry the bearings as this has a tendency to spin the bearings.

3. Check the bearings for excessive play between the inner and outer races. Lubricate the bearings with oil and spin them slowly by hand. There should be no rough spots and the bearing should exhibit a smooth action. If it does not, replace the bearing with a new one.

4. Inspect the oil seals for leaking or damaged lips and replace them as necessary.

IMPORTANT: *Always press in cartridge-type needle bearings with the lettered side up. Check the bearings after installation to be sure that they move freely.*

Installation

1. Slip the ball bearing onto the crankshaft and seat it in place against the lower shoulder of the crankshaft. Install the shims, if any were removed.

2. Install the two oil seals on the crankshaft with the lips facing downward and the plate spacer on the crankshaft with the notches toward the bottom.

NOTE: *Smaller horsepower models have only one oil seal and no spacer.*

3. Replace the oil seal in the upper end cap using a tool of equal diameter. This should be pressed in with an arbor press.

4. Install the roller bearing.

5. Replace the ball bearing, using an arbor press or other suitable press. Be sure that the bearing is not cocked.

6. Install the oil seal.

7. Temporarily install the end cap on the crankshaft, being careful not to damage the oil seal.

8. Tap the end cap down so that it seats against the end of the cylinder block. Install the retaining screws and check the end-play between the crankshaft bearing journal thrust face and the inner race of the ball bearings. Tap the crankshaft either way to be sure of a true reading. The end-play should be 0.008–0.012 in.

9. If too much end-play registers, re-

move the shims; if too little end-play exists, add shims. It is important that shims be equally spaced between the upper and lower ball bearings to keep the connecting rod journal centerlines in the center of the cylinder bore.

Reed Block (1 Cylinder Models)

REMOVAL

1. The reed block can be removed without removing the powerhead.
2. Remove the strainer cover from the carburetor and remove the carburetor mounting nuts.
3. Disengage the choke lever from the choke shutter by pulling the choke lever forward.
4. Remove the carburetor. Tilt it toward the port side of the engine and pull it forward.
5. Remove the reed block by pulling it forward, off the carburetor mounting studs.

INSPECTION

1. Check to be sure that all of the reeds lie flat.
2. Be sure that no reeds are broken or warped.

INSTALLATION

1. Refer to the accompanying illustration for correct installation and assembly of the reeds. Care must be taken to be sure that the reeds are centered and square with the reed block.

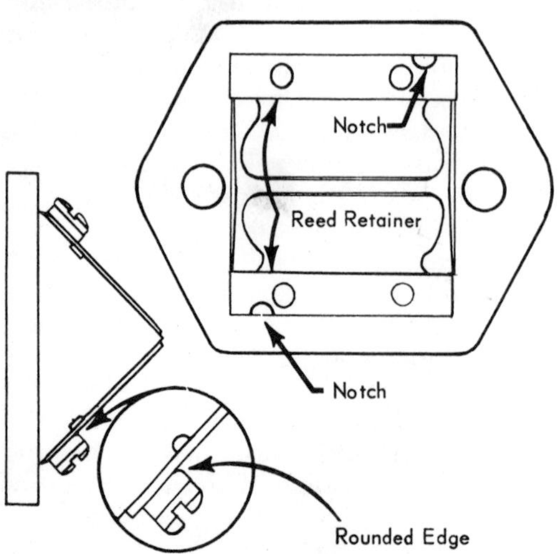

Reeds centered and square with the reed block (© Kiekhaefer Mercury)

2. The reeds have an identification notch. Install the reed with the notch positioned as shown. The rounded edge of the reed retainer should be toward the reed to prevent breakage.
3. Late Merc 39 models have both the reed and reed retainer notched. Install the reeds and reed retainers as shown.

Separating Crankcase and Cylinder Block—All Models

DISASSEMBLY

1. Remove the powerhead and flywheel.
2. Remove the exhaust manifold cover plate and remove the cover and baffle plate.
3. Remove the cylinder block covers and intake deflectors.

NOTE: *These covers do not have to be removed unless cleaning of the exhaust and water cooling chambers is desired.*

4. Remove the upper end cap.
5. Remove all nuts securing the crankcase to the cylinder block.
6. Remove the lower end cap.
7. Separate the crankcase from the cylinder block by prying the two apart at the special recesses provided.

Separating the crankcase and cylinder block (© Kiekhaefer Mercury)

8. Remove the crankshaft, piston, and connecting rod assembly.

CLEANING AND INSPECTION

1. Inspect the cylinder block for cracks and general condition.
2. Remove carbon and varnish with a fine wire wheel attached to an electric drill.
3. Finish-hone the cylinder walls slightly to seat new rings.

4. On engines which display evidence of overheating, check the bore for an out-of-round condition, using an inside micrometer. If the bore exceeds 0.005–0.006 in. out of round, bore the cylinders 0.015 in. oversize and install oversize pistons. This operation should be done only by Kiekhaefer Mercury or a well-equipped machine shop with qualified personnel.

Finish Honing

1. Follow the manufacturer's directions for use of the hone and lubrication during honing.

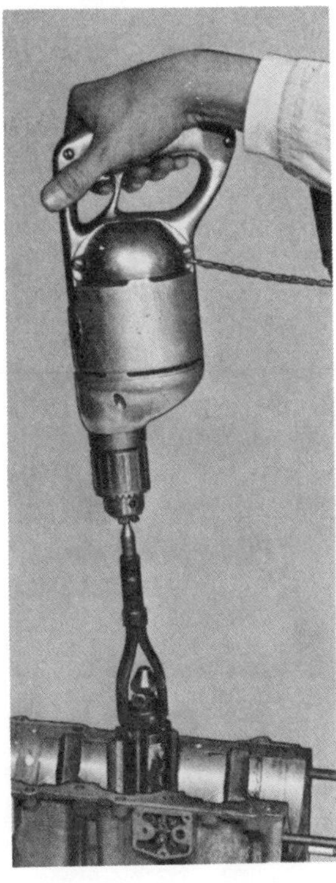

Finish honing the cylinder block (© Kiekhaefer Mercury)

2. Start stroking at the smallest diameter. Maintain firm stone pressure against the cylinder walls.

3. Localize the stroking at the smallest diameter until the drill speed is constant throughout the length of the bore. Stroke at a rate of thirty complete cycles per minute to produce the best crosshatch pattern. Expand the stone as necessary to compensate for stock removal and stone wear.

4. Use a coarse grit for the roughing operation. The softer the material, the coarser the grit that can be used for roughing. Leave approximately 0.002 in. for finishing cast iron.

5. For the finishing operation, finer grit stones are used to bring the cylinder to the desired size and to produce the desired finish.

6. For best results, a continuous flow of honing oil should be pumped into the work. If this is not practical, apply oil generously and frequently with an oil can.

7. After honing, clean the cylinder bores with hot water and detergent. Scrub them well and rinse with hot water. Bores should be swabbed several times with light engine oil and wiped with a clean, dry cloth. Do not clean with kerosine or gasoline.

Assembly

1. Install the crankshaft, piston, and connecting rod assembly.

2. Coat the joint face of the crankcase with gasket sealer for good metal-to-metal contact.

3. Set the crankcase over the cylinder block, insert the bolts, and attach nuts and washers. Do not tighten them.

4. Install the center main bearing locking screws, with tab washer, through the respective hole in the crankcase, to hold the center main bearing.

5. Align the opening of the valve-type center main bearing with that of the crankcase fuel intake opening, so that they are evenly centered.

6. Start tightening with A and follow with B roller-type center main. (See illustration in "Tightening Sequences.")

7. Crimp the locktab washers after torqueing to specification.

8. Install the end caps, being careful not to damage the oil seal. Coat the face of the O-ring with New Multipurpose Lubricant. Check crankshaft end-play.

9. Place the proper screws in the end cap, but do not tighten them.

10. Tighten the crankcase bolts, according to the appropriate illustration in the specifications section, to the proper torque figure.

11. Tighten the end cap screws evenly.

12. Rotate the crankshaft several times to be sure that all parts in the powerhead are free to move.

13. Install the intake port covers and cylinder block cover. Use new gaskets before installing.

Checking crankshaft end-play (© Kiekhaefer Mercury)

14. The intake port covers have a beveled face toward the front of the intake passage toward the crankcase. Install the gasket on the manifold and baffle plate. Install the gasket for the outside cover.

15. Tighten the cylinder block covers and exhaust manifold screws, using the appropriate illustration in the specifications. Torque to the proper figure.

Pistons—All Models

Removal

1. Perform steps 1–7 of "Separating the Crankcase and Cylinder Block" (disassembly).

Power dome-type piston (© Kiekhaefer Mercury)

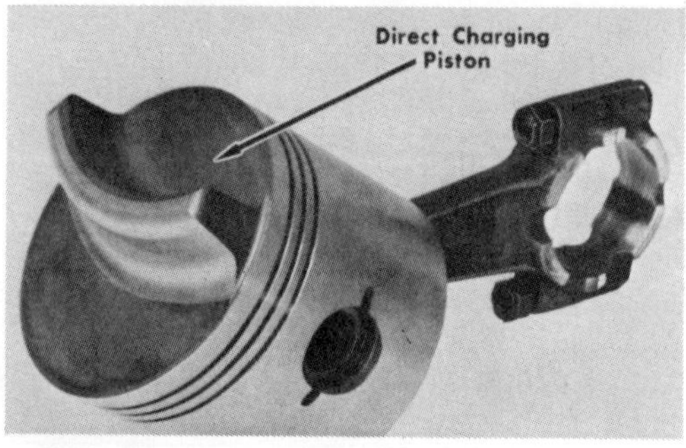

Direct charging type piston (© Kiekhaefer Mercury)

2. Punch-mark or otherwise identify each piston and cylinder so that the piston can be returned to its original cylinder.

3. Remove the crankshaft and the piston and connecting rod assembly from the cylinder block.

4. Remove the piston rings from the pistons using a piston ring expander.

5. Do not attempt to disassemble the lockrings and wrist pins from the piston. A special tool is needed to hold the wrist pin bearings in place.

Cleaning and Inspection

1. Check the pistons for scoring and cracking.

2. Inspect the ring grooves for wear, burn, and distortion. It is recommended practice, when piston rings are removed, to install new ones.

3. Before replacing piston rings, clean the grooves in the pistons. Varnish and carbon deposits should be removed from the top of the piston with a soft, wire brush.

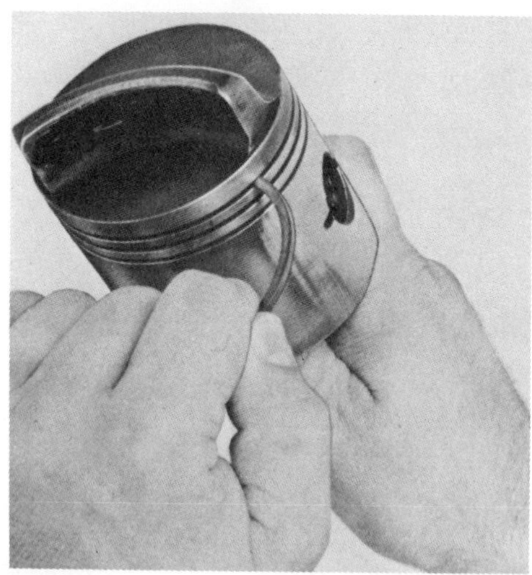

Clearing piston ring grooves (© Kiekhaefer Mercury)

4. To assure positive seating of the piston rings, hone or deglaze the cylinders when the pistons are removed.

5. Remove burrs from the piston skirt by polishing with crocus cloth.

6. If the engine has been submerged, check the wrist pin and boss. In the event of submersion, it will probably be necessary to remove the wrist pin by removing the locktabs on each end and driving the wrist pin out with a soft drift.

NOTE: *Wrist pins are not sold separately.*

7. Pistons that are 0.015 in. oversize are available from Mercury for installation to overbored cylinders. It is recommended that cylinders be rebored 0.015 in. oversize if score marks exceed 0.0075 in. in depth.

INSTALLATION

1. Installation is the reverse of removal. A piston ring compressor should be used when installing the piston and ring assemblies into the cylinder. Be sure that the crankshaft is installed correctly. If a piston ring compressor is not available, carefully compress the piston rings by hand.

Checking piston rings when installed (© Kiekhaefer Mercury)

Connecting Rods

REMOVAL FROM CRANKSHAFT

1. Remove the crankshaft and the piston and connecting rod assembly from the cylinder block as detailed above.

2. Remove the connecting rod locknuts, allowing separation of the connecting rod from the rod cap.

NOTE: *Mark the front of the pistons and, immediately after removing the connecting rods from the crankshaft, rematch the rod and cap, observing the raised matchmarks on the side of the rod and cap. It is also good practice to number the connecting rods, so that they are returned to their original crankshaft journals.*

3. Remove the connecting rods from the crankshaft.

CLEANING AND INSPECTION

1. Check for rust (explained under "Crankshaft").

2. Check rods for alignment by placing the rods on a flat surface. If light can be seen under any part of the machined surface, the rod is probably bent and should be replaced.

3. It is necessary that all bearings be kept separate and returned to the original connecting rod. This is especially true of the Merc 1250.

4. Do not attempt to clean Merc 1250 connecting rods by polishing them.

5. Do not polish the crankshaft journals.

INSTALLATION ON THE CRANKSHAFT

1. Open the matched connecting rod and cap, one at a time.

2. Place a small amount of New Multipurpose Lubricant on each half of the connecting rod bearing race to hold the bearing in place. Do not mix bearings from different connecting rods.

3. Place the bearing retainer race in the connecting rod, where applicable.

4. Install the roller bearings around each side for assembly. Always count roller bearings to be sure that none have been lost. Never intermix new and old roller bearings in the same connecting rod.

5. Install the connecting rod cap so that the knob markings match perfectly.

6. Install the connecting rod nuts and torque them to specification.

7. After torqueing the nuts, rotate the connecting rod to be sure that it rotates freely. If it rotates roughly, remove the rod

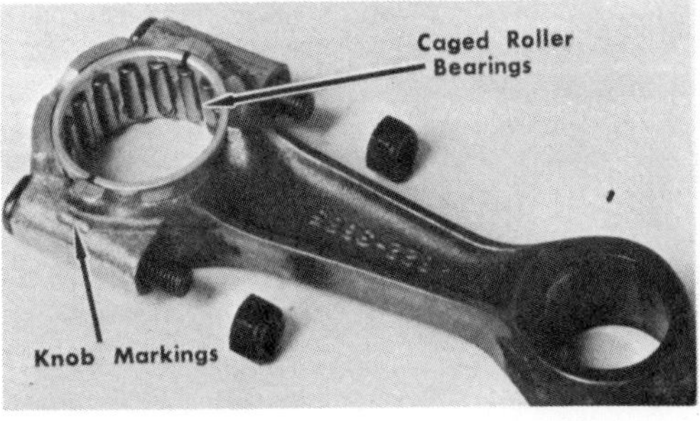

Connecting rod with caged roller bearings (© Kiekhaefer Mercury)

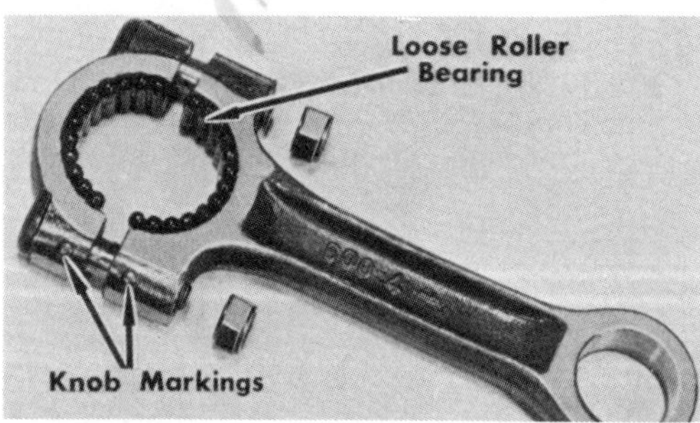

Connecting rod with loose roller bearings (© Kiekhaefer Mercury)

and check the bearing race and rollers.

8. Repeat the procedure for the other rods.

9. Always recheck the matchmarks (knob markings) on the rod to assure a correct and perfect match.

Center Main Bearing

Reed Valve and Valve Cage

Removal

1. Remove the crankshaft.
2. The reed valve-type center main bearing can be removed by extracting the two phillips head screws securing the assembly. Be careful not to bend or distort the reed valves or reed valve stops.
3. Rematch the bearing halves immediately after removal.
4. Remove the reed valves and reed valve stops by removing the cap screws.

Cleaning and Inspection

1. Be sure that the inside diameter is not sprung.
2. Check the wear from the reed valves on face of the block.
3. Resurface the reed valve cage on a lapping plate after removing the locating pins.
4. Inspect for bent, chipped, or damaged reeds.

Adjustment

1. When replacing reed valves on the bearing, be sure that the left reed valve is set on the left side and the right reed on the right side. Right and left are determined by viewing from the point end of the valve stop.
2. Adjust the reeds on the center main bearing so that the reeds are set squarely over their respective openings and are at "no preload." This means that the reed valves should not adhere tightly to the seat, but have a slight opening, never more than 0.007 in.
3. Tighten the reed stop screws.

Reed valve stop setting (© Kiekhaefer Mercury)

4. Check all reed valves for the proper opening. See the specifications section. Always check for proper opening. Excessive opening can cause breakage and minimal opening can cause fuel starvation at high rpm.

Installation

1. Lubricate with New Multipurpose Lubricant.
2. When installing, align the locking screw holes in the crankcase cover and bearing.
3. Replace the bearing and reed valve cage on the crankshaft. Tighten the two screws to assure a tight fit.
4. Recheck the reed valve clearance.
5. Install the crankshaft as detailed.
6. Install the reed block gasket and reed block on the carburetor mounting studs.
7. Install the carburetor gasket.
8. Tilt the carburetor toward the port side and engage the mounting flange with the port stud. Tilt the carburetor down so that the slotted mounting hole is completely down on the stud.

   NOTE: *If the carburetor is not completely engaged with the mounting stud, difficulty will arise when trying to synchronize the linkage.*
9. Install and tighten the carburetor mounting nuts.
10. Pull the choke lever forward and engage it with the choke shutter.
11. Install the strainer and strainer cover and tighten the retaining screws.

Center Main Bearing—All Models

REMOVAL

1. Bearing halves are machine-mated and should not be intermixed.
2. Remove the crankshaft.
3. Remove the screws which hold the bearing halves together.
4. Separate the bearing halves from the crankshaft. The rear half of the bearing has a dowel pin holding the inner race of the bearing. Tap lightly to remove.

Removing and installing center main bearing outer race (© Kiekhaefer Mercury)

Removing and installing center main bearing rollers (© Kiekhaefer Mercury)

5. Remove the lockring from the inner races.
6. Separate the inner races, being careful to catch all of the roller bearings.

CLEANING AND INSPECTION

1. Needle bearings should always be replaced at overhaul or whenever rust is present.
2. Inspect the oil seals for leaking or damaged lips.

ASSEMBLY

1. Lubricate the inner races of the bearing with New Multipurpose Lubricant.
2. Space the roller bearings equally around the inner bearing races. Be sure that all the bearings are replaced.
3. Install the bearings and inner race over the crankshaft and install the snap-rings around the races.
4. Rotate several times to be sure that the roller bearings do not bind.
5. Place the dowel in position and install the bearing halves on the inner race.
6. Install the bearing with the word "top" uppermost. This will allow the internal bleed systems to function.
7. Install the screws and tighten securely.

Lower Unit

The lower unit consists of the motor leg (long or short model) which houses the driveshaft, water pump, and water tubes. The gear housing is located immediately below the motor leg and houses the pinion gears and propeller shaft, which turn the propeller. The lower units for Merc 39, 40, 60, 75, 110, and 200 are virtually identical, except for minor differences in isolated cases.

GEAR HOUSING

Removal

1. Drain the lubricant from the gear housing by removing the filler hole screw and vent screw. Do not lose the washers under the screws. Replace the washers and screws after draining.
2. Remove the propeller.
3. Remove the locknut from the leading edge of the gear housing.
4. Remove the locknut from the center bottom side of the cavitation plate. On Merc 200's, remove the anode plate.

5. Separate the gear housing from the driveshaft housing (motor leg).

Installation—Short Shaft Models

1. If the water intake-to-powerhead tube was removed with the gear housing, coat the upper end of the tube with New Multipurpose Quicksilver Lubricant and slip it into the rubber seal in the bottom cowl. Be sure it enters the recess in the powerhead.
2. Lubricate the bottom end of the water tube with New Multipurpose Lubricant.
3. Apply a heavy coat of New Multipurpose Lubricant to the driveshaft splines.
4. Be sure that the shift lever and the lower unit are in Forward gear.
5. Insert the driveshaft into the driveshaft housing and align the water tube with the water pump body outlet. Align the driveshaft splines with the crankshaft and slide into place while joining the housings.

   NOTE: *Be sure that the water intake tube enters the plastic guide in the water pump body guide and the rubber seal in the water pump cover.*
6. Move the shift control lever into Neutral and Forward to be sure that the lower shift shaft splines are engaged.
7. Pull lightly on the starter rope to rotate the propeller shaft. This will allow the driveshaft splines to enter the crankshaft.
8. Install and tighten the elastic stop nuts.

Installation—Long Shaft Models

1. On early models, if the nylon block was dislodged the powerhead must be removed to install the nylon block on the driveshaft of long-shaft models. On later models, the nylon block is secured by a screw.
2. Remove the powerhead.
3. Perform steps 1 and 2 of the preceding procedure.
4. Insert the driveshaft part way into the driveshaft housing.
5. Reach through the exhaust opening on the bottom cowl and install the nylon block on the driveshaft.
6. Join the gear housing and driveshaft housing.
7. Be sure that the water intake tube enters the plastic water tube guide in the water pump body recess and the rubber seal in the water pump cover.
8. Shift the motor into Neutral and Forward to be sure that the lower shift shaft splines are aligned.
9. Install and tighten the elastic stop nuts.
10. Before installing the powerhead, check to be sure that the nylon block is wedged lightly between the driveshaft housing and the driveshaft. The radius side of the block should face the rear of the engine.
11. Lubricate the driveshaft splines with a heavy coat of New Multipurpose Lubricant.
12. Install the powerhead.
13. Turn the flywheel to seat the driveshaft and crankshaft splines.
14. Reinstall the anode plate if applicable.
15. Refill the gearcase with new lubricant.

Propeller Installation—All Models

1. Place the collar guide into the propeller hub, with the shoulder in the recess of the propeller.

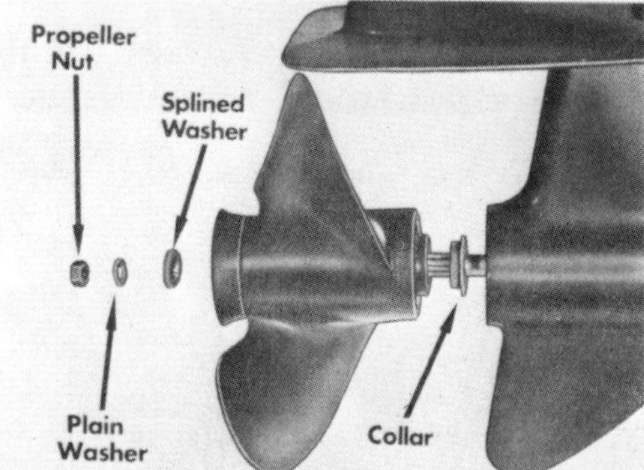

Propeller removal and installations (© Kiekhaefer Mercury)

2. Lubricate the propeller shaft splines.
3. Slide the propeller onto the shaft aligning the splines.
4. Replace the splined washer, plain washer, and propeller nut. Tighten the nut.

Water Pump

Removal

1. Remove the gear housing and position it upright in a vise with soft jaws.
2. Remove the driveshaft O-ring and centrifugal slinger from the driveshaft.
3. Unbolt and remove the water pump body assembly.

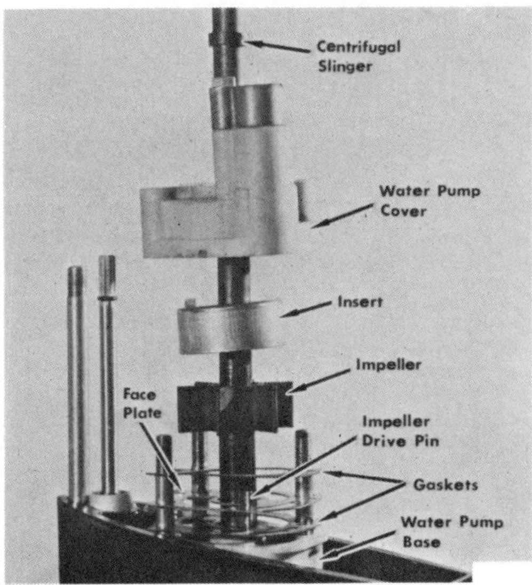

Exploded view of water pump components (© Kiekhaefer Mercury)

4. Remove the water pump cover and water pump face plate.
5. Remove the impeller and impeller drive pin.
6. Check the impeller and water pump insert closely for wear or damage.
7. Remove the water pump base assembly and water intake tube.
8. Remove the O-ring and oil seal from the base plate assembly and watch for shims under the base assembly.

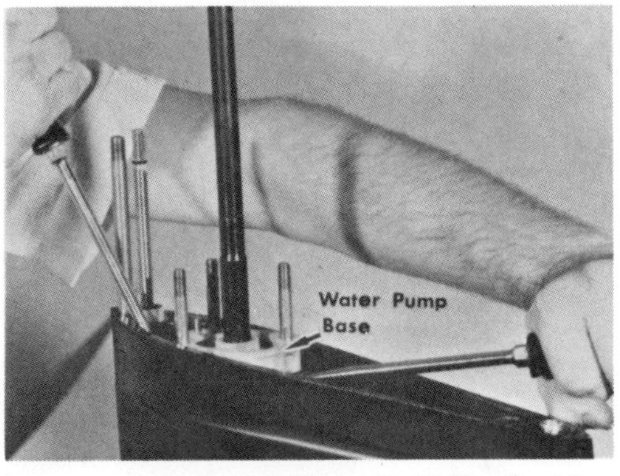

Removing water pump base (© Kiekhaefer Mercury)

INSTALLATION

1. Install the water pump base assembly in the gear housing.
2. There should be no play between the bearing and water pump base assembly. Depress the base assembly and place a feeler gauge between the gear housing and water pump body. If the measured gap is 0.010 in., remove a 0.010 in. shim. If the measured gap is 0.005 in., remove a 0.005 in. shim. This will produce a zero gap which should not be altered.
3. Insert the stainless steel water pump cartridge into the pump body.
4. Place the drive pin in the driveshaft, holding it in position with a dab of New Multipurpose Lubricant.
5. Check the condition of the impeller and install a new one if the blades are worn or cracked.
6. Turn the driveshaft clockwise, at the same time seating the impeller. Be sure that the drive pin engages the groove of the impeller.
7. Install the stainless steel face plate, wave washer, water pump cover assembly, and water intake tube.
8. Install the two locknuts and tighten them evenly.
9. Install the plastic water tube guide in the pump body recess.
10. Install the driveshaft slinger and driveshaft O-ring.
11. Check the forward gear backlash (at least 0.003–0.005 in.) between the forward gear and the pinion gear. If it is too tight, remove the forward gear shim until the correct backlash is obtained. If too little, add shims until it is correct. The gears should fully engage each other the length of the tooth. Shimming of the driveshaft ball bearing may be necessary to obtain the correct backlash if this cannot be accomplished by shimming the forward gear.

4 · Outboard Marine Corporation (Evinrude and Johnson)

Introduction

The first Outboard Marine Corporation (OMC) outboard motor was designed by one of the founders of the corporation in 1909. In 1921, OMC engineers designed and patented the first propeller to incorporate thru-hub exhaust. A year later, in 1922, model "A," Johnson's first production outboard was introduced, a two-cylinder model developing two horsepower. Johnson introduced their first single-cylinder production model, the J—25 in 1929. The J—25 developed the magnificent total of 1.5 horsepower, but more importantly, provided the design breakthrough to single-cylinder outboards.

There are many notable design features on the present line of smaller OMC out-

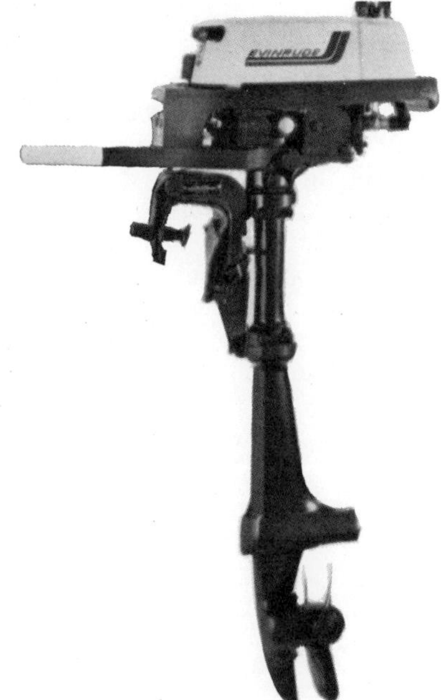

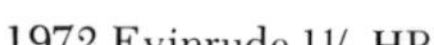
1972 Evinrude 1½ HP

1972 Evinrude 9½ HP

1972 Evinrude 18 HP

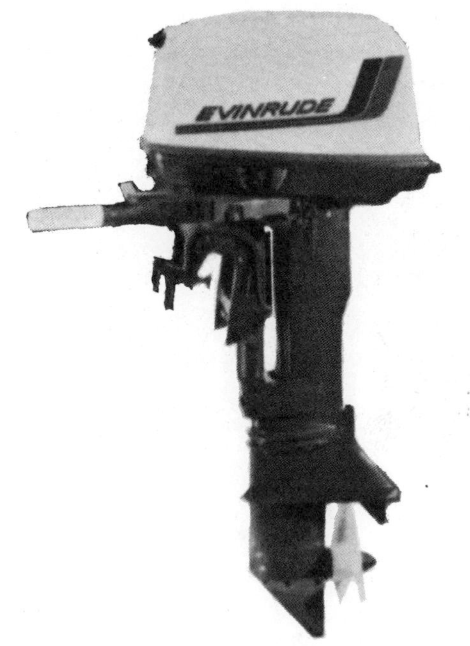

1972 Evinrude 25 HP

1972 Johnson 2 HP

1972 Johnson 4 HP

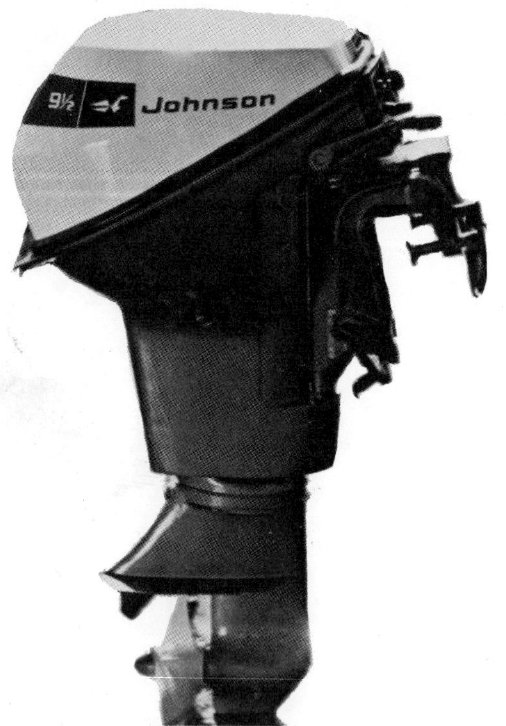

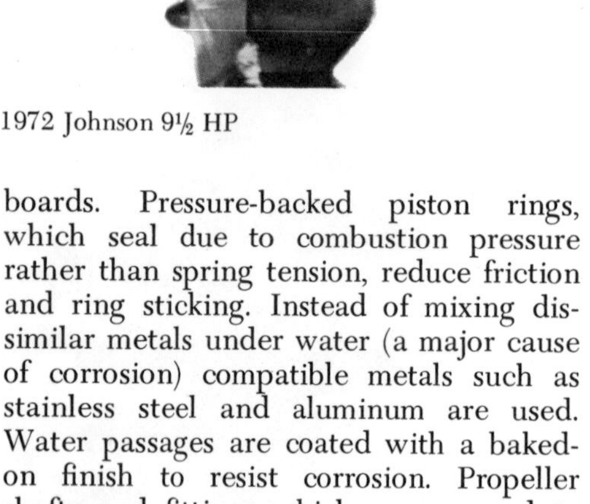

1972 Johnson 9½ HP

1972 Johnson 20 HP

boards. Pressure-backed piston rings, which seal due to combustion pressure rather than spring tension, reduce friction and ring sticking. Instead of mixing dissimilar metals under water (a major cause of corrosion) compatible metals such as stainless steel and aluminum are used. Water passages are coated with a baked-on finish to resist corrosion. Propeller shafts and fittings which are exposed to salt water are made from stainless steel.

The service procedures contained in this chapter have been compiled from Evinrude service manuals, since service procedures for Evinrude and Johnson outboards are virtually identical. Some relatively minor specifications vary between the two manufacturers, but otherwise, service procedures and specifications remain common to each.

Model Identification

Year	*Model (hp)*	*No. of Cyls*	*Displacement (cu in.)*
1966	3	2	5.28
	5	2	8.84
	6	2	8.84
	9.5	2	15.2
	18	2	22.0
1967	3	2	5.28
	5	2	8.84
	6	2	8.84
	9.5	2	15.2
	18	2	22.0
1968	1.5	1	2.64
	3	2	5.28
	5	2	8.84
	6	2	8.84
	9.5	2	15.2
	18	2	22.0
1969	1.5	1	2.64

Year	*Model (hp)*	*No. of Cyls*	*Displacement (cu in.)*
1969	4	2	5.28
	6	2	8.84
	9.5	2	15.2
	18	2	22.0
	25	2	22.0
1970	1.5	1	2.64
	4	2	5.28
	6	2	8.84
	9.5	2	15.2
	18	2	22.0
	25	2	22.0
1971	2	1	2.64
	4	2	5.28
	6	2	8.84
	9.5	2	15.2
	18	2	22.0
	25	2	22.0

General Engine Specifications

Year	Model (hp)	HP (OBC) (@ rpm)	Full Throttle rpm Range	Bore (in.)	Stroke (in.)	Carburetion	Fuel/Oil Ratio①
1966	3	3.0 @ 4000	3500–4500	1.5625	1.3750	1—bbl	50 / 1
	5	5.0 @ 4000	3500–4500	1.9375	1.5000	1—bbl	50 / 1
	6	6.0 @ 4500	4000–5000	1.9375	1.5000	1—bbl	50 / 1
	9.5	9.5 @ 4500	4000–5000	2.5000	2.2500	1—bbl	50 / 1
	18	18.0 @ 4500	4000–5000	2.5000	2.2500	1—bbl	50 / 1
1967	3	3.0 @ 4000	3500–4500	1.5625	1.3750	1—bbl	50 / 1
	5	5.0 @ 4000	3500–4500	1.9375	1.5000	1—bbl	50 / 1
	6	5.0 @ 4500	4000–5000	1.9375	1.5000	1—bbl	50 / 1
	9.5	9.5 @ 4500	4000–5000	2.3125	1.8125	1—bbl	50 / 1
	18	18.0 @ 4500	4000–5000	2.5000	2.2500	1—bbl	50 / 1
1968	1.5	1.5 @ 4000	3500–4500	1.5625	1.3750	1—bbl	50 / 1
	3	3.0 @ 4000	3500–4500	1.5625	1.3750	1—bbl	50 / 1
	5	5.0 @ 4000	3500–4500	1.9375	1.5000	1—bbl	50 / 1
	6	6.0 @ 4500	4000–5000	1.9375	1.5000	1—bbl	50 / 1
	9.5	9.5 @ 4500	4000–5000	2.3125	1.8125	1—bbl	50 / 1
	18	18.0 @ 4500	4000–5000	2.5000	2.2500	1—bbl	50 / 1
1969	1.5	1.5 @ 4000	3500–4500	1.5625	1.3750	1—bbl	50 / 1
	4	4.0 @ 4500	4000–5000	1.5625	1.3750	1—bbl	50 / 1
	6	6.0 @ 4500	4000–5000	1.9375	1.5000	1—bbl	50 / 1
	9.5	9.5 @ 4500	4000–5000	2.3125	1.8125	1—bbl	50 / 1
	18	18.0 @ 4500	4000–5000	2.5000	2.2500	1—bbl	50 / 1
	25	25.0 @ 5500	5000–6000	2.5000	2.2500	1—bbl	50 / 1
1970	1.5	1.5 @ 4000	3500–4500	1.5625	1.3750	1—bbl	50 / 1
	4	4.0 @ 4500	4000–5000	1.5625	1.3750	1—bbl	50 / 1
	6	6.0 @ 4500	4000–5000	1.9375	1.5000	1—bbl	50 / 1
	9.5	9.5 @ 4500	4000–5000	2.3125	1.8125	1—bbl	50 / 1
	18	18.0 @ 4500	4000–5000	2.5000	2.2500	1—bbl	50 / 1
	25	25.0 @ 5500	5000–6000	2.5000	2.2500	1—bbl	50 / 1
1971	2	2.0 @ 4500	4000–5000	1.5625	1.3750	1—bbl	50 / 1
	4	4.0 @ 4500	4000–5000	1.5625	1.3750	1—bbl	50 / 1
	6	6.0 @ 4500	4000–5000	1.9375	1.5000	1—bbl	50 / 1
	9.5	9.5 @ 4500	4000–5000	2.3125	1.8125	1—bbl	50 / 1
	18	18.0 @ 4500	4000–5000	2.5000	2.2500	1—bbl	50 / 1
	25	25.0 @ 5500	5000–6000	2.5000	2.2500	1—bbl	50 / 1

① For 6 gallon tanks, add 1 pint lubricant to 6 gallons (5 Imperial) of gasoline.
For 3 gallon tanks, add ½ pint lubricant to 3 gallons (2.5 Imperial) of gasoline.

Tune-Up Specifications

Year	Model (hp)	Spark Plugs Type AC	AL	CH	Gap (in.)	Compression Pressure (psi)	Ignition Type	Breaker Point Gap (in.) ▲
1966	3	M24K	A21X	J4J	0.030	①	Fly Mag	0.020
	5	M24K	A21X	J4J	0.030	①	Fly Mag	0.020
	6	M24K	A21X	J4J	0.030	①	Fly Mag	0.020
	9.5	M42K	A21X	J4J	0.030	①	Fly Mag	0.020
	18	M42K	A21X	J4J	0.030	①	Fly Mag	0.020
1967	3	M42K	A21X	J4J	0.030	①	Fly Mag	0.020
	5	M42K	A21X	J4J	0.030	①	Fly Mag	0.020
	6	M42K	A21X	J4J	0.030	①	Fly Mag	0.020
	9.5	M42K	A21X	J4J	0.030	①	Fly Mag	0.020
	18	M42K	A21X	J4J	0.030	①	Fly Mag	0.020
1968	1.5	M42K	A21X	J4J	0.030	①	Fly Mag	0.020
	3	M42K	A21X	J4J	0.030	①	Fly Mag	0.020
	5	M42K	A21X	J4J	0.030	①	Fly Mag	0.020
	6	M42K	A21X	J4J	0.030	①	Fly Mag	0.020
	9.5	M42K	A21X	J4J	0.030	①	Fly Mag	0.020
	18	M42K	A21X	J4J	0.030	①	Fly Mag	0.020

Tune-Up Specifications (cont.)

Year	Model (hp)	Spark Plugs Type AC	AL	CH	Gap (in.)	Compression Pressure (psi)	Ignition Type	Breaker Point Gap (in.) ▲
1969	1.5	M42K	A21X	J4J	0.030	①	Fly Mag	0.020
	4	M42K	A21X	J4J	0.030	①	Fly Mag	0.020
	6	M42K	A21X	J4J	0.030	①	Fly Mag	0.020
	9.5	M42K	A21X	J4J	0.030	①	Fly Mag	0.020
	18	M42K	A21X	J4J	0.030	①	Fly Mag	0.020
	25	M42K	A21X	J4J	0.030	①	Fly Mag	0.020
1970	1.5	M42K	NA	J4J	0.030	①	Fly Mag	0.020
	4	M42K	NA	J4J	0.030	①	Fly Mag	0.020
	6	M42K	NA	J4J	0.030	①	Fly Mag	0.020
	9.5	M42K	NA	J4J	0.030	①	Fly Mag	0.020
	18	M42K	NA	J4J	0.030	①	Fly Mag	0.020
	25	M42K	NA	J4J	0.030	①	Fly Mag	0.020
1971	2	M44C	NA	J6J	0.030	①	Fly Mag	0.020
	4	M44C	NA	J6J	0.030	①	Fly Mag	0.020
	6	M44C	NA	J6J	0.030	①	Fly Mag	0.020
	9.5	M42K	NA	J4J	0.030	①	Fly Mag	0.020
	18	M42K	NA	J4J	0.030	①	Fly Mag	0.020
	25	M42K	NA	J4J	0.030	①	Fly Mag	0.020

AC—AC
AL—Autolite
CH—Champion
NA—Not applicable
Fly Mag—Flywheel Magneto

▲—0.020 in. (used points); 0.022 in. (new points)
①—All cylinders within 15 psi of each other

Marine Specifications

Year	Model (hp)	Weight (lbs) ▲	Standard Propeller Diameter (in.)	Pitch (in.)	Rotation (facing bow)	Transom Height Recommended (in.) Long Shaft	Short Shaft
1966	3	37–39	8	4½	L	15	20
	5	42–43	8	7½	L	15	20
	6	51–52	8	7¼	R	15	20
	9.5	60–61	8¼	8½	R	15	20
	18	77	9¼	11	R	15	20
1967	3	33–37	8	5½	L	15	20
	5	41–42	8	7½	L	15	20
	6	51–52	8	7¼	R	15	20
	9.5	60–61	8¼	8½	R	15	20
	18	79–81	9	10½	R	15	20
1968	1.5	19	7¼	4½	L	15	NA
	3	33–37	8	5½	L	15	20
	5	41–42	8	7½	R	15	20
	6	51–52	8	7¼	R	15	20
	9.5	60–61	8¼	8½	R	15	20
	18	79–81	9	10½	R	15	20
1969	1.5	20	7¼	4½	L	15	NA
	4	33–35	8	5½	L	15	20
	6	51–52	8	7¼	R	15	20
	9.5	60–61	8⅛	8	R	15	20
	18	80–82	9	10	R	15	20
	25	80–84	9	10	R	15	20
1970	1.5	20	7¼	4½	L	15	NA
	4	33–35	8	5½	R	15	20
	6	51–52	8	7¼	R	15	20
	9.5	60–61	8⅛	8	R	15	20
	18	80–82	9	10	R	15	20
	25	81–84	9	10	R	15	20

Marine Specifications (cont.)

Year	Model (hp)	Weight (lbs) ▲	Standard Propeller Diameter (in.)	Standard Propeller Pitch (in.)	Standard Propeller Rotation (facing bow)	Transom Height Recommended (in.) Long Shaft	Transom Height Recommended (in.) Short Shaft
1971	2	23	7¼	4½	L	15	NA
	4	35	8	5½	L	15	20
	6	51–52	8	7¼	R	15	20
	9.5	60–61	8⅛	8	R	15	20
	18	81–83	9	10	R	15	20
	25	82–84	9	10	R	15	20

▲—Weight may vary depending on equipment
L—Left-hand rotation; R—Right-hand rotation

Torque Specifications

Year	Model (hp)	Flywheel Nut (ft lbs)	Connecting Rod (in. lbs)	Cylinder Head ▲ (in. lbs)	Crankcase to Cylinder Block (in. lbs) Upper and Lower	Crankcase to Cylinder Block (in. lbs) Center	Spark Plugs (ft lbs)
1966	3	30–40	60–66	60–80	60–80	60–80	20–21
	5	40–45	60–66	60–80	60–80	60–80	20–21
	6	40–45	60–66	60–80	60–80	60–80	20–21
	9.5	40–45	90–100	96–120	120–145	120–145	20–21
	18	40–45	180–186	96–120	110–130	120–130	20–21
1967	3	30–40	60–66	60–80	60–80	60–80	17–21
	5	40–45	60–66	60–80	60–80	60–80	17–21
	6	40–45	60–66	60–80	60–80	60–80	17–21
	9.5	40–45	90–100	96–120	120–145	120–145	17–21
	18	40–45	180–186	96–120	110–130	120–130	17–21
1968	1.5	22–25	60–66	60–80	60–80	60–80	17–21
	3	30–40	60–66	60–80	60–80	60–80	17–21
	5	40–45	60–66	60–80	60–80	60–80	17–21
	6	40–45	60–66	60–80	60–80	60–80	17–21
	9.5	40–45	90–100	96–120	120–145	120–145	17–21
	18	40–45	180–186	96–120	120–145	120–145	17–21
1969	1.5	22–25	60–66	60–80	60–80	60–80	17–21
	4	30–40	60–66	60–80	60–80	60–80	17–21
	6	40–45	60–66	60–80	60–80	60–80	17–21
	9.5	40–45	90–100	96–120	120–145	120–145	17–21
	18	40–45	180–186	96–120	120–145	120–145	17–21
	25	40–45	180–186	96–120	110–130	120–130	17–21
1970	1.5	22–25	60–66	60–80	60–80	60–80	17–21
	4	30–40	60–66	60–80	60–80	60–80	17–21
	6	40–45	60–66	60–80	60–80	60–80	17–21
	9.5	40–45	90–100	96–120	120–145	120–145	17–21
	18	40–45	180–186	96–120	110–130	120–130	17–21
	25	40–45	180–186	96–120	110–130	120–130	17–21
1971	2	22–25	60–66	60–80	60–80	60–80	17–21
	4	30–40	60–66	60–80	60–80	60–80	17–21
	6	40–45	60–66	60–80	60–80	60–80	17–21
	9.5	40–45	90–100	96–120	120–145	120–145	17–21
	18	40–45	180–186	96–120	110–130	120–130	17–21
	25	40–45	180–186	96–120	110–130	120–130	17–21

▲—Recheck torque on the cylinder head screws, after the motor has been run to operating temperature and cooled so it is comfortable to the touch.

NOTE: *Due to the extensive use of aluminum and white metal to resist corrosion, these torque specifications must be adhered to strictly. When tightening two or more screws on the same part, do not tighten screws fully one at a time. To avoid distortion, tighten all screws to ⅓ of specified torque, to ⅔ of specified torque, and then torque completely.*

Crankshaft, Piston, and Ring Specifications

Year	Model (hp)	Crankshaft (in.) Journal Diameter Upper	Center	Lower	End-Play	Pistons (in.) Piston to Cylinder Clear	Oversize(s)	Rings (in.) Ring to Groove Clearance	End-Gap
1966	3	0.6849–0.6854	0.6849–0.6854	0.6849–0.6854	0.010–0.020	0.0013–0.0025	0.020	0.001–0.0035	0.005–0.015
	5	0.8080–0.8085	0.8075–0.8080	0.8080–0.8085	0.007 (max)	0.0018–0.0030	0.020	0.001–0.0035	0.005–0.015
	6	0.8080–0.8085	0.8075–0.8080	0.8080–0.8085	0.007 (max)	0.0018–0.0030	0.020	0.001–0.0035	0.005–0.015
	9.5	0.8120–0.8125	0.8113–0.8118	0.8120–0.8125	0.007 (max)	0.0030–0.0045	0.020, 0.040	0.001–0.0035	0.007–0.017
	18	0.9995–1.0000	0.9995–1.0000	0.9995–1.0000	0.007 (max)	0.0030–0.0045	0.020, 0.040	0.001–0.0035	0.007–0.017
1967	3	0.6849–0.6854	0.6849–0.6854	0.6849–0.6854	0.0007–0.0017	0.0013–0.0025	0.020	0.001–0.0035	0.005–0.015
	5	0.8080–0.8085	0.8075–0.8080	0.8080–0.8085	0.002–0.010	0.0018–0.0030	0.020	0.001–0.0035	0.005–0.015
	6	0.8080–0.8085	0.8075–0.8080	0.8080–0.8085	0.002–0.010	0.0018–0.0030	0.020	0.001–0.0035	0.005–0.015
	9.5	0.8120–0.8125	0.8113–0.8118	0.8120–0.8125	0.007 (max)	0.0030–0.0045	0.020, 0.040	0.001–0.0035	0.007–0.017
	18	0.9995–1.0000	0.9995–1.0000	0.9995–1.0000	0.007 (max)	0.0030–0.0045	0.020, 0.040	0.001–0.0035	0.007–0.017
1968	1.5	0.6849–0.6854	NA	0.6849–0.6854	——	0.0013–0.0025	0.020	0.001–0.0035	0.005–0.015
	3	0.6849–0.6854	0.6849–0.6854	0.6849–0.6854	0.0007–0.0017	0.0013–0.0025	0.020	0.001–0.0035	0.005–0.015
	5	0.8080–0.8085	0.8075–0.8080	0.8080–0.8085	0.002–0.010	0.0018–0.0030	0.020	0.001–0.0035	0.005–0.015
	6	0.8080–0.8085	0.8075–0.8080	0.8080–0.8085	0.002–0.010	0.0018–0.0030	0.020	0.001–0.0035	0.005–0.015
	9.5	0.8120–0.8125	0.8113–0.8118	0.8120–0.8125	——	0.0030–0.0045	0.020, 0.040	0.001–0.0035	0.007–0.017
	18	0.9995–1.0000	0.9995–1.0000	0.9995–1.0000	0.009–0.023	0.0030–0.0045	0.020, 0.040	0.001–0.0035	0.007–0.017
1969	1.5	0.7497–0.7502	NA	0.7497–0.7502	——	0.0043–0.0055	0.020	0.001–0.0035	0.005–0.015
	4	0.7515–0.7520	0.6849–0.6850	0.6859–0.6850	0.0007–0.0017	0.0043–0.0055	0.020	0.001–0.0035	0.005–0.015
	6	0.8080–0.8085	0.8075–0.8080	0.8080–0.8085	——	0.0018–0.0030	0.020	0.001–0.0035	0.005–0.015
	9.5	0.8120–0.8125	0.8127–0.8132	0.8120–0.8125	——	0.0035–0.0050	0.020, 0.040	0.001–0.0035	0.007–0.017
	18	0.9995–1.0000	0.9995–1.0000	0.9995–1.0000	0.009–0.023	0.0032–0.0047	0.020, 0.040	0.002–0.0040	0.007–0.017
	25	0.9995–1.0000	0.9995–1.0000	0.9995–1.0000	0.009–0.023	0.0032–0.0047	0.020, 0.040	0.002–0.0040	0.007–0.017
1970	1.5	0.7497–0.7502	NA	0.7497–0.7502	——	0.0043–0.0055	0.020	0.002–0.0040	0.005–0.015
	4	0.7515–0.7520	0.6849–0.6854	0.6849–0.6854	0.0007–0.017	0.0020–0.0080	0.020	0.002–0.0040	0.005–0.015
	6	0.8075–0.8080	0.8075–0.8080	0.8075–0.8080	——	0.0018–0.0030	0.020	0.001–0.0035	0.005–0.015
	9.5	0.8120–0.8125	0.8127–0.8132	0.8120–0.8125	——	0.0035–0.0050	0.020, 0.040	0.001–0.0035	0.007–0.017
	18	0.9995–1.0000	0.9995–1.0000	0.9995–1.0000	0.009–0.023	0.0033–0.0045	0.020, 0.040	0.002–0.0040	0.007–0.017
	25	0.9995–1.0000	0.9995–1.0000	0.9995–1.0000	0.009–0.023	0.0033–0.0045	0.020, 0.040	0.002–0.0040	0.007–0.017
1971	2	0.7497–0.7502	NA	0.7497–0.7502	——	0.0043–0.0055	0.020	0.002–0.0040	0.005–0.015
	4	0.7515–0.7520	0.6849–0.6850	0.6849–0.6850	0.0007–0.017	0.0008–0.0020	0.030	0.002–0.0040	0.005–0.015
	6	0.8075–0.8080	0.8075–0.8080	0.8075–0.8080	——	0.0018–0.0030	0.030	0.002–0.0040	0.005–0.015
	9.5	0.8120–0.8125	0.8127–0.8132	0.8120–0.8125	——	0.0035–0.0050	0.030	0.001–0.0035	0.007–0.017
	18	0.9995–1.0000	0.9995–1.0000	0.9995–1.0000	0.009–0.023	0.0032–0.0048	0.030	0.002–0.0040	0.007–0.017
	25	0.9995–1.0000	0.9995–1.0000	0.9995–1.0000	0.009–0.023	0.0032–0.0048	0.030	0.002–0.0040	0.007–0.017

NA—Not Applicable
——Not Available

Standard Screw Torque Chart

Standard Screw Size	Torque In. Lbs	Ft Lbs
no. 6	7–10	——
no. 8	15–22	——
no. 10	25–35	2–3
no. 12	35–45	3–4
¼ in.	60–80	5–7
5/16 in.	120–140	10–12
⅜ in.	220–240	18–20
7/16 in.	340–360	28–30

NOTE: *Due to the extensive use of aluminum and white metal to resist corrosion, torque specifications must be adhered to strictly. When tightening two or more screws on the same part, do not tighten screws one at a time. To avoid distortion, tighten all screws to ⅓ specified torque, to ⅔ specified torque, then torque completely.*

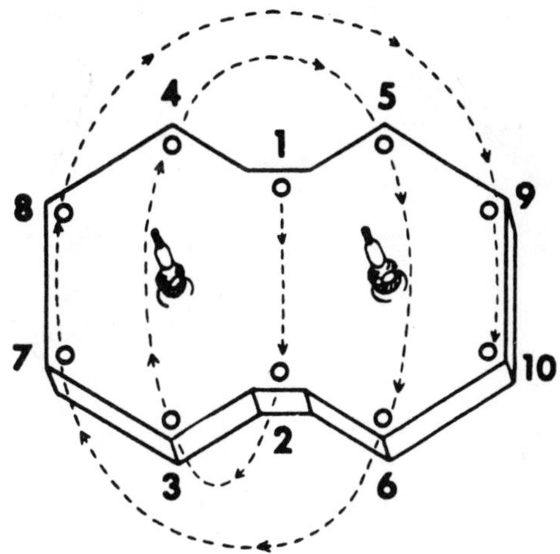

Cylinder head—1966–71 5, 6, 18, and 25 HP (© Outboard Marine Corporation)

Torque Sequences

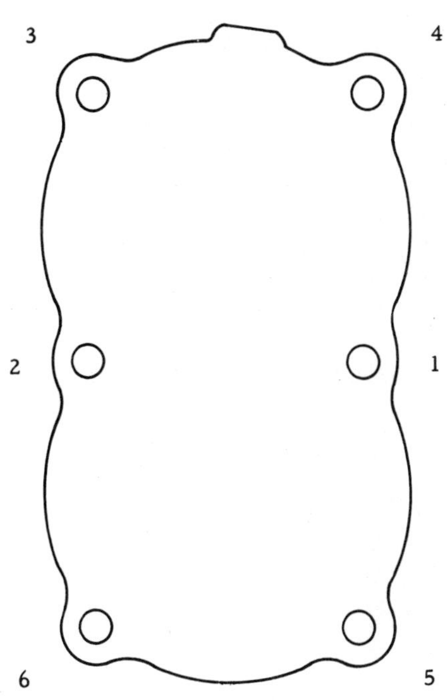

Cylinder head—1966–71 3 HP (© Outboard Marine Corporation)

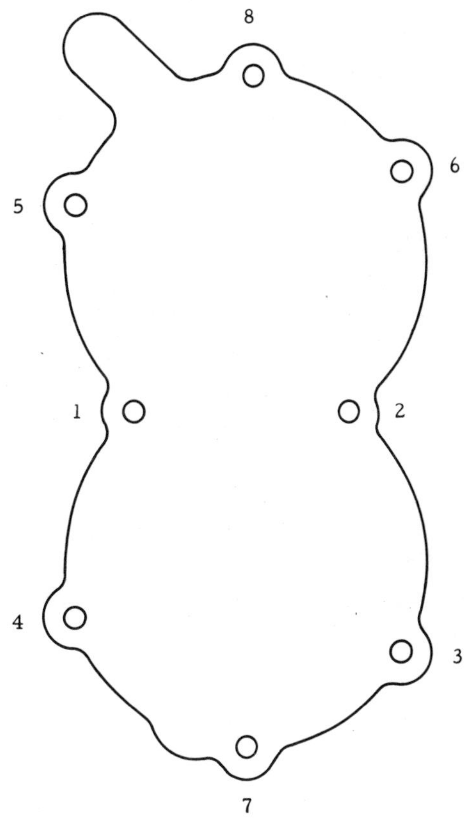

Cylinder head—1966–71 9.5 HP (© Outboard Marine Corporation)

Wiring Diagrams

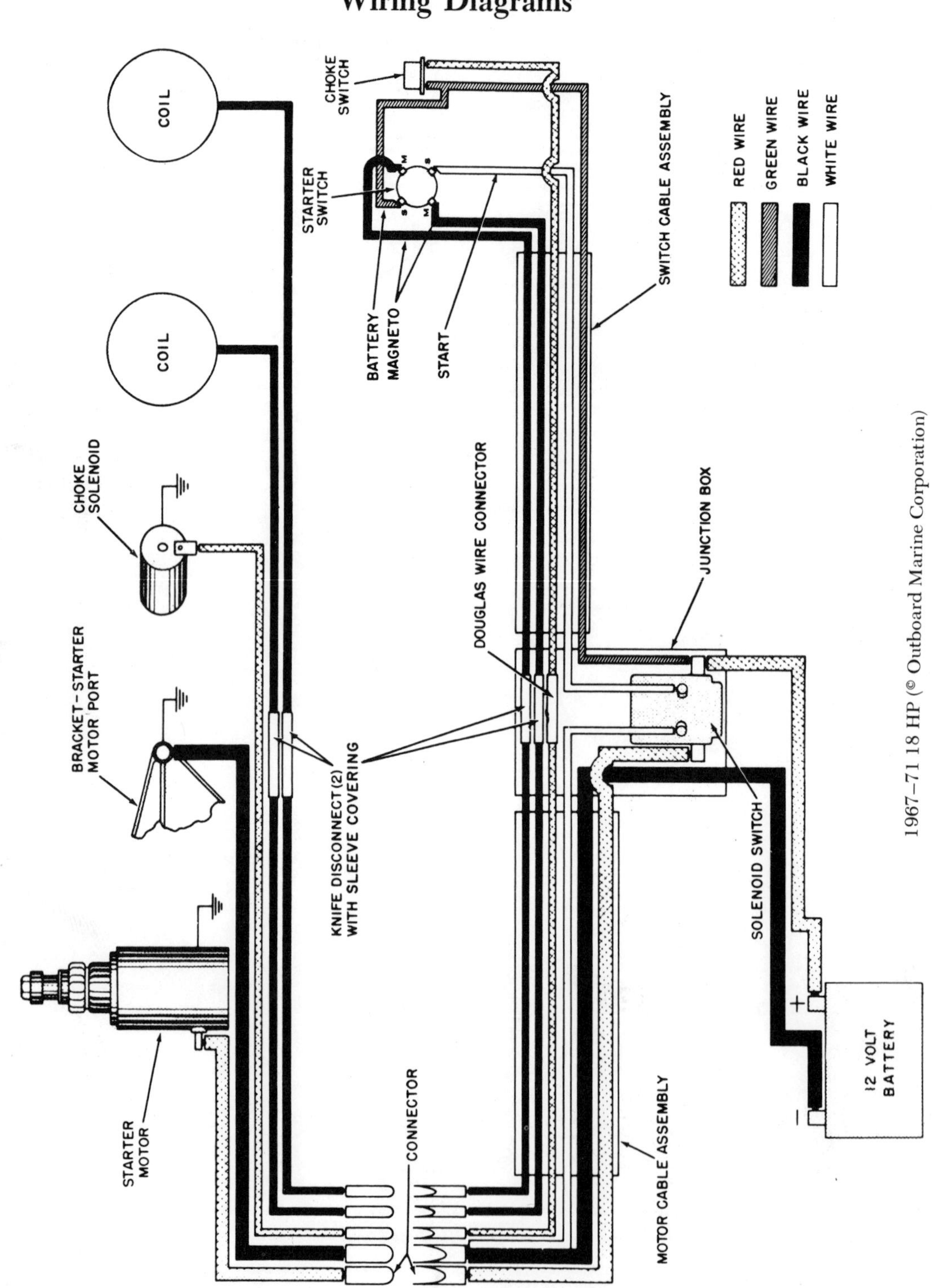

1967–71 18 HP (© Outboard Marine Corporation)

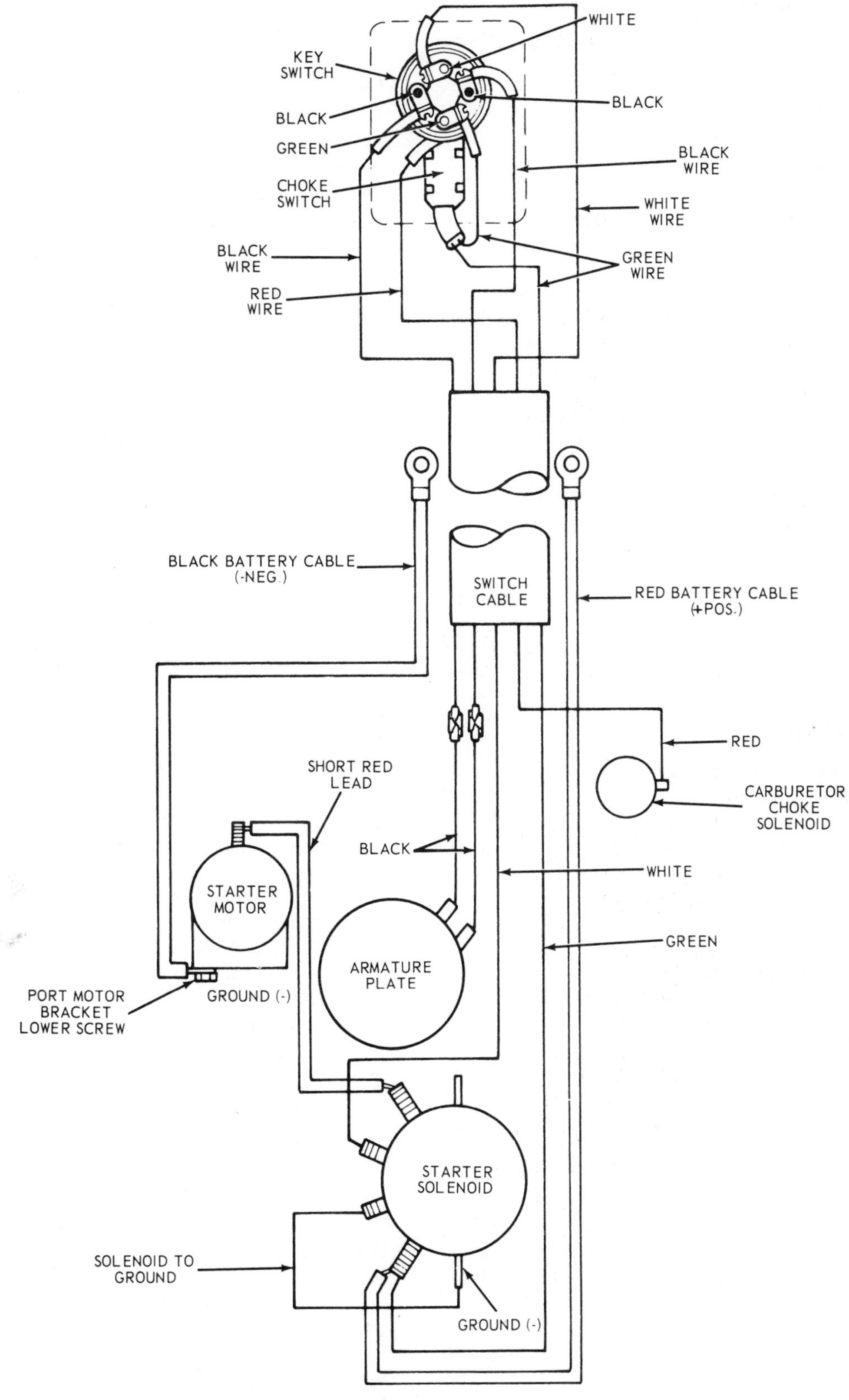

1969–71 18 and 25 HP (© Outboard Marine Corporation)

General Maintenance and Lubrication

GENERAL MAINTENANCE

Tune-Up And / Or Winterizing

The following procedure can be followed for a mid-season tune-up or for end-of-season winterizing.

1. Remove the exhaust covers and cylinder head(s). Slowly rotate the flywheel and visually inspect the pistons, rings, and cylinders for wear, free movement, or excessive carbon buildup.

NOTE: *Piston ring condition should be determined before continuing. Gum and varnish can be removed with an application of OMC Engine Cleaner.*

2. If pistons and rings are in satisfactory condition, remove all carbon and reinstall the exhaust covers.
3. Clean the carbon from the cylinder head and the top of the pistons. Replace the upper bearing crankshaft seal. Reinstall the cylinder head using a new gasket.
4. Remove all spark plugs and inspect each one. Clean all serviceable plugs and set each to the correct gap. Replace plugs as necessary. Install all spark plugs and torque them to specification.
5. Inspect and test the ignition coil, points, and ignition wires (depending on equipment). Replace parts as necessary and set the point gap.
6. Inspect all carburetors and the automatic choke.
7. Inspect the fuel pump and fuel lines. Replace any fuel lines which are cracked or rotted. Replace the fuel filter element and gasket.
8. Synchronize the carburetor linkage.
9. Inspect the electric shift operation (if equipped).
10. Check the condition of the propeller for nicks, scratches, bent blades, and correct pitch. Remove the propeller and lubricate the propeller shaft splines. If equipped, inspect the condition of the drive key and replace it if necessary. Reinstall the propeller.
11. Drain and refill the gearcase and thoroughly lubricate all components of the motor.
12. Tighten all screws and nuts to the specified torque.
13. Tank-test or boat-test the motor and adjust the low-speed jets on the carburetor. Check the cooling system operation. After the motor has cooled until it is comfortable to the touch, retorque the cylinder head screws.

NOTE: *Steps 14 and 15 should only be performed when winterizing the motor.*

14. Run the engine at idle and disconnect the fuel line. Rapidly inject rust preventive oil through the carburetor throat(s) until the engine smokes profusely. This will lubricate the internal moving parts of the motor.
15. Fog the motor for storage using OMC Accessory Rust Preventive Oil. Store the motor in a clean, dry area in an upright position.

Battery Care

OMC outboards are designed to be operated with a twelve-volt battery.

The first step in determining the condition of a battery is to make a visual inspection. Broken, cracked, or distorted covers or containers may be evidence of improper care, installation, or application of the battery. Inspect the battery for excessive corrosion of the battery cables or terminals. Replace cables and clean terminals as necessary.

NOTE: *An application of petroleum jelly will prevent corrosion on the battery terminals.*

The battery should be kept fully charged at all times. Check the state of charge with a hydrometer approximately every two weeks. If the battery has been standing for thirty days or more, it should be recharged before placing it back in service. Refer to the introductory chapter of this book for further battery care.

Battery Installation

Install the battery near the motor. For mounting the battery, use a Coast Guard approved battery box (available as an OMC accessory) and securely fasten it to the boat.

Correct battery polarity is extremely important. The battery must be connected so that the negative (−) post is connected to the ground. If the positive (+) post is connected to ground, the rectifier diodes will be damaged.

Checking Thermostat Operation

The thermostat is housed in the thermostat housing in the cylinder head. The thermostat is closed when starting a cold motor, preventing the water pump from circulating water in the cooling system, although limited circulation and air discharge is permitted through a bleed valve in the thermostat. When temperatures in the powerhead and cooling system reach 145° F, the thermostat opens, allowing heated water to pass through the water discharge and fresh water to be drawn in through the water intake. The thermostat continues to regulate the powerhead temperature, by opening and closing as additional fresh water is required.

Thermostat removed from housing (© Outboard Marine Corporation)

Powerhead temperature is best checked by operating the motor on a boat or in a test tank. Two Markal Thermomelt sticks are necessary to check powerhead temperature: a 125° F stick and a 163° F stick. Run the motor to operating temperature and hold the 125° F stick against the powerhead. The 125° F stick should melt and

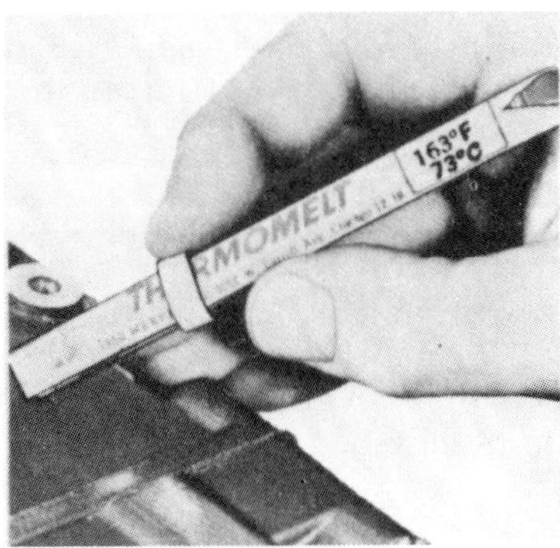

Checking engine temperature with a thermomet stick (© Outboard Marine Corporation)

the 163° F stick should not melt. If the 125° F stick does not melt, the thermostat is probably stuck and the motor is running too cold. If the 163° F stick also melts, check for a defective water pump or thermostat or a leaking water system. Any of the above defects should be checked and corrected as quickly as possible, to prevent further costly damage to the motor.

Propeller Selection

Next to the selection of a motor and boat, the most important decision to be made is what propeller to install on your motor. The standard propeller is usually satisfactory for general purposes and all-around use. However, it is wise to check and be sure that your motor is running in the recommended operating range (see specifications) with any propeller that is being used. The procedure for checking this factor of boat performance is included in the introductory chapter of this book.

The propellers listed are available from OMC as alternate or spare propellers.

Lubrication and Fuel

FUELS

Fuel Recommendations

Use any regular grade of automotive gasoline in your motor. Higher octane fuels may be used but will generally offer no advantages over regular grade gasoline. When operating your motor in any country other than the United States or Canada, use any gasoline that will perform satisfactorily in an automotive engine.

OMC (Johnson or Evinrude) outboard motor oil is recommended. A reputable outboard 50/1 lubricant can be used, as long as it is BIA (Boating Industry Association) certified for service TC-W (two-cycle, water-cooled). Any outboard lubricant which meets the above conditions will perform satisfactorily. Automotive oils should not be used except in extreme emergencies. Should an emergency of this type arise, use only SAE 30 oil with a container marked "Service ML-MM" or "Service MM." Avoid the use of oils marked as "ML" or multiviscosity oils such as 10W—30. It should be recognized that

Propeller Chart

hp	Year	Boat Size and Recommendation	Boat Speed (mph)	Part No.	Material	No. of Blades	Diameter	Pitch
1½ and 2	68–70	General Usage		313689	Al	3	7¼ in.	4½ in.
	68–70	General Usage		384664 kit	Al	3	7¼ in.	4½ in.
	71	General Usage		316557	Al	3	7¼ in.	4½ in.
3 and 4	52–70	General Usage		314806	Al	3	6¼ in.	5½ in.
weedless	52–70	General Usage		203919	Al	2	6⅛ in.	6¼ in.
	71	General Usage		316651	Al	3	6⅜ in.	5½ in.
3 and 4 right angle	64 thru	Heavy Loads		310208	Al	3	8 in.	4½ in.
		General Usage		315858	Al	3	8 in.	5½ in.
5	50–53	General Usage		375689	Al	2	8 in.	7¼ in.
	65 thru	General Usage		380104	Al	3	8 in.	7½ in.
6	54–65	General Usage		376968	Al	2	8 in.	7¼ in.
	66 thru	General Usage		380958	Al	2	8 in.	7¼ in.
9½	64 thru	General Usage		383315	Al	3	8⅛ in.	8 in.
18 and 25 (69 thru)		14–16 ft Boats Heavy Loads	10–22	379717	Al	3	9 in.	9 in.
		12–16 ft Boats General Usage	20–30	383629	Al	3	9 in.	10 in.
		12–14 ft Boats Extremely Weedy	20–30	592959	Al	3	9 in.	10 in.

automotive oils are formulated for use in automotive engines and outboard oils are designed specifically for two-cycle, water-cooled outboards.

NOTE: *Additive compounds, such as "tune-up" compounds, "tonics," "friction reducing" compounds, etc., are unnecessary and are not recommended for use in OMC outboards. OMC engine cleaner or OMC rust preventive oil are recommended as additives.*

Fuel Mixing Procedure

Always use fresh gasoline. When filling an empty (or almost empty) tank, put approximately one gallon of gasoline into the tank and add the recommended amount of oil. Shake vigorously to be sure that the fuel is thoroughly mixed and add the balance of the gasoline.

Add one part oil to fifty parts of gasoline, or, to each six gallon tank (five gallons Imperial) add one pint of oil.

LUBRICATION

Gear Housing

Refer to the following chart for the frequency of lubrication and for the recommended type of lubricant.

CAUTION - DO NOT
REMOVE PIVOT PIN

Lubricating the gear housing (© Outboard Marine Corporation)

1. Remove the plugs and gasket assemblies marked "Oil Level" and "Oil Drain" from the starboard side of the gear housing.
2. With the propeller shaft in a normal running position, allow the oil to drain from the gear housing.
3. Fill the gear housing with the recommended lubricant until grease appears at the oil level hole.
4. Install the oil level plug before removing the lubricant filler tube from the oil drain hole. This allows the oil drain plug to be installed without lubricant loss.

Lubrication Chart—1 1/2 HP

Lubrication Point	*Lubricant*	*Frequency (Period of Operation)* *Fresh Water*	*Salt Water #*
1. Gearcase	OMC Type C	Check level after first 10 hours of operation and every 50 hours of operation thereafter. Add lubricant if necessary.	Same as Fresh Water
		Drain and refill every 100 hours of operation or once each season, whichever occurs first.	Same as Fresh Water
2. Steering Handle Pivot	OMC Type A	60 days	30 days
3. Throttle Cam, Carburetor and Choke Linkage	OMC Type A	60 days	30 days
4. Clamp Screw	OMC Type A	60 days	30 days

Some areas may require more frequent lubrication.

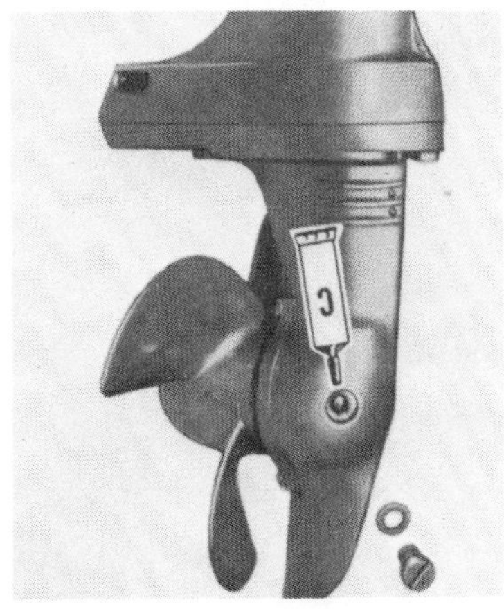

Gearcase lubrication—1½ HP (© Outboard Marine Corporation)

Magneto cam, carburetor, and choke lubrication—1½ HP (© Outboard Marine Corporation)

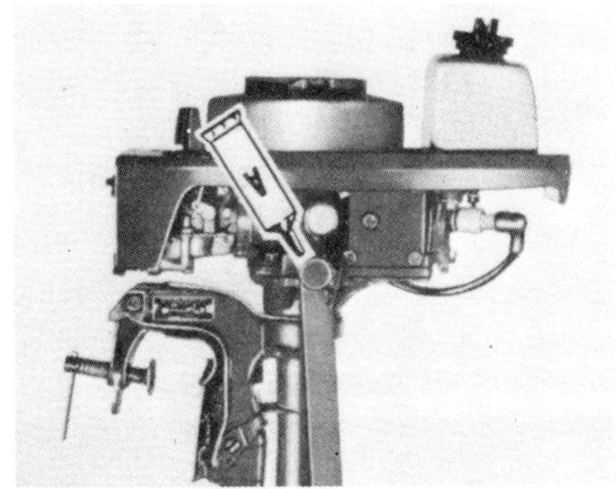

Steering handle lubrication—1½ HP (© Outboard Marine Corporation)

Clamp screw lubrication—1½ HP (© Outboard Marine Corporation)

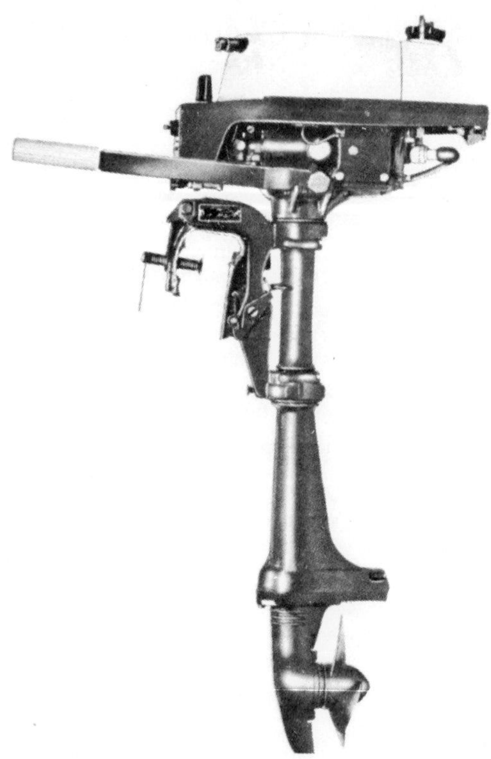

Port-side view—1½ HP (© Outboard Marine Corporation)

Lubrication Chart—3 and 4 HP

Lubrication Point	*Lubricant*	*Frequency (Period of Operation)* *Fresh Water*	*Salt Water #*
1. Steering Handle Pivot	OMC Type A	60 days	30 days
2. Clamp Screw	OMC Type A	60 days	30 days
3. Gearcase	OMC Type C Capacity 2.9 ozs	Check level after first 10 hours of operation and every 50 hours of operation thereafter. Add lubricant if necessary.	Same as Fresh Water
		Drain and refill every 100 hours of operation or once each season, whichever occurs first.	Same as Fresh Water
4. Starter Pinion	OMC Type A	60 days	30 days
5. Cam Follower	OMC Type A	60 days	30 days
6. Carburetor Linkage and Choke Rod	OMC Type A	60 days	30 days
7. Swivel Bracket (remove steering friction [vent] screw)	OMC Type A	60 days	30 days

Some areas may require more frequent lubrication.

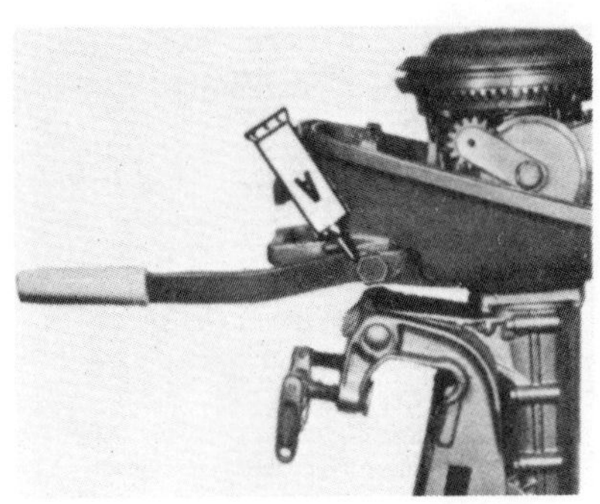

Steering handle pivot lubrication—3 and 4 HP (© Outboard Marine Corporation)

Starter pinion lubrication—3 and 4 HP (© Outboard Marine Corporation)

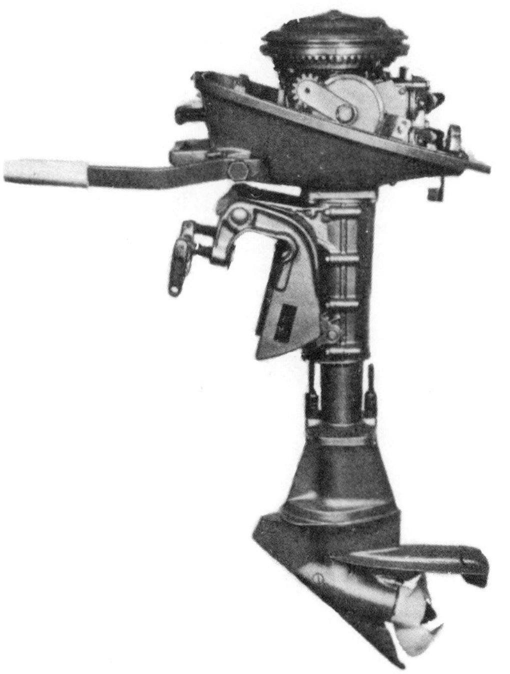

Port-side view—3 and 4 HP (© Outboard Marine Corporation)

Starboard-side view—3 and 4 HP (© Outboard Marine Corporation)

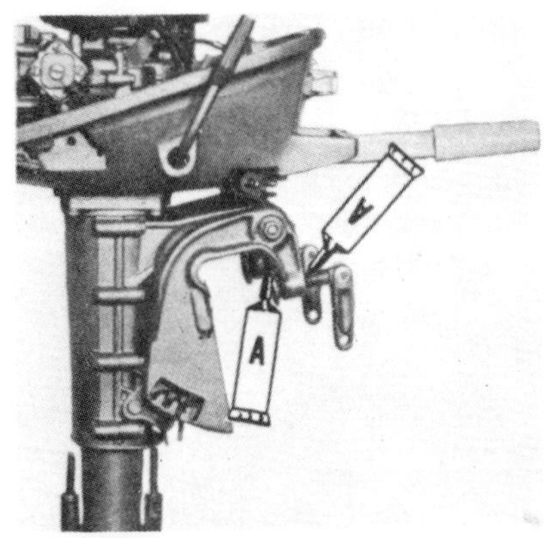

Clamp screw lubrication—3 and 4 HP (© Outboard Marine Corporation)

Cam follower lubrication—3 and 4 HP (© Outboard Marine Corporation)

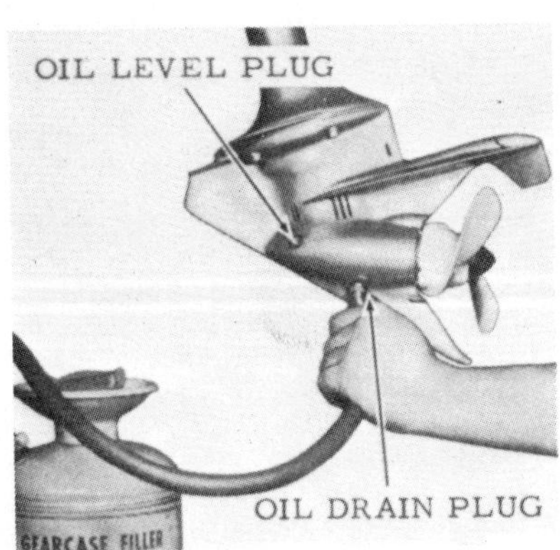

Weedless gearcase lubrication—3 and 4 HP (© Outboard Marine Corporation)

Carburetor linkage and choke rod lubrication—3 and 4 HP (© Outboard Marine Corporation)

Standard gearcase lubrication—3 and 4 HP (© Outboard Marine Corporation)

Swivel bracket lubrication—3 and 4 HP (© Outboard Marine Corporation)

Lubrication Chart—5 and 6 HP

Lubrication Point	*Lubricant*	*Frequency (Period of Operation)* Fresh Water	Salt Water #
1. Carburetor Linkage	OMC Type A	60 days	30 days
2. Cam Follower and Choke Linkage	OMC Type A	60 days	30 days
3. Clamp Screws	OMC Type A	60 days	30 days
4. Swivel Bracket Fitting	OMC Type A	60 days	30 days
5. Vertical Throttle Shaft Bearing	SAE 90 Oil	60 days	30 days
6. Vertical Throttle Shaft Bottom and Gears	OMC Type A	60 days	30 days
7. Gearcase	OMC Type C Capacity 8.5 ozs	Check level after first 10 hours of operation and every 50 hours of operation thereafter. Add lubricant if necessary.	Same as Fresh Water
		Drain and refill every 100 hours of operation or once each season, whichever occurs first.	Same as Fresh Water
8. Throttle Shaft Bearings and Gears—Front	OMC Type A	60 days	30 days
9. Shift Lever	OMC Type A	60 days	30 days

Some areas may require more frequent lubrication.

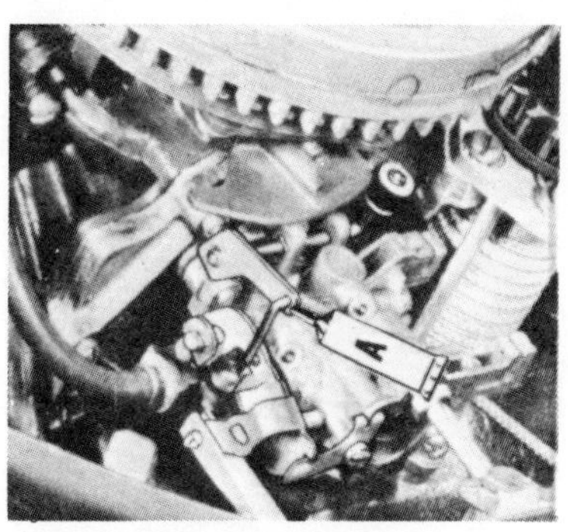

Carburetor linkage lubrication—5 and 6 HP (© Outboard Marine Corporation)

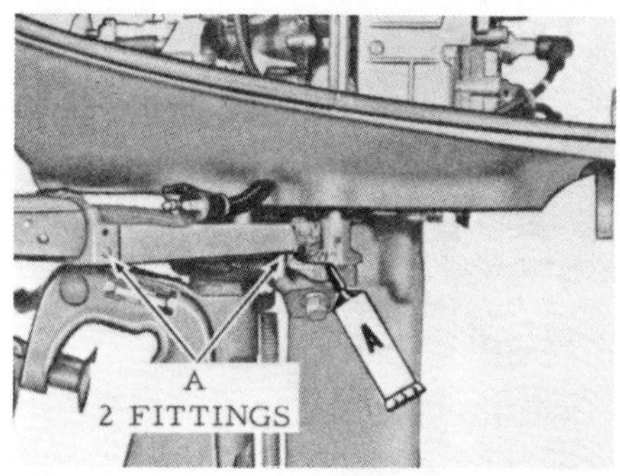

Throttle shaft and gears lubrication—5 and 6 HP (© Outboard Marine Corporation)

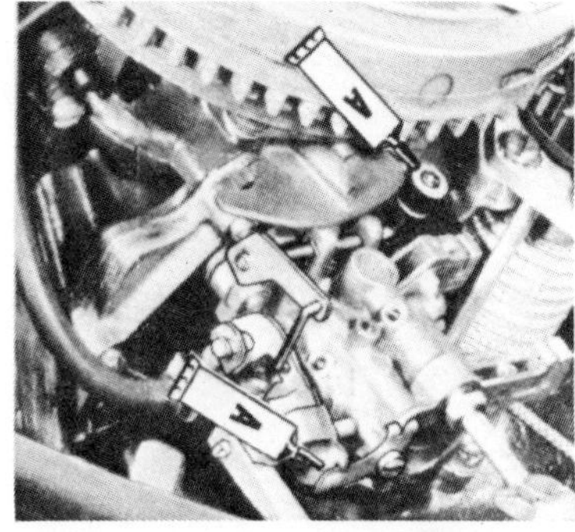

Cam follower and choke linkage lubrication—5 and 6 HP (© Outboard Marine Corporation)

Throttle shaft and bearing lubrication—5 and 6 HP (© Outboard Marine Corporation)

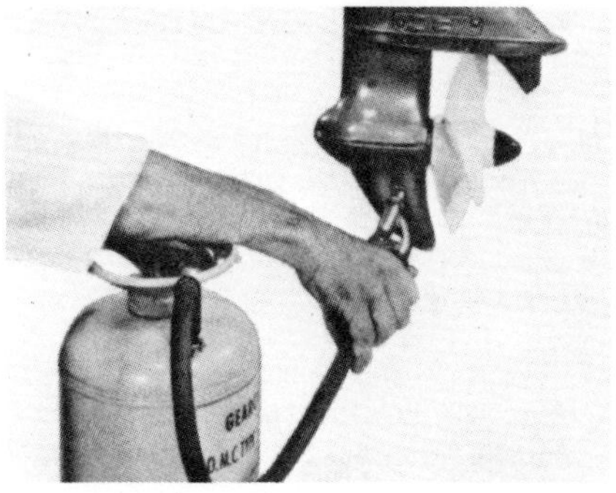

Gearcase lubrication—5 and 6 HP (© Outboard Marine Corporation)

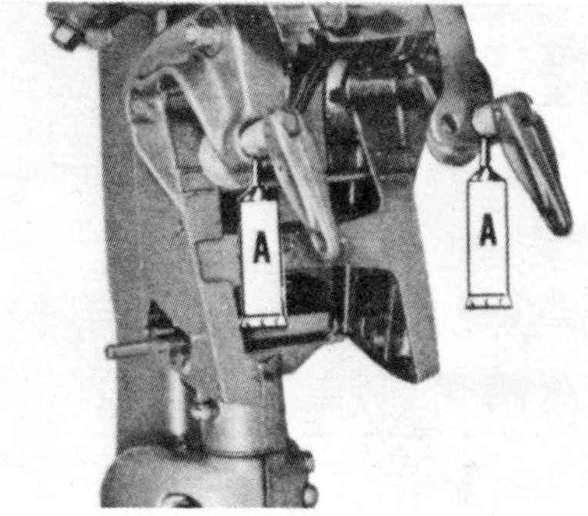

Clamp screw lubrication—5 and 6 HP (© Outboard Marine Corporation)

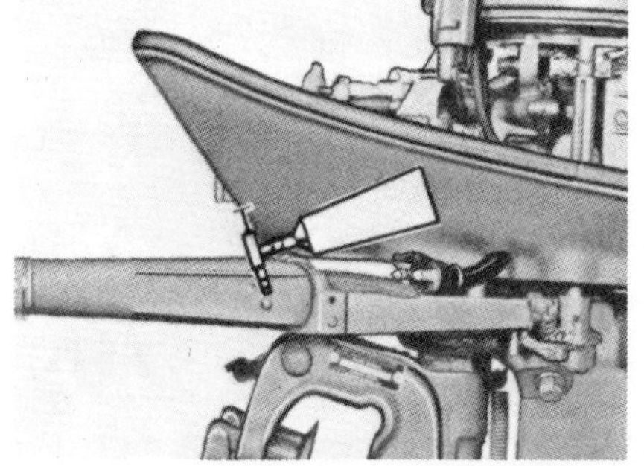

Front throttle shaft bearings and gear lubrication —5 and 6 HP (© Outboard Marine Corporation)

Swivel bracket lubrication—5 and 6 HP (© Outboard Marine Corporation)

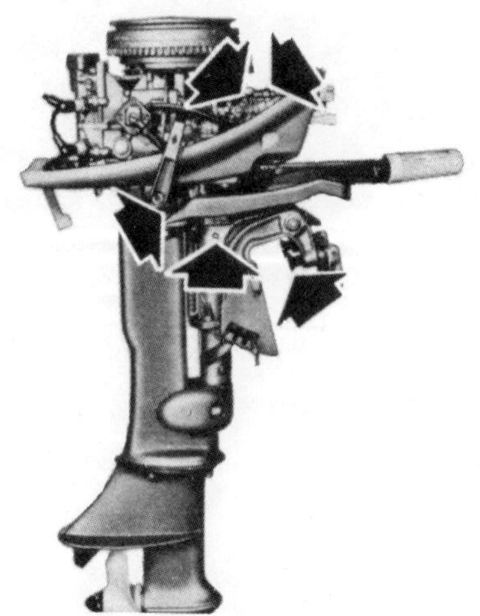

Starboard-side lubrication points—5 and 6 HP (© Outboard Marine Corporation)

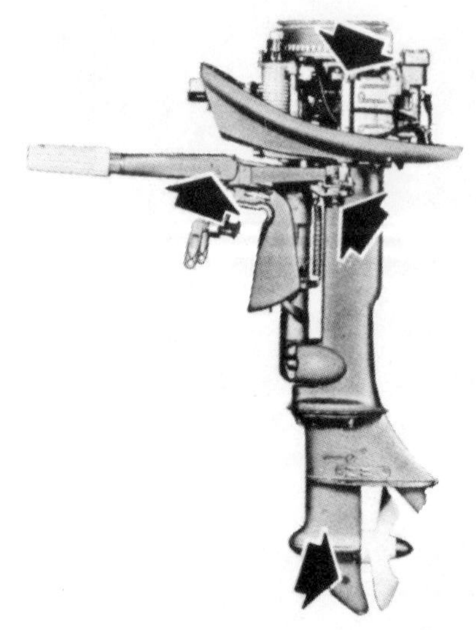

Port-side lubrication points—5 and 6 HP (© Outboard Marine Corporation)

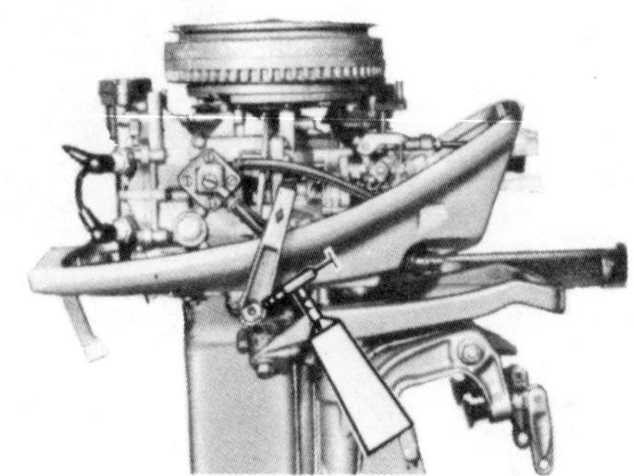

Shift lever lubrication—5 and 6 HP (© Outboard Marine Corporation)

Lubrication Chart—9 1/2 HP

Lubrication Point	*Lubricant*	*Frequency (Period of Operation)* *Fresh Water*	*Salt Water #*
1. Carburetor and Choke Linkage	OMC Type A	60 days	30 days
2. Throttle Linkage	OMC Type A	60 days	30 days
3. Clamp Screws	OMC Type A	60 days	30 days
4. Friction Ratchet	OMC Type A	60 days	30 days
5. Tilt Adjust Rack and Pinion	OMC Type A	60 days	30 days
6. Gearcase	OMC Type C	Check level after first 10 hours of operation and every 50 hours of operation thereafter. Add lubricant if necessary. Drain and refill every 100 hours of operation or once each season, whichever occurs first.	Same as Fresh Water
7. Swivel Bracket (2 fittings)	OMC Type A	60 days	30 days
8. Throttle Shaft (3 fittings)	OMC Type A	60 days	30 days
9. Shift Lever (2 fittings)	OMC Type A	60 days	30 days

Some areas may require more frequent lubrication.

Carburetor and choke linkage—9½ HP (© Outboard Marine Corporation)

Throttle linkage lubrication—9½ HP (© Outboard Marine Corporation)

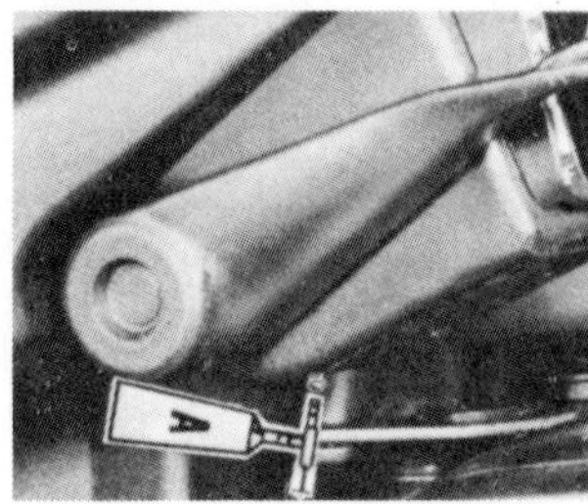

Shift lever lubrication—9½ HP (© Outboard Marine Corporation)

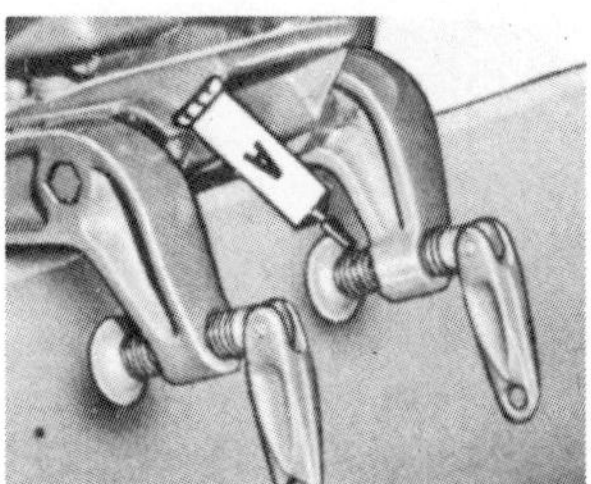

Clamp screw lubrication—9½ HP (© Outboard Marine Corporation)

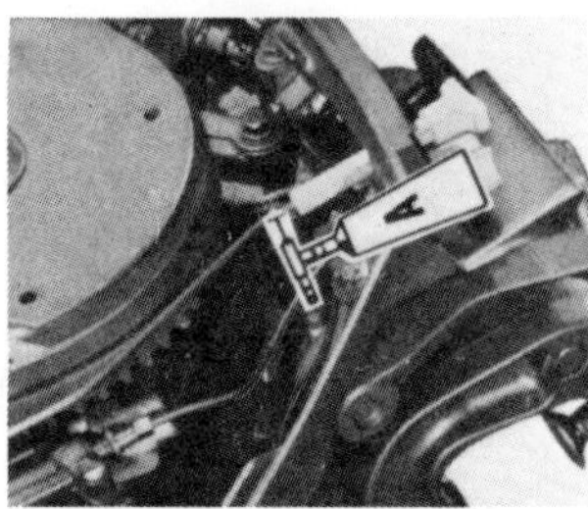

Shift lever lubrication—9½ HP (© Outboard Marine Corporation)

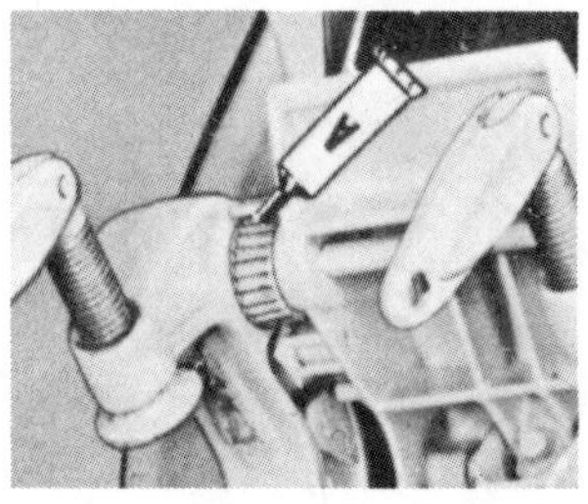

Friction ratchet lubrication—9½ HP (© Outboard Marine Corporation)

Throttle shaft lubrication—9½ HP (© Outboard Marine Corporation)

Rack and pinion tilt adjustment—9½ HP (© Outboard Marine Corporation)

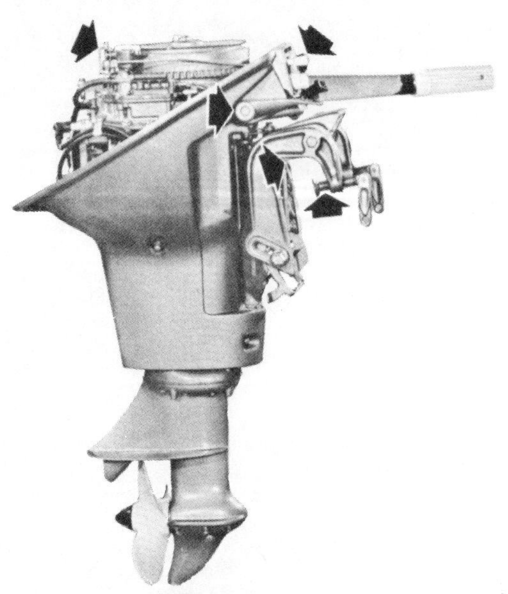

Starboard-side lubrication points—9½ HP (© Outboard Marine Corporation)

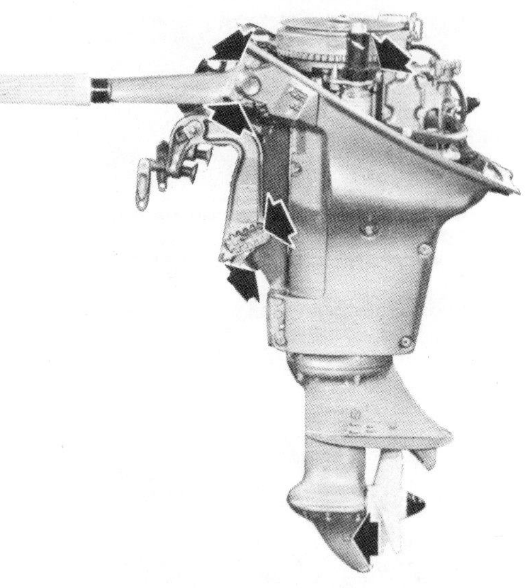

Port-side lubrication points—9½ HP (© Outboard Marine Corporation)

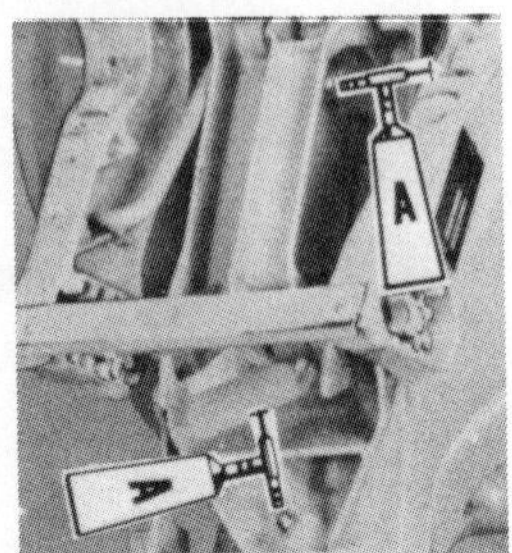

Swivel bracket lubrication—9½ HP (© Outboard Marine Corporation)

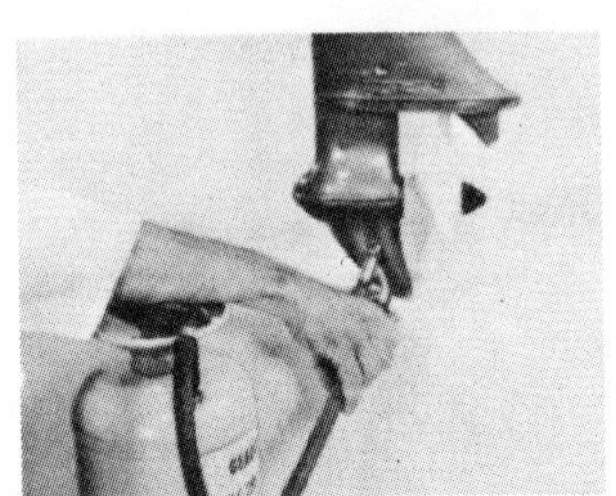

Gearcase lubrication—9½ HP (© Outboard Marine Corporation)

Lubrication Chart—18 and 25 HP

Lubrication Point	*Lubricant*	*Frequency (Period of Operation)* *Fresh Water*	*Salt Water #*
1. Cam Follower Linkage	OMC Type A	60 days	30 days
2. Throttle Shaft Bearings	SAE 90 Oil	60 days	30 days
3. Throttle Shaft Bushings and Gears	OMC Type A	60 days	30 days
4. Choke Linkage	OMC Type A	60 days	30 days
5. Swivel Bracket Fittings and Reverse Lock	OMC Type A	60 days	30 days
6. Gearcase	OMC Type C Capacity 8.3 ozs	Check level after first 10 hours of operation and every 50 hours of operation thereafter. Add lubricant if necessary.	Same as Fresh Water
		Drain and refill every 100 hours of operation or once each season.	Same as Fresh Water
7. Gear Shift Lever Shaft and Lockout	OMC Type A	60 days	30 days
8. Clamp Screws	OMC Type A	60 days	30 days

Some areas may require more frequent lubrication.

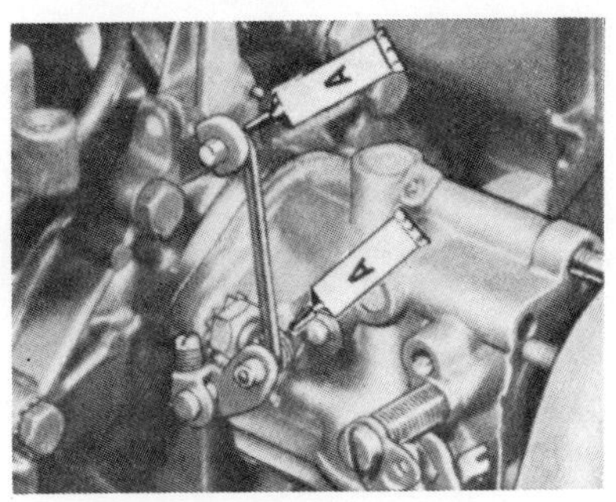

Cam follower and linkage lubrication—18 and 25 HP (© Outboard Marine Corporation)

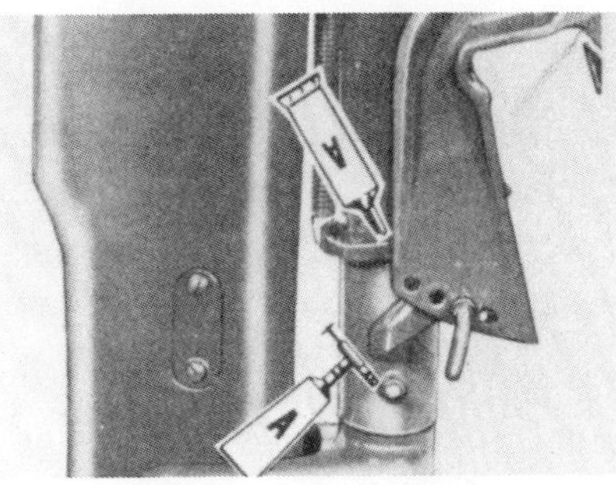

Swivel bracket and reverse lock lubrication—18 and 25 HP (© Outboard Marine Corporation)

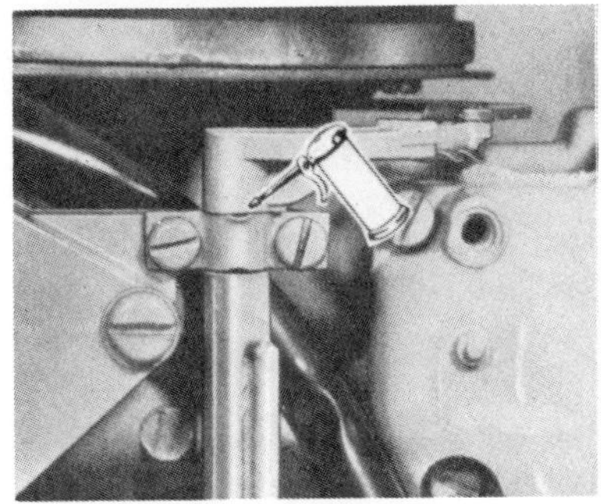

Throttle shaft bearing lubrication—18 and 25 HP (© Outboard Marine Corporation)

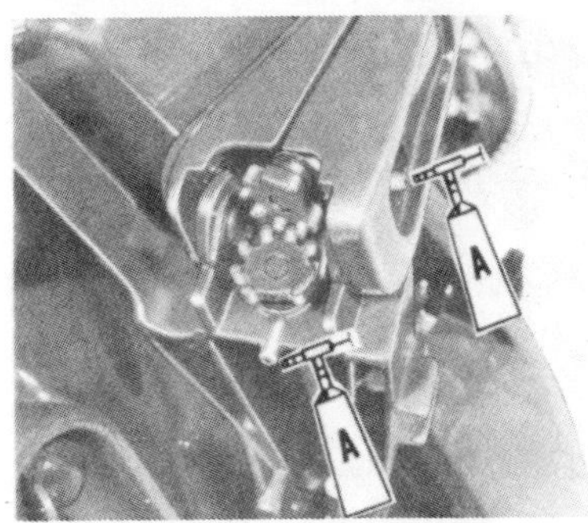

Throttle shaft and gear lubrication (at handle)—18 and 25 HP (© Outboard Marine Corporation)

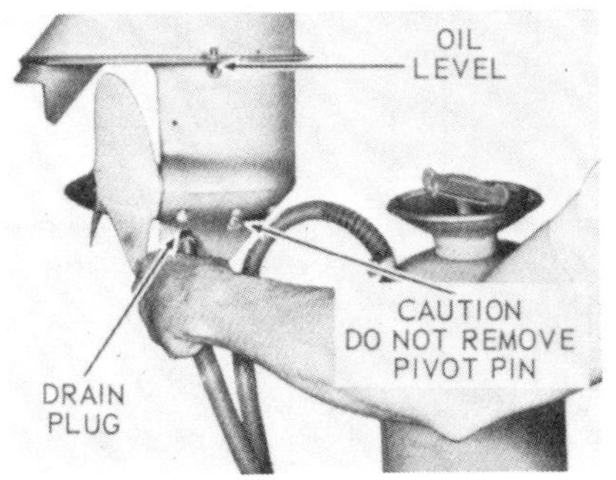

Gearcase lubrication—18 and 25 HP (© Outboard Marine Corporation)

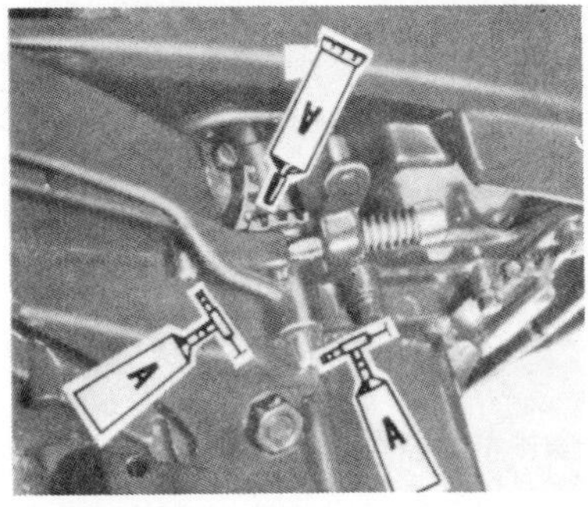

Throttle shaft and gear lubrication—18 and 25 HP (© Outboard Marine Corporation)

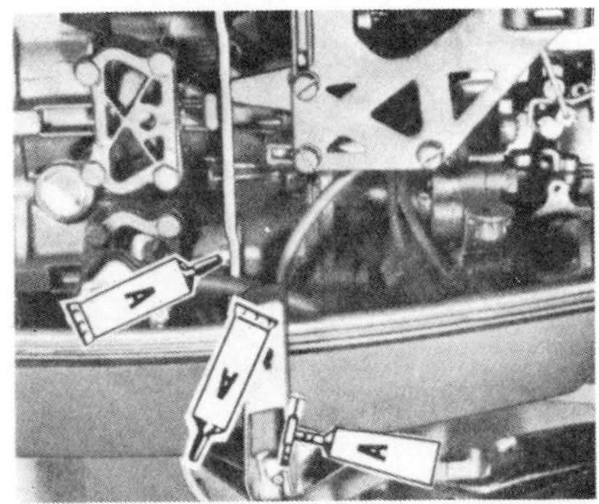

Gearshift lever and lockout lubrication—18 and 25 HP (© Outboard Marine Corporation)

Choke linkage lubrication—18 and 25 HP (© Outboard Marine Corporation)

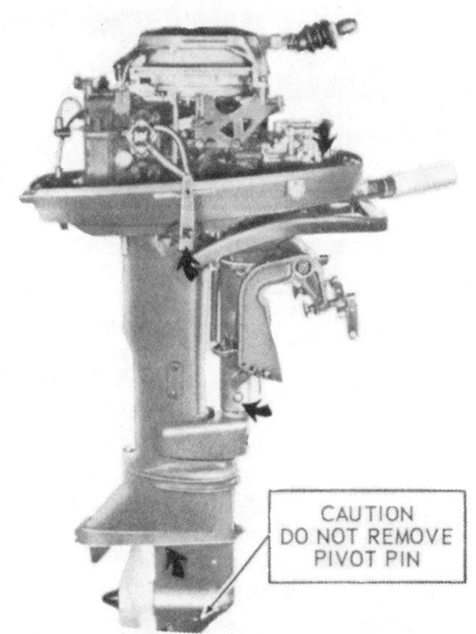

Starboard-side lubrication points—18 and 25 HP (© Outboard Marine Corporation)

Port-side lubrication points—18 and 25 HP (© Outboard Marine Corporation)

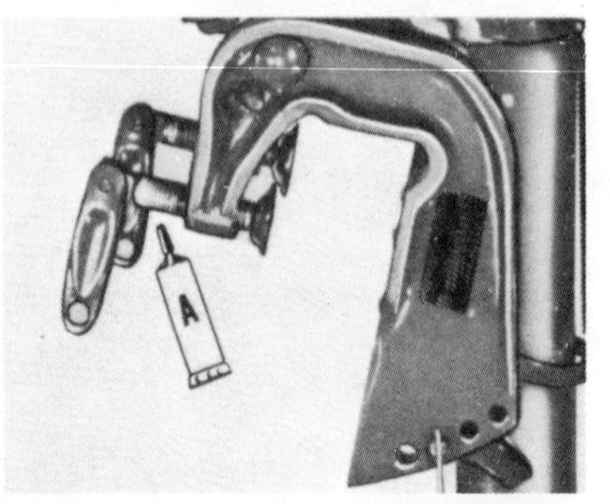

Clamp screw lubrication—18 and 25 HP (© Outboard Marine Corporation)

TYPES OF LUBRICANT

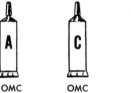

OMC TYPE "A" | OMC TYPE "C" | OIL CAN SAE 90 | GREASE GUN OMC TYPE "A"

OMC lubrication—all models (© Outboard Marine Corporation)

EXTERNAL LUBRICANTS

Three types of lubricants are recommended by Outboard Marine Corporation for use on their outboards. Engine oil (SAE 90) is recommended for use on throttle shaft bearings as shown in the previous illustrations. OMC Type A lubricant, available in either a tube or grease gun is recommended for use on clamp screws, linkages of all types, swivel bracket fittings, bushings and gears, and almost any type of external fitting.

OMC Type C lubricant is recommended for use in the gearcase and is the only type lubricant approved for this use. Do not, under any circumstances, use a corrosive hypoid-type lubricant in the gearcase. If in doubt concerning any particular lubricant, consult an OMC dealer.

Fuel System

CARBURETOR AND INTAKE MANIFOLD

Removal

1½ HP

The fuel system on these models consists of a fuel tank mounted on the powerhead, a fuel filter inside the fuel tank and a single barrel carburetor with high- and low-speed adjustable jets. A fuel shut-off valve is positioned in the fuel line directly below the fuel filter.

1. Shut off the fuel supply at the fuel shut-off valve.
2. Remove the low-speed adjusting knob.
3. Remove the motor cover, after removing the port and starboard cover screws and the two screws at the control panel.
4. Disconnect the fuel hose at the carburetor.
5. Remove the two attaching nuts and remove the carburetor.
6. Remove four screws and remove the intake manifold, leaf valves, and gaskets from the powerhead.

Carburetor attaching nuts—1½ HP (© Outboard Marine Corporation)

Intake manifold attaching screws—1½ HP (© Outboard Marine Corporation)

2 HP

These models use a fuel tank mounted on the power head, a fuel filter inside the fuel tank, and a single-barrel carburetor with high- and low-speed adjustable jets. A fuel shut-off valve is positioned in the fuel line directly below the fuel filter.

1. Shut off the fuel supply at the fuel shut-off valve.
2. Remove the low-speed adjustment knob.
3. Remove the screws holding the rewind starter.
4. Disconnect the fuel hose at the carburetor.
5. Remove the screws holding the control panel to the carburetor and the screws at the fuel tank support bracket at the powerhead. Align the speed control knob with the slot in the control panel support bracket.
6. Remove the support bracket and fuel tank.
7. Remove the carburetor attaching nuts and remove the carburetor.
8. Remove the four screws and the intake manifold, leaf valves, and gaskets from the powerhead.
9. At this time, the fuel tank may be removed from the support bracket.

3 HP (1966–67)

These models use the same type of fuel system as the 1½ and 2 hp models, except that the high-speed jet is fixed, with only the low-speed jet adjustable.

1. Shut off the fuel supply at the fuel shut-off valve.
2. Remove the choke knob.
3. Remove the port and starboard motor covers.
4. Remove the air silencer.

Air silencer and cam follower—3 HP (1966–67) (© Outboard Marine Corporation)

Carburetor fuel line connection and attaching nuts—3 HP (1966–67) (© Outboard Marine Corporation)

5. Detach the cam follower spring from the intake manifold.

6. Disconnect the fuel hose at the carburetor.

7. Remove the two attaching nuts and remove the carburetor from the manifold.

8. Remove the intake manifold, leaf valve assembly, and gasket from the powerhead.

Manifold and leaf valve removal—3 HP (1966–67) (© Outboard Marine Corporation)

3 HP (1968) AND 4 HP

These models use a remote fuel tank, diaphragm-type fuel pump, and single-barrel carburetor with high- and low-speed adjustable jets.

1. Remove the motor cover.

2. Remove the high- and low-speed adjustment knobs. Remove the retaining pin and choke knob.

3. Remove the cam follower.

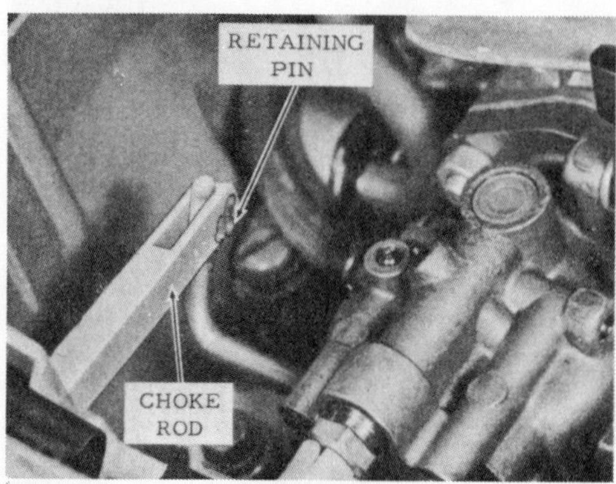

Choke rod removal—3 HP (1968) and 4 HP (© Outboard Marine Corporation)

4. Disconnect and plug the fuel hose at the carburetor.

5. Remove the attaching nuts and carburetor.

6. Remove the intake manifold, leaf valves, and gaskets from the powerhead.

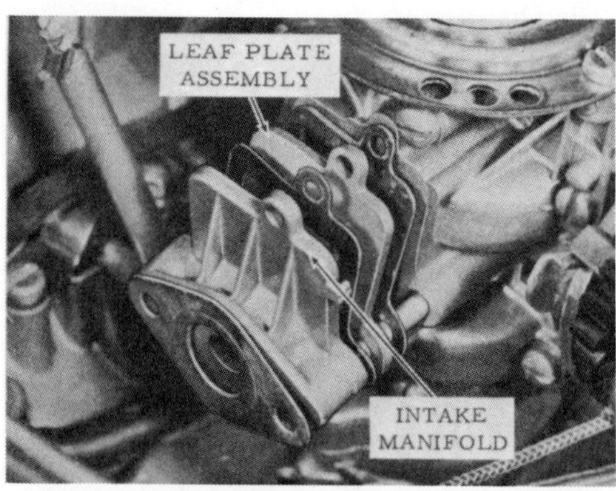

Manifold and leaf valve removal—3 HP (1968) and 4 HP (© Outboard Marine Corporation)

5 HP

These models use a remote fuel tank, diaphragm-type fuel pump, and single-barrel carburetor with fixed high-speed jets and adjustable low-speed jets.

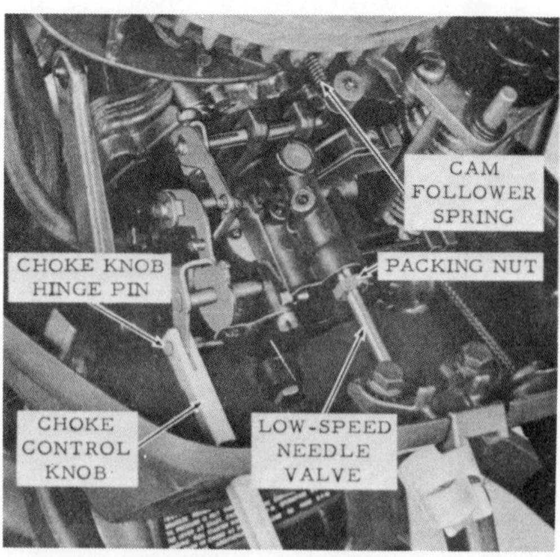

Carburetor components—5 HP (© Outboard Marine Corporation)

1. Remove the low-speed adjustment knob. Remove the choke knob hinge pin and choke control knob.

2. Remove the cam follower spring from the throttle cam follower.

3. Remove the manual starter.

4. Disconnect and plug the fuel hose at the carburetor.

5. Remove the throttle lever.

6. Remove the two nuts attaching the carburetor to the intake manifold. Remove the carburetor and gasket from the manifold.

7. Remove the seven attaching screws, intake manifold, leaf valves and gaskets from the powerhead.

Intake manifold mounting screws—5 HP (© Outboard Marine Corporation)

6 HP

These models use a remote fuel tank, diaphragm-type fuel pump, and single-barrel type carburetor with a fixed high-speed jet and an adjustable low-speed jet.

1. Remove the low-speed adjustment knob. Remove the choke hinge pin and remove the choke control shaft.

2. Disconnect the fuel line at the carburetor and plug the line.

3. Remove two screws and set the manual starter aside.

4. Remove the attaching nuts from the carburetor and remove the carburetor from the manifold.

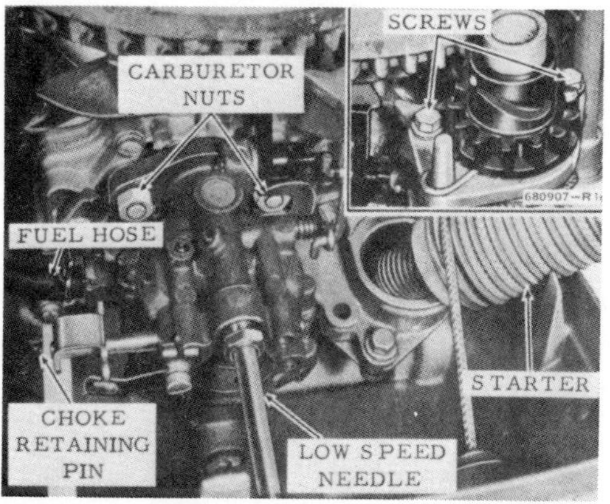

Carburetor removal—6 HP (© Outboard Marine Corporation)

5. Remove seven screws attaching the intake manifold and remove the intake manifold, leaf valves, and gasket from the powerhead.

Intake manifold attaching screws—6 HP (© Outboard Marine Corporation)

9½ HP

These models use remote fuel tanks, diaphragm-type fuel pumps, and single-barrel carburetors with fixed high-speed jets and adjustable low-speed jets.

1. Remove the fuel line from the carburetor and plug the line.

2. Disconnect the choke linkage by lifting the rod from the bellcrank.

Carburetor linkage and fuel connection—9½ HP (© Outboard Marine Corporation)

3. Unhook the cable-to-cover spring from the low-speed jet.

4. Pull the low-speed knob from the jet and feed the end of the cable through the control panel.

5. Remove five screws attaching the carburetor to the intake manifold. Swing the stabilizer bracket aside and remove the carburetor.

6. Remove the screws attaching the leaf plate base to the intake manifold and remove the leaf plate base from the manifold.

Leaf plate mounting screws—9½ HP (© Outboard Marine Corporation)

18 AND 25 HP

These models use a remote fuel tank, a diaphragm-type fuel pump, and a single-barrel carburetor with a fixed high-speed jet and adjustable low-speed jet.

1. Remove the shoulder screw and choke lever to remove the choke lever from the carburetor. Lift up on the choke arm and remove the choke control knob from the carburetor.

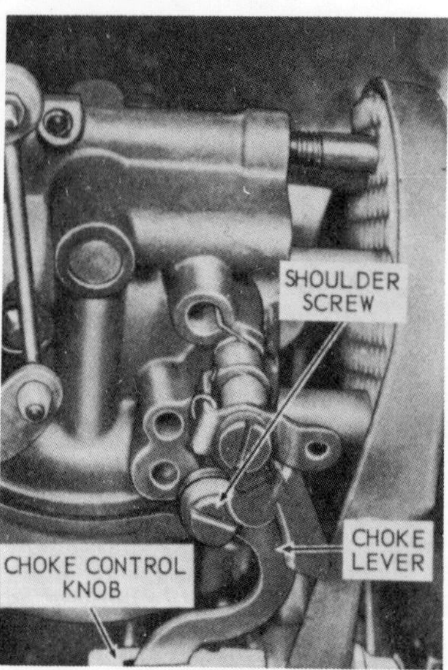

Choke knob removal—18 and 25 HP (© Outboard Marine Corporation)

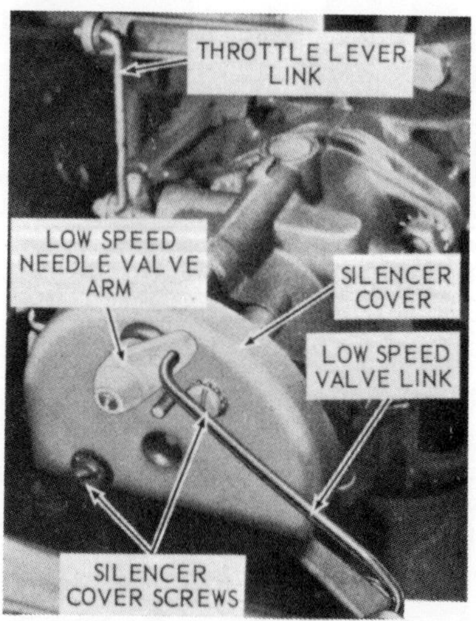

Carburetor linkage—18 and 25 HP (© Outboard Marine Corporation)

2. Remove the low-speed adjustment arm.

3. Remove the air silencer cover.

4. Disconnect the cam follower to throttle lever link.

5. Disconnect the fuel line at the fuel pump and plug the fuel pump fitting and the fuel line.

6. Remove two nuts and lockwashers attaching the carburetor to the intake manifold.

7. Remove the carburetor and gaskets from the manifold.

8. Remove the eight screws attaching the intake manifold to the powerhead. Remove the intake manifold.

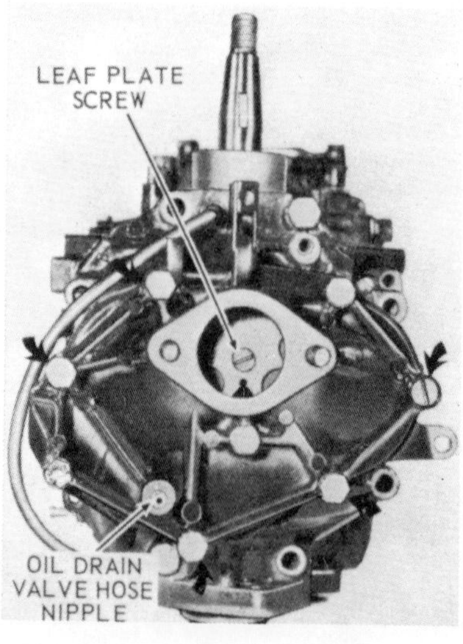

Leaf plate screw location—18 and 25 HP (© Outboard Marine Corporation)

9. Remove the leaf plate assembly and gasket.

Installation

1½ HP

1. Place a new gasket between the intake manifold and the crankcase and attach the intake manifold to the crankcase.
2. Install the leaf valve assembly. Install the carburetor on the mounting studs and reconnect the fuel line.
3. Further installation is the reverse of removal.
4. Perform adjustments as necessary.

2 HP

1. Place a new gasket between the intake manifold and crankcase and attach the intake manifold and leaf valve assembly to the crankcase.
2. Install the carburetor in position, with a new gasket, and fasten it in place.
3. Reconnect the fuel line to the carburetor.
4. Further installation is the reverse of removal.
5. Perform all necessary adjustments.

3 HP (1966–67)

1. Place a new gasket between the intake manifold and leaf valves and attach these components to the powerhead. Do not tighten the manifold screws until the carburetor is in place.
2. Using a new gasket, install the carburetor.
3. Install the cam follower spring.
4. Reconnect the fuel line to the carburetor.
5. Reinstall the air silencer.
6. Perform all necessary adjustments.

3 HP (1968) AND 4 HP

1. Place a new gasket between the intake manifold and leaf plate assembly and install these on the powerhead. Do not tighten the intake manifold screws until after the carburetor has been installed.
2. Install the carburetor with a new gasket.
3. Reconnect the fuel line to the carburetor.
4. Install the choke rod.
5. Further installation is the reverse of removal.
6. Adjust the carburetor as necessary.

5 HP

1. Attach the leaf plate and intake manifold to the crankcase with screws and using new gaskets.
2. Install the carburetor on the intake manifold studs with a new gasket.
3. Reconnect the fuel line between the fuel pump and carburetor.
4. Install the cam follower spring.
5. Further installation is the reverse of removal.
6. Adjust the carburetor as necessary.

6 HP

1. Attach the leaf plate and intake manifold to the crankcase with new gaskets.
2. Install the carburetor on the intake manifold studs, using a new gasket.
3. Reconnect the fuel hose to the carburetor.
4. Attach the manual starter.
5. Further installation is the reverse of removal.
6. Perform all adjustments as necessary.

9½ HP

1. With a new gasket, install the intake manifold and leaf valves to the crankcase. Using a new gasket, install the carburetor on the mounting studs of the intake manifold. Swing the stabilizer bracket into position and insert the carburetor attaching screws. Tighten the flathead screw first to prevent distortion.
2. Install the choke knob and rod.
3. Install the low-speed needle cable through the control panel, but do not install the knob until after the carburetor has been adjusted.
4. Install the cable for the cover spring.
5. Further installation is the reverse of removal.
6. Perform all carburetor adjustments.

18 AND 25 HP

1. With a new gasket, install the leaf plate assembly on the crankcase.
2. Install the intake manifold, using a new gasket.
3. Install the carburetor and new gasket on the intake manifold studs and tighten the attaching nuts.
4. Reconnect the fuel line.
5. Install the throttle lever link and cam follower spring. Attach the silencer to the carburetor body.
6. Install the choke knob.

7. Perform all carburetor adjustments.
8. Further installation is the reverse of removal.

Carburetor Overhaul

Single-Barrel Types

1. Drain the carburetor by removing the screw plug in the bottom of the float chamber.

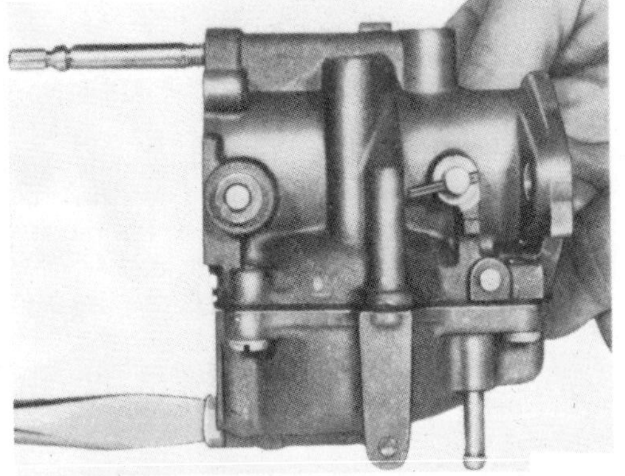

Removing the drain plug (© Outboard Marine Corporation)

2. Remove the screw(s) in the adjusting needles to permit removal of the adjusting knob(s).
3. Remove the control panel from the carburetor.
4. If the carburetor is equipped with a fixed, high-speed jet, remove this from the carburetor body. This should be done carefully to avoid damaging the jet.

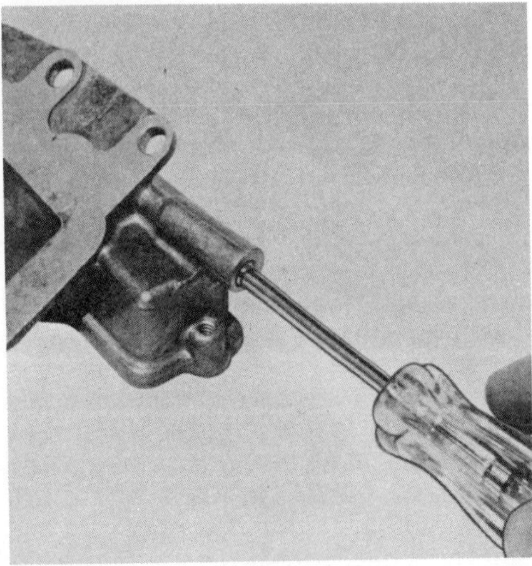

Removing the fixed high-speed jet (© Outboard Marine Corporation)

5. Remove the low-speed needle packing nut and low-speed needle valve from the carburetor. To remove the needle, temporarily replace the adjusting knob.

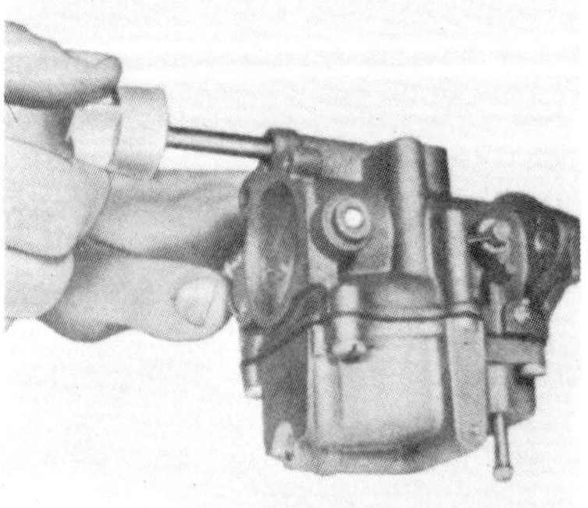

Removing the needle valve (© Outboard Marine Corporation)

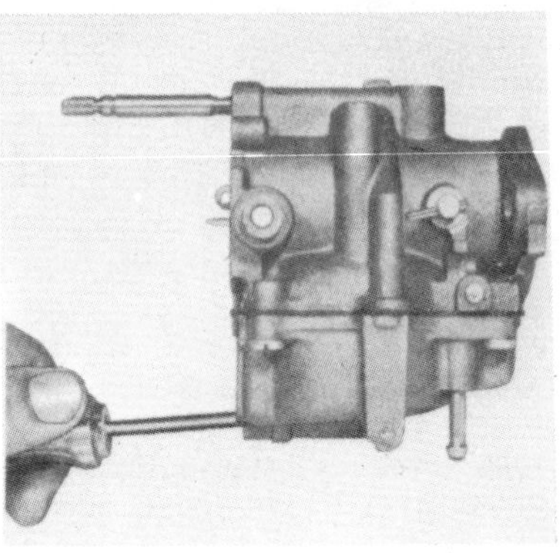

Removing the fixed-jet orifice plug (© Outboard Marine Corporation)

6. If the carburetor is equipped with an adjustable high-speed jet, remove the packing nut and remove it in the same manner as used for the low-speed jet.
7. Remove all needle valve packing and washers, being careful of the threads.
8. Remove the float chamber and gasket from the carburetor body.
9. Remove the nylon hinge pin and remove the float and float arm.
10. Remove the float valve, float valve seat, and gasket from the carburetor body. Unscrew the high-speed nozzle.
11. Scribe the choke cover to assure correct assembly. Remove the automatic choke cover (if equipped). Remove the choke solenoid and plunger. Do not remove the choke housing.
12. Clean all parts, except the cork float, in carburetor solvent and blow dry with compressed air or air-dry. Do not dry

parts with a cloth. Flush all passages in the carburetor with solvent to be sure all gum and varnish is removed. Do not attempt to clean the small passages in the carburetor with pieces of wire or the like.

13. Inspect the float and arm for wear or damage. If the float is oil-soaked, discard it and install a new one. Adjust the float level to specifications (see "Float Level Specifications"). Hold the body so that the weight of the float closes the valve.

14. Inspect the intake needle valve for wear or grooves. If any are found, replace the float valve assembly.

15. Check the needle valve seat for nicks, scratches, or wear. The valve seat and needle are a matched set; if either is worn, both parts must be replaced.

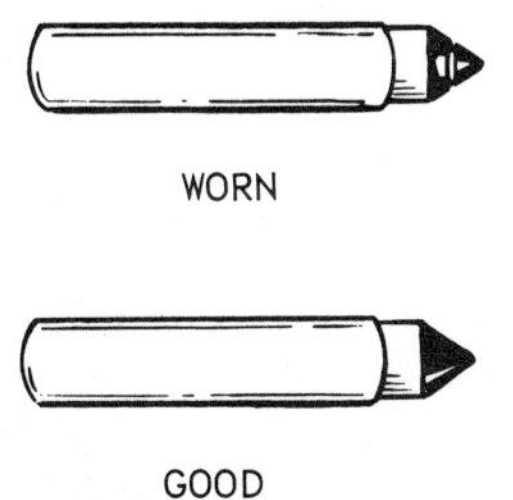

Intake needle valve wear (© Outboard Marine Corporation)

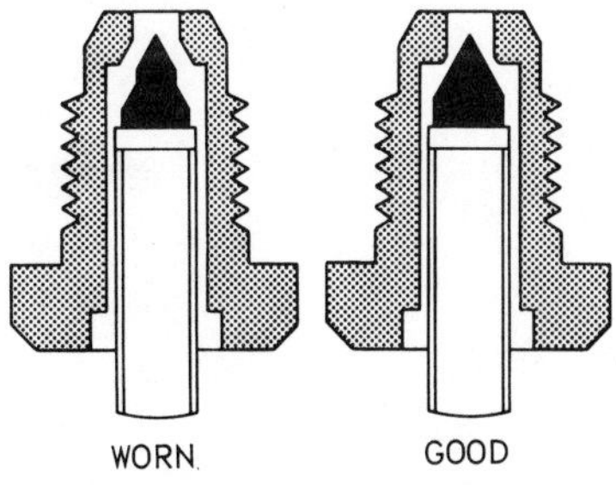

Intake needle valve seat wear (© Outboard Marine Corporation)

16. Check the throttle and choke shafts for excessive play. These are staked in place at assembly and, while replacement of these shafts is possible, carburetor body replacement is recommended.

17. Check the core plugs for leakage. If leakage is slight, a sharp rap with a hammer and flat punch will normally correct the situation. If leakage persists, drill a 1/8 in. hole in the plug and carefully pry the plug out. Apply a drop of sealant to the new plug and flatten the new plug to a tight fit.

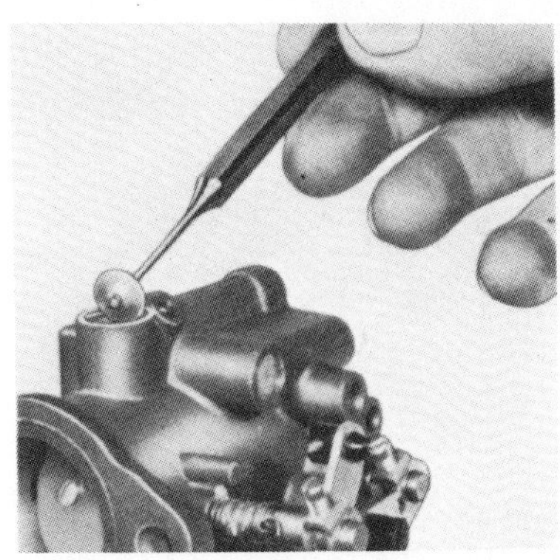

Removing the core plug (© Outboard Marine Corporation)

18. Inspect the leaf valves, which must be free of all gum and varnish. The leaves must be perfectly flat and free from distortion. Under no circumstances should the leaves be repaired or flexed by hand.

19. Assemble the carburetor in a clean area, using new gaskets and O-rings.

20. Install the high-speed nozzle and new carburetor boss gasket in the float chamber. Replace the float valve, seat and gasket, float, and hinge pin.

21. Turn the carburetor body upside down so that the weight of the float closes the needle. The top of the float should be even with the rim of the casting.

22. Reassemble the float chamber to the carburetor body.

23. If so equipped, install the high-speed orifice plug and screw plug.

24. Install the packing and packing washers, followed by the low-speed needle. Install the low-speed needle, turning it in carefully until it lightly contacts the seat. Do not overtighten. Back the needle out 7/8 of a turn.

25. Install the packing nut and tighten it until the needle can just be turned using finger pressure.

26. If the carburetor is equipped with an adjustable high-speed jet, perform steps 24 and 25 to replace the high-speed adjustable jet.

27. If so equipped, replace the non-adjustable high-speed jet.

28. Check the choke for free operation and be sure that the valves move freely.

29. Assemble the automatic choke. Be sure that the choke plunger moves freely.

30. The importance of keeping the leaf valves free cannot be overemphasized. The leaf is so designed that it maintains constant contact with the leaf plate and will

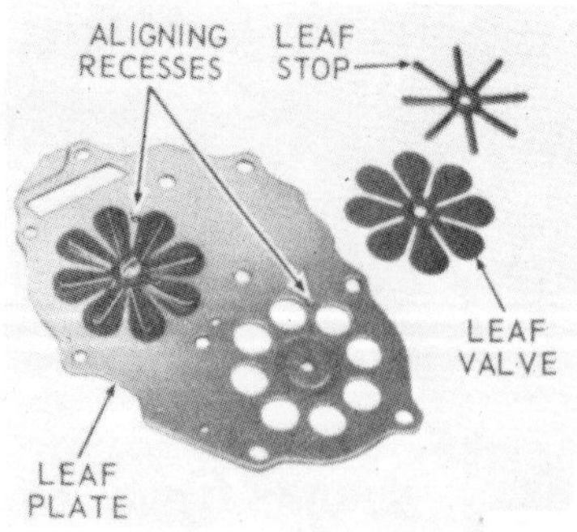

Leaf valve assembly—9½–25 HP (© Outboard Marine Corporation)

spring away under predetermined pressure.

31. Replace the control panel assembly and the adjusting knobs.

Adjustments

1½ AND 2 HP

Throttle Cam

1. Set the speed control lever at "stop."
2. Slowly advance the control until the cam follower just begins to open the throttle.
3. The mark on the cam and the point of contact on the cam follower should now be aligned.

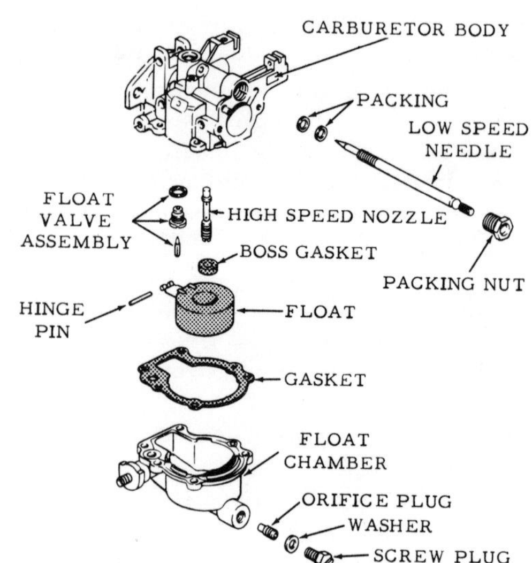

Exploded view of single-barrel carburetor (© Outboard Marine Corporation)

4. If not, loosen the cam mounting screws and set the cam so that, without play in the linkage, the throttle valve is closed. The mark on the throttle cam should align with the flat, port side of the cam follower just as the follower makes contact with the cam. Retighten the cam screws.

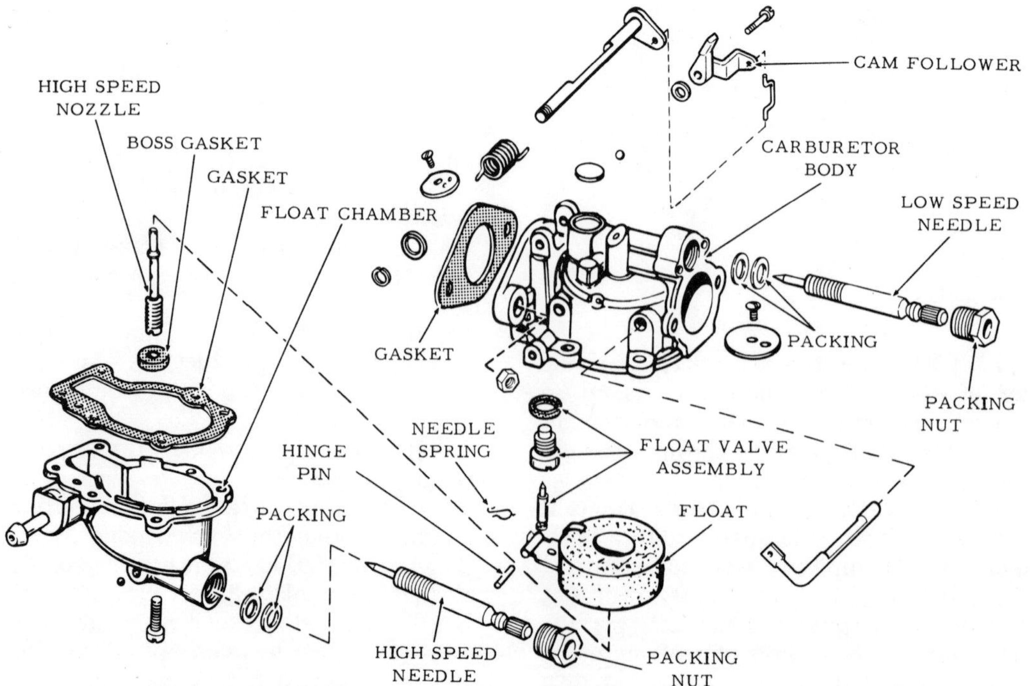

Exploded view of single-barrel carburetor (© Outboard Marine Corporation)

Float Level Adjustments

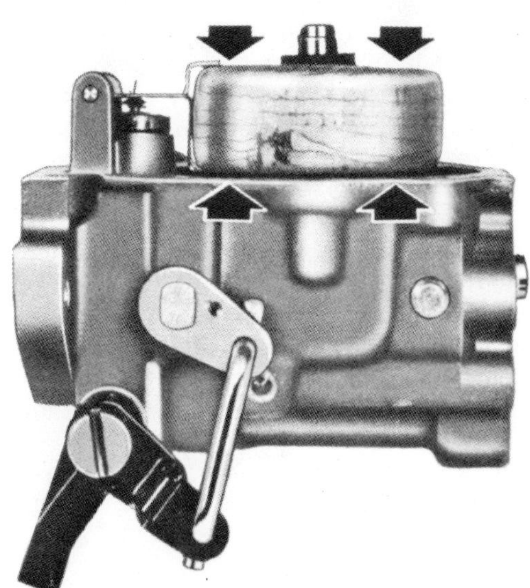

Float level adjustment—1½, 2, 3, 4, and 5 HP models. The float should be parallel and flush with the casting. Bend the metal tab to make adjustment (© Outboard Marine Corporation)

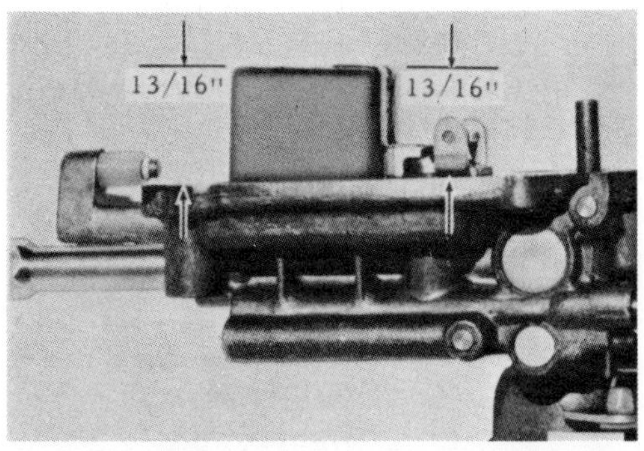

Float in the closed position—9½ HP models. The float should be parallel and flush with the casting. To adjust, level the metal tab (© Outboard Marine Corporation)

High- and Low-Speed Needles

1. Seat the high-speed needle gently. Do not force the needle into the seat. Seat the low-speed needle in the same manner.
2. Back the high-speed needle out one-half turn and the low-speed needle 1¼ turns.
3. Start the engine. Allow it to reach normal operating temperature.
4. Run the engine at full throttle and adjust the high-speed needle until the best rpm setting is obtained.
5. With the motor at a low speed, run the motor on a boat or in a test tank.

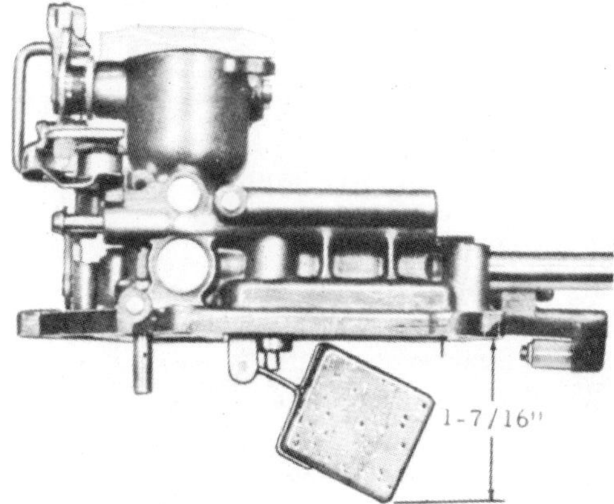

Float drop adjustment—9½ HP Models (© Outboard Marine Corporation)

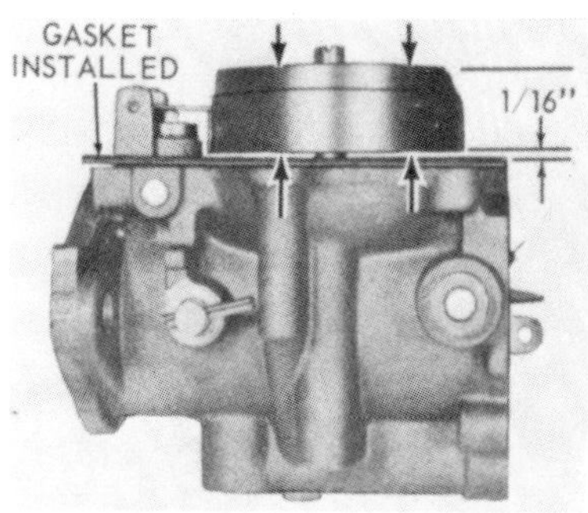

Float level adjustment—18 and 25 HP models. The float should be parallel to and $\frac{1}{16}$ in. above the casting with gasket installed. Bend the tab to make adjustment (© Outboard Marine Corporation)

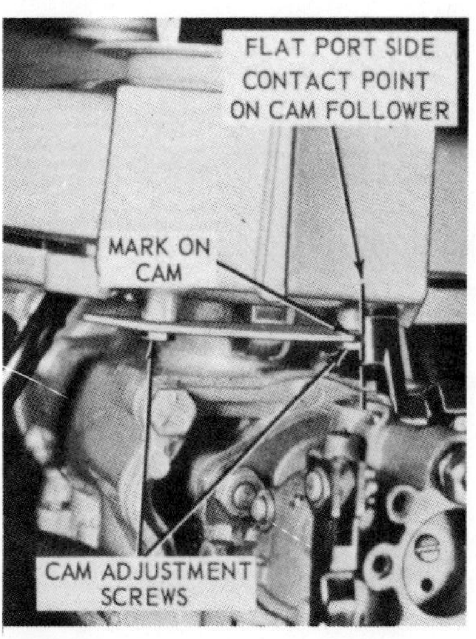

Throttle cam adjustment—1½ HP and 2 HP (© Outboard Marine Corporation)

6. Adjust the low-speed needle until the highest rpms and smoothest performance are obtained. Allow fifteen seconds for the motor to respond to each adjustment.

7. After the low-speed setting has been established, adjust the high-speed setting again.

8. Install the adjustment knobs without disturbing the position of the needles. Position each knob so that the boss is pointing straight up.

9. With the throttle cam and needle valves adjusted correctly, the motor should idle at approximately 550 rpm.

3 HP (1966–67)

Throttle Cam

1. Set the speed control at "stop."

2. Slowly advance the speed control until the cam follower shaft just begins to open the throttle.

3. The front edge of the cam should be aligned with the center of the shaft.

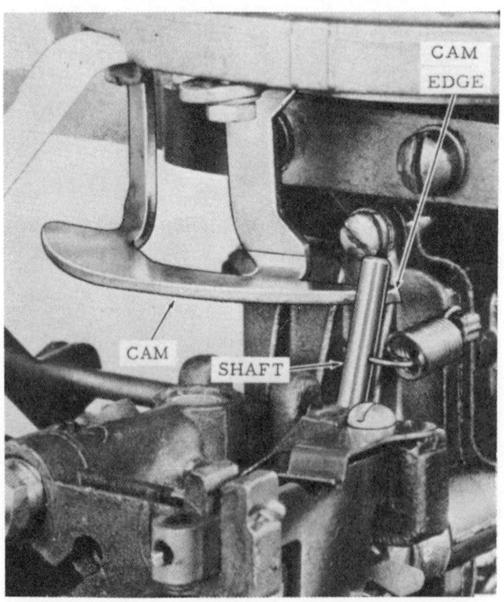

Throttle cam adjustment—3 HP (1966–67) (© Outboard Marine Corporation)

4. If the adjustment is not correct, loosen the cam adjusting screw and set the cam so that, with no play in the linkage, the throttle valve is closed as the marks align. Retighten the mounting screw.

5. With the cam correctly adjusted, the motor should idle at approximately 550 rpm.

Low Speed Needle

1. Loosen but do not remove the screw in the center of the low-speed adjusting knob. Pull the knob out so that it clears the stop on the needle shaft.

2. Retighten the screw and gently seat the needle in its seat. Do not force the needle.

3. Turn the needle out $1\frac{1}{4}$ turns.

4. Start the motor and warm it thoroughly.

5. Adjust the knob until the fastest and smoothest operation is obtained. Allow fifteen seconds for the motor to respond to each adjustment. The motor should idle around 550 rpm.

6. After reinstalling the motor covers, position the knob in the normal running position and tighten the screw.

3 HP (1968) AND 4 HP

Throttle Cam

1. See this procedure under the section for $1\frac{1}{2}$ hp motors.

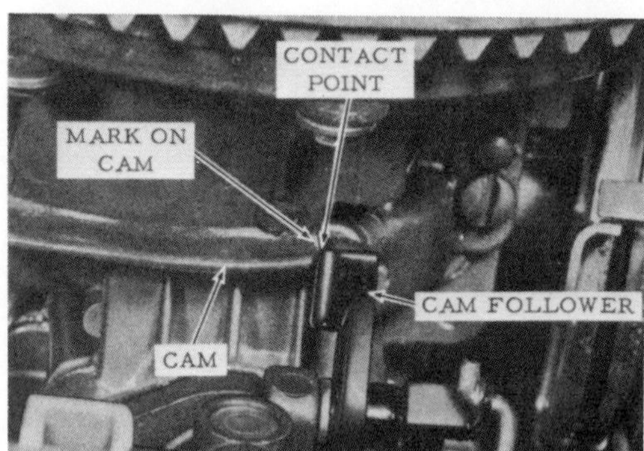

Throttle cam adjustment—3 HP (1968) and 4 HP (© Outboard Marine Corporation)

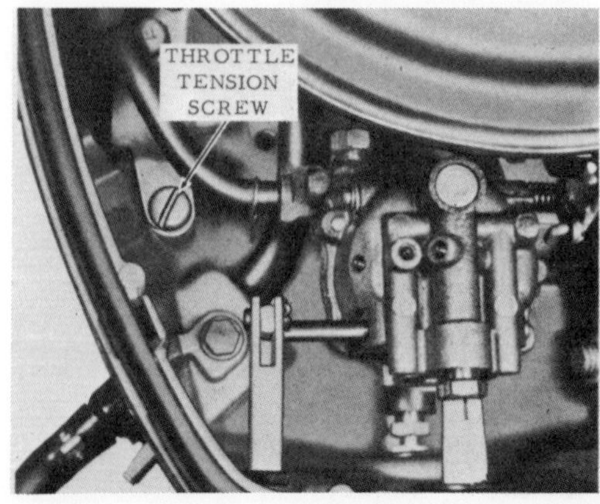

Throttle tension adjustment screw—3 HP (1968) and 4 HP (© Outboard Marine Corporation)

High- and Low-Speed Needles

1. This procedure is identical to that listed for 1½ hp motors, except that the high-speed needles should be backed out ¾ turn.

Throttle Tension

1. Throttle tension is correct when the motor speed remains constant and the throttle lever retains its position. To adjust the throttle tension, tighten the tension adjustment screw as necessary.

5 and 6 HP

Throttle Cam

1. If the throttle does not close, either the throttle return spring is too weak and should be replaced or the throttle or linkage is binding.
2. To adjust the throttle cam, advance the throttle control to the position where the leading edge of the cam follower is opposite the mark on the throttle cam. At this point, the throttle valve should be closed.
3. If it is not closed, adjust it by advancing the throttle control. The mark on the throttle cam must be directly behind the rounded starboard edge of the cam follower just as the throttle begins to open.
4. Loosen the screws holding the cam to the armature base. Push the cam toward the rear of the motor then pull the cam forward until it contacts the cam follower. The choke knob must be all the way in.
5. Tighten all screws and check the adjustment. The throttle valve should just begin to open as the flat port side of the cam follower passes the mark on the cam.

Throttle cam adjustment—5 and 6 HP (© Outboard Marine Corporation)

Low-Speed Needle

1. Seat the low-speed needle in the seat. Do not force the needle into the seat.
2. Back the needle out ¾ turn.
3. Start the motor and allow it to reach operating temperature.
4. Adjust the low-speed knob until the motor runs at its fastest and smoothest. Allow fifteen seconds for the motor to respond to each adjustment.
5. Replace the low-speed knob on the needle in the normal running position. Do not disturb the position of the needle when installing the knob.
6. With the low-speed needle and cam correctly adjusted, the motor should idle at approximately 550 rpm in gear.

9½ HP

Throttle Linkage and Cam Follower

1. Loosen the cam follower adjustment screw.
2. Move the cam follower so that it just contacts the throttle control cam. Rotate the magneto so that the cam follower aligns with the mark on the throttle control cam.
3. Be sure that the throttle valve is fully closed and rotate the throttle lever roller against the cam follower. Tighten the throttle lever to the throttle shaft.
4. Be sure that the adjustment settings are not disturbed when tightening the screws.

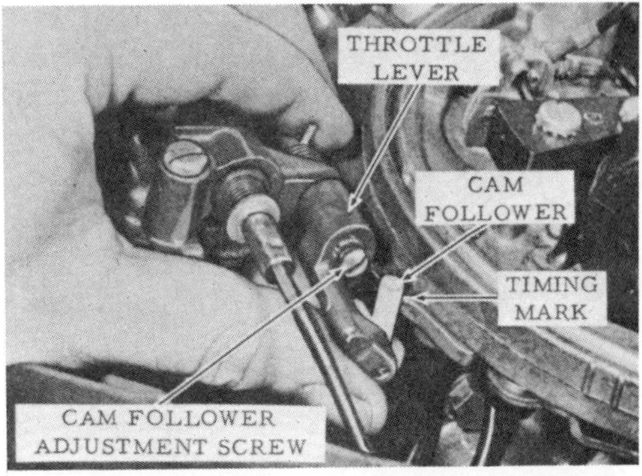

Throttle cam adjustment—9½ HP (© Outboard Marine Corporation)

Low-Speed Needle

1. Seat the needle valve in a clockwise direction until it is fully closed. Do not force the needle into the seat.
2. Back the needle out ¾ turn.

3. Start the motor and allow it to reach operating temperature.

4. With the motor in gear, run the motor at half-throttle briefly to clear the cylinders.

5. Keep the motor in gear and retard the throttle to idle. Turn the low-speed needle clockwise to lean it out until the motor begins to stall from an overly lean mixture. Richen the mixture by turning the needle counterclockwise until the cylinders begin to load up from a mixture that is too rich. Set the motor between these two settings where it runs fastest and smoothest.

6. Replace the low-speed adjusting knob midway between lean and rich. Be careful not to disturb the position of the needle when replacing the adjusting knob.

7. Adjust the idle adjustment knob to idle the motor at 550 rpm in gear.

18 and 25 HP

Throttle Cam

1. If the throttle does not close, either the throttle return spring is weak or the linkage is binding.

2. To adjust the throttle cam follower, advance the throttle control to the point where the cam follower roller is centered between the two marks on the throttle cam. At this point, the throttle valve should be closed. If not, adjust as follows.

3. Advance the throttle control to the position where the roller is centered between the two marks.

4. Loosen the throttle shaft arm screw. Hold the cam follower tight against the cam and tighten the throttle shaft arm screw. The throttle valve should just begin to open after the edge of the roller passes the second mark on the cam.

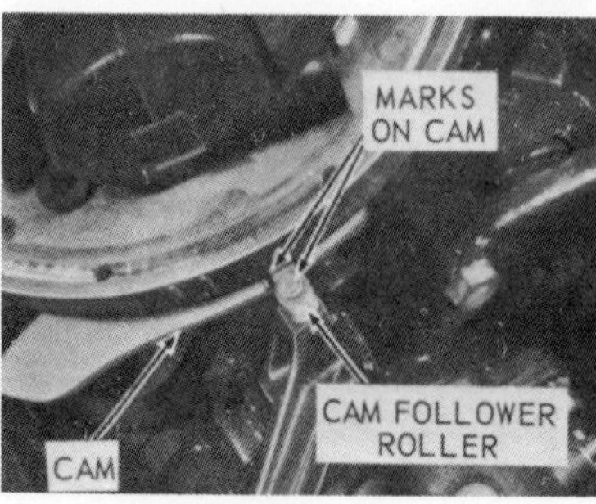

Throttle cam adjustment—18 and 25 HP (© Outboard Marine Corporation)

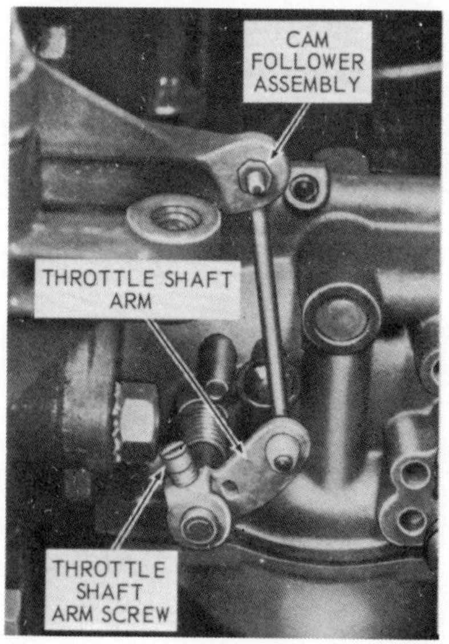

Throttle shaft arm screw location—18 and 25 HP (© Outboard Marine Corporation)

Low-Speed Needle

1. See this same procedure for the 9½ hp models.

OIL DRAIN VALVE

The oil drain valve ordinarily requires little or no service. However, when servicing the motor, the valve should be removed and cleaned. If gum or varnish is found in the crankcase when the powerhead is disassembled, it is likely that gum and varnish will be found in the oil drain valve. The valve should be removed and cleaned in OMC Accessory Engine Cleaner or a similar substitute.

Be sure that the oil drain valve leaf seats against the leaf plate. Check the spacing between the leaf and the leaf stop. Bend the leaf stop to obtain a clearance of 0.040 in.

FUEL PUMP AND FUEL FILTER

Models with Remote Fuel Tank

Before servicing the fuel pump, remove and clean the fuel filter and install a new filter element. Remove the fuel line from the fuel tank and blow through all passages and lines with compressed air. Restriction or clogging may be the cause of inadequate fuel delivery and this could cure it, eliminating unnecessary replacement of the fuel pump. If the trouble still

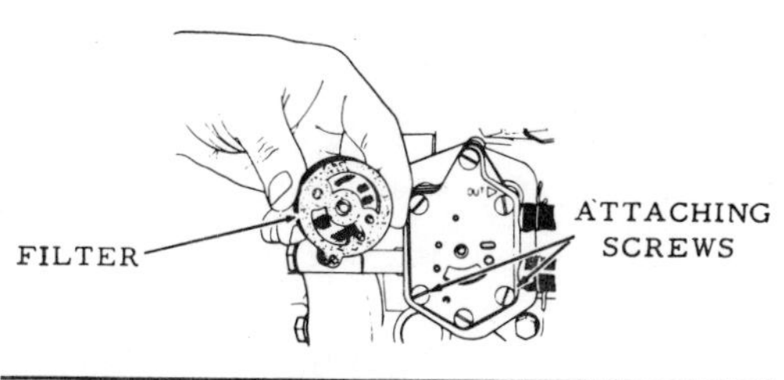

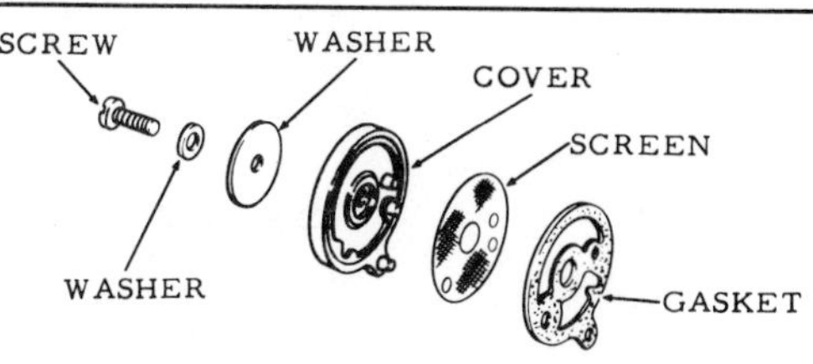

Typical fuel filter (remote tank models) (© Outboard Marine Corporation)

exists, the fuel pump is probably malfunctioning and should be replaced.

NOTE: *On models with an integral fuel tank, the fuel filter is located on the inside end of the fuel shut-off valve. It may be removed from the tank by unscrewing it for cleaning.*

REMOVAL

1. Disconnect the hoses from the filter and pump assembly.
2. Remove the screws which attach the pump and filter assembly to the powerhead or air silencer and remove the fuel pump and filter.

CLEANING AND INSPECTION

1. The fuel pump components are not serviceable. If a malfunction exists, replace the complete pump.
2. Inspect the filter for sediment accumulation. The filter can be removed by unscrewing the filter cap and removing the cap.

FUEL TANK

Integral Tank Models

INSTALLATION

REMOVAL

1. Shut off the fuel supply at the fuel shut-off valve and at the vent cap.
2. Remove the spark plug wire and grommet.
3. Disconnect the fuel line below the fuel shut-off valve. Plug the line and the tank.
4. Remove the screws attaching the fuel tank to the support bracket and remove the tank.

INSTALLATION

1. Installation is the reverse of removal.

Remote Tank Models

All remote fuel tanks, hoses, primer bulbs, fuel level indicators, and the upper housing and valves are serviced in an identical manner.

UPPER HOUSING AND LEVEL INDICATOR

Inspection and Repair

1. The fuel level indicator is mounted in the upper housing. The entire upper housing assembly can be removed by removing the attaching screws and lifting the assembly from the tank. Be careful not to damage the float or screen on the end of the fuel line.
2. Check for free movement of the indicator on the indicator pin. Remove the pin from the indicator support by compressing the free end and pulling it out.
3. Be sure that the float arm is straight and that the float is not oil-soaked.
4. Remove the screws holding the indicator support to the upper housing.
5. Lift out the lens and clean it with thinner.
6. The release valves must seat tightly to prevent fumes from escaping, but must open a clear passage for air to enter when the fuel hose is connected. The release

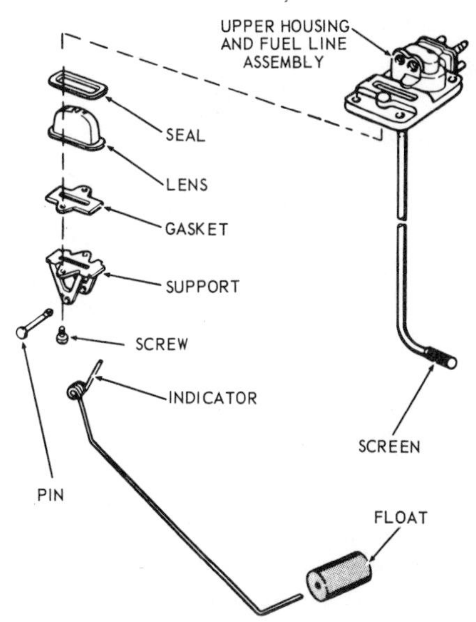

Fuel tank level indicator—remote tank (© Outboard Marine Corporation)

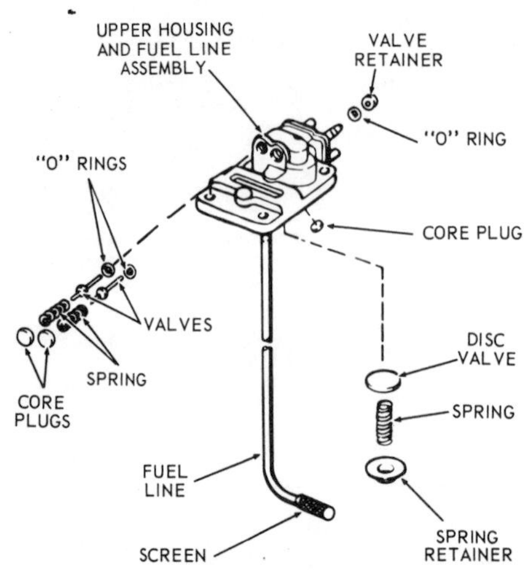

Fuel tank upper housing—remote tank (© Outboard Marine Corporation)

Fuel tank upper housing showing drain screw—remote tank (© Outboard Marine Corporation)

valves are best cleaned by removing the core plugs and disassembling them.

7. Replace the O-rings to be sure of a good fit.

8. The air intake disc valve must seat tightly to prevent fumes from escaping, but must allow air to enter. The disc valve spring retainer is staked in place and may be removed by filing off the burrs. Restake the new one in place with a small punch.

Hose and Primer Bulb

Clamps

1. To release the clamp, grip the clamp with pliers and bend the overlapping hook backward.

2. To install the clamps, grip the clamp with pliers and apply slight pressure to the hook on the top side with a screwdriver. Squeeze the clamp with pliers until the hooks interlock.

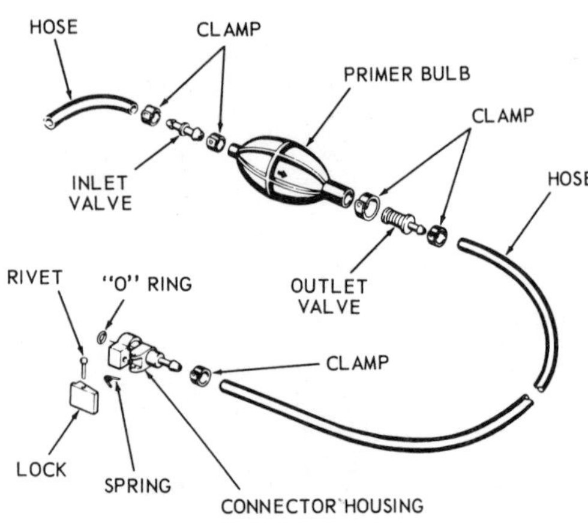

Fuel hose and primer bulb assembly—remote tank (© Outboard Marine Corporation)

Connector Housings

Installation of the O-ring in the fuel hose connectors requires the use of two fabricated tools; one to hold the plunger down and one to remove the O-ring. Both of these instruments are illustrated and can be made from 16 gauge ($^1/_{16}$ in. diameter) wire. Form a small hook on the bottom of the longer tool with about a $^1/_{16}$ in. radius. Be sure there are no burrs on the ends to scratch the O-ring seats or plungers.

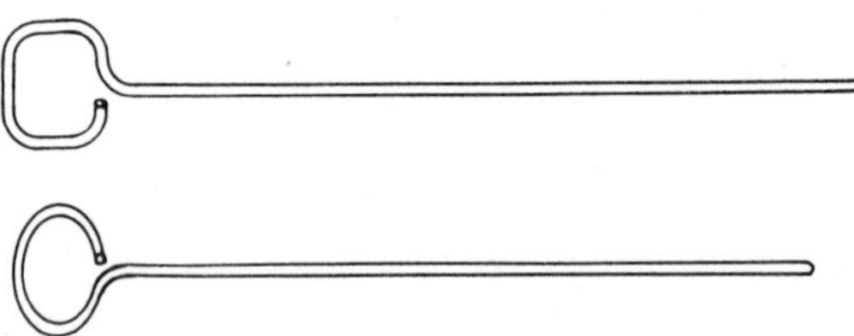

O-ring tools (can be fabricated) (© Outboard Marine Corporation)

O-Ring Removal

1. Place the connector housing in a vise between two wood blocks.

2. Push the plunger down with the straight instrument.

3. Insert the hooked instrument between the O-ring and its seat with the hook in a horizontal position.

4. Twist the hook to grasp the O-ring.

5. Carefully (to avoid scratching the plunger) pull the O-ring out of the housing.

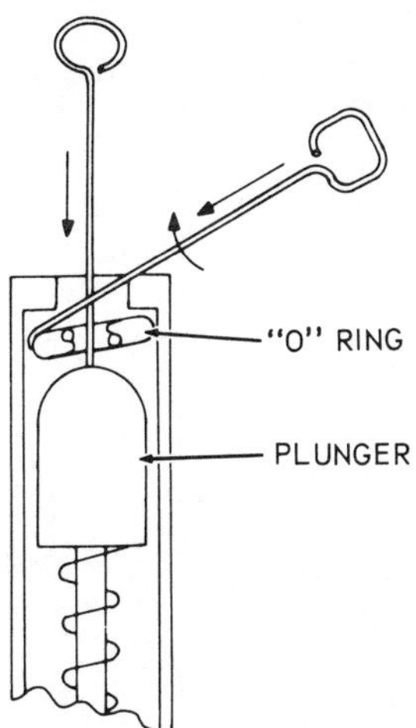

Removing the O-ring from connector housing (© Outboard Marine Corporation)

O-Ring Installation

1. Place a drop of oil on the O-ring.
2. Place the O-ring on the face of the connector.
3. Push the plunger down with the straight instrument.
4. Pinch the O-ring together with your fingers and gently push it into position.

Fuel Hose

When assembling the fuel hose, check for cracks in the primer bulb or the hose. The primer bulb must be installed so that the fuel flows from the shorter length to the longer length. Fuel flow through the primer bulb is indicated by an arrow.

Electrical System

THEORY OF OPERATION

The ignition system of all outboards covered in this chapter consists of a flywheel-type magneto connected to the spark plugs by high-tension leads. The magneto is a self-contained electrical generating unit consisting of an armature plate and two ignition coil and lamination assemblies, condensers, and breaker points. A permanent magnet cast into the flywheel completes the assembly.

The magneto uses the fast-moving flywheel magnet and stationary coils to generate an electric current sufficient to jump the spark plug air gap.

Each ignition coil consists of two coils; one a primary (relatively few turns of heavy-gauge copper wire), and the other a secondary (many turns of thin copper wire). One end of both the primary and secondary coil is connected to the core (ground). The other end of the primary coil is connected to the insulated stationary breaker point. The other end of the secondary coil is connected to the spark plug leads. The coil core and movable breaker point are grounded on the armature base.

When the poles of the magnet sweep past the first and center legs of the core, a magnetic flow is momentarily established in the core, assuming a direction from the North pole of the permanent magnet to the South pole. As the poles sweep further along, the magnetic flow breaks down. An electric charge is induced in the coils by the rapid development and collapse of current in the center leg. The current flows through the closed breaker points, and sets up its own magnetic flow in the center leg of the core. As two opposing magnetic flows are created, the cam on the crankshaft opens the breaker points and the flow collapses. To hasten the collapse, a condenser absorbs the current that would normally arc the breaker points. This rapid collapse induces sufficient voltage in the secondary circuit to jump the spark plug gap.

MAGNETO REMOVAL

1½ HP

1. Remove the motor cover by removing the port and starboard motor covers, and remove the control panel screws.
2. Twist the high-tension leads off the spark plugs in a counterclockwise direction.
3. Using an automotive flywheel holder, remove the flywheel nut. Remove the starter rope pulley and, using an appropriate puller, remove the flywheel.
4. Remove the exhaust cover screw and detach the armature plate ground wire. Remove the screw below the armature plate. Remove this screw before attempting to remove the armature plate.
5. Lift the armature plate from the

Armature plate ground wire—1½ HP (© Outboard Marine Corporation)

crankcase. Remove the bushing which has a tongue engaging the groove in the crankshaft.

Armature plate removal—1½ HP (© Outboard Marine Corporation)

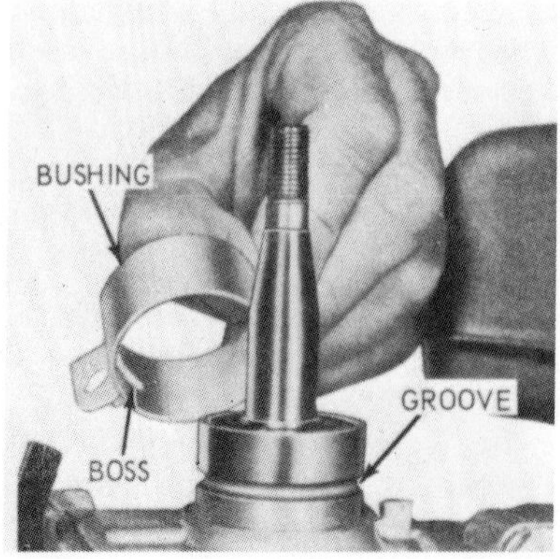

Bushing removal showing tongue and groove—1½ HP (© Outboard Marine Corporation)

2 HP

1. Remove the rewind starter housing.
2. Twist the high-tension leads from the sparks by twisting counterclockwise.
3. Using an automotive flywheel holder, remove the flywheel nut and pull the flywheel from the crankshaft, with a suitable puller.
4. Remove the exhaust cover screw and detach the armature plate ground wire. Do not remove the armature plate before removing the screw located below the armature plate.

Armature plate ground wire and armature plate screw—2 HP (© Outboard Marine Corporation)

5. Lift the armature plate from the crankcase. Remove the bushing which engages the groove in the crankcase by means of a projection.

3 HP (1966–67)

1. Remove the port and starboard motor covers.
2. Remove the four screws attaching the starter to the powerhead. Lift the starter from the gas tank.
3. Twist the leads off the spark plugs in a counterclockwise direction.
4. Disconnect the fuel hose at the fuel shut-off valve. Remove the fuel tank from the mounting plate.

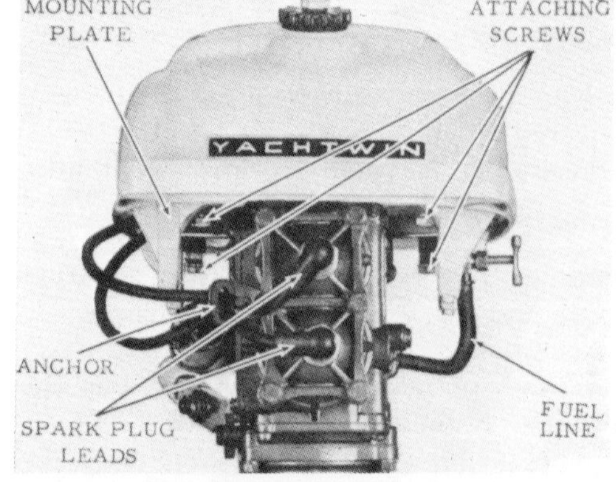

Fuel tank removal—2 HP (1966–67) (© Outboard Marine Corporation)

5. Using an automotive flywheel holder, remove the flywheel nut. Using a suitable puller, pull the flywheel from the crankshaft.

6. Remove the magneto from the powerhead.

Magneto removal—3 HP (1966–67) (© Outboard Marine Corporation)

3 HP (1968) and 4 HP

1. Remove the motor cover.
2. Twist the leads off the spark plugs in a counterclockwise direction.
3. Disconnect the throttle lever-to-armature link.
4. Using an automotive flywheel holder, remove the flywheel nut and three screws. With a suitable puller, remove the flywheel from the crankshaft.
5. Loosen the four phillips head screws and remove the magneto from the powerhead.

Flywheel removal—3 HP (1968) and 4 HP (© Outboard Marine Corporation)

Spark plug wire loom and throttle lever link (insert)—3 HP (1968) and 4 HP (© Outboard Marine Corporation)

5 HP

1. Twist the leads off the spark plugs in a counterclockwise direction. Remove the wire loom from the side of the powerhead.
2. Using an automotive-type flywheel holder, remove the flywheel nut and three screws. Using a suitable puller, remove the flywheel from the crankshaft.
3. Remove the throttle link retainer and link.

Armature link—5 HP (© Outboard Marine Corporation)

4. Loosen the phillips screws attaching the magneto to the powerhead. Lift the magneto from the powerhead.

6 HP

1. Twist the leads off the spark plugs in a counterclockwise direction and remove the wire loom from the side of the powerhead.
2. Using an automotive flywheel holder,

Magneto arm and link removal—9½ HP (© Outboard Marine Corporation)

remove the flywheel nut and three screws. Using a suitable puller, remove the flywheel from the crankshaft.

Armature link—6 HP (© Outboard Marine Corporation)

3. Remove the armature link spring clip. Loosen the four phillips head screws attaching the magneto armature plate to the powerhead.

4. Lift the magneto assembly from the powerhead.

9½ HP

1. Using an automotive-type flywheel holder, remove the flywheel nut and pull the flywheel from the crankshaft with the aid of a suitable puller.

2. Disconnect the stop switch leads. Lift up two electrical connectors and slide them apart.

3. Twist the leads off the spark plugs in a counterclockwise direction.

4. Remove the retainer and pivot arm screw from the magneto arm and link.

Magneto arm and link removal—9½ HP (© Outboard Marine Corporation)

5. Loosen the four screws attaching the magneto armature plate to the retaining ring. Lift the magneto armature plate from the powerhead.

18 and 25 HP

1. Remove the starter by removing the three attaching screws.

2. Twist the leads off the spark plugs in a counterclockwise direction.

3. Remove the spark plug wire loom from the cylinder head.

4. Using an automotive-type flywheel holder, remove the flywheel nut and three screws. With the aid of a puller, remove the flywheel from the crankshaft.

5. Disconnect the stop switch leads by pulling the electrical connections apart.

6. Remove the armature link spring clip. Loosen the screws attaching the magneto armature plate to the powerhead. Lift the magneto assembly from the powerhead.

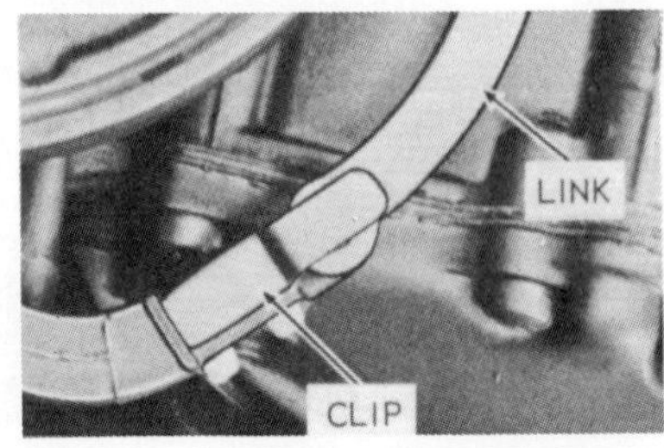

Armature link and clip—18 and 25 HP (© Outboard Marine Corporation)

Disassembly—All Models

1. All components can now be removed from the armature plate. Remove the attaching screws to accomplish this. The spark plug high-tension leads can be pulled from the coil and lamination assemblies.

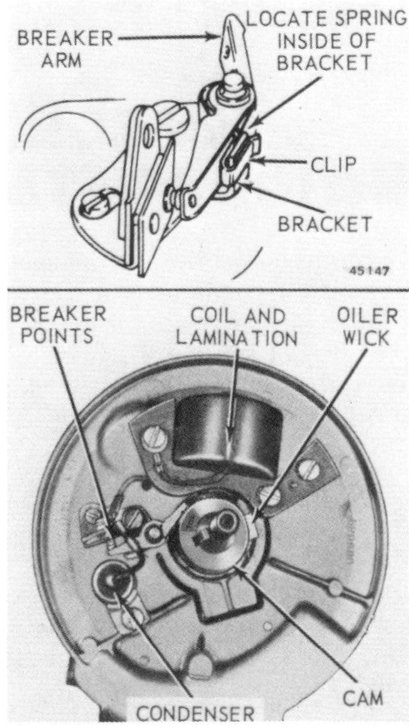

Magneto armature plate and breaker point assembly—1½ and 2 HP (© Outboard Marine Corporation)

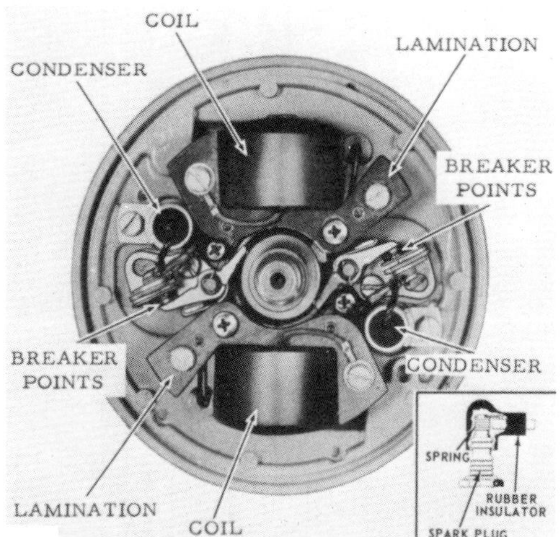

Magneto used on 1968 3, 4, 5, and 6 HP and 1966–67 3 HP (© Outboard Marine Corporation)

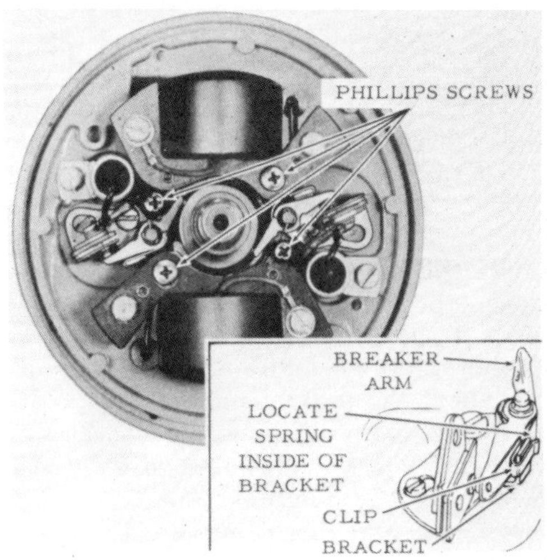

Magneto used on 9½ HP (© Outboard Marine Corporation)

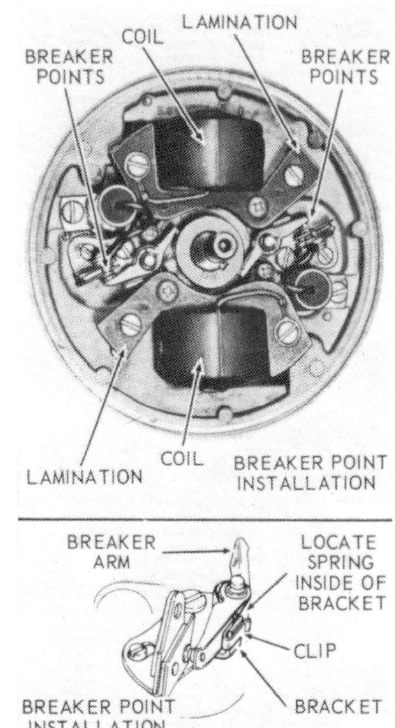

Magneto used on 18 and 25 HP (© Outboard Marine Corporation)

Ignition System Component Inspection

1. Inspect the spark plugs for cracked porcelains or badly worn electrodes. Clean the electrodes with a point file. Do not sandblast the spark plugs. Adjust the gap

to specification by bending the side electrode. Before installing the spark plugs, clean the spark plug seat and install new gaskets. Tighten the spark plugs by hand and tighten them to the specified torque.

2. Examine the breaker points for corrosion or unusual wear. Breaker points in questionable condition should be replaced. Check the action of the spring and the free movement of the arm. If the points are in need of cleaning, use trichloroethylene or alcohol. Even the oil from a person's hands can affect the performance of the points. Check the points for good electrical contact and check and adjust the breaker point setting as described later.

3. Coils, condensers, and breaker points can be accurately tested with an ignition tester or other specialized equipment. About the only test that can be performed with reasonable results, without special equipment, is the condenser test. Instructions for testing the condenser are given in chapter one.

Assembly of Magneto

1. Reassemble the components that were removed from the armature plate, following the reverse order of disassembly.

2. Correct location of the coil and lamination assemblies is governed by machined mounting surfaces on the armature plate. The heels of the coil laminations should be flush with the machined surfaces.

3. Alignment of the magneto coils is simplified by the use of a special coil locating ring, which is machined to fit over the four bosses. The locating ring is helpful, but not absolutely necessary.

Coil locating ring (special tool) (© Outboard Marine Corporation)

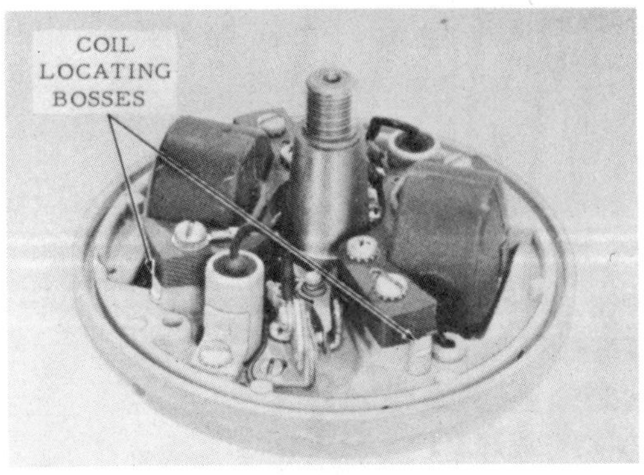

Coil locating basses (© Outboard Marine Corporation)

4. Reconnect all leads to the magneto; be sure that the connections are clean and tight. Bend the condenser leads down so that they do not rub the flywheel.

5. Be sure that a new oiler wick is installed under the forward coil.

Installation—All Models

1. If the flywheel key was removed, install the key in the crankshaft keyway with the single mark on the side of the key facing down. If the key is not installed in this position, the engine timing will be late (retarded).

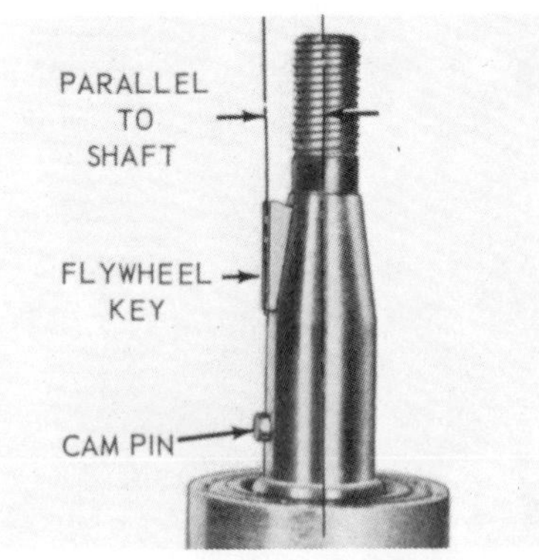

Flywheel key and cam pin installed (© Outboard Marine Corporation)

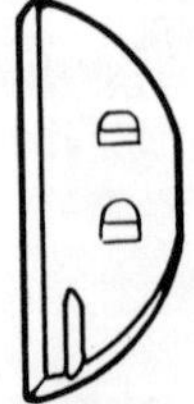

Flywheel key showing single mark which faces down (© Outboard Marine Corporation)

2. Install the breaker cam on the crankshaft with the word "top" facing up.

3. Apply a coat of OMC Type A lubricant to the magneto support and retaining ring or the inside diameter of the armature plate liner.

4. Install the magneto support and retaining ring or the armature plate liner on the powerhead. The magneto support ring should be installed with the tapered side down. Align the screw holes of the magneto support ring to correspond with the holes in the magneto.

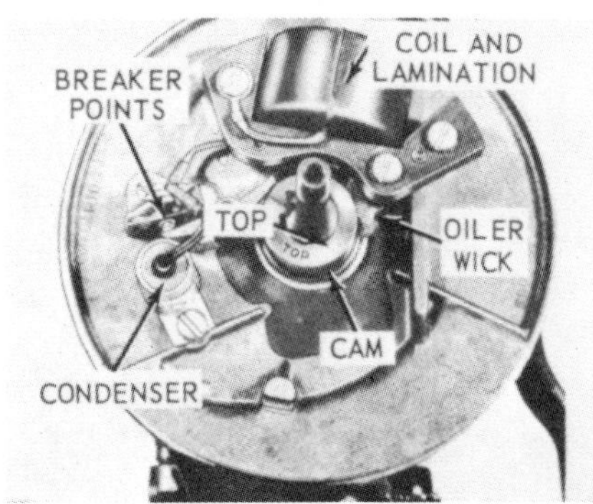

Armature plate installed (© Outboard Marine Corporation)

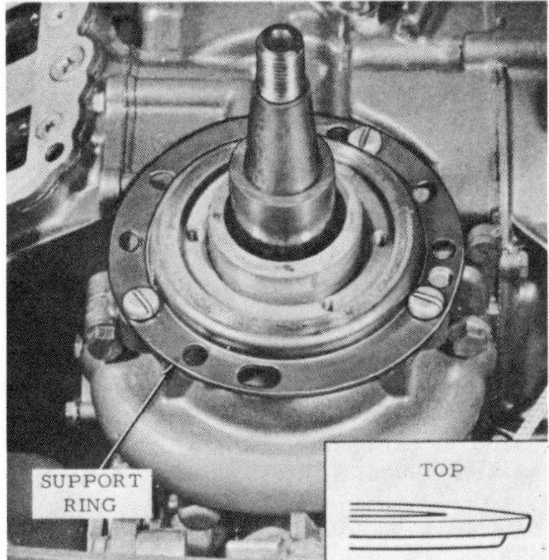

Magneto support ring installed (© Outboard Marine Corporation)

5. Do not add oil or grease the wick.

6. Place the magneto in position over the crankshaft. Do not damage the breaker arms on the cam and do not bend the cam follower. If the motor is equipped with an armature plate instead of magneto support, install the armature plate in position with the liner tab in the slot of the armature plate hub.

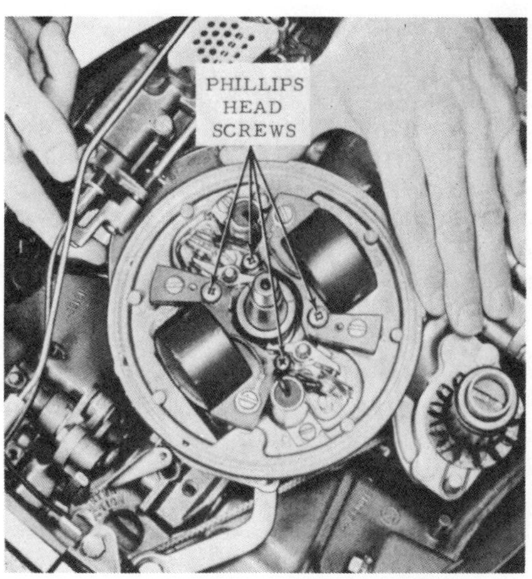

Magneto installed (© Outboard Marine Corporation)

7. Be sure that the cam follower is not jammed by the throttle control cam. Insert the screw and tighten it just enough to hold the plate in any selected position but not tight enough to cause it to turn with effort.

NOTE: *This step applies only to models with an armature plate.*

8. Install the throttle link and retainer.

9. Check the breaker point settings as described later.

10. Check the crankshaft and flywheel tapers for any traces of oil. The tapers must be perfectly dry and clean. Swab the tapered surfaces with solvent and blow them dry.

11. Install the flywheel and screws and tighten the nut to the specified torque.

12. Connect the spark plug wires to the spark plugs and be sure of a tight electrical connection.

13. If equipped, install the spark plug wire looms on the side of the powerhead.

ADJUSTMENTS

Engine Timing

The engine timing is fixed between two predetermined points on all models up to and including the 25 hp model. There is no adjustment to the engine timing and none should be attempted.

Breaker Point Adjustment

1½ AND 2 HP

1. To adjust the breaker points, the magneto must be installed and the flywheel must be removed.

2. Rotate the crankshaft in a clockwise direction (to avoid damage to the water pump impeller) and place the breaker arm on the high point of the cam.

3. Turn the eccentric screw until a gap of 0.020 in. (used points) or 0.022 in. (new points) is established. Measure the gap with a clean, non-oily feeler gauge.

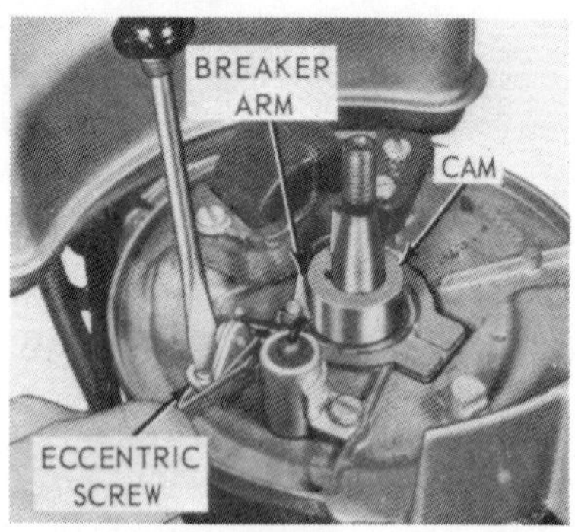

Adjusting the breaker points—1½ and 2 HP (© Outboard Marine Corporation)

4. Tighten the locking screw and rotate the crankshaft several revolutions (clockwise direction only) and recheck the breaker point gap.

5. Reinstall the flywheel.

3–25 HP

NOTE: *There are two methods of adjusting the breaker points detailed in this procedure, one with the use of a special tool available from OMC dealers (by special order), and the other without using the special tool.*

1. To adjust the breaker points by either method, the magneto must be installed and the flywheel must be removed.

2. Disconnect all leads from the breaker point assemblies. Note that there are two sets of points, one for each cylinder.

3. Connect a battery-powered test light between the breaker plate and the forward breaker point screw terminal. A suitable test light can be fashioned using the materials and directions as given in chapter one.

4. Place the special timing fixture on

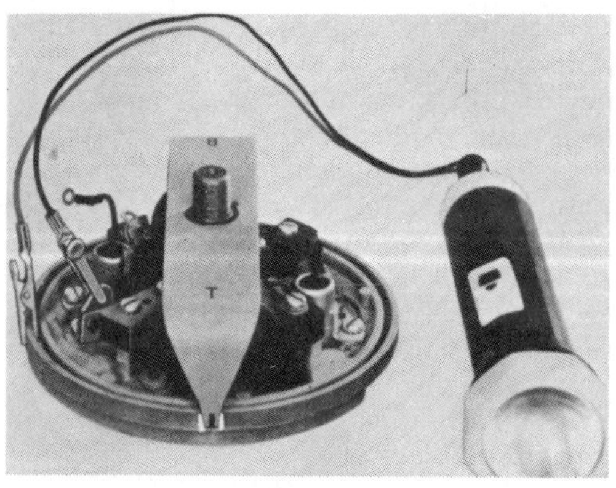

Connections for checking point gap with battery-powered test light (© Outboard Marine Corporation)

the crankshaft. Rotate the timing fixture in a clockwise direction until the side of the fixture marked "T" is aligned with the first projection of the armature plate.

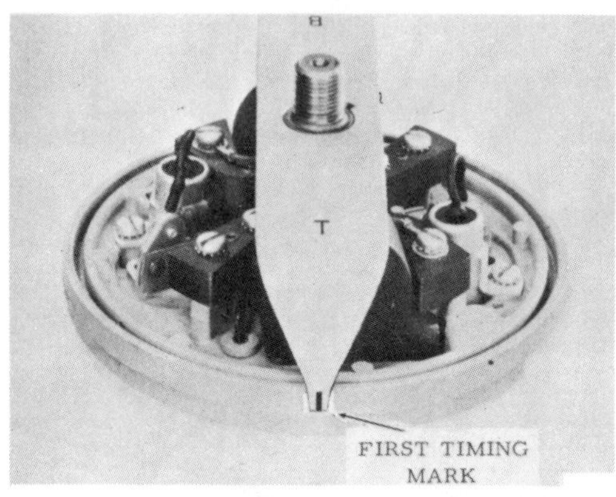

Timing fixture aligned with first projection (© Outboard Marine Corporation)

5. Move the timing fixture back and forth until the exact instant at which the points close is indicated by the test light. The points should break open when the timing fixture pointer is midway between the two projections on the armature plate.

6. If the adjustment is not correct, align the timing fixture and the first timing mark. Adjust the points by means of the eccentric screw until the test light indicates a closed circuit.

NOTE: *If new points have been installed, adjust the points to break open at the first timing mark, to allow for seating of the fiber breaker block.*

7. Recheck the timing (steps 5 and 6).

8. If the timing fixture is not available, use a feeler gauge to adjust the point gap.

Rotate the crankshaft in a clockwise direction, until the breaker arm is on the high lobe of the cam (fully open). With the eccentric screw, adjust the point gap to 0.020 in. (used points) or 0.022 in. (new points).

9. Recheck the adjustment after rotating the crankshaft through several revolutions in a clockwise direction only.

10. Regardless of which procedure is used, rotate the crankshaft 180° and set the other set of points.

11. Connect all leads that were removed and install the flywheel. Tighten the flywheel nut to the specified torque.

STARTER MOTOR

Maintenance operations on the starter motor are generally limited to periodic inspection for tight mountings. Unless it is certain that the starter motor is defective, do not remove it for overhaul. In general, starter motor removal procedures are alike among OMC models. The following procedure can be used for all models, noting minor variations among models.

Starter motor (© Outboard Marine Corporation)

Removal

1. Disconnect and tag the lead(s) from the starter motor.

2. Depending on equipment, either detach the starter and mounting bracket from the crankcase or remove the thru-bolts from the starter.

3. If the former method is chosen, remove the starter and bracket, and separate the motor from the bracket.

4. If the latter method (step 2) is chosen, the starter can now be dropped from the starter drive housing. If it is necessary to remove the starter drive housing, remove the ring gear cover, loosen the screw, and remove the starter drive housing.

Installation

1. Installation is the reverse of removal.

AUTOMATIC REWIND STARTER

The manual starter engages the powerhead flywheel, by means of three pawls, when the rope handle is pulled. A coil spring is wound as the handle is pulled and then unwinds, pulling the rope back.

NOTE: *Do not release the handle at the end of each pull, allowing it to snap back. Serious damage can occur.*

Gear drive manual starter (© Outboard Marine Corporation)

Removal

1. Disconnect the locking lever assembly by removing the screw holding the locking lever to the starter housing.

2. Remove the attaching screws and lift the mechanism from the powerhead.

Disassembly

1. Pull out the rope and tie a knot in the end of it.

2. Pry the rope from the handle.

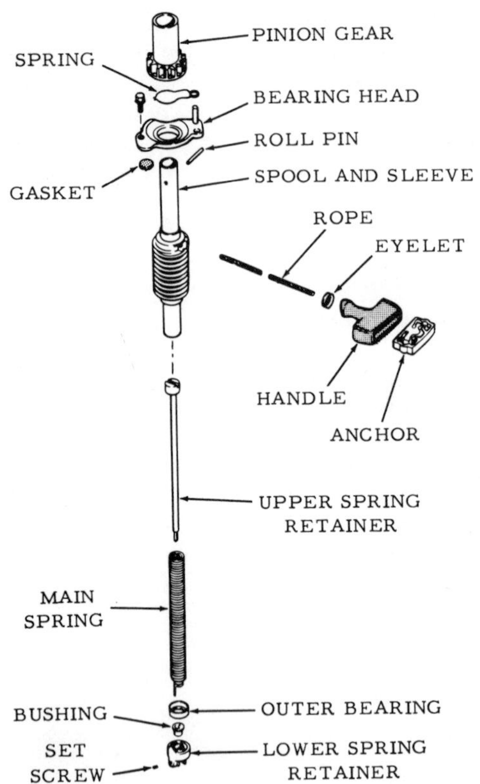

Exploded view of manual starter (© Outboard Marine Corporation)

3. Remove the handle, release the knot and, very gently, ease the starter drum back until the spring is fully unwound. It is an excellent idea to wear safety glasses and heavy gloves when overhauling rewind starters of this type.

4. Remove the starter spindle screw, washer, and pawl retainers.

5. Remove the spindle, spring washer, friction ring, pawls, and nylon bushing.

6. Jar the housing (bottom side down) on the workbench to dislodge the spring and pulley.

Inspection

1. Wash the metal components in solvent and allow them to air-dry.

2. Inspect the spring for broken end loops or weak tension.

3. Examine the pawls for wear.

4. Inspect the rope and discard it if it is frayed or worn. A new rope should be cut to 73¾ in. from nylon stock.

5. Examine the pulley and housing eye for sharp edges which could cut the rope.

Assembly

1. Be sure to wear heavy gloves when assembling the mechanism.

2. Attach an end of the spring to the pin on the drum and carefully wind the spring in a counterclockwise direction.

3. When the spring is wound tight, very carefully release the spring about one turn or until the loop in the spring aligns with the hole drilled in the edge of the pulley. Slide a pin through the pulley and spring loop.

4. Install the pulley and spring into the starter housing and be sure that the outside spring loop is on top of its appropriate stud in the housing.

5. Press down on the pulley so that the stud moves into the spring loop, forcing the pin out.

6. Tie a knot in one end of the rope. Be sure that the rope is 73¾ in. long. With an open flame, burn each end of the nylon rope to prevent it from fraying.

7. Lubricate the spindle and install it in the pulley.

8. Turn the starter pulley counterclockwise to be sure that the starter spring is fully wound. Allow it to unwind one turn so that the pulley rope hole aligns with the housing rope hole.

9. Insert the rope through the pulley and pull it through the starter housing. Tug hard on the end of the rope to seat the knot in the pulley.

10. Tie a knot in the rope and allow the pulley to rewind.

11. Install the bushing in the pulley. Install the pawls and lock them in place. Attach the friction spring, spring washer, and spindle.

12. Install the spindle washer and screw.

13. Attach a piece of wire to the end of the rope and thread it into the handle and pull it through. It may need some lubrication.

14. Attach the rope to the handle and untie the knot. Allow the rope to wind up on the pulley.

15. Activate the mechanism to be sure that it works properly. The pawls should pivot out to engage the flywheel ratchet and return to their original positions.

Installation

1. Align the starter with the powerhead and attach it with three screws.

2. Attach the locking lever with the screw and washer.

Powerhead

The powerhead consists of the cylinder block, crankcase, pistons, connecting rods, and crankshaft. It is either a single-cylinder or a twin-cylinder (mounted vertical) in-line type, with the cylinder heads combined in one casting. A split crankcase and cylinder block make servicing the powerhead relatively easy.

REMOVAL

1½ HP

1. Remove the motor cover, carburetor, manifold, and fuel tank.
2. Remove the flywheel, magneto cam, armature plate, and spark plug.
3. Remove the six screws attaching the powerhead to the motor leg. Lift the powerhead off the exhaust housing.

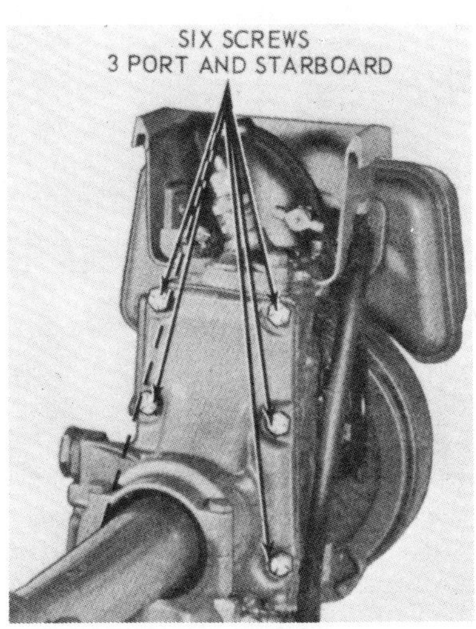

Powerhead attaching screws—1½ and 2 HP (© Outboard Marine Corporation)

2 HP

1. Remove the starter, carburetor, manifold, and fuel tank.
2. Remove the flywheel, magneto cam, armature plate, and spark plug.
3. Remove the six screws attaching the powerhead to the motor leg and remove the powerhead.

3 HP (1966–67)

1. Remove the carburetor, leaf valves, and manifold.
2. Remove the flywheel, fuel tank, and magneto.
3. Remove the fuel tank mounting plate.
4. Remove the four screws attaching the powerhead adaptor to the exhaust housing. Lift the powerhead and adaptor from the exhaust housing and motor leg.
5. Remove the five screws attaching the adaptor to the powerhead. Separate the adaptor and water tube from the powerhead.

Exhaust housing screws—3 HP (1966–67) (© Outboard Marine Corporation)

Mounting plate screws—3 HP (1966–67) (© Outboard Marine Corporation)

Adaptor attaching screws—3 HP (1966–67) (© Outboard Marine Corporation)

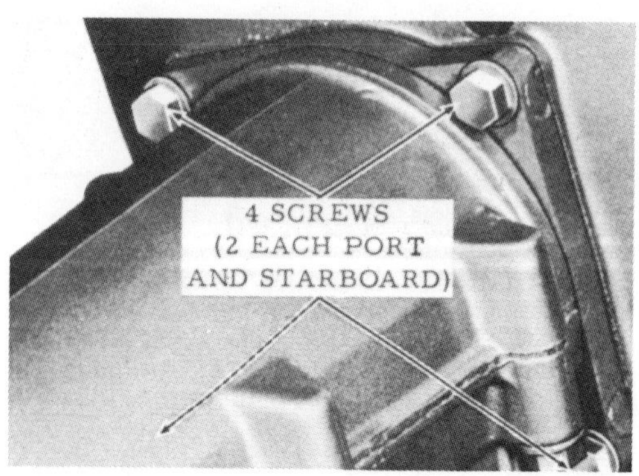

Exhaust housing-to-lower motor cover screws—3 HP (1968) and 4 HP (© Outboard Marine Corporation)

3 HP (1968) and 4 HP

1. Remove the carburetor, leaf valves, and manifold.
2. Remove the flywheel, spark plugs, and magneto.
3. If the starter does not require service, leave it on the crankcase.
4. Remove the four screws attaching the lower motor cover to the exhaust housing. Lift the powerhead from the exhaust housing. The water tube is attached to the lower motor cover with a compression sleeve and nut.

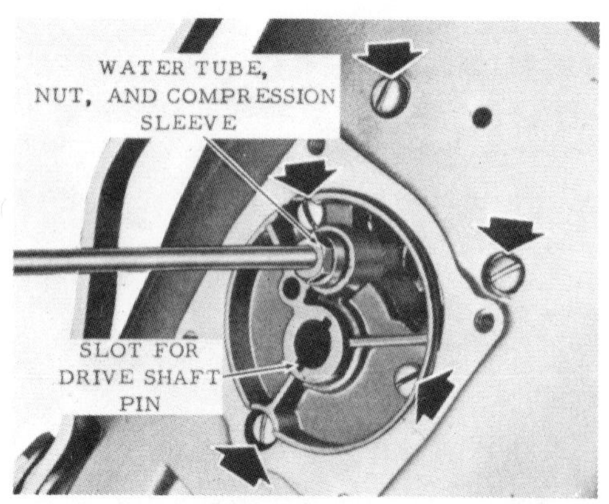

Lower motor cover attaching screws—3 HP (1968) and 4 HP (© Outboard Marine Corporation)

5. The folding model has a pin through the driveshaft. Rotate the crankshaft clockwise to align the pin with the slot in the lower motor cover while lifting the powerhead.
6. Remove the five screws attaching the lower motor cover to the powerhead.

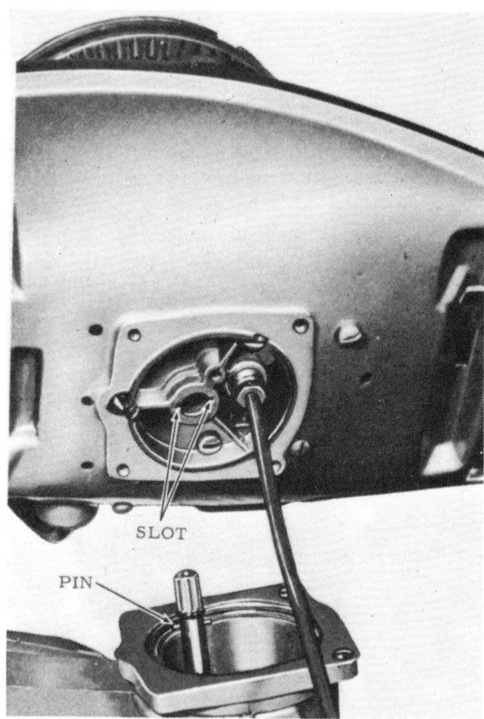

Slot in lower motor cover—3 HP (1968) and 4 HP (© Outboard Marine Corporation)

5 HP

1. Remove the manual starter.
2. Remove the carburetor, leaf valves, fuel pump and fuel filter, and fuel lines.
3. Remove the flywheel and magneto.
4. Remove the retaining ring and armature plate support.
5. Remove the five screws and two nuts attaching the powerhead to the adaptor block and the housing.
6. Remove the powerhead from its mounting.

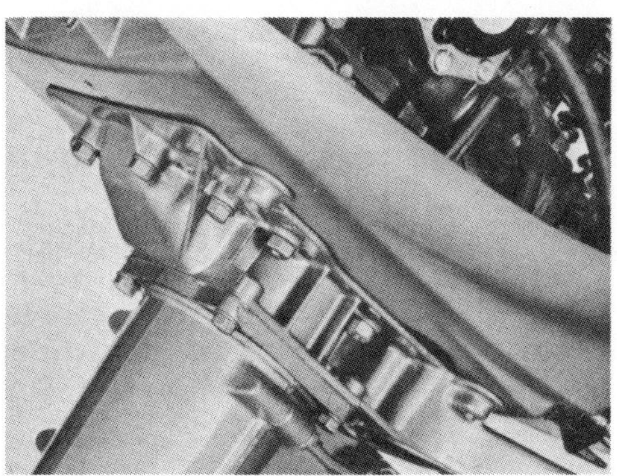

Powerhead attaching screws—5 HP (© Outboard Marine Corporation)

6 HP

1. Remove the carburetor, leaf valves, fuel pump and filter, and fuel lines.
2. Remove the flywheel and magneto. Remove the starter.
3. Disconnect and remove the throttle control lever by removing the screws and clamps. Lift the lever from the lower motor cover.
4. Remove the retaining ring and armature plate support.
5. Remove the seven screws attaching the powerhead to the exhaust housing.

Powerhead attaching screws—6 HP (© Outboard Marine Corporation)

9½ HP

1. Remove the flywheel and magneto.
2. Remove the carburetor, leaf valves, and fuel pump and filter.
3. Remove the exhaust relief hose and clamp from the exhaust cover.
4. Remove the upper and lower gearcase.
5. Remove the shift rod lever and shaft by first unscrewing the detent screw and pulling the shift lever from the lower starboard cover.

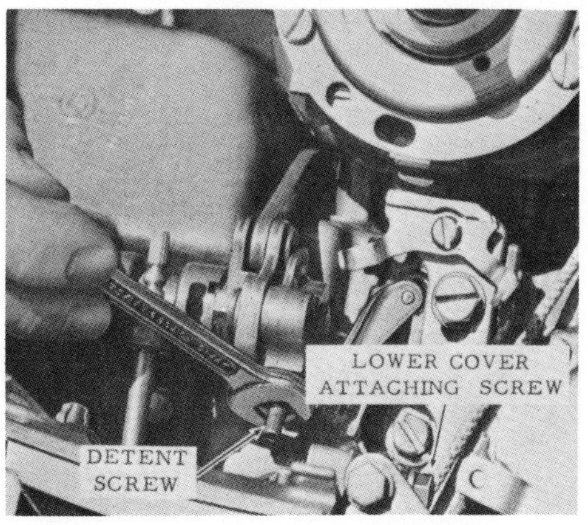

Shift lever removal—9½ HP (© Outboard Marine Corporation)

6. Remove the starboard lower cover. Remove the port and starboard-side friction plate screws. Remove the one nut and screw from the starboard side first. Remove the five screws from the port side.

Starboard lower cover attaching screws—9½ HP (© Outboard Marine Corporation)

7. Loosen the screws securing the port-side stabilizer bracket to the exhaust cover. Depress the bracket and swing it away from the powerhead.

8. Remove the two screws and nuts, and separate the powerhead and exhaust housing from the port-side lower cover.

Exhaust housing attaching screws—9½ HP (© Outboard Marine Corporation)

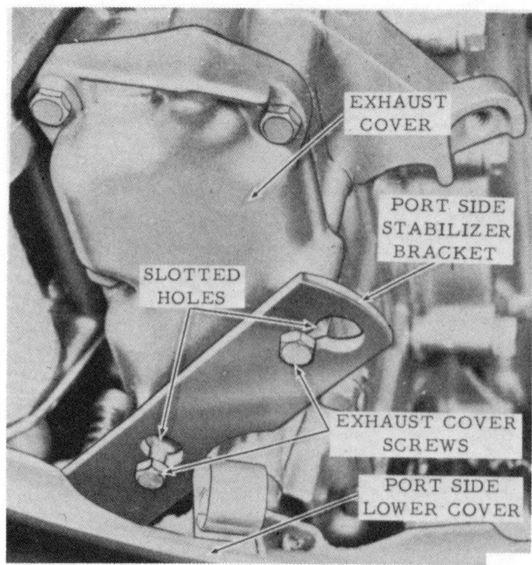

Port-side stabilizer bracket removal—9½ HP (© Outboard Marine Corporation)

9. Remove the starboard side upper rubber mount and the two cotter pins attaching the clevis to the shift rod.

10. Remove the seven screws attaching the exhaust housing to the powerhead.

18 and 25 HP

1. Remove the carburetor, leaf valves, fuel pump, fuel filter, and fuel lines.
2. Remove the starter, flywheel, and magneto. Remove the spark plugs.
3. Remove the armature plate support and retaining ring.
4. Remove the port and starboard-side starter mounting brackets. The throttle lever will detach with the port-side starter bracket.
5. Remove the shifter lock spring and shifter lockscrew.
6. Remove the seven screws securing the powerhead to the exhaust housing.
7. Lift the powerhead up to disengage the crankshaft and driveshaft. Remove the powerhead.

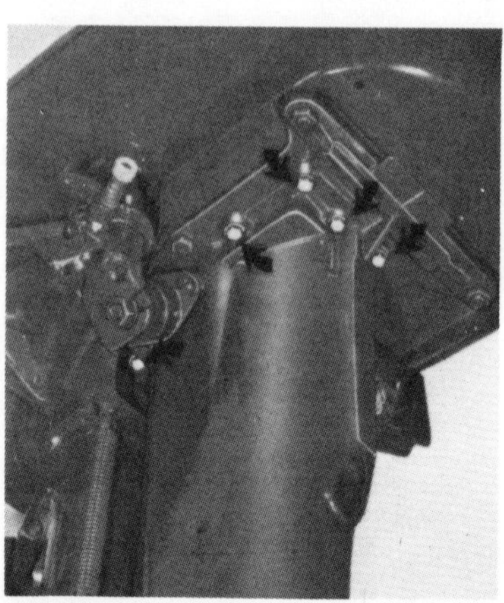
Powerhead attaching screws—18 and 25 HP (© Outboard Marine Corporation)

DISASSEMBLY

Single-Cylinder Models

The following procedures apply to single-cylinder powerheads (1½ and 2 hp). There may exist minor differences between specific models, although, service procedures, in general, remain similar.

1. Remove the cylinder head and gasket from the powerhead.
2. Remove the cover plate screws and the exhaust cover and gasket.
3. Straighten out any of the locktabs which are bent up against the connecting rod screws. If the locktabs are broken off, it is imperative that they be found, preferably before the motor is assembled. These pieces of locktab (if they are broken) have

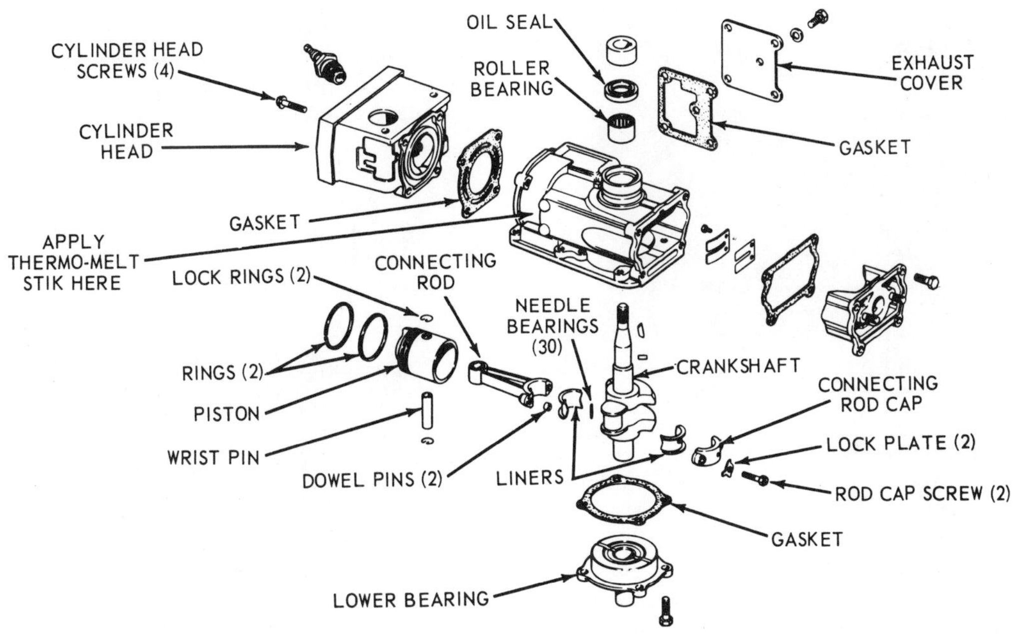

Exploded view of single-cylinder powerhead (© Outboard Marine Corporation)

been known to cause great havoc. Remove the connecting rod screws.

4. Remove the connecting rod cap and thirty needle bearings. Immediately count the needle bearings to be sure that they are all present. Do not lose the two dowel pins.

5. Remove the four screws holding the lower main bearing housing and remove the lower main bearing housing.

Exhaust cover removed—single-cylinder models (© Outboard Marine Corporation)

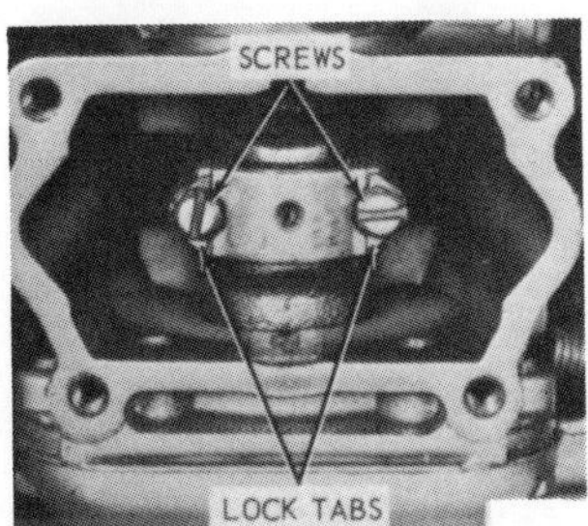

Connecting rod screws and lock tabs—single-cylinder models (© Outboard Marine Corporation)

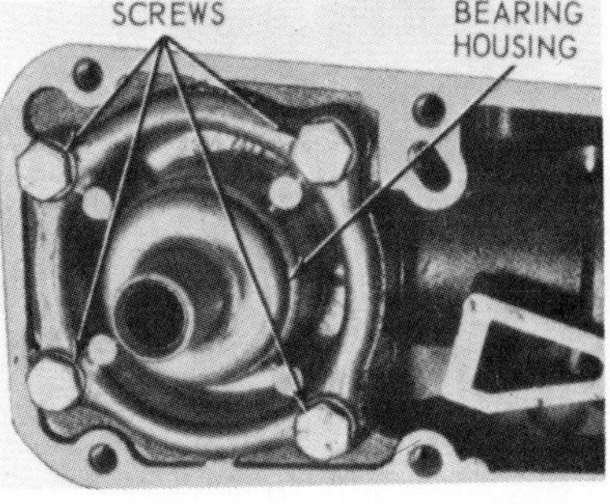

Lower bearing housing removal—single-cylinder models (© Outboard Marine Corporation)

6. Remove the crankshaft through the bottom of the crankcase.

7. Reinstall the rod on the cap and remove the piston and rod through the front of the crankcase.

8. Remove the piston rings from the pistons by prying the ends loose and breaking the rings free. Do not try to save the rings. Install a new set of rings each time the powerhead is overhauled.

9. If it is necessary to remove the piston from the connecting rod, remove the

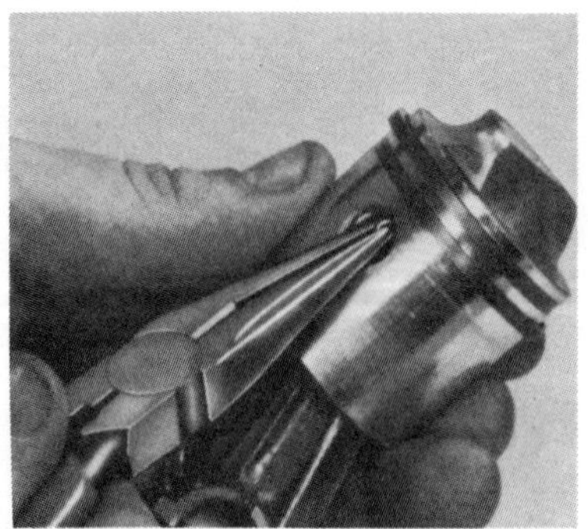

Removing wrist pin retaining ring—single-cylinder models (© Outboard Marine Corporation)

wrist pin retaining rings, and drive the wrist pin out of the piston and connecting rod bushing.

NOTE: *One side of the piston is marked with an L on the inside. When the wrist pin is removed, the L side of the piston must be pointing up and the driving tool applied to the loose end. Be careful not to distort the piston.*

Single-cylinder piston marked L (© Outboard Marine Corporation)

10. The upper and main bearing seal can be removed by supporting the crankcase properly and pushing them out with a suitable tool.

TWO CYLINDER MODELS

1. Remove the lift bracket, cylinder head, and cylinder head gasket. Remove the lower main bearing seal housing (if equipped).

2. Remove the bypass covers and gaskets.

3. Remove the inner and outer exhaust covers and gaskets. If pitting is encountered on the inner exhaust plate, install a new plate at assembly.

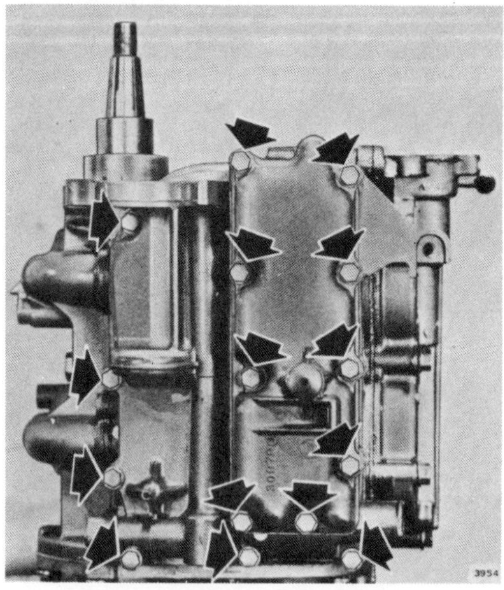

Exhaust cover attaching screws—two-cylinder models (© Outboard Marine Corporation)

4. Loosen the clamps and remove the oil return hose from the crankcase.

5. Drive the taper pins from the back to the front of the crankcase.

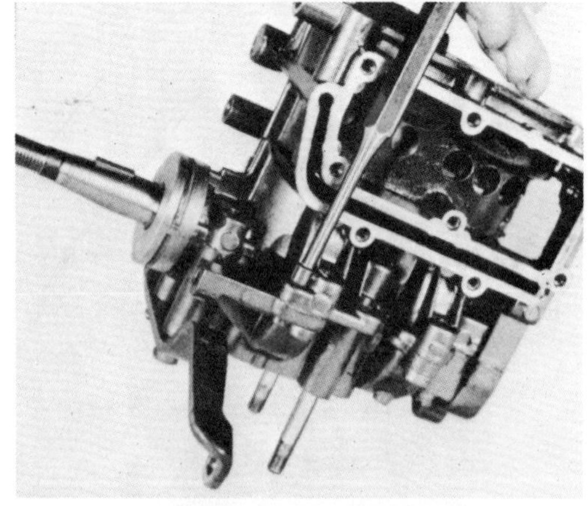

Removing the taper pins—two-cylinder models (© Outboard Marine Corporation)

6. Remove the screws attaching the crankcase to the cylinder block. Tap the top end of the crankshaft with a rubber mallet or rawhide mallet to break the seal between crankcase and cylinder block.

Removing the crankcase screws—two-cylinder models (© Outboard Marine Corporation)

7. Lift the crankcase from the cylinder block.

8. Remove the oil drain valve from the crankcase for cleaning and inspection.

9. Remove the connecting rod caps and needle bearings.

NOTE: *The connecting rod caps and connecting rods are matched assemblies. Mark each connecting rod cap, connecting rod, piston, cylinder, and bearing component to assure correct mating when they are assembled.*

10. Remove the snap-ring from the end of the crankshaft and remove the seal components.

Connecting rod caps removed—two-cylinder models (© Outboard Marine Corporation)

GASKETS
CAP
CYLINDER
BLOCK
OUTER
EXHAUST
COVER
INNER
EXHAUST
COVER
CRANKSHAFT
CRANKCASE
CYLINDER
HEAD
OIL
DRAIN
VALVE
RINGS
OIL
RETURN
HOSE
PISTONS
BEARINGS
AND
LINERS
WRIST
PINS
CONNECTING
RODS AND CAPS

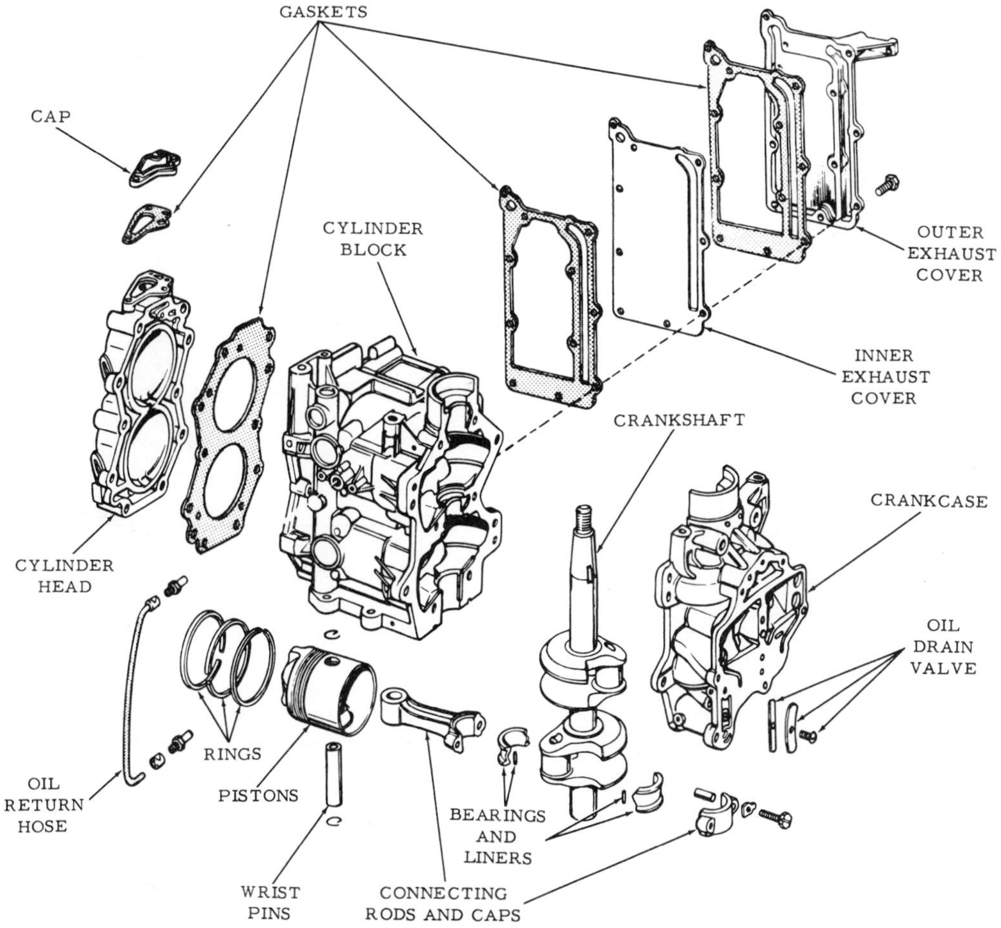

Exploded view of two-cylinder models (© Outboard Marine Corporation)

11. Lift the crankshaft from the cylinder block and lay it on a clean cloth to avoid damage. Slide the center bearing retaining ring aside and separate the center bearing halves.

Crankshaft removal—two-cylinder models (© Outboard Marine Corporation)

12. Reinstall the matched caps on the connecting rods and remove the matched caps and connecting rods from the cylinders.

13. Remove the rings from the pistons. Do not try and save the rings; new rings should be installed at each overhaul.

14. It is possible to remove the pistons from the connecting rods. However, the

Two cylinder piston marked "loose" (© Outboard Marine Corporation)

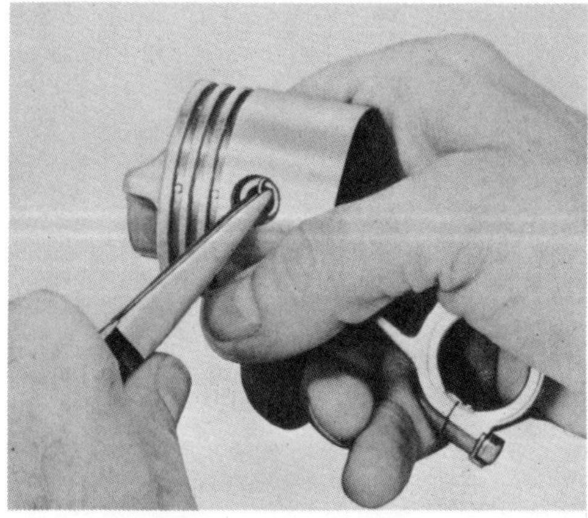

Removing wrist pin retaining rings (© Outboard Marine Corporation)

better procedure is to replace the connecting rod, piston, and bearing assembly if this is necessary. One side of the piston is marked "loose" on the inside. Remove the retaining rings from the wrist pins. Drive the wrist pin out from the side of the piston marked "loose." Be careful that the piston is not distorted.

Cleaning and Inspection—All Models

Cylinder Block and Crankcase

1. Check all cylinder walls for wear and check cylinder ports for carbon accumulation. Cylinder walls wear depending on lubrication and operating conditions. The major portion of wear is above the ports and the area covered by ring travel.

2. Check the cylinders for out-of-round. If wear is greater than 0.003 in., replace the cylinder block or have the block rebored and install oversize pistons. (See specifications.)

3. Carbon accumulation on the walls of the exhaust ports restricts the flow of exhaust gases and has a large effect on the motor's performance. Carefully scrape the carbon from the cylinder heads and exhaust ports with a scraper or blunt instrument. Avoid getting carbon in the water jackets.

4. Before installing the pistons in the cylinders, break the glaze on the cylinder walls with a cylinder hone. A few up-and-down motions of the hone should remove the glaze. Do not scratch the cylinder walls.

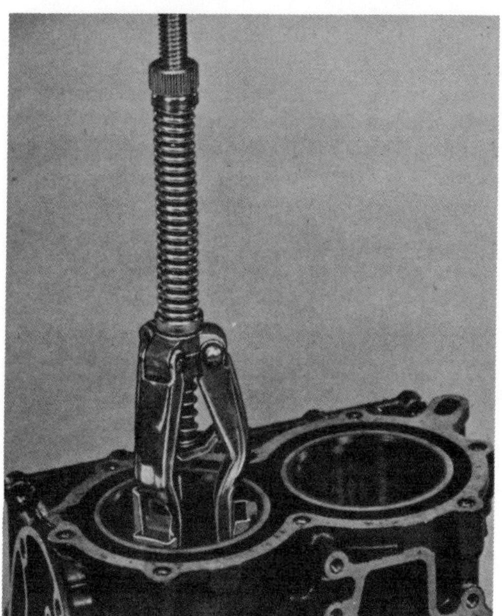

Breaking the cylinder glaze (© Outboard Marine Corporation)

Gasket Surfaces

1. Remove all traces of dried cement with trichloroethylene. Check all gasket faces for straightness.

2. To check for flatness, use a straightedge or lay a sheet of no. 120 emery paper on a sheet of plate glass. Place the part to be surfaced on the emery cloth and move it back and forth slowly as indicated in the illustration. Be sure to exert even pressure. If the surface is warped, the high spots will take on a dull polish while the low spots will retain the original finish. Continue surfacing until the entire area has a dull polish. Finish surfacing with no. 180 emery cloth in the same manner.

Surfacing the cylinder head (© Outboard Marine Corporation)

Bearings

1. Keep the bearings free of dirt and oil when servicing.

2. Wash all bearings in solvent until they are clean and free of dirt and sludge. Air-dry the bearings; do not spin them to dry, as this will cause irreparable harm.

3. Bearings rust easily and should be lubricated immediately with light, clean oil.

4. Discard any bearings showing any of the following:

   a. Rusted balls, rollers, or races;

   b. Fractured rings;

   c. Worn or abraded surfaces;

   d. Badly discolored balls, rollers, or races. (This is usually due to inadequate lubrication.)

Seals

1. Replace the upper crankcase head seal. Seat the new seal with the lip facing in and flush with the top of the crankcase head.

2. Replace the lower crankcase head seal.

Pistons

1. Check the pistons for roundness, scoring, or wear. The pistons' skirts must be perfectly round to prevent exhaust gases from entering the compression chamber.

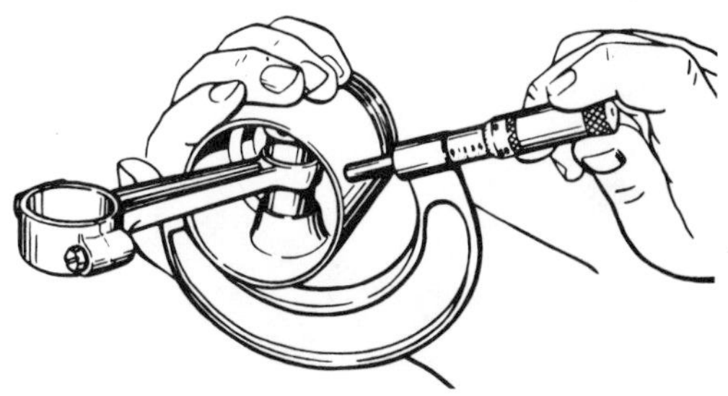

Checking pistons with a micrometer (© Outboard Marine Corporation)

2. Carefully remove all carbon deposits.

3. Scrape carbon from the ring grooves, using a piece of an old ring. Do not damage the ring grooves or the lower ring lands.

4. Remove carbon from inside the piston head.

5. Before installing new piston rings, check the piston ring gap by installing the ring in its bore and seating it squarely with the bottom of a piston. Check the ring groove clearance with a feeler gauge.

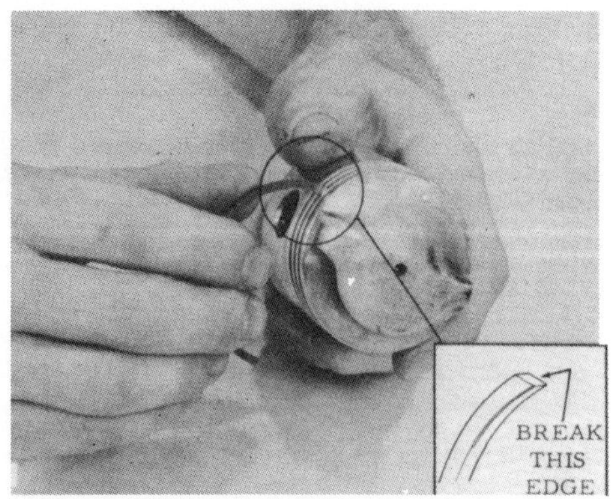

Cleaning carbon from the ring grooves (© Outboard Marine Corporation)

Checking ring gap (© Outboard Marine Corporation)

Checking ring-to-groove clearance (© Outboard Marine Corporation)

ASSEMBLY

Single-Cylinder Models

1. Proceed slowly and make no forced assemblies unless press fits are specified. Make no trial assemblies and be sure that all parts are clean and free of dirt, grit, and grease. Coat all bearing surfaces with light oil before assembly.
2. Always use new gaskets throughout.
3. Install the piston on the rod as shown in the illustration.

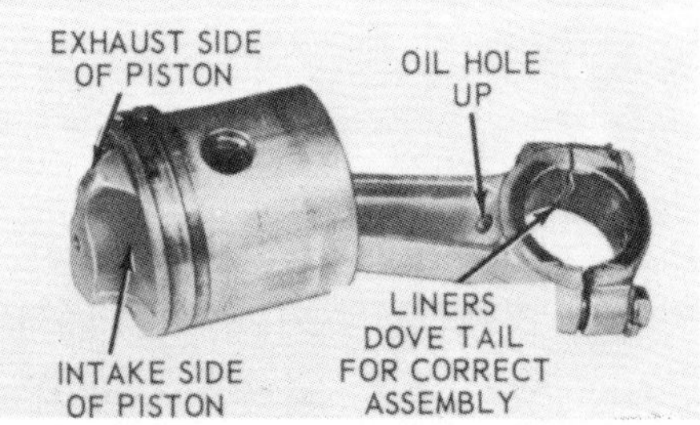

Correct piston and connecting rod assembly—single-cylinder models (© Outboard Marine Corporation)

4. Apply a coat of oil to the wrist pin and install the wrist pin through the slip-fit side of the piston. Place the connecting rod in position and heat the piston slightly to make wrist pin installation easier.
5. Replace the wrist pin retaining rings, making sure that they are seated in the groove.
6. Install the upper main bearing through the bottom of the crankcase. Press against the lettered side of the case until it is flush with the inside of the crankcase. Be sure that the needles in the upper main bearing are not lost.
7. Install the oil seal with the lip down, until flush with the crankcase.
8. Coat the piston and cylinder bore with oil and install the piston and connecting rod through the front of the crankcase, until the piston ring grooves are exposed. The intake deflector must face the intake port.
9. Install the piston rings on the piston. Spread each ring with a ring expander and slip it into place in the ring groove. The ring grooves are pinned to prevent the edges of the rings from catching on the edge of the ports and to stagger the ring gaps.
10. Carefully install the piston and rings into the cylinder bore. A ring compressor works best for this but is not absolutely necessary. The rings can be compressed by hand and carefully worked into the cylinders.
11. Remove the connecting rod cap.
12. Oil the crankshaft and install it in

the crankcase. Do not disturb the needles in the bearing or the upper bearing seal.

13. Install the lower bearing housing with a new gasket and tighten the screws to the specified torque.

14. If removed, install the bearing liners in the connecting rod and cap.

15. The connecting rod cap may be turned endwise. To aid correct assembly, small bosses are cast on the matching sides of the rod and cap. When replacing the needle bearing inserts, be sure that the dove-tailed ends match when the rod and cap match.

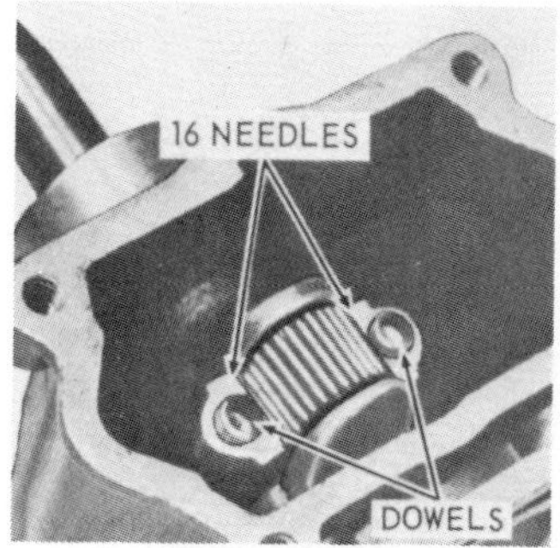

Installing needle on crankshaft journal—single-cylinder models (© Outboard Marine Corporation)

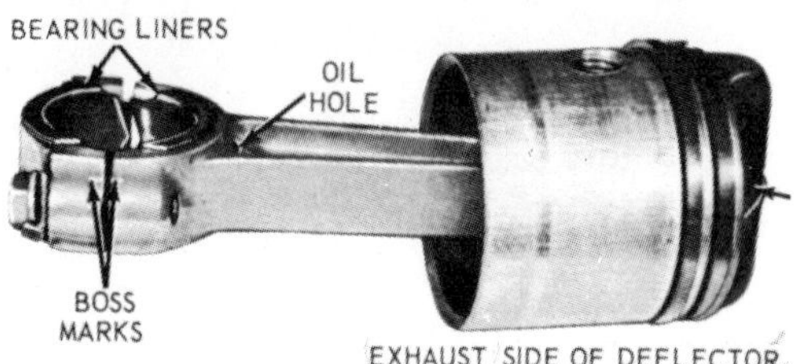

Correct connecting rod alignment—single-cylinder models (© Outboard Marine Corporation)

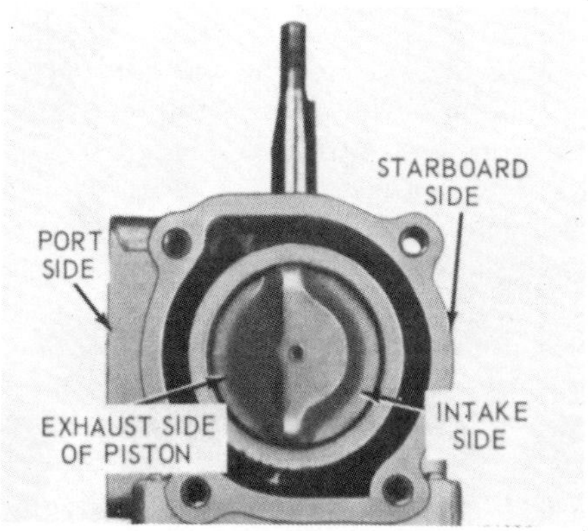

Piston installation—single-cylinder models (© Outboard Marine Corporation)

16. Apply a coat of OMC Needle Bearing Grease to the connecting rod liner and place fourteen needles in the connecting rod.

17. Move the piston up so that the connecting rod bearings are against the crankshaft journal.

18. Apply OMC Needle Bearing Grease to the crankshaft journal and load sixteen needle bearings onto the crankshaft journal and then install the rod cap.

19. Be sure that the connecting rod dowel pins are in place before attaching the connecting rod cap.

20. Install the lockplates on the screws and torque the screws to specifications.

21. Check to be sure that all needles are in place and that the rod is not binding, but floating freely. Insert a small rod or wire through the oil hole in the cap. It will not be possible to touch the crankshaft journal if the correct number of needles has been used. Bend the lockplates up on the connecting rod screws.

22. Install the cylinder head using a new gasket. Torque the cylinder head bolts to specification.

23. Install the exhaust cover, using a new gasket.

24. Install the magneto cam drive pin and cam. Be sure that the top of the cam marked "top" is facing up.

2 Cylinder Models

1. Proceed slowly and do not force parts unless press-fits are specified. Do not test-assemble parts. Be sure that all parts are clean and free of dirt and grit. Use new gaskets and seals throughout.

2. Install the piston rings on each piston and be sure they fit freely. The ring gaps are staggered to prevent loss of compression. The ring grooves are pinned to locate the gaps.

3. Coat the cylinders and pistons with oil and install the piston and connecting rod assemblies, with the intake side of the piston deflector toward the intake port. Avoid the use of automotive-type ring compressors as these frequently damage the pistons and rings through improper alignment of the rings.

4. Replace the main journal bearings on the crankshaft and place the O-rings in position on the upper and lower bearings.

5. Remove the rod caps from the connecting rods. Apply a coat of OMC Needle Bearing Grease to the connecting rod

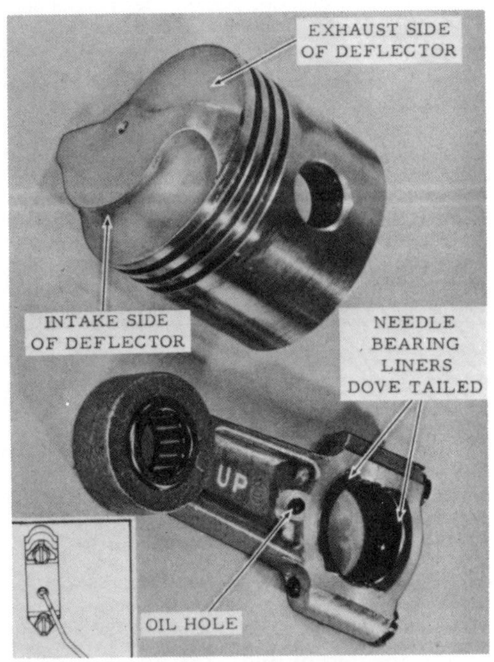

Correct piston and rod assembly—two-cylinder models (© Outboard Marine Corporation)

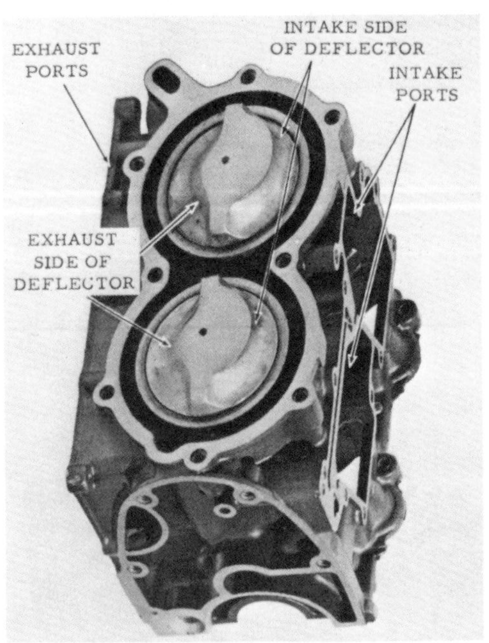

Correct piston installation—two-cylinder models (© Outboard Marine Corporation)

bearing area. Place the retainer half and fourteen roller bearings on each rod.

6. Place the crankshaft in position on the cylinder block and align the dowel pins with the main bearings.

7. Apply OMC Needle Bearing Grease to the crankpins and install roller bearings and the remaining sixteen roller bearings in each retainer.

8. Install the connecting rod caps. These are not interchangeable between rods, nor may they be turned endwise. Small raised dots are provided to assist in matching the sides of the rod and cap.

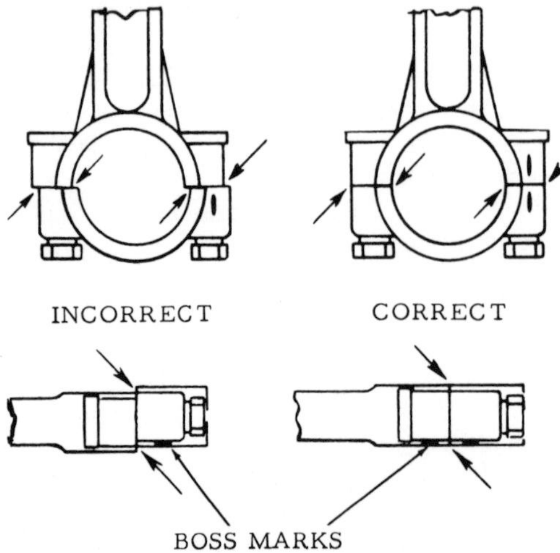

Correct rod and cap alignment—two-cylinder models (© Outboard Marine Corporation)

9. Tighten the connecting rod screws to the specified torque.

10. The crankcase face is grooved for proper installation of a new seal. The seal should be seated in the groove and cut somewhat longer than is necessary, to obtain a good seal against both ends of the crankcase. Run a fine bead of Sealer 1000 in the groove, before installing the seal. After the sealer has set, trim the ends of the seal, leaving approximately 1/32 in. on each end for a good butt.

11. Apply a thin line of Sealer 1000 to the crankcase face.

12. Install the crankcase on the cylinder block and install the screws finger-tight. Install the crankcase taper pins, driving them in carefully with a hammer.

13. Rotate the crankshaft and check for binding between the crankshaft and bearings or the connecting rods and bearings.

14. Torque all crankcase screws to the specified torque.

15. Install the cylinder head and lifting bracket. Tighten the cylinder head bolts to the specified torque in the sequence illustrated in the specifications.

NOTE: *Retorque the cylinder head screws after the motor has cooled to the point where it is comfortable to the touch.*

16. Replace the inner and outer exhaust covers. Install all screws finger-tight before torqueing.

17. Install the by-pass covers. The upper by-pass cover has tapped holes for mounting the fuel pump.

18. Install the oil return hose on the crankcase and tighten the clamps.

19. The oil drain valve ordinarily requires little service; however, if the motor is serviced, remove and clean the oil drain valve and screen. If gum or varnish is found in the crankcase, it is likely there will be similar substances in the drain valve. Be sure that the leaf seats squarely against the leaf plate.

INSTALLATION

1½ and 2 HP

1. Using a new gasket, secure the powerhead to the exhaust housing with the six screws.
2. Install the fuel tank, intake manifold, and carburetor.
3. Install the spark plug, magneto, and flywheel.

3 HP (1966–67)

1. Using a new gasket, secure the powerhead to the adaptor with five screws.
2. The upper end of the water tube anchors to the powerhead adaptor with a rubber grommet. It is not necessary to remove the gearcase to install the water tube.
3. Install a new gasket on the exhaust housing and apply liquid soap or oil to the end of the water tube. Install a new upper grommet on the water tube. The grooves in the grommet engage the flanges in the powerhead adaptor.
4. Slip the lower end of the water tube into the water pump grommet and position the upper grommet on top of the exhaust housing gasket.
5. Align the driveshaft pin with the groove at the bottom of the adaptor housing. Carefully lower the powerhead onto the exhaust housing so that the flanges in the adaptor slip into the slots in the upper water tube grommet. Rotate the powerhead slightly to engage the driveshaft splines with the crankshaft splines. Attach the powerhead to the exhaust housing and torque the screws to specifications.
6. Install the leaf valve assembly, intake manifold, and carburetor.
7. Install the magneto and flywheel. Perform all necessary adjustments.

3 HP (1968) and 4 HP

1. Using a new gasket, secure the lower motor cover to the powerhead.
2. Install a new exhaust housing gasket. Apply oil to the end of the water tube. Assemble the powerhead to the exhaust housing and be sure the water tube enters the grommet.
3. Attach the powerhead to the exhaust housing and torque the screws to specifications.
4. Install the leaf valves, intake manifold, and carburetor.
5. Install the magneto and flywheel.
6. Install the starter.

5 HP

1. Install a new gasket on the powerhead adaptor.
2. Install the powerhead on the adaptor. Do not damage the splined ends of the crankshaft or driveshaft. Rotate the powerhead slightly as it is lowered onto the exhaust housing. This will help engage the driveshaft and crankshaft splines.
3. Install the armature plate support and retaining ring.
4. Install the carburetor and other fuel system components.
5. Install the manual starter.
6. Install the magneto and other ignition system components.
7. Install the flywheel and perform all necessary adjustments.

6 HP

1. Installation of the powerhead is the same as that for the preceding (5 hp) models, with one exception. Be sure to replace the throttle control arm.

9½ HP

1. Check the exhaust housing alignment.
2. Install the shift rod boot and plate in the exhaust housing. Oil the water tube and install the nut, washer, and O-ring on the upper end.
3. Slide the water tube through the

opening in the boot and position the upper end in the exhaust housing flange.

4. Oil the shift rod and install the seal and guide.

5. Insert the rod down through the boot, positioning the seal and guide in the exhaust housing flange.

6. Install the gasket and pilot ring on the crankcase. Install the exhaust housing on the powerhead while holding the bottom end of the shift rod.

7. Attach the link to the shift rod.

8. Attach the shift rod connector to the upper shift rod.

9. Replace all rubber mounts and the exhaust housing seal.

10. Install the powerhead and exhaust housing on the port-side lower cover. Position the port-side stabilizer bracket over the exhaust cover screws. Slide it upward until it seats.

11. Attach the upper and lower gearcase assembly.

12. Connect the shift rod linkage and assemble the starboard lower cover.

13. Install the leaf valves and other fuel system components. Swing the stabilizer bracket into position over the carburetor.

14. Replace the magneto and flywheel and perform all necessary adjustments.

18 and 25 HP

1. Install new gaskets in position on the exhaust housing.

2. Install the powerhead, rotating the crankshaft in a clockwise direction, to engage the splines of the crankshaft with the driveshaft splines. Do not rotate the driveshaft, as damage to the water pump may result.

3. Install the attaching screws.

4. Install the armature plate support and retaining ring. Install the port and starboard starter mounting brackets.

5. Install the shifter lock and shifter lock spring.

6. Install the leaf plate assembly, carburetor, and other fuel system components.

7. Replace the magneto and other ignition system components. Install the manual starter.

8. Perform all necessary adjustments.

9. Install the flywheel.

BREAK-IN PERIOD

A rebuilt or overhauled motor should be treated as a new motor. Follow the break-in procedure and lubrication recommendations for a brand new motor.

Lower Unit

The lower unit, located immediately below the powerhead, consists of the exhaust housing and the gearcase. The exhaust housing contains the water tubing for cooling purposes, water pump, and the driveshaft. The gearcase holds the propeller shaft, pinion gears, and the lower portion of the driveshaft.

1½ AND 2 HP

Gearcase Removal

1. Remove the two screws attaching the gearcase to the exhaust housing.

2. Withdraw the gearcase carefully to avoid damaging the water tube and driveshaft.

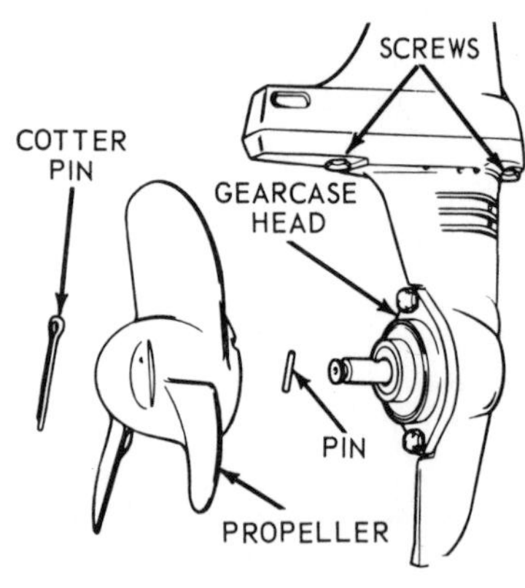

Gearcase removal—1½ and 2 HP (© Outboard Marine Corporation)

Water Pump Removal

1. Remove the cotter pin, propeller, and drive pin.

2. Drain the gearcase.

3. Remove the water pump screws and lift the water pump cover and driveshaft off the gearcase. Remove the water tube and grommet from the cover.

4. Lift the water pump impeller from the chamber in the gearcase.

Water Pump Installation

1. Install the impeller pin in the driveshaft. Lubricate and install the impeller on the driveshaft. Rotate the impeller clock-

Water pump screws—1½ and 2 HP (© Outboard Marine Corporation)

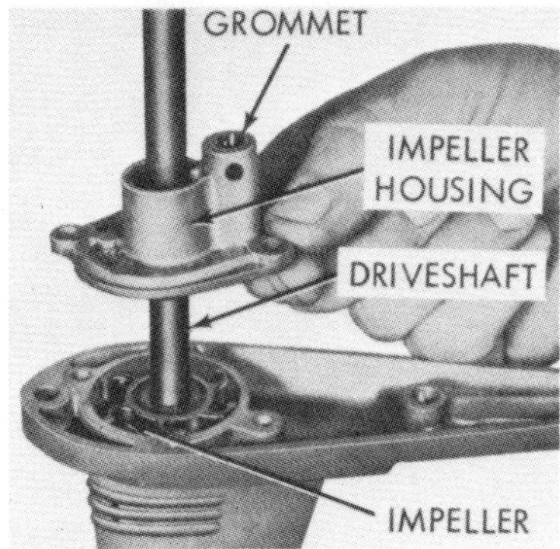

Removing the water pump—1½ and 2 HP (© Outboard Marine Corporation)

wise to seat the impeller on the drive pin. Attach the pump cover to the gearcase.

2. Oil and install a new water tube grommet.

Gearcase Installation

1. Lubricate the water tube grommet.
2. Lubricate the top splines of the driveshaft.
3. Install the gearcase, being careful to align the water tube grommet with the water tube, and the driveshaft splines with the crankshaft splines.
4. Turn the flywheel clockwise to align the driveshaft and crankshaft splines.
5. Attach the gearcase to the exhaust housing with screws that have been coated with sealant.
6. Install the propeller, drive pin, and cotter pin after lubricating the propeller shaft.

Lower Unit Adjustments

TILT FRICTION

1. Tilt the motor and adjust the screw so that it will remain in the tilted position, but can be let down with little effort.

Tilt friction adjustment—1½ and 2 HP (© Outboard Marine Corporation)

STEERING FRICTION

1. Adjust the steering friction screw to obtain minimum steering effort, but tight enough to prevent the motor from turning when the handle is released.

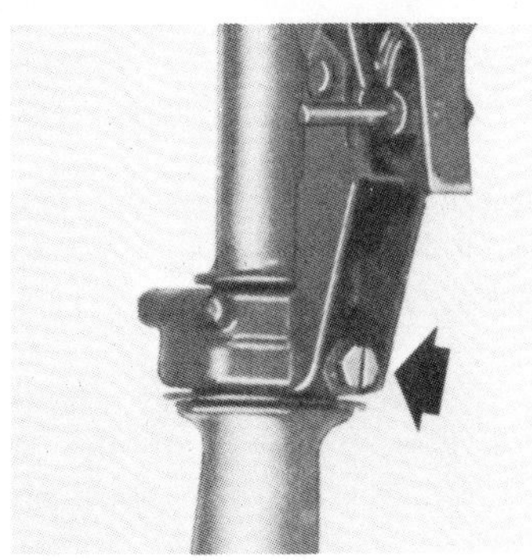

Steering friction adjustment—1½ and 2 HP (© Outboard Marine Corporation)

3, 4, AND 5 HP

Powerhead and Exhaust Housing Removal—3 and 4 HP

1. On the rigid lower-unit model, remove the four housing-to-adaptor screws. Lift the powerhead from the exhaust housing. The water tube and upper grommet will slip out of the powerhead adaptor.
2. On folding lower-unit models, align the upper driveshaft pin with the slot in the powerhead adaptor. Lift the powerhead off the exhaust housing. The water tube and grommet will slide free.
3. Remove the exhaust housing from the swivel bracket.
4. If it is necessary to replace the upper driveshaft, the pin at the bottom of the upper driveshaft must be removed before the upper driveshaft can be removed.
5. Remove the grommets from the upper and lower exhaust housings by compressing them.

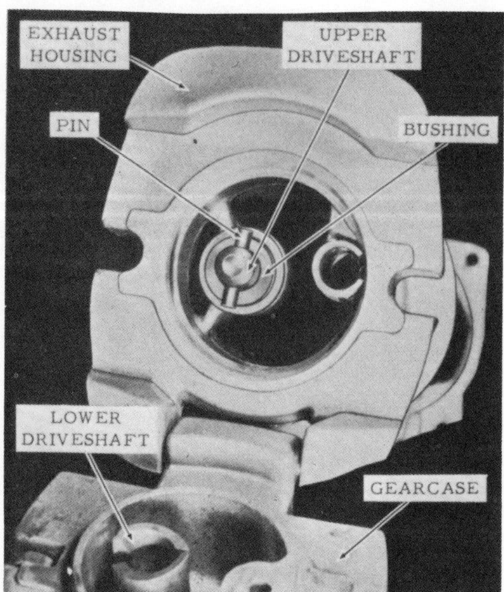

Driveshaft pin—3 and 4 HP (© Outboard Marine Corporation)

Gearcase and Exhaust Housing Removal—5 HP

1. Remove the four housing-to-adaptor screws.
2. Lift the powerhead and adaptor and the lower motor cover off the exhaust housing. The water tube will probably stay in the exhaust housing. Remove the water tube from the powerhead adaptor.
3. The exhaust housing may be removed from the swivel bracket by removing the screws and lifting the exhaust housing out of the bracket.

Swivel bracket screws—5 HP (© Outboard Marine Corporation)

Gearcase Removal—3, 4, and 5 HP

1. It is possible to remove the gearcase without removing the powerhead or exhaust housing.
2. Remove the screws attaching the gearcase to the exhaust housing.
3. Carefully withdraw the gearcase to avoid damaging the driveshaft or water tube.

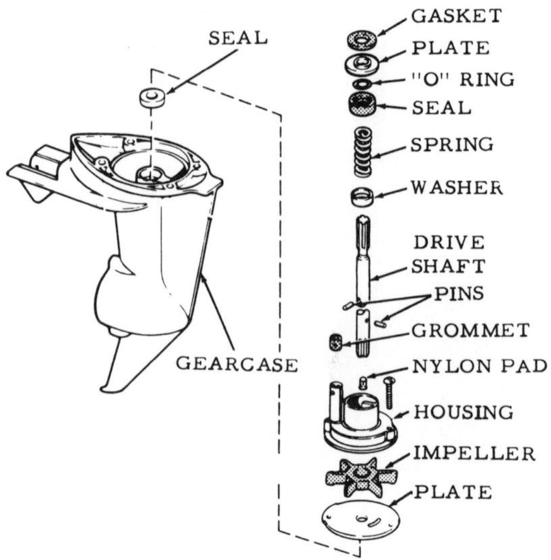

Exploded view of gearcase—1½–5 HP (© Outboard Marine Corporation)

Water Pump Replacement—3, 4, and 5 HP

1. Water pump replacement (disassembly and assembly) procedures are identical to those for the 1½ and 2 hp models.

Gearcase and Exhaust Housing Assembly—3 HP

1. On folding models, align the grommet locking guides with the holes in the grommet seats in the upper and lower exhaust housings. Install the grooved grommet on the water tube and install the water tube into the top of the upper exhaust housing and the grommet at the bottom.
2. If the driveshaft nylon sleeve and/or bushing was removed, carefully press a new one into place.
3. Install the driveshaft assembly into the exhaust housing and secure it with a

pin through the driveshaft at the bottom of the upper exhaust housing.

4. On the folding or rigid model, attach the gearcase extension, if used, with screws dipped in sealant.

5. Place housing linings and new O-rings in position on the exhaust housings.

6. Coat the inside of the swivel bracket halves with OMC type A lubricant. Apply a thin line of sealant between the swivel bracket halves and install on the exhaust housing. Use screws dipped in sealant.

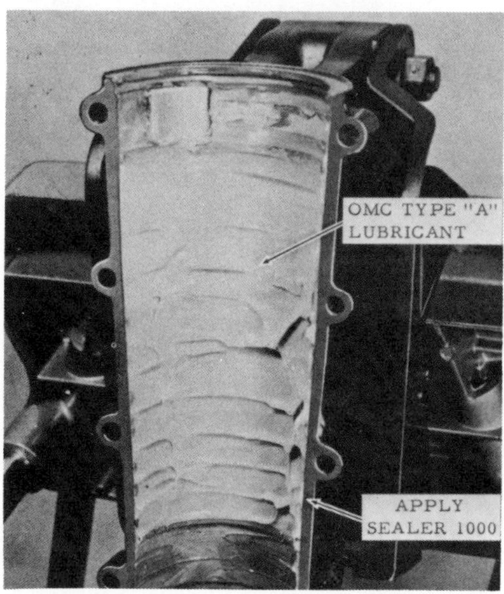

Lubricant applied to the swivel bracket—3 HP (© Outboard Marine Corporation)

7. Remove the co-pilot screw (if equipped) and fill the swivel bracket with OMC Type A lubricant.

8. Install the water tube and powerhead.

9. Install the gearcase on the extension housing or gearcase extension, if used. Use oil or liquid soap in the water tube grommet and insert the tube into the grommet. Turn the flywheel clockwise to align the driveshaft and crankshaft splines. Attach the gearcase with screws and sealant.

10. Fill the gearcase with the specified lubricant.

Gearcase and Exhaust Housing Installation—5 HP

1. For these models, perform steps 4–10 of the preceding procedure, ignoring the folding and rigid models.

Lower Unit Adjustments

TILT FRICTION—3, 4, AND 5 HP

1. Tilt the motor up as far as it will go. Tighten the tilt bolt until the motor will remain in a tilted position, but can be returned to a drive position, with little effort.

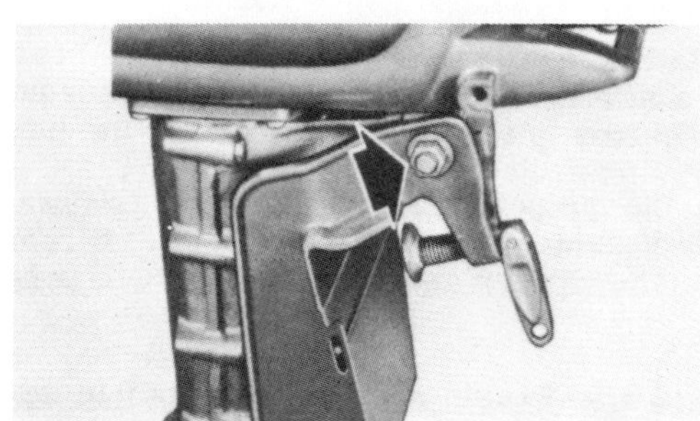

Tilt friction adjustment—3, 4, and 5 HP (© Outboard Marine Corporation)

CO-PILOT FRICTION—3 AND 4 HP

1. The co-pilot adjusting screw is located beneath the powerhead on the front, port side of the swivel bracket.

2. Adjust the screw for minimum steering effort, but tight enough to prevent the motor from turning in the swivel bracket when the tiller handle is released.

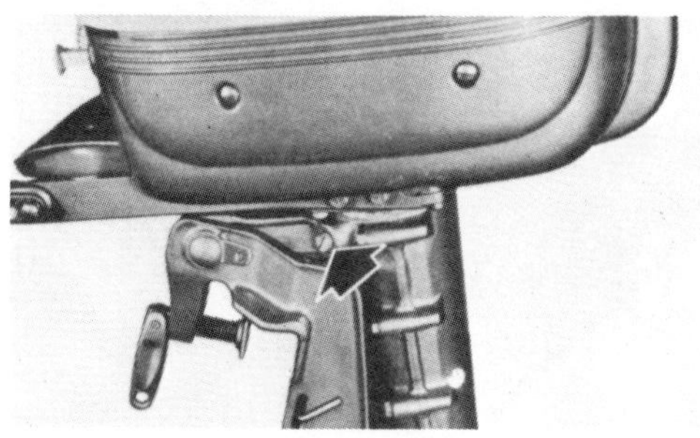

Co-pilot adjustment—3 and 4 HP (© Outboard Marine Corporation)

STEERING FRICTION—5 HP

1. The steering friction adjustment is identical to the "Co-Pilot Adjustment" for 3 and 4 hp models.

6 AND 9½ HP

Gearcase Removal—6 HP

1. Remove the upper motor cover and disconnect the spark plug wires.

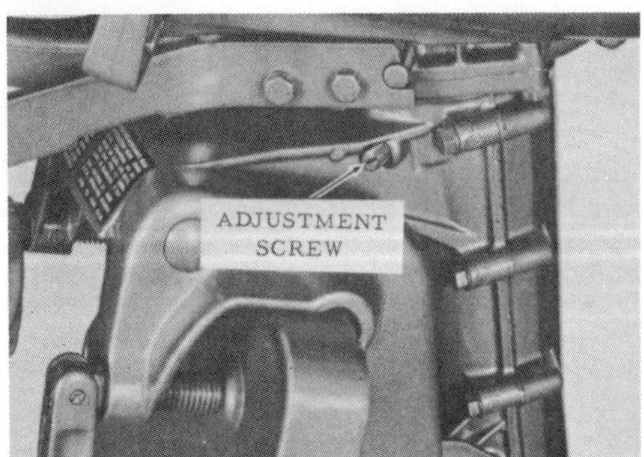

Steering friction adjustment—5 HP (© Outboard Marine Corporation)

2. Place the gearshift in Forward.
3. Remove the screws attaching the gearcase to the gearcase extension or exhaust housing.
4. Rotate the propeller to align the pin in the driveshaft with the slot in the exhaust housing.
5. Drop the gearcase sufficiently to expose the shift rod connector.
6. Remove the lower connector screw from the shift rod connector.
7. Remove the upper and lower gearcase assembly from the exhaust housing or gearcase extension.

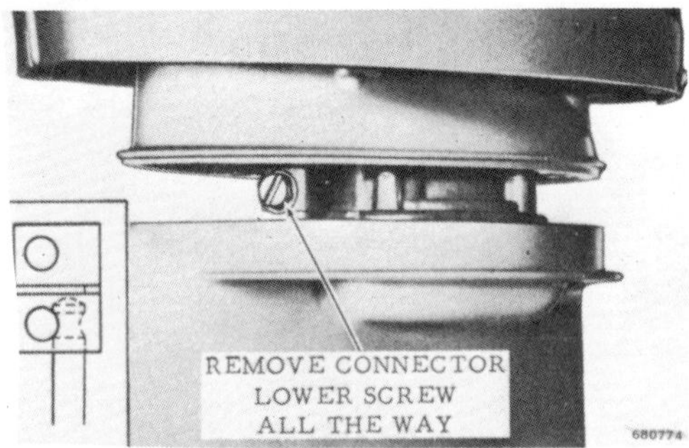

Shift rod connector screw—6 HP (© Outboard Marine Corporation)

Gearcase Removal—9½ HP

1. Place the gearshift in Forward.
2. Remove the screws attaching the gearcase to the gearcase extension or the exhaust housing.
3. Drop the gearcase sufficiently to expose the shift rod connector and remove the lower screw.
4. Remove the upper and lower gearcase from the exhaust housing or gearcase extension. Be careful not to damage the driveshaft splines.

Water Pump Replacment—6 and 9½ HP

1. Remove the propeller.
2. Remove the water pump screws and rollpin.
3. Lift the water pump plate and bearing housing from the driveshaft.

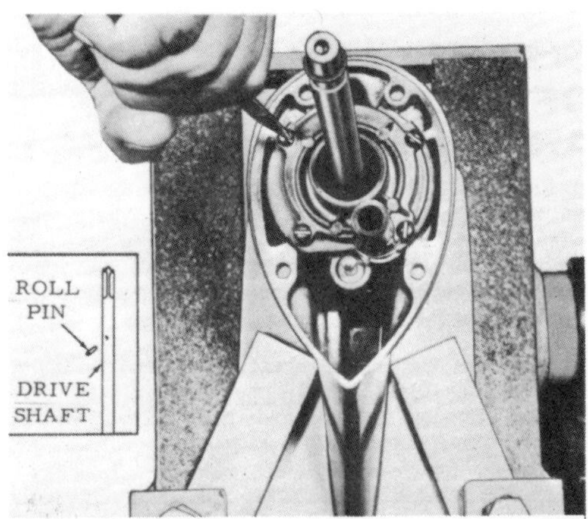

Water pump attaching screws—6 and 9½ HP (© Outboard Marine Corporation)

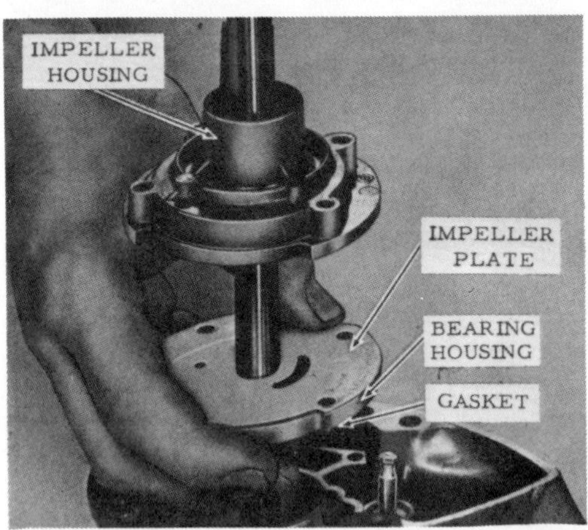

Water pump removal—6 and 9½ HP (© Outboard Marine Corporation)

4. Install a new grommet in the impeller housing water tube outlet.
5. Install the bearing housing on the gearcase with a new gasket.
6. Install the impeller plate over the bearing housing. Install the pump housing and impeller on the driveshaft.
7. Place the driveshaft with the impeller housing in the gearcase. Rotate the driveshaft to engage the pinion gear. Install the impeller pin and position the impeller over the pin.

8. Attach the impeller housing to the gearcase.
9. Install the screws and rollpin.

Gearcase Installation—6 HP

1. Lubricate and install the water tube in the exhaust housing grommet.
2. Position the gearcase beneath the exhaust housing. Align the pin in the driveshaft with the slot in the exhaust housing. Carefully slide it upward until the water tube slides into the grommet in the water pump and the lower shift rod enters the connector.
3. Install the shift rod connector screw.
4. Attach the gearcase to the exhaust housing.
5. Install the powerhead.
6. Lubricate the propeller shaft and install the propeller with a new cotter pin and drive pin.
7. Fill the gearcase with the specified lubricant.
8. Touch up any paint scratches with spray enamel.

Gearcase Installation—9½ HP

1. Lubricate the driveshaft splines and place the gearcase in position beneath the exhaust housing. Rotate the flywheel clockwise to engage the driveshaft and crankshaft splines.
2. Further installation is the same as the preceding procedure (steps 2–8).

Lower Unit Adjustments

Shift Lever—9½ HP

1. Shift the motor into Reverse. Loosen the screw attaching the shift rod clevis to the shift shaft bracket. Move the shift linkage to be sure that the detent spring has engaged. Adjust the shift lever to register at the Reverse mark, but leave a ⅛ in. clearance between the lever and cover.

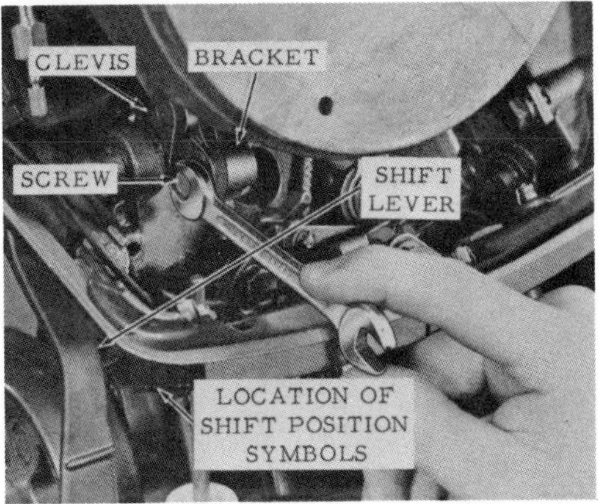

Shift lever adjustment—9½ HP (© Outboard Marine Corporation)

Tilt Friction and Steering Friction—6 and 9½ HP

1. Tilt friction and steering friction are the same as for other models.

Tilt friction adjustment—6 and 9½ HP (© Outboard Marine Corporation)

Steering friction adjustment—6 and 9½ HP (© Outboard Marine Corporation)

18 AND 25 HP

Gearcase Removal

1. It is possible to remove the lower gearcase assembly without removing the powerhead from the motor leg.
2. If disassembly of the exhaust housing is required, the powerhead will have to be removed.
3. Remove the upper motor cover and disconnect the spark plug wires.
4. Remove the exhaust housing cover plate to expose the shift rod connector. Remove the connector screw.

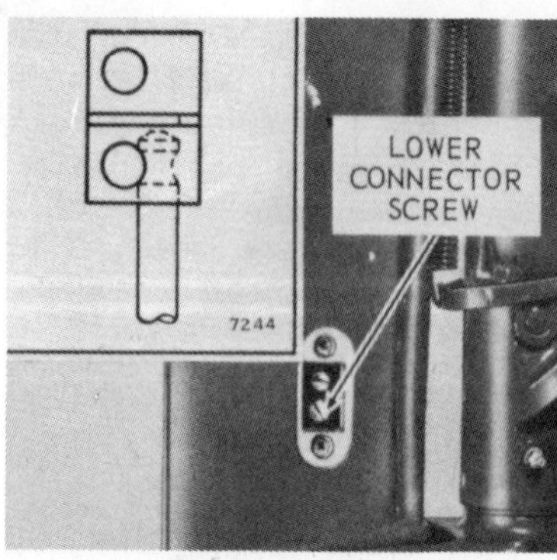

Shift rod connector—18 and 25 HP (© Outboard Marine Corporation)

5. Remove the screws attaching the gearcase to the exhaust housing.

6. Remove the gearcase assembly from the exhaust housing, being careful not to damage the driveshaft.

Water Pump Replacement

1. Water pump replacement on 18 and 25 hp models is quite similar to the procedure used for 6 and 9½ hp models. There may exist one or two small differences between models, but they are basically alike in design, operation, and serviceability.

Gearcase Installation

1. Install a new O-ring on the driveshaft. Lubricate the upper end of the driveshaft and lower end of the water tube.

2. Place the shift lever in Forward.

3. Slide the gearcase up to align with the exhaust housing.

4. Look between the gearcase housings (upper and lower) to be sure that the water tube enters the grommet of the water pump housing.

5. Check to see that the lower shift rod enters the connector.

6. Rotate the flywheel slightly to engage the crankshaft splines with the driveshaft splines.

7. Attach the gearcase to the extension housing.

8. Install the connector screw, making certain that it engages the notch in the rod.

9. Install the cover plate and new gasket.

10. Lubricate the propeller shaft and install the propeller, drive pin, and cotter pin.

11. Fill the gearcase with the specified lubricant.

12. Touch up any paint scratches on the lower unit.

Lower Unit Adjustments

Gearshift

1. Place the shift handle in Neutral and be sure that the propeller rotates.

2. Move the shift handle to Forward gear. Note the point at which the shifter dog engages Forward gear (rotate the propeller). Note also where the shift lever pin engages the forward detent in the shifter lock.

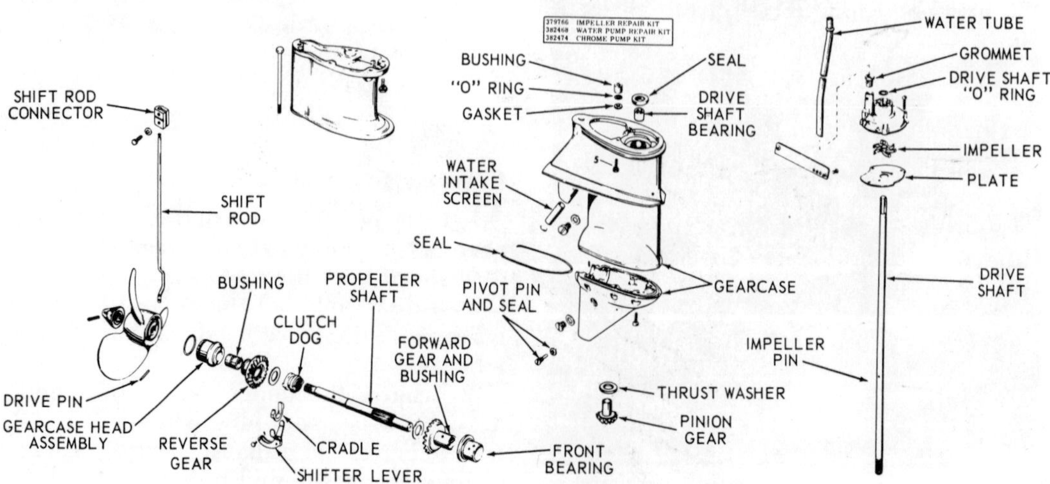

Exploded view of lower unit—18 and 25 HP (© Outboard Marine Corporation)

LAKEHEAD BOAT BASIN, INC.
ROY HALVORSON, INC. 1
940 MINNESOTA AVENUE INV 051484
DULUTH, MN 55802 05/12/90
722-4015

ITEM NO.	QTY	PRICE	AMOUNT
305191	1	14.75	$14.75
CLUTCH DOG			
302493	1	0.65	$.65
O RING			
311598	2	0.45	$.90
WASHER			
MISC	1	1.00	$1.00
MISC			
OIL PR	1	2.88	$2.88
PREMIUM BLEND 11 OZ			

303879 8.65

Jack - Link

LAKEHEAD BOAT BASIN, INC.
ROY HALVORSON, INC. 2
940 MINNESOTA AVENUE INV 051484
DULUTH, MN 55802 05/12/90
722-4015

ITEM NO.	QTY	PRICE	AMOUNT
321469	1	12.40	$12.40
RUBBER MOUNT			
303880	2	7.65	$15.30
RUBBER MOUNT			
331812	1	10.85	$10.85
RUBBER MOUNT			

AMT TND $62.84 SUBTOTAL $58.73
CHANGE $.00 TAX $4.11
FREIGHT $.00
TOTAL $62.84

!!!!!!THINK SPRING!!!!!!!

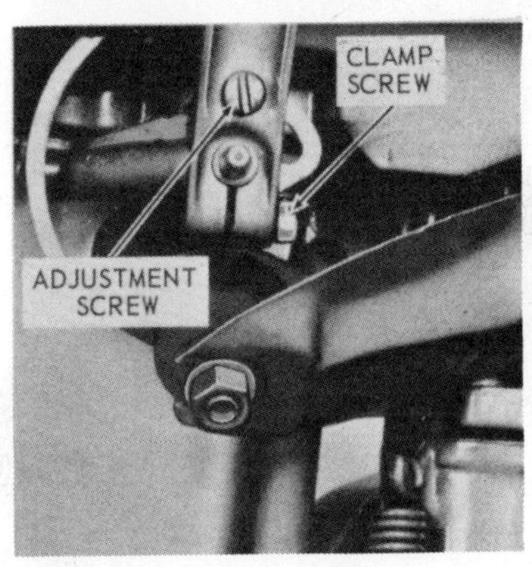

Gearshift adjustment—18 and 25 HP (© Outboard Marine Corporation)

3. Repeat the operation for Reverse.

4. The shifter lever should stop an equal distance from the Neutral detent, but closer to Neutral in Forward gear.

5. Loosen the adjustment screw and adjust it as required.

Tilt Friction

1. Tilt friction adjustment is the same as for previous models.

Steering Friction

1. Steering friction is the same operation as for other models.

Appendix

Safety Afloat

BOATING SAFETY COURSES

As an aid to boating safety, wise boatmen know the value of becoming involved in a voluntary education program so that they will better understand their responsibilities on the water. The Coast Guard Auxiliary offers any boatman the opportunity to obtain instruction in seamanship, smallcraft handling, and safety practices aloft. Qualified members of the Coast Guard Auxiliary present each of the following courses:

1. Outboard Motorboat Handling—primarily for outboard operators with the emphasis on safety. Covers the fundamental rules of boat handling, equipment requirements, and common-sense courtesy.
2. Safe Boating—provides instruction in the elements of seamanship, navigation, rules of the road, and boating safety for outboards and inboards.
3. Basic Seamanship and Smallboat Handling—provides a practical and comprehensive study of boating, seamanship, navigation, piloting (charts and compass), rules of the road, safe motorboat operation, and accident prevention. Those who successfully complete this course are awarded the U.S. Coast Guard Auxiliary Basic Smallboat Seamanship Certificate.

To obtain information on any of the above courses, write to the director of the Auxiliary located in your district (see list of U.S. Coast Guard Districts) or contact any member of the Coast Guard Auxiliary Flotilla nearest you.

In addition to the above courses, U.S. Power Squadrons and the American National Red Cross offer free courses for any boater.

Troubleshooting Emergencies Afloat

SAFETY PRECAUTIONS

Wise boatmen take a tip from professional sailors who know the value of being prepared for emergencies. By studying the following sections, and familiarizing yourself and at least one other person with them, your reactions in an emergency situation will be fast and may save a life. Before venturing into any waters, it is wise to check the following items. Remember, that it is not necessary to be on the open seas, to encounter an emergency. Many boating accidents occur each year on protected waters, inland waterways, and lakes or rivers.

1. Check the weather.
2. Advise someone of your destination.
3. Check your fuel supply and be sure that you carry enough fuel for a round trip.
4. Be sure that you have lifesaving equipment for all hands.

SAFE LOAD CAPACITIES

The Outboard Boating Club of America has calculated weight capacity specifications as a guide for small craft operators. Most manufacturers display this information on a plate somewhere on their boats. These are recommended weight capacities for cruising in good weather and calm water. It is still the responsibility of the operator to exercise caution and sound judgment regarding the capacity of his craft. In the absence of capacity plates, the following formulae will help to determine the capacity of boats of more or less standard design.

CAPACITY (NUMBER OF PERSONS)

The number of persons that your boat can carry in good weather conditions without crowding can be calculated as follows:

L=Length Overall (feet)
B=Maximum Width (feet)

$\frac{L \times B}{15} =$ ——number of persons

(to the nearest whole number).

CAPACITY (WEIGHT)

The weight capacity of your boat, taking into account the weight of people, engine, fuel, and gear can be calculated as follows:

L=Length Overall (feet)
B=Maximum Width (feet)
De=Minimum Effective Depth of Boat (feet). "De" should be measured at the lowest point that water can enter. This takes into account low transom cutouts or acceptable engine wells.

$7.5 \times L \times B \times De =$ ——pounds for persons, engines, fuel, and gear.

MINIMUM NECESSARY EQUIPMENT

The states and the Federal Government have established minimum equipment requirements, which, by law, must be carried at all times. The following chart sets down additional equipment which is recommended for various classes of boats and various types of waters. "D" designates items which are desirable and "E" indicates essential items. Common sense and experience will dictate any changes to this recommended equipment list.

	Class A (to 16′)			*Class I (16′–26′)*			*Class 2 (26′–40′)*		
Item	*Open waters*	*Semi-protected*	*Protected*	*Open waters*	*Semi-protected*	*Protected*	*Open waters*	*Semi-protected*	*Protected*
Anchor(s)	E	E	E	E	E	E	E	E	E
Anchor cable (line, chain, etc.)	E	E	E	E	E	E	E	E	E
Bailing device (pump, etc.)	E	E	E	E	E	E	E	E	E
Boat hook	—	—	—	D	D	D	E	E	E
Bucket (fire fighting/bailing)	E	E	E	E	E	E	E	E	E
Coast pilot	—	—	—	D	D	—	D	D	—

Item	Class A (to 16′) Open waters	Semi-protected	Protected	Class I (16′–26′) Open waters	Semi-protected	Protected	Class 2 (26′–40′) Open waters	Semi-protected	Protected
Compass	E	E	D	E	E	D	E	E	E
Course protractor or parallel rules	D	D	—	E	E	D	E	E	E
Deviation table	D	D	—	E	E	D	E	E	E
Distress signals	E	E	E	E	E	E	E	E	E
Dividers	D	D	—	E	E	D	E	E	E
Emergency rations	E	—	—	E	—	—	E	—	—
Emergency drinking water	E	D	—	E	D	—	E	D	—
Fenders	D	D	D	D	D	D	D	D	D
First-aid kit and manual (10- to 20-unit)	E	E	E	E	E	E	E	E	E
Flashlight	E	E	E	E	E	E	E	E	E
Heaving line	—	—	—	—	—	—	D	D	D
Lantern, kerosine	—	—	—	—	—	—	D	D	D
Light list	D	D	—	E	E	D	E	E	E
Local chart(s)	E	D	—	E	E	E	E	E	E
Megaphone or loud hailer	—	—	—	—	—	—	D	D	D
Mooring lines	E	E	E	E	E	E	E	E	E
Motor oil and grease (extra supply)	—	—	—	D	D	D	D	D	D
Nails, screws, bolts, etc.	D	D	D	D	D	D	D	D	D
Oars, spare	E	E	E	E	E	E	—	—	—
Radar, reflector, collapsible	D	D	—	D	D	—	D	D	—
Radio direction finder	—	—	—	D	—	—	D	—	—
Radio, telephone	D	—	—	D	D	—	D	D	—

Item	Class A (to 16')			Class I (16'–26')			Class 2 (26'–40')		
	Open waters	*Semi-protected*	*Protected*	*Open waters*	*Semi-protected*	*Protected*	*Open waters*	*Semi-protected*	*Protected*
Ring buoy(s) (additional)	D	D	D	D	D	D	D	D	D
RPM table	—	—	—	D	D	D	D	D	D
Sounding device, (lead line, etc.)	D	D	—	D	D	D	E	E	E
Spare batteries	D	D	D	D	D	D	D	D	D
Spare parts	E	D	—	E	E	D	E	E	D
Tables, current	—	—	—	—	—	—	—	D	D
Tables, tide	—	—	—	—	—	—	—	D	D
Tools	E	D	—	E	E	D	E	E	D

COAST GUARD COURTESY EXAMINATIONS

You are required by law to carry certain equipment on board at all times, while underway, depending on the class of your boat and method of power. While there is no obligation, any boat owner or operator may request a free Courtesy Motorboat Examination from the Coast Guard Auxiliary or U.S. Coast Guard. If your boat is properly equipped, you will receive the Auxiliary's Official Courtesy Motorboat Examination decal. If your boat is improperly equipped, you will be so advised.

NOTE: *If you are advised that your boat is improperly equipped, NO report is made to any law enforcement agency. You are advised of deficiencies so that they can be corrected.*

WEATHER AND STORM SIGNALS

Wise boatmen are always aware of the weather, since, for the most part, you are at the mercy of the prevailing conditions when on the open seas or large bodies of water. Before venturing onto any body of water, it is wise to check the weather and sea condition as well as the forecast for your area. Weather forecasts are available from the U.S. Weather Bureau Office in your area, as well as from radio stations and newspapers. On the Great Lakes, Atlantic, Gulf, and Pacific coasts, all Coast Guard stations and some yacht clubs fly storm signals. Small craft warnings, in particular, should never be ignored. Remember, also, that many areas of the country, and especially coastal areas, are subject to sudden squalls and the dreaded "northeasters" even in the presence of optimistic forecast. These squalls and northeast storms can arise suddenly; all small craft should seek the nearest shelter at the first sign of foul weather. It is poor practice to try to weather a storm when shelter is available. If it is impossible to reach shelter, however, the best practice is to keep the bow into the wind. Under no circumstances should you allow the craft to become broadside to large waves.

Storm Signals

The storm signals following are descriptive of the type of weather indicated. All boatmen should become familiar with their meaning and the location (in your area) from which they are flown.

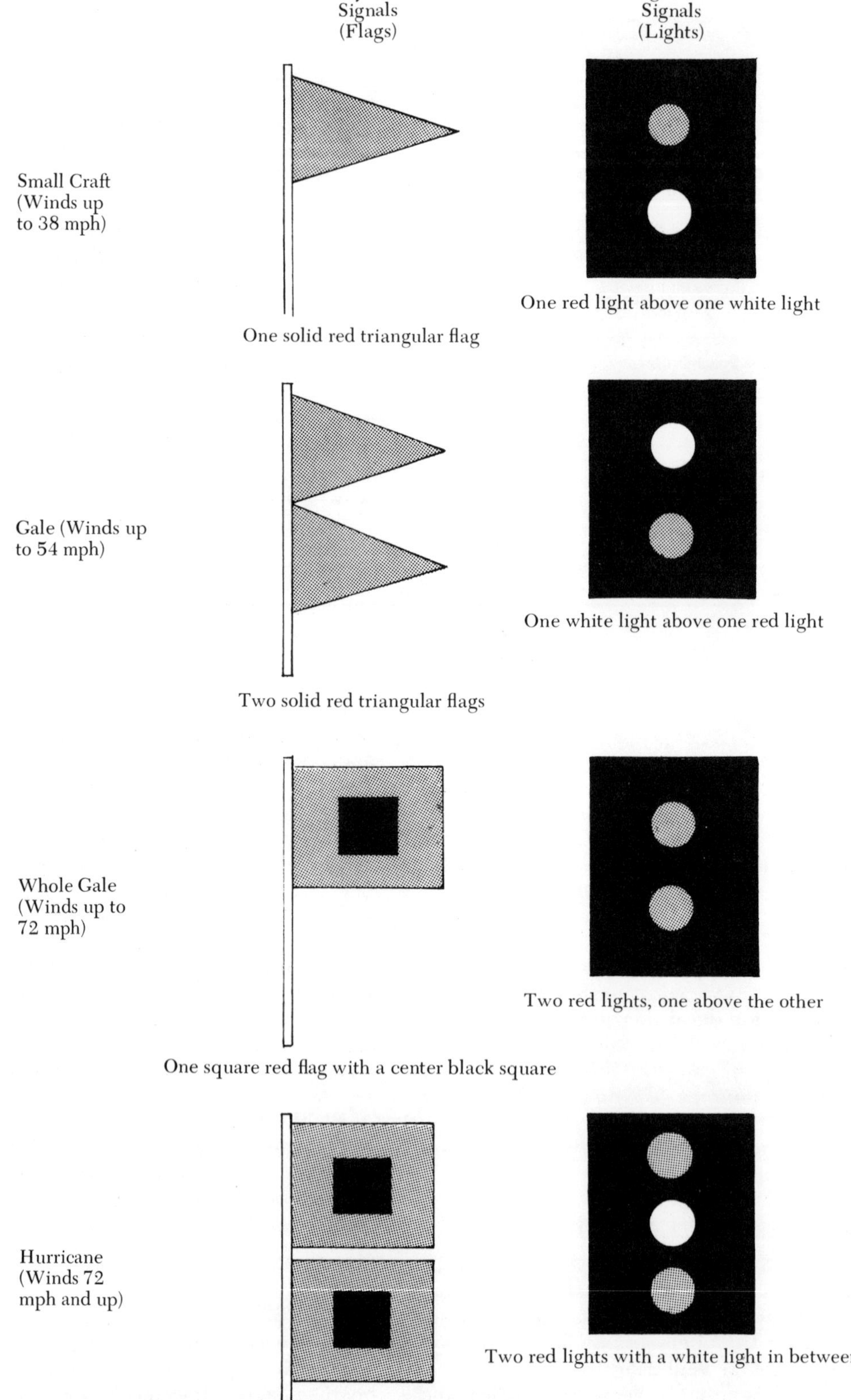

Daytime Signals (Flags)
Nighttime Signals (Lights)
Small Craft (Winds up to 38 mph)
One solid red triangular flag
One red light above one white light
Gale (Winds up to 54 mph)
Two solid red triangular flags
One white light above one red light
Whole Gale (Winds up to 72 mph)
One square red flag with a center black square
Two red lights, one above the other
Hurricane (Winds 72 mph and up)
Two square red flags with a center black square in each flag
Two red lights with a white light in between

NOTE: *This table includes general statements about the weather and can be very useful. However, the latest Weather Bureau forecast should be used whenever available. These forecasts are available on scheduled marine radiotelephone broadcasts, commercial radio stations, and from Weather Bureau Offices.*

Wind Barometer Chart

Wind Direction	*Barometer Reduced to Sea Level*	*Character of Weather*
SW to NW	30.10 to 30.20 and steady	Fair, with slight temperature changes for 1 or 2 days.
SW to NW	30.10 to 30.20 and rising rapidly	Fair followed within 2 days by rain.
SW to NW	30.20 and above and stationary	Continued fair with no decided temperature change.
SW to NW	30.20 and above and falling slowly	Slowly rising temperature and fair for 2 days.
S to SE	30.10 to 30.20 and falling slowly	Rain within 24 hours.
S to SE	30.10 to 30.20 and falling rapidly	Wind increasing in force, with rain within 12 to 24 hours.
SE to NE	30.10 to 30.20 and falling slowly	Rain in 12 to 18 hours.
SE to NE	30.10 to 30.20 and falling rapidly	Increasing wind and rain within 12 hours.
E to NE	30.10 and above and falling slowly	In summer, with light winds, rain may not fall for several days. In winter, rain in 24 hours.
E to NE	30.10 and above and falling fast	In summer, rain probably in 12 hours. In winter, rain or snow with increasing winds will often set in when the barometer begins to fall and the wind set in NE.
SE to NE	30.00 or below and falling slowly	Rain will continue 1 or 2 days.
SE to NE	30.00 or below and falling rapidly	Rain with high wind, followed within 36 hours by clearing and, in winter, colder.
S to SW	30.00 or below and rising slowly	Clearing in a few hours and fair for several days.
S to E	29.80 or below and falling rapidly	Severe storm imminent, followed in 24 hours by clearing and, in winter, colder.
E to N	29.80 or below and falling rapidly	Severe NE gale and heavy rain; winter, heavy snow and cold wave.
Going to W	29.80 or below and rising rapidly	Clearing and colder.

Beaufort Wind Scale

Wind Force	*Wind Velocity (Knots)*	*Water Condition*	*Wind Condition*
1	1–3	Ripples	Light air
2	4–6	Small wavelets	Light breeze
3	7–10	Wavelets crest	Gentle breeze
4	11–16	Small waves	Moderate breeze
5	17–21	Moderate waves	Fresh breeze
6	22–27	Many whitecaps	Strong breeze
7	28–33	Foam flies	Moderate gale
8	34–40	——	Fresh gale
9	41–47	——	Strong gale
10	48–55	——	Whole gale
11	56–66	——	Storm
12	66 and up	——	Hurricane

NOTE: *This is a traditional scale used to estimate wind force from wind and water conditions.*

DISTRESS PROCEDURES

Distress Signals

Searching for a vessel in distress is a time-consuming procedure when there is insufficient information on which to base the search. Your chances of receiving assistance is greatly increased if you know the recognized distress signals and have the proper equipment.

Radiotelephones are the best piece of equipment for communicating distress, and should be carried by all vessels which are used for off-shore cruising. Pleasure craft, merchant vessels, Coast Guard ships, and monitoring stations listen on 2182 kilocycles, which is a calling and distress frequency. Occasionally, 2638 or 2738 kilocycles may not be busy and may bring assistance sooner. However, in an emergency, you may use any frequency available. In an extreme emergency, the spoken word MAYDAY (international code word for needing emergency assistance) stands a good chance of being heard in most areas. The spoken word MAYDAY should not be used unless immediate assistance is required.

Many search craft today are also equipped with radar; however, wood and plastic boats do not make good radar targets. A radar reflector of the small collaps-

DISTRESS INFORMATION SHEET

When requesting assistance from the Coast Guard furnish the following information after establishing communications

SPEAK SLOWLY AND CLEARLY

__________ This is __________
(Coast Guard Station being called) (Your boat's name and radio call sign)

I am __________ in position __________
(Nature of distress—Disabled, sinking, grounded, etc.) (Latitude and

____
longitude bearing (True or Magnetic) and distance from a prominent point of land)

I have __________ persons aboard. I am in __________
(Number) (Immediate or no immediate danger)

My boat is __________, __________, __________, __________
(Length and type) (Type of rig) (Color of hull) (Color of topside)

I request __________ assistance.
(Source of assistance—Coast Guard or commercial)

I will standby __________ OVER
(Radio frequency)

ible type positioned high on the craft will infinitely increase your chances of radar detection.

The latest distress signal for small craft on waters of the United States is the act of standing as high as possible on the craft and SLOWLY RAISING AND LOWERING THE ARMS OUTSTRETCHED TO EACH SIDE. This is a distinctive signal, not likely to be mistaken for a greeting. It is important to remember that when in need of emergency assistance, any signal that will attract attention is acceptable. However, your chances are enhanced by using any of the recognized distress signals, which are shown following.

Recognized Distress Signals

Signal	*Inland Rules*	*Great Lakes Rules*	*Western Rivers*	*International Rules* *
A gun or other explosive fired at intervals of about a minute	Yes (day and night)	Yes (day and night)	Yes (day and night)	Yes
A continuous sounding with any fog-signal apparatus	Yes (day and night)	Yes (day and night)	Yes (day and night)	Yes
Rockets or shells, throwing red stars fired one at a time at short intervals				Yes
Signal made by radiotelegraphy or by any other signaling methods consisting of the group ···———··· (SOS) in Morse Code				Yes
A signal sent by radiotelephony consisting of the spoken word "Mayday"				Yes
The International Code signal of distress indicated by N.C.			Yes (day)	Yes
A signal consisting of a square flag having above or below it a ball or anything resembling a ball		Yes (day)	Yes (day)	Yes
Flames on the vessel (as from a burning tar barrel, oil barrel, etc.)	Yes (night)	Yes (night)	Yes (night)	Yes
A rocket parachute flare showing a red light				Yes
Rockets or shells, bursting in the air with a loud report and throwing stars of any color or description, fired one at a time at short intervals			Yes (day and night)	
A continuous sounding with steam whistle			Yes (day and night)	
Rockets or shells, throwing stars of any color or description fired one at a time at short intervals		Yes (day and night)		

* International rules do not distinguish between day and night use of signals.

Reporting Emergencies

In general, the search and rescue responsibilities of the U.S. Coast Guard include conducting harbor checks, searches for missing craft, effecting emergency repairs, towing to the nearest port of safe anchorage, and furnishing emergency medical assistance or evacuation, depending on circumstances.

To assist the Coast Guard in search and rescue operations, remember the following points.

1. When requesting assistance by radio, provide information listed on the form shown on p. 220.
2. Advise someone of your itinerary, and at the first opportunity, notify those concerned of any change in plans.
3. Do not use MAYDAY in voice distress communications unless immediate assistance is required.

Man Overboard

The following procedures are recommended in the event of a man overboard.

1. Keep calm. Do not panic or allow others to panic.
2. Swing the stern of the boat away from the man. This reduces the danger of his being injured by a propeller.
3. Throw the man a lifesaving device as soon as possible. A ring buoy is best, since these are easiest to handle in the water. However, speed may be essential, and any device is better than none.
4. Keep the man in view at all times. If another person is available, have him act as a lookout. At night, direct the best possible light on the man in the water.
5. Maneuver to approach the man from downwind or into the sea. The particular maneuver that you use to approach the man will depend on circumstances (physical condition of the man in the water, availability of assistance, maneuvering room, etc.).
6. If capable assistance is available, it might be best to have that person put on a life jacket and go into the water to assist the person overboard. The person entering the water should not do so without attaching himself to the craft with a line.
7. Assist the man in boarding the boat. In small boats, the best way to take a person aboard from the water is over the stern. This will avoid capsizing and shipping water on small craft, which are sensitive to weight distribution. Common sense dictates that the propeller should be stopped or the engine shut off.

Fire Afloat

Fire on the water is a terrifying experience. In a real sense the person is trapped. He has a choice of staying with a burning boat or jumping into unfamiliar surroundings. Either prospect is less than pleasant. The first thought should be to stay calm and assess the situation. More can be done in the first few minutes, than in the next few hours.

Fire extinguishers such as dry chemical, carbon dioxide, and foam are most effective on oil or grease fires, when the extinguisher is directed at the base of the flames. Vaporizing liquids (chlorobromomethane and carbon tetrachloride) should not be used in confined areas, because of the danger to health. Burning items such as wood, mattresses, and rags should be extinguished by water. (Throwing them over the side is as good a method as any.)

If the fire occurs in a relatively closed space, it can be confined by closing all hatches, doors, vents, and ports to cut off the oxygen supply.

Maneuvering the craft can also be a great aid in controlling fires. Reducing speed will help to minimize the fanning effect of the wind. To help in preventing the spread of the fire, keep the fire downwind by maneuvering the boat according to the position of the fire and direction of wind.

The following steps should be taken (not necessarily in order) in the event of fire.

1. Apply the extinguishing agent by:
   a. Fire extinguisher,
   b. Discharging the fixed smothering system, or
   c. Applying water to wood or similar materials.
2. If practical, burning materials should be thrown over the side.
3. Reduce the air supply by:
   a. Maneuvering the craft to reduce the effect of wind, and
   b. Closing hatches, ports, vents, and doors if the fire is in an area where this will be effective.
4. Make preparations for abandoning the craft:
   a. Put on lifesaving devices;
   b. Signal for assistance by radio or other means.

Capsizing

Many ships and boats involved in accidents have continued to float for long periods of time. If your boat capsizes, do not leave it. There are many reasons for this school of thought. Generally, a damaged boat can be sighted more easily than a swimmer in the water.

NOTE: *Information pertaining to Minimum Necessary Equipment, Coast Guard District Offices, Weather and Storm Signals, Wind Barometer Chart, and Distress Procedures is taken from the Recreational Boating Guide, CG-340, United States Coast Guard. This pamphlet is for sale from the Superintendent of Documents, United States Government Printing Office at 40 cents per copy.*

General Conversion Table

Multiply by	*To Convert*	*to*	
2.54	Inches	Centimeters	0.3937
30.48	Feet	Centimeters	0.0328
0.914	Yards	Meters	1.094
1.609	Miles	Kilometers	0.621
0.645	Square Inches	Square cm	0.155
0.836	Square Yards	Square meters	1.196
16.39	Cubic Inches	Cubic cm	0.061
28.3	Cubic Feet	Liters	0.0353
1.152	Knots/Hour	MPH	0.8684
2.113	Liters	US Pints	0.473
1.057	Liters	US Quarts	1.06
0.21998	Liters	Imp. Gallons	4.54
0.2642	Liters	US Gallons	3.785
0.4536	Pounds	Kilograms	2.2045
0.068	PSI	Atmospheres	14.7
	To Obtain	*From*	*Multiply by*

NOTE: *1 cm = 10 mm; 1 mm = 0.0394 in.*
1 Imp. Gallon = 1.2 US Gallons = 4.5459 liters
1 US Gallon = 0.833 Imp. Gallon = 3.78543 liters

Conversion—Common Fractions to Decimals and Millimeters

Inches			Inches			Inches		
Common Fractions	*Decimal Fractions*	*Millimeters (approx.)*	*Common Fractions*	*Decimal Fractions*	*Millimeters (approx.)*	*Common Fractions*	*Decimal Fractions*	*Millimeters (approx.)*
1/128	0.008	0.20	11/32	0.344	8.73	43/64	0.672	17.07
1/64	0.016	0.40	23/64	0.359	9.13	11/16	0.688	17.46
1/32	0.031	0.79	3/8	0.375	9.53	45/64	0.703	17.86
3/64	0.047	1.19	25/64	0.391	9.92	23/32	0.719	18.26
1/16	0.063	1.59	13/32	0.406	10.32	47/64	0.734	18.65
5/64	0.078	1.98	27/64	0.422	10.72	3/4	0.750	19.05
3/32	0.094	2.38	7/16	0.438	11.11	49/64	0.766	19.45
7/64	0.109	2.78	29/64	0.453	11.51	25/32	0.781	19.84
1/8	0.125	3.18	15/32	0.469	11.91	51/64	0.797	20.24
9/64	0.141	3.57	31/64	0.484	12.30	13/16	0.813	20.64
5/32	0.156	3.97	1/2	0.500	12.70	53/64	0.828	21.03
11/64	0.172	4.37	33/64	0.516	13.10	27/32	0.844	21.43
3/16	0.188	4.76	17/32	0.531	13.49	55/64	0.859	21.83
13/64	0.203	5.16	35/64	0.547	13.89	7/8	0.875	22.23
7/32	0.219	5.56	9/16	0.563	14.29	57/64	0.891	22.62
15/64	0.234	5.95	37/64	0.578	14.68	29/32	0.906	23.02
1/4	0.250	6.35	19/32	0.594	15.08	59/64	0.922	23.42
17/64	0.266	6.75	39/64	0.609	15.48	15/16	0.938	23.81
9/32	0.281	7.14	5/8	0.625	15.88	61/64	0.953	24.21
19/64	0.297	7.54	41/64	0.641	16.27	31/32	0.969	24.61
5/16	0.313	7.94	21/32	0.656	16.67	63/64	0.984	25.00
21/64	0.328	8.33